BIOGRAPHICAL ENCYCLOPEDIA OF
20th-Century
World Leaders

BIOGRAPHICAL ENCYCLOPEDIA OF
20th-Century
World Leaders

Volume 3

Herriot – Mankiller

Editor
John Powell
Pennsylvania State University, Erie

Marshall Cavendish
New York • London • Toronto • Sydney

Marshall Cavendish Corporation
99 White Plains Road
Tarrytown, New York 10591-9001

© 2000 Marshall Cavendish Corporation
Printed in the United States of America
09 08 07 06 05 04 03 02 01 00   5 4 3 2 1

Library of Congress Cataloging-in-Publication Data

Biographical encyclopedia of 20th-century world leaders / John Powell
p. cm.
   v. cm.
   Includes bibliographical references and index.
   1. Heads of state Biography Encyclopedias.   2. Statesmen Biography Encyclopedias.   3. Biography 20th century Encyclopedias.   I. Powell, John, 1954-   . II. Title:
Biographical encyclopedia of twentieth-century world leaders
   ISBN 0-7614-7129-4 (set)
   ISBN 0-7614-7132-4 (vol. 3)
   D412.B56   1999
   920'.009'04—dc21

                                                  99-34462
                                                  CIP

CONTENTS

Key to Pronunciation vii

Édouard Herriot 675
Chaim Herzog 678
Rudolf Hess 682
Heinrich Himmler 685
Paul von Hindenburg 688
Hirohito 692
Adolf Hitler 695
Oveta Culp Hobby 699
Ho Chi Minh 702
Oliver Wendell Holmes, Jr. 706
Harold Holt 709
Erich Honecker 712
Herbert Hoover 715
J. Edgar Hoover 719
Félix Houphouët-Boigny 722
John Howard 725
Victoriano Huerta 728
Charles Evans Hughes 730
William Morris Hughes 733
Cordell Hull 737
Hubert H. Humphrey 741
Hussein I 744
Saddam Hussein 748
Hayato Ikeda 752
İsmet İnönü 755
Itō Hirobumi 758
Jesse Jackson 762
Cheddi Jagan 765
Jiang Qing 767
Jiang Zemin 770
Mohammed Ali Jinnah 774
Joseph-Jacques-Césaire Joffre 777
John XXIII 779
John Paul II 782
Lyndon B. Johnson 785
Barbara Jordan 789
Juan Carlos I 792
János Kádár 795
Constantine Karamanlis 798
Rashid Karami 800

Kenneth Kaunda 803
Karl Kautsky 807
Paul Keating 810
Frank B. Kellogg 813
George F. Kennan 816
John F. Kennedy 819
Robert F. Kennedy 823
Jomo Kenyatta 827
Aleksandr Fyodorovich Kerensky 831
Albert Kesselring 835
John Maynard Keynes 837
Ruhollah Khomeini 841
Nikita S. Khrushchev 845
Kim Il Sung 849
Ernest Joseph King 853
Martin Luther King, Jr. 856
William Lyon Mackenzie King 860
Jeane Kirkpatrick 863
Henry A. Kissinger 866
Horatio Herbert Kitchener 870
Ralph Klein 873
Helmut Kohl 875
Juscelino Kubitschek 879
Robert M. La Follette, Jr. 881
Henri-Marie La Fontaine 885
Fiorello Henry La Guardia 887
Christian Lous Lange 890
Julia C. Lathrop 892
Wilfrid Laurier 894
Pierre Laval 897
Bonar Law 901
T. E. Lawrence 903
Le Duc Tho 906
Lee Kuan Yew 909
Vladimir Ilich Lenin 912
Jean-Marie Le Pen 916
René Lévesque 919
Lin Biao 921
Li Peng 923
Maksim Maksimovich Litvinov 926
Liu Shaoqi 929
David Lloyd George 932

Henry Cabot Lodge 936
Huey Long 939
Erich Ludendorff 942
Patrice Lumumba 945
Albert Lutuli 947
Douglas MacArthur 950
Ramsay MacDonald 954
Samora Moisès Machel 958
Harold Macmillan 960
Francisco Madero 964
Ramón Magsaysay 966

Datuk Seri Mahathir bin Mohamad 968
John Major 971
Makarios III 975
Malcolm X 978
Georgi M. Malenkov 982
Nelson Mandela 985
Winnie Mandela 989
Wilma P. Mankiller 992

Index 997

Key to Pronunciation

As an aid to users of the *Biographical Encyclopedia of 20th-Century World Leaders*, guides to pronunciation for all profiled leaders have been provided with the first mention of the name in each entry. These guides are rendered in an easy-to-use phonetic manner. Stressed syllables are indicated by capital letters.

Letters of the English language, particularly vowels, are pronounced in different ways depending on the context. Below are letters and combinations of letters used in the phonetic guides to represent various sounds, along with examples of words in which those sounds appear and corresponding guides for their pronunciation.

Symbols	Pronounced As In	Spelled Phonetically
a	answer, laugh	AN-sihr, laf
ah	father, hospital	FAH-thur, HAHS-pih-tul
aw	awful, caught	AW-ful, kawt
ay	blaze, fade, waiter	blayz, fayd, WAYT-ur
ch	beach, chimp	beech, chihmp
eh	bed, head, said	behd, hehd, sehd
ee	believe, leader	bee-LEEV, LEED-ur
ew	boot, loose	bewt, lews
g	beg, disguise, get	behg, dihs-GIZ, geht
i	buy, height, surprise	bi, hit, sur-PRIZ
ih	bitter, pill	bih-TUR, pihl
j	digit, edge, jet	DIH-jiht, ehj, jeht
k	cat, kitten, hex	kat, KIH-tehn, hehks
o	cotton, hot	CO-tuhn, hot
oh	below, coat, note	bee-LOH, coht, noht
oo	good, look	good, look
ow	couch, how	kowch, how
oy	boy, coin	boy, koyn
s	cellar, save, scent	SEL-ur, sayv, sehnt
sh	issue, shop	IH-shew, shop
uh	about, enough	uh-BOWT, ee-NUHF
ur	earth, letter	urth, LEH-tur
y	useful, young	YEWS-ful, yuhng
z	business, zest	BIHZ-ness, zest
zh	vision	VIH-zhuhn

BIOGRAPHICAL ENCYCLOPEDIA OF
20th-Century
World Leaders

Édouard Herriot

Born: July 5, 1872; Troyes, France
Died: March 26, 1957; Lyon, France

French political leader, president of Chamber of Deputies (1936-1940) and three-time premier

Édouard Herriot (ay-DWAHR eh-RYOH) was a statesman, politician, and scholar. He was premier of France three times, all of them relatively brief. Repeatedly elected to the Chamber of Deputies, Herriot was its leader when Nazi Germany invaded and occupied France. He protested the government's collaboration with Germany, and he was arrested and deported. Herriot became known as a writer and scholar as well as a statesman. In 1904 he published *Madame Recamer and Her Friends. A Short History of French Letters* followed in 1905. About twenty years later he wrote *The Life and Times of Beethoven* and *The United States of Europe.* Herriot was elected into the French Academy in 1946.

Mayor of Lyon

Herriot began his long political career by serving on the Lyon city council in 1905. In 1906 he was elected mayor, a position he held for nearly fifty years even though he also held national office. In 1942 his term ended with arrest by the occupying German forces. He was returned to the mayor's office at the end of World War II in 1945. He continued there until his death in 1957. His administration provided Lyon with excellent municipal services, growth, and continued prosperity. His friendship with noted architect Tony Garnier influenced Herriot's vision of postwar urban life. Lyon's Tony Garnier Hall and Gerland Stadium are lasting contributions of their collaboration.

Leader in National Government

Herriot became a member of the General Counsel in 1910 and senator for the region of Rhône in 1912. Between December, 1916, and March, 1917, he became minister of public works in the cabinet of Aristide Briand. During World War I (1914-1918), his ability to organize transportation and other support services were vital to France. In 1919 Herriot left the national Senate and was elected to the Chamber of Deputies, the other house in the National Assembly. His persuasive speeches helped him to become a power-

Édouard Herriot *(Archive Photos)*

675

Édouard Herriot (seated) in 1955, an elder statesman and president of France's Radical Socialist Party. He is clasping hands with Mendes France, former French premier. *(AP/Wide World Photos)*

ister of foreign affairs and promoted diplomatic recognition of the Soviet Union. Unpopular financial policies ended the first ministry in 1925. Herriot's second ministry lasted only three days. His third stint as premier (and foreign minister) began in June, 1932, but this ministry ended six months later when the Chamber of Deputies refused to pay the United States the December installment of its war debt from World War I. After briefly serving as vice premier, Herriot was elected president of the Chamber of Deputies in June of 1936.

ful member of the legislature and president of the Radical Party.

After World War I, Édouard Herriot led the Cartel des Gauches, a left-wing coalition of Radicals and Socialists that won the elections of May, 1924. He began serving as premier in the first of three ministries that June. He also served as min-

World War II

Nazi Germany invaded and occupied France in 1940. Philippe Pétain, who was then eighty-four, replaced Paul Reynaud as premier of France. With German support, he established a new government in Vichy in central France. When the Chamber of Deputies and Senate voted

The Chamber of Deputies, 1936-1940

During the Third Republic of France (1875-1940), the National Assembly consisted of the Senate and the Chamber of Deputies. The National Assembly resembled the British Parliament, but the chief executive's power was limited by the Chamber of Deputies. If the chamber failed to support the president's actions, he had to resign.

In 1940 Nazi forces invaded France and created a puppet government in Vichy. On July 9, 1940, the Chamber of Deputies voted 395 to 3 to give their authority to Philippe Pétain. The president of the chamber, Édouard Herriot refused to participate in the vote. The Senate voted 569 to 80 in favor of the Vichy government. Pétain dissolved the permanent bureaus of the Senate and Chamber of Deputies in 1942. Senate president Jules Jeanneney and Herriot lodged a joint protest. Herriot was arrested and deported as a direct result of this action.

to give full power to Pétain, Herriot refused to give consent. Six months after Pétain and his deputy Pierre Laval took power, Herriot was abruptly removed from office after being mayor of Lyon for thirty-five years. Soon after, the Vichy government asked him to name all Jewish deputies. Herriot replied, "I don't know any Jewish deputies, or Catholic deputies, or free-thinking deputies. I only know elected deputies."

In 1942 the Vichy government dissolved the permanent offices of the Chamber of Deputies and the Senate. Herriot and Senate president Jules Jeanneney lodged formal protests. A few weeks later, the government decreed that citizens who were "dangerous for national defense" could be arrested. This law was used to arrest Herriot and detain him in France and then in Germany. Soviet troops freed him at the war's end in 1945.

Bibliography

Morgan, Ted. *An Uncertain Hour: The French, the Germans, the Jews, the Klaus Barbie Trial, and the City of Lyon, 1940-1945*. New York: William Morrow, 1990.

Prager, Arthur, and Emily Prager. *World War II Resistance Stories*. New York: Franklin Watts, 1979.

Wilhelm, Maria. *For the Glory of France: The Story of the French Resistance*. New York: Julian Messner, 1968.

Barbara Frisbie

Chaim Herzog

Born: September 17, 1918; Belfast, Ireland
Died: April 17, 1997; Tel Aviv, Israel

Israeli soldier and statesman, president of Israel (1983-1993)

Chaim Herzog (KI-yihm HURT-zog) was the son of a Polish Orthodox rabbi and the daughter of a Lithuanian rabbi who also had a younger son, Yaacov. The elder Herzog was appointed chief rabbi of Ireland, where the family lived for eighteen years. Chaim was thoroughly grounded in religious observance and Bible study and attended Hebrew school daily. After his bar mitzvah, Herzog chose to attend yeshiva (talmudic academy) in Palestine. Later, his father was appointed chief rabbi of Palestine. Herzog gradu-

ated from the University of London in 1941 with a bachelor of laws degree and immediately volunteered for the British army. In the army he received intense training as an intelligence officer. In 1947 he returned to Palestine and married Aura Ambache, with whom he had three sons.

Military Service

Herzog's military career began when he was sixteen and still in yeshiva. He joined the underground military organization Haganah, knowing that he could be hanged for joining by the British mandate authorities but believing in the justice of the Jewish cause. The Haganah eventually grew into the Israel Defense Forces, but in the 1930's it was frequently used by British occupiers as a police force to help control Arab uprisings. After active duty in World War II, Herzog rejoined the Haganah as chief of its new unit to monitor the U.N. Special Commission on Palestine. When the U.N. General Assembly granted statehood to Israel in November, 1947, Herzog became the direct liaison between the Jewish and British authorities, eventually negotiating directly with Arab representatives in an attempt to establish peace. After the British withdrew from Palestine, Herzog was called up to save the city of Jerusalem during the War of Independence.

Herzog was formally released from the Israel Defense Forces in 1962. That same year he began to appear on Israeli radio and the British Broadcasting Corporation (BBC) as a military commentator, and his broadcasts guided the Israelis through the Six-Day War of 1967. He was appointed military governor of the West Bank after the war. Herzog strove to reach accommodation with Jordan's King Hussein, but Hussein refused Israeli attempts to negotiate.

Chaim Herzog *(Library of Congress)*

Ambassador Under Siege

Herzog arrived in New York as Israeli ambassador to the United Nations in August, 1975, at a time when the Arab countries were united with the Soviet bloc in an effort to suspend Israel from the organization. The Soviet bloc and more than one hundred nonaligned groups were equally hostile. Because of Herzog's powerful speeches and strong support by Henry A. Kissinger on behalf of the United States and its European allies, the effort to oust Israel failed.

In his second year as ambassador, 1976, an Air France plane was hijacked by Palestinian and German terrorists and flown to Entebbe, Uganda. Jews were separated from non-Jews, and all non-Israeli passengers were released. Under the leadership of Israeli prime minister Yitzhak Rabin and Shimon Peres, the Israel Defense Forces rescued the hostages in a lightning strike; they saved every hostage but one. The Israeli forces returned home to a tumul-

Chaim Herzog (right) being sworn in as Israel's president, May, 1983. With him are former president Yitzhak Navon (left) and Knesset speaker Menachem Savidor. *(AP/Wide World Photos)*

tuous welcome and world adulation. Led by the Organization of African Unity, three countries—Benin, Tanzania, and Libya—introduced a resolution to the U.N. Security Council demanding that Israel offer Uganda full compensation for damages inflicted. Refuting all who attacked Israel, Herzog spoke powerfully against terrorism, and the resolution was not adopted.

U.N. General Assembly Resolution 3379

Most developing Asian and African countries banded with the Arab bloc against what they called the "First World," and their frustration gave new impetus to anti-Israeli sentiments. In the mid-1970's Cuba, Somalia, and Benin submitted an amendment to the U.N. Human Rights Committee's resolution attacking racism and apartheid; it stated that "Zionism is a form of racism and racial discrimination." Although

the resolution was attacked as "an obscene act" by the U.S. representative, it passed on the first vote. Galvanized into action, Herzog delivered a dynamic speech before the final vote and ended by holding the resolution in his hands and tearing it up. On November 10, 1975, Resolution 3379 passed, but Israel won many friends during the battle. The resolution was rescinded on December 16, 1991.

The Israeli Intelligence Service

Chaim Herzog attended the University of London in 1938 to read for the bar, and there he joined the officer's training corps. In November, 1942, he volunteered for the British army. He was sent to the Intelligence Corps Training Depot in Yorkshire, then to the Officer's Basic Course in Intelligence. By the time he returned to Jerusalem in 1947, he had directed many intelligence projects, was sure of himself as a military leader, and was a strong supporter of the Labor Party.

The Israel Defense Forces had no professional intelligence service. In 1948 Prime Minister David Ben-Gurion appointed Herzog deputy director of military intelligence to establish a service that would meet the requirements of the new state of Israel. Herzog created a vast research operation, and then a security and counterintelligence division based on the British system. He delineated responsibilities among the various civilian, military, and political security agencies and defined the duties of the Mossad, responsible for foreign intelligence.

In 1959 Ben-Gurion called upon Herzog for a new job; that of director of military intelligence. Herzog launched a program to computerize the agency and educate the staff in technology, which gave Israel a marked advantage over other countries in the region. The Soviet Union was carefully monitored, and Israeli military intelligence was used by many Western intelligence agencies. Herzog also expanded military intelligence to include African countries, many of which he considered a direct threat to Israel. In January, 1962, he concluded his service as director of military intelligence and presented an analysis for the coming year. He estimating that the Arabs would be ready for war with Israel in five years' time, 1967. He was correct.

In 1994 former Israeli president Chaim Herzog addresses the World Economic Development Congress in Madrid, Spain. *(Reuters/Desmond Boyland/Archive Photos)*

President Herzog

Herzog represented the Labor Party in the Knesset (Israel's parliament) in 1981, and during his service he worked to improve domestic economic and social affairs. He improved Israel's communication network, fought for improved transportation, and emphasized the importance of tourism to Israel. He also streamlined higher education and upgraded the status of technical colleges.

On May 5, 1983, Herzog was sworn in as the sixth president of the state of Israel. Although the actual power of the Israeli president is limited, he was heavily involved in coalition-building activities behind the scenes. Endowed with faultless English and an urbane manner, Herzog enhanced Israel's standing abroad. He was the first Israeli head of state to visit Germany and China, and he paid a reconciliation visit to Spain marking five hundred years since Spain's expulsion of the Jews. Herzog addressed fifteen parliaments, challenged the media on unfair criticism, and built bridges between Israel and Jewish communities around the world.

On February 23, 1988, the Knesset officially voted Herzog president for a second term by 116 votes out of 120, a historic majority. He served ten years as president, covering the terms of four prime ministers; Menachem Begin, Yitzhak Shamir, Rabin, and Peres. Herzog's created closer diplomatic relations with foreign governments, especially in Africa, and promoted trade relations. Insisting that he was the president of "all Israelis," he visited the Arab and Druze minorities as well as Jewish settlers in the administered areas. His term of office saw the country through some of its most pressing problems, including the rise of the Orthodox Party's "Who is a Jew" legislation, which threatened to split world Jewry, and the *Intifada*, which broke out in 1987.

Bibliography

Herzog, Chaim. *The Arab-Israeli Wars*. New York: Random House, 1983.

_____. *Living History*. New York: Pantheon Books, 1996.

Peres, Shimon. *Battling for Peace*. London: Weidenfeld and Nicholson, 1969.

Sheila Golburgh Johnson

Rudolf Hess

Born: April 26, 1894; Alexandria, Egypt
Died: August 17, 1987; West Berlin, West Germany (now Berlin, Germany)

Adolf Hitler's secretary and deputy in the 1930's

Walter Richard Rudolf Hess (VAHL-tur RIHK-hahrt REW-dohlf HEHS) was born in Alexandria, Egypt, the son of a prosperous German merchant and exporter. He joined the German army in 1914 and fought in World War I, being twice wounded. After the army he learned to fly and joined the Freikorps, a right-wing organization for former soldiers; the Freikorps put down communist uprisings in Germany. As early as 1920, Hess had become a devoted follower of Adolf Hitler after hearing him speak in a Munich beer hall. Later, both men were arrested for the Munich "beer-hall putsch" in 1923. They were imprisoned in Landsberg prison until 1925. There Hitler dictated *Mein Kampf* (my struggle) to Hess, who also edited the book and made contributions regarding the proposed organization of the Nazi Party and about *Lebensraum*, the policy of increasing German territory at the expense of other nations.

Hess in the Nazi Party

Hess studied political science at the University of Munich, where he became strongly influenced by the Thule Society, a secret anti-Semitic group dedicated to Nordic supremacy and the policy of *Lebensraum*. During this period of Hess's indoctrination into the Nazi Party, he proved to be a formidable fighter against paramilitary Marxists and other agitators who attempted to disrupt Hitler's speeches. From 1921 to 1941 Hess was a dedicated member of the Nazi Party. He was made deputy to the führer in April, 1933, and later Reich minister without portfolio, member of the Reichstag, member of the Council of Ministers for Defense of the Reich, and a general in both the SS (the *Schutzstaffel*, the Nazi security echelon) and SA (*Sturmabteilung*, or storm troopers).

Despite the frequent appearance of Hess at huge public rallies and his role of dramatically announcing Hitler himself, Hess was never given real authority because of his lack of comprehension of the machinations of power and policies. Neither did he assume any initiative in party matters or policies. What power Hess did have was further curtailed by the pervasive political intrigue among top Nazis. They constantly schemed for personal power and political position. A subordinate, Martin Bormann, was eventually successful in replacing Hess, and as a result Hitler gradually distanced himself from Hess.

Rudolf Hess *(Library of Congress)*

Final Mission

In 1941 Hess made a secret flight to Scotland. Some historians believe that he was attempting to prove his devotion to Hitler and the Nazi cause by planning to negotiate a peace treaty with Britain. Hess certainly knew that Germany planned to invade Russia on June 22, 1941, which would create a second front in the war. Hess apparently wanted to convince the British that Germany only wanted *Lebensraum* for the German people and did not intend to destroy a "fellow" Nordic nation. Presumably he had been encouraged by British intelligence and by correspondence with the duke of Hamilton.

At any rate, Hess made a spectacular 900-mile (1,400-kilometer) solo flight on May 11, 1941, flying a Messersschmidt 110 from Ausburg to Scotland. Secret landing lights were supposed to guide him to his landing site, but they had been extinguished. Hess was therefore forced to para-

Rudolf Hess (second from right) and other Nazi officials; Nazi leader Adolf Hitler (left) is wearing traditional Bavarian *lederhosen. (Library of Congress)*

chute and was captured by a farmer with a pitchfork. Hess was held as a prisoner of war in Britain and displayed signs of mental instability. Later he was given a life sentence at the Nuremberg Trials. At the time of his death in 1987, a presumed suicide, Hess was the last Nazi war criminal being held at the Spandau prison in Berlin.

The Hess Mission to Scotland

Rudolf Hess's now-famous secret flight to Scotland in May, 1941, remains one of the most interesting mysteries of World War II. Scottish, Polish, and Russian documents have provided proof that Prime Minister Winston Churchill knew of Hess's mission twenty-four hours before his arrival. (British records will not be released until 2017.) Some scholars suspect that Adolf Hitler wanted Hess to commence peace negotiations with Britain, since Hitler could not openly offer peace without damaging German morale. However, it is not known for certain whether Hitler had advance knowledge of Hess's flight or whether Hess was acting on his own. Documents attest that the Allied group seeking to sue for peace included European royal households, specifically those delegated to meet Hess: the earl of Suffolk, the duke of Buccleuch, General Sikorsky, Guards Officer Colonel Pilcher, and the king's brother, the duke of Kent, who had been offered the Polish throne.

Rudolf Hess in November, 1946, at the war-crimes trials in Nuremberg, Germany. *(Library of Congress)*

Bibliography

Costello, John. *Ten Days to Destiny*. New York: William Morrow, 1991.

Hess, Wolf Rudiger. *My Father Rudolf Hess*. Newport Beach, Calif.: Noontide Press, 1984.

Posner, Gerald. *Hitler's Children*. New York: Random House, 1991.

John Alan Ross

Heinrich Himmler

Born: October 7, 1900; Munich, Germany
Died: May 23, 1945; Lüneburg, Germany

Public official in Nazi Germany, leader of the SS

Heinrich Himmler (HIN-rihk HIHM-lur) was the second of three sons of Gebhard Himmler, a Bavarian high school teacher, and Anna Maria Himmler, a devoted Catholic homemaker. He obtained a good humanistic education in Munich and in Landshut. In 1917 he was accepted as an officer candidate, but World War I ended in 1918 before he obtained a commission or experienced combat. After the war he earned a degree in agriculture from the Institute of Technology in Munich. In 1928 he married Margarete Boden and established a small poultry farm near Munich. One year later their only daughter, Gudrun, was born.

Party Activist

Himmler was deeply disturbed by Germany's defeat in World War I, and in 1922 he joined a paramilitary group organized by Ernst Röhm, a decorated army officer. The following year, he became a member of Adolf Hitler's Nazi Party. On November 9, 1923, Himmler marched with Röhm's organization in support of Hitler's futile attempt to overthrow the government in Munich. After 1923 Himmler joined the National Socialist Freedom Movement and became the secretary of Gregor Strasser in Landshut, Bavaria. Both became members of the reestablished Nazi party in 1925. In 1926 Himmler followed Strasser to Munich to become deputy propaganda leader of the Nazi Party. Between 1926 and 1930, Himmler played a major role in coordinating the party's national propaganda campaigns.

SS and Police Leader

Himmler was also interested in the *Schutzstaffel*, or SS, which emerged after 1925 to protect Hitler and other leading Nazi speakers. In 1929 Himmler took over the small SS organization under the supervision of Ernst Röhm, the commander of the party's storm troopers (the *Sturmabteilung*, or SA). Himmler devoted himself completely to establishing the SS as the racial elite within the Nazi Party. When Hitler took control of the German government on January 30, 1933, there were about fifty thousand men in the SS.

Heinrich Himmler on an inspection tour of the Dachau concentration camp. *(Archives of the Simon Wiesenthal Center)*

Heinrich Himmler (right) with Nazi führer Adolf Hitler. *(Library of Congress)*

War and Extermination

With the outbreak of World War II in September, 1939, Himmler's powers increased greatly. The concentration camps held increasing numbers of prisoners, and Himmler was appointed Reich commissioner for the strengthening of Germandom. This position gave him powers over the resettlement of all ethnic Germans in eastern Europe. War also provided the cover for the beginning of mass murder. In late 1939, special SS units killed thousands of Poles, and Hitler approved a euthanasia program that was responsible for the deaths of thousands of Germans with physical and mental handicaps. Beginning with the invasion of the Soviet Union in June, 1941, other special SS units initiated the Holocaust by shooting hundreds of thousands of Russian Jews. In 1942 Himmler ordered the construction of three camps, Belzec, Treblinka, and Sobibor, to exterminate Polish Jews. Himmler also build two additional camps in Majdanek and Auschwitz, which exploited the

Between 1933 and 1934, Himmler gained control over the political police of the German states, and in 1936 he was officially appointed head of Germany's police forces. After Himmler helped purge Röhm's SA in 1934, the SS was made an independent organization. In that year Himmler also gained control over all concentrations camps in Germany. By 1939 the SS had expanded to a quarter of a million members.

The "Final Solution"

On January 20, 1941, at Wannsee, Berlin, Reinhard Heydrich presided over a conference of fifteen leading Nazi officials to coordinate plans for the Final Solution, a euphemism for the elimination of all Jews from Europe. Heydrich made it clear that Adolf Hitler had given Heinrich Himmler primary responsibility for implementing the Final Solution. The decision to kill Europe's Jews was first implemented by Hitler and Himmler in the summer of 1941, when special mobile SS units followed the German army into Russian. By the fall of 1942 they had killed at least 1.5 million Jews. Himmler witnessed a mass shooting near Minsk in August, 1941, and was shaken by the experience. He ordered an alternative method of killing. Mobile gas trucks were utilized; they used carbon monoxide gases produced by the motors to asphyxiate the victims. Later, hydrogen cyanide (Zyklon B gas) was used in the extermination camps. Between March, 1942, and October, 1943, at least 1.7 million Jews were gassed at Belzec, Sobibor, and Treblinka. An additional 2 million or more perished at Majdanek and Auschwitz-Birkenau.

labor of inmates and exterminated those unable to work.

Between 1943 and 1945, Himmler accumulated additional offices. He was appointed minister of the interior in 1943 and became the head of Germany's Home Army in 1944. In late 1944 and early 1945, he commanded the Upper Rhine and Vistula army groups. Himmler was one of the most powerful men in the Third Reich, but he was dismissed from all of his duties on April 29, 1945, after Hitler discovered that he was negotiating with Western representatives. After he was captured by the British military at the war's end, Himmler committed suicide on May 23, 1945.

Bibliography

Breitman, Richard. *The Architect of Genocide*. New York: Knopf, 1991.

Padfield, Peter. *Himmler*. New York: Holt, 1991.

Smith, Bradley F. *Heinrich Himmler: A Nazi in the Making, 1900-1926*. Stanford, Calif.: Hoover Institution Press, 1971.

Johnpeter Horst Grill

Paul von Hindenburg

Born: October 2, 1847; Posen, Prussia (now Pozznan, Poland)
Died: August 2, 1934; Neudeck, Germany (now in Poland)

German military leader and statesman, president of German Republic (1925-1933)

Paul Ludwig Hans Anton von Beneckendorff und von Hindenburg (POWL LEWT-vihk HAHNS AHN-tohn BEH-neh-kehn-dohrf oont fon HIHN-dehn-bewrk) was descended on his father's side from generations of soldiers and landholders. Young Paul enrolled in the Prussian Cadet Corps at age eleven and fought bravely in the Austro-Prussian War of 1866 and the Franco-Prussian War of 1870-1871. Subsequently, Hindenburg did peacetime staff and regimental duty, married a general's daughter, and retired from the army in 1911 as a lieutenant general.

The Soldier

Three weeks after the outbreak of war in 1914,

Paul von Hindenburg *(Library of Congress)*

Hindenburg was named commander of the German Eighth Army, which found itself outnumbered by unexpectedly large Russian forces invading East Prussia. His chief of staff, Major General Erich Ludendorff, capably shifted troops as the new commanders defeated one Russian army at Tannenberg and another at the Masurian Lakes (both in 1914). Given Germany's failure to win decisively over France in the west, these eastern victories became doubly important to Germans now facing a long war.

The reports of the Battle of Tannenberg made General Hindenburg—soon promoted to field marshal—into a national hero. Fan mail and gifts poured in, children, streets and towns were named for him, and hammering nails into his wooden likeness became a popular fund-raising event. The massive and stolid general replaced the kaiser as a national icon. Germans put their trust in Hindenburg because they needed to believe in ultimate victory.

Continuing victories on the eastern front elevated Hindenburg and Ludendorff to overall command of the army in August, 1916. Hindenburg was made chief of the kaiser's general staff, with Ludendorff as first quartermaster-general. Militarily they managed important but limited success in several theaters of the war. The 1917 Russian Revolution gave Germany a significant chance to end the war in the east on easy terms and concentrate its forces on defeating France and Britain in 1918. However, Ludendorff's haggling over eastern annexation demands as "fruits" of German victory delayed troop withdrawals. Meanwhile, the 1917 campaign of submarine warfare in the Atlantic, which Hindenburg and Ludendorff demanded in order to starve out England, instead brought the United

Paul von Hindenburg (seated, center right) at the ceremonies opening the new Reichstag (parliament) in 1933, the year before his death. New chancellor Adolf Hitler is seated behind him to his right. *(Library of Congress)*

Tannenberg and the Eastern Front

The German victory at Tannenberg over the Russian Second Army under General Alexander Samsonov owed much to the initial concentration orders issued by Lieutenant Colonel Max Hoffmann before Paul von Hindenburg and Erich Ludendorff arrived. However, Ludendorff certainly accomplished much at Tannenberg. Hindenburg's contribution was preventing Ludendorff and Hoffmann from overcorrecting their own plans. They thought that his role was superfluous, whereas he felt they were only arranging technical details for his judgment.

Throughout the eastern front battles, the German commanders had the best equipment, the best-trained army, and were themselves the best generals. They were limited by their inferior numbers, by the poor roads, deep mud, and severe climate of the region, and by the fact that their right wing depended on an ineffective Austrian army. The Russian army suffered from inferior equipment and a critical shortage of noncommissioned officers. Germany won the war on the Russian front in a military sense but was not able to avoid defeat in terms of the war as a whole.

The Depression and Adolf Hitler

The 1929 world money crisis ended the American credits that were sustaining the German economy. Socialist chancellor Hermann Müller's cabinet members were not supported by their own political parties, and they resigned on March 27, 1930. The next chancellor, Heinrich Brüning of the Center Party, governed under Paul von Hindenburg's presidential emergency powers, thereby ending parliamentary democracy. By reducing unemployment payments at a time when the number of unemployed was rising rapidly, Brüning lost support in the September 30, 1930, elections; Nazi Reichstag membership jumped from 12 to 107. Brüning's 1932 proposal for restoring the monarchy may have ended Hindenburg's support for him. Franz von Papen was named chancellor in a bid to gain Nazi support under aristocratic leadership, but the feudal approach seemed out of place as Ger-

man unemployment reached crisis levels, peaking at six million in January of 1933.

The Nazis became the largest party in the Reichstag, with 230 members elected in July of 1932, although only 196 in November. The brief chancellorship of General Kurt von Schleicher ended when former chancellor Papen negotiated the compromise of a predominantly bourgeois cabinet that he hoped might control Hitler. Hindenburg then reluctantly appointed Hitler chancellor on January 30, 1933. By then the worst of the Depression was ending. Also, while earlier administrations had limited public works because of tight budgets, Hitler's economic mastermind Hjalmar Schacht, used separate accounts and blocked currencies to make possible the greater government spending needed to stimulate the economy and reduce unemployment.

States into the war. The 1918 German offensive in the west was well directed but lacked the numbers needed to overcome the American reinforcements. When the Allies gained the initiative, Hindenburg on October 3, 1918, requested the German government to seek an armistice. President Woodrow Wilson's terms led to Ludendorff's resignation. As revolution spread across Germany, Hindenburg on November 9 supported the generals who persuaded the kaiser to abdicate and seek refuge in Holland in order to prevent a German civil war.

Hindenburg, continuing in command of the army, advised the provisional government to accept the Allied armistice terms. He then brought home the western armies in good order and oversaw eastern defense. In 1919 he gave a subordinate the responsibility of recommending that the new German republic accept the unpopular Versailles Treaty. Later, Hindenburg publicly endorsed the view that the German army lost the war because it had been "stabbed in the back" by traitorous elements on the home front. From 1919 to 1925 he was retired and showed no wish to return to public life.

The Statesman

On the death of President Friedrich Ebert in 1925, Hindenburg reluctantly agreed to become a "patriotic fusion" candidate for the second round of balloting, which he won with a plurality. Fearing a return of the old order in Germany, the world press predicted, "today Hindenburg, tomorrow the Kaiser," but this was a mistaken forecast. Hindenburg reasoned that as a soldier he had been bound by his oath to the kaiser, but as president, it was his duty to support and protect the republic. This he did, to the grudging satisfaction of the liberals and the disappointment of monarchists and right-wing extremists. Hindenburg was for a time a fortunate head of state. American loans under the Dawes Plan covered Germany's reparations debts and supported economic recovery, while Foreign Minister Gustav Stresemann negotiated the 1925 Locarno Treaty, which brought Germany membership in the League of Nations in 1926. Unfortunately, Stresemann's death on October 3, 1929, removed the republic's ablest statesman. In addition, shortly thereafter, the New York stock market crash signaled the beginning of a major world depression.

Between 1930 and 1933, Germany's constitutional government broke down. The Nazis became the largest political party in the Reichstag, and old age diminished Hindenburg's stamina and mental faculties. In spite of this, in 1932 the eighty-four-year-old general was reelected president for another seven-year term, defeating Nazi Adolf Hitler and Communist Ernst Thälmann. The fact that the "Weimar parties" had no better candidate was, in fact, a measure of their weakness and desperation. After several clumsy attempts to find a political alternative, Hindenburg in early 1933 reluctantly appointed Hitler chancellor

Hindenburg acquiesced as Nazi propaganda made him a symbol of "tradition" in the Third Reich. The president was paraded, revered, and flattered, but he was also increasingly isolated from political realities. His death and his burial at Tannenberg were material for Nazi propaganda in 1934. Later his remains were reburied at St. Elizabeth Church, Marburg, Germany.

When he lived, Hindenburg was generally admired, or at least respected, for his character and sense of patriotic duty. Posterity has been less impressed by these virtues and more mindful of the fact that his last years served as a transition to the murderous dictatorship of Adolf Hitler.

Bibliography

Asprey, Robert. *The German High Command at War*. New York: William Morrow, 1991.

Dorpalen, Andreas. *Hindenburg and the Weimar Republic*. Princeton, N.J.: Princeton University Press, 1964.

Hindenburg, Paul von. *Out of My Life*. 2 vols. New York: Harper and Brothers, 1921.

Ludendorff, Erich. *Ludendorff's Own Story*. 2 vols. New York: Harper and Brothers, 1920.

Wheeler-Bennett, John. *Hindenburg, the Wooden Titan*. London: Macmillan, 1936.

K. Fred Gillum

Hirohito

Born: April 29, 1901; Tokyo, Japan
Died: January 7, 1989; Tokyo, Japan

Emperor of Japan (1926-1989)

Hirohito (hee-roh-hee-toh) was the eldest male child of Yoshihito, the emperor of Japan from 1912 to 1926. Educated by private tutors and at Peers' School, Hirohito acquired a good foundation in the liberal arts. After completing his formal studies in 1921, he took a six-month tour of Europe, where he was especially impressed by the British system of limited monarchy. He married Princess Nagako in January, 1924. In contrast to his father, he was committed to a monogamous view of marriage and the family. His son and heir, Prince Akihito, was born in 1933.

Early Shōwa Reign

In 1926 Hirohito ascended the throne. It was a time when Japan was becoming increasingly democratic, and he took the name Shōwa (or enlightened peace) for his reign. Despite the wish contained in this title, Japan soon embarked on a path of militarism. Following a major bank crisis of 1927, the new Japanese premier, General Giichi Tanaka, began to expand Japan's military presence in Manchuria and northeastern China. Hirohito himself was committed to filling the role of a constitutional monarch who would generally not interfere with the policies of the cabinet ministers. He neither defended nor opposed expansionism. Ironically, ultranationalist groups preached unquestioned obedience to the emperor and opposed constitutional democracy.

The advent of the Great Depression in 1929 promoted the further growth of militaristic and expansionist policies. Following the Japanese invasion of the Chinese region of Manchuria in 1931, the Japanese military established the puppet state of Manchukuo. Ultranationalist fanatics were responsible for a number of political assassinations during the 1930's, and the assassination of Prime Minister Tsuyoshi Inukai on May 15, 1932, marked the end of cabinets led by political parties and the beginning of bureaucratic cabinets that were increasingly dominated by the military. These authoritarian regimes required public schools to teach the duty of unquestioned patriotism, and they forced the universities to dismiss liberal professors with democratic ideas.

Only on a very few occasions did Hirohito directly intervene in political affairs. On February 26, 1936, he took a firm stand against an attempted *coup d'état* led by the "Imperial Way Faction" of young ultranationalist officers. Although the coup failed, right-wing military leaders maintained control over the government.

Hirohito *(Library of Congress)*

World War II

War between Japan and China began in 1937, and Japan soon incorporated much of eastern Asia into what it called a "Co-prosperity Sphere." Hirohito has been criticized for endorsing the foreign policies that led to the war. Apparently, his position was that the government had already decided to go to war and that he had merely been asked for his formal approval. According to his understanding of the constitution, he was obligated to support the policies of his cabinet regardless of his personal views. Hirohito was kept informed about the general orientation of Japanese military policy, but apparently he never knew about the means used, such as the brutal treatment of prisoners of war.

The Japanese surprise attack on the U.S. naval base at Pearl Harbor on December 7, 1941, brought the United States and its allies into war with Japan. The war came to an end in 1945, after the United States dropped two atomic bombs on Japan in August. Hirohito was asked to participate in a special meeting of the Supreme War Council to consider the surrender terms offered by the victorious Allies. Because the political and military members of the council were deadlocked

Hirohito in 1926, before observing a review of the Japanese navy that climaxed his enthronement as emperor. *(Library of Congress)*

about whether to surrender, the prime minister requested that the emperor make the final decision. Hirohito advised surrender. In an unprecedented radio broadcast of August 15, Hirohito explained the reasons for the decision to the Japanese population.

The Japanese Invasion of Manchuria

In the early twentieth century, many Japanese leaders viewed the Chinese region of Manchuria as a source of industrial raw materials, and a location for a growing Japanese population. After 1917 it was also seen as a buffer against the Soviet Union. In 1919 the Japanese army became guardian of the leased South Manchurian Railway. On September 18, 1931, Japanese army officers claimed that the Chinese had set off an explosion on the railroad near Mukden, and they began the conquest of Manchuria. It was completed early in 1932. The government in Tokyo was only informed after military operations had started,

but it accepted them as an accomplished fact.

The Chinese government, weakened by civil wars, appealed to the League of Nations for international support. When the league's Lytton Commission ruled in favor of China, the Japanese government simply withdrew from the League of Nations. Although China's deposed emperor, Pu-yi, was installed as emperor of Manchuria, renamed "Manchukuo," in 1934, the region remained under the control of the Japanese army. Japan's occupation of Manchuria was the first major step toward the expansionism that led to World War II.

Emperor Hirohito's Renunciation of Divinity

Although the Japanese Shinto religion traditionally taught that the emperor of Japan was divine, Hirohito explicitly denied his divinity in a statement of January 1, 1946. He declared that the ties between the emperor and the people were based on "mutual trust and affection" and that they did not "depend upon mere legends and myths."

At the end of World War II in 1945, American forces had occupied Japan. Hirohito's repudiation of divinity was important in the context of the efforts of the American occupation to establish a democratic constitution for Japan. Although the repudiation apparently reflected the desires of the emperor, General Douglas MacArthur and American officials had made it known that they wanted the emperor to make such a statement. At the time many Americans wanted to abolish the imperial institution completely, and it is possible that the statement helped preserve the institution. Most Japanese were not shocked by Hirohito's statement, because a common concept of imperial divinity was that the emperor was a great person worthy of profound respect.

Postwar Reign

Early during the American occupation, many Americans believed that Hirohito should be tried as one of Japan's war criminals, but General Douglas MacArthur and other authorities determined that he was not responsible for the conduct of the war. This decision was extremely popular in Japan. Hirohito appeared to agree with the reforms under the American occupation (1945-1952), and his renunciation of claims of divinity was in keeping with the orientation of these goals. The Constitution of 1947 changed the emperor from a sovereign ruler to a "symbol of the state" and recognized that sovereignty resides in the people.

In keeping with the constitutional change, Hirohito played the part of a democratic monarch, meeting with regular citizens and allowing the imperial family to be photographed. He visited scenes of disaster and inspected Japan's postwar construction. Crown Prince Akihito broke tradition by marrying a commoner rather than a member of a noble family. Hirohito visited Western Europe in 1971 and the United States in 1975, the first time that a reigning emperor had visited foreign countries. A recognized authority in marine biology, he appeared to symbolize the technological and scientific changes of the new Japan.

Hirohito's reign of sixty-two years was the longest of any Japanese emperor in recorded history, and it was a period of great upheaval and change. Although Hirohito did nothing to counteract Japanese expansionism before and during World War II, most historians agree that he was not responsible for those policies. Following the war, he quietly supported democratic reforms in a dignified manner, and he became a symbol for the postwar modernization of Japan.

Bibliography

Behr, Edward. *Hirohito: Behind the Myth*. New York: Vintage Books, 1990.

Hoyt, Edwin. *Hirohito: The Emperor and the Man*. New York: Praeger, 1992.

Irokawa, Kaikichi. *The Age of Hirohito*. New York: Free Press, 1995.

Kawahara, Toshiaki. *Hirohito and His Times: A Japanese Perspective*. Tokyo: Kodansha International, 1990.

Large, Stephen. *Emperors of the Rising Sun: Three Biographies*. Tokyo: Kodansha International, 1997.

Thomas T. Lewis

Adolf Hitler

Born: April 20, 1889; Branau am Inn, Austro-Hungarian Empire
Died: April 30, 1945; Berlin, Germany

Dictatorial leader of Nazi Germany, as chancellor (1933) and führer (1934-1945)

Adolf Hitler (AH-dohlf HIHT-lur) was the son of a customs official of the Austro-Hungarian Empire and a peasant girl. He attended *Realschule* but never graduated. Hitler began earning his living in Vienna by painting picture-postcards and portraits. In 1913 he immigrated to Munich, where he continued to paint. When World War I erupted in August, 1914, Hitler enlisted and served for four years, participating in many of the battles on the western front. He earned the Iron Cross (both first and second class) for bravery in action. After the war, Hitler decided on a career in politics.

The Struggle for Power

In September, 1919, Hitler joined a small political party. He quickly became the undisputed führer (leader) of the party and began to attract members through his mesmeric oratorical ability. At a mass meeting in February, 1920, Hitler changed the name of the party to the National Socialist German Workers' Party (generally referred to as the Nazi Party, or Nazis). Hitler also acquired a newspaper to spread his views, which featured two principle themes. First, he denounced the Treaty of Versailles, the peace treaty ending World War I, which placed many restrictions and enormous financial burdens on Germany. Second, he denounced the Jews, whom he blamed for all the ills of Germany.

In November, 1923, Hitler led an uprising in Munich (sometimes called the beer-hall putsch) that failed. The Bavarian authorities imprisoned Hitler and several other leaders. Hitler served nine months in Landsberg Fortress, where he wrote *Mein Kampf* (my struggle). The book explained Hitler's worldview, and it concluded that his movement must come to power legally, not through force.

After his release from prison in late 1924, Hitler rebuilt his movement. In 1930 the Great Depression came to Germany, swelling the ranks of the dissatisfied, many of whom turned to Nazism. In January, 1933, President Paul von Hindenburg appointed Hitler as chancellor of Germany. Hitler convinced the German parliament to pass the Enabling Act, which granted him dictatorial powers for twelve months. While Hitler was concentrating on rebuilding the German economy, Hindenburg died. Hitler declared the offices of

Adolf Hitler *(Archive Photos)*

695

Adolf Hitler addressing a Nazi rally in April, 1938. *(Library of Congress)*

Through strict wage and price controls and through a rearmament program which rejuvenated the German armed forces, he essentially eliminated unemployment. Through political regimentation of most aspects of German life, he involved Germans in building a prosperous nation.

By 1939 the German economy was booming. Everyone who wanted to work had a job. Germany had regained its status as a great power among the nations. German citizens had paid a high price for economic security, however. The Gestapo (secret police) arrested any political dissidents. The German government had placed severe restrictions on the rights of Jews. Most ominous of all, Hitler had became reckless in his diplomatic affairs, risking war to gain his ends.

president and chancellor to be merged, and he became the führer of Germany.

Hitler as Dictator

Between 1933 and 1939, Hitler through his speeches inspired hope in the German people.

Mein Kampf

While imprisoned in Landsberg Fortress in 1924, Adolf Hitler wrote the first volume of *Mein Kampf* (my struggle), which was published in 1925. Hitler wrote that, just as individuals within a species engage in a struggle for survival, so do the races of humankind. When a race ceases to expand, it will atrophy and die. (This was essentially Hitler's version of the concept of social Darwinism.) The German or Aryan race must struggle for living space for an expanding population. Hitler saw Marxism, with its emphasis on internationalism and the unity of the human race, as being a fundamental misunderstanding

of the nature of the world that must be eliminated. He wrote that the Jews are an antirace and claimed that they were the cause of most of the problems of Germany and the world: They must be eliminated from German educational, cultural, political, and economic life, he wrote, if not driven from Germany completely. The publishers of *Mein Kampf* eventually translated it into most of the world's major languages. The book became a best-seller in Germany, for a time the only book to outsell the Bible. Hitler never deviated from the principles laid out in his book, pursuing them to the end of his life.

Fortress Europe

Adolf Hitler intended to turn Europe into a region completely independent of the rest of the world, capable of producing all the raw materials and manufactured goods necessary for a modern industrial region. He desired to make it impregnable to attack, describing the ideal result as *Festung Europe*, or fortress Europe. Toward this end, he fortified the most vulnerable areas of the Continent, especially France. There he ordered the beaches fortified with tank impediments, camouflaged artillery, and machine-gun emplacements. To command the "Atlantic wall" he chose one of Germany's most famous generals, Erwin Rommel.

World War II

Hitler had several foreign-policy goals that he wanted to accomplish. In 1936 he remilitarized the German Rhineland, an action prohibited by the Treaty of Versailles. In 1938 he merged Germany and Austria. Hitler nearly provoked a war in 1938 by demanding that the Sudetanland region of Czechoslovakia be ceded to Germany, but the British prime minister, Neville Chamberlain, acceded to Hitler's demands. Then, in 1939, Hitler demanded a settlement of what he called the "Polish question." When the French and British refused to grant his demands, Hitler signed a nonaggression pact with the Soviet Union. On September 1, 1939, Germany invaded Poland. The French and British immediately declared war on Germany, and World War II began. Poland fell quickly.

In 1940 Hitler launched an attack against western Europe. The smaller nations succumbed to the German Blitzkrieg. In June, France capitulated, leaving the British to face Germany alone. Hitler elected not to invade the British Isles, trying instead to bomb the nation into submission. The resulting "Battle of Britain" was inconclusive. The United States gave the British "all aid short of war" during 1940 and 1941. American president Franklin D. Roosevelt sent the British vital supplies, resulting in an undeclared naval war in the North Atlantic between German submarines and the U.S. navy.

German führer Adolf Hitler (left) studying a map of the Russian campaign in 1941; General Gerd von Rundstedt is in the foreground. *(National Archives)*

On June 22, 1941, the Germans attacked the Soviet Union. The German army overran vast portions of the Soviet Union, driving to within 20 miles (32 kilometers) of Moscow before the Russian winter and the resistance of the Red Army finally halted them on December 6, 1941. The next day, the Japanese attacked Pearl Harbor, drawing the United States into World War II both in Europe and the Pacific.

In 1942 the Germans suffered disastrous defeats at Stalingrad in Russia and El Alamein in North Africa. In 1944 the British, Canadians, and Americans successfully invaded France at Normandy (the D day invasion). By this time, Hitler had become a virtual recluse and was addicted to prescription drugs. In July, 1944, some of his generals tried unsuccessfully to assassinate him. His survival left him convinced that God had spared him to achieve final victory. He determined to fight on.

Hitler's Last Days

During the last months of his life, Hitler tried desperately to turn the tide of the war. He unleashed new weapons against Britain, the V-1 and V-2 rockets, which took many lives but had no effect on the course of the war. In December, 1944, Hitler used his last reserves of troops in an offensive against the British and American forces in Belgium. After the failure of the offensive, Hitler retreated to his bunker, located below the chancellory building in Berlin. There Hitler spent his final days. When the Red Army broke through the German defenses around Berlin in 1945, Hitler had to admit that the end had come. He married his long-time mistress Eva Braun. The couple bid farewell to the people who shared their last stronghold and retired into their bedroom, where they committed suicide.

Hitler's Legacy

Although Hitler accomplished much for Germany in the years before World War II, his name will live in infamy for the forty to eighty million people who died during World War II, including many of the Jews of Europe. The people of the world will forever associate Hitler's name with what the Jews term the Shoah, called the Holocaust in popular literature. The Germans rounded up the Jews of Europe and sent them to concentration camps in Poland, where millions of them were murdered.

Hitler's foreign policy deliberately risked, and finally provoked, war. When it came, the war spread virtually throughout the world. Millions of soldiers and innocent civilians from all the belligerent nations died as a result of Hitler's obsession with revising the terms of the Treaty of Versailles, gaining living space for the German people, and making Europe free of Jews. By the end of World War II, Germany and indeed much of Europe were utterly devastated by the effects of the war.

Bibliography

Fest, Joachim. *Hitler*. New York: Harcourt Brace Javanovich, 1974.

Steinert, Marlis. *Hitler: A Biography*. New York: W. W. Norton, 1997.

Stone, Norman. *Hitler*. Boston: Little, Brown, 1980.

Toland, John. *Adolf Hitler*. Garden City, N.Y.: Doubleday, 1976.

Paul Madden

Oveta Culp Hobby

Born: January 19, 1905; Killeen, Texas
Died: August 16, 1995; Houston, Texas

U.S. public official, director of Women's Army Corps (1942-1945), first secretary of health, education, and welfare (1953-1955)

Oveta Culp Hobby (oh-VEE-tah KUHLP HO-bee), born Oveta Culp, was the daughter of a well-known lawyer in Texas. Following in her father's footsteps, she obtained an education in law at Mary Hardin Baylor College and the University of Texas. She became active in public affairs at an early age, becoming Houston's assistant city attorney in 1925—when she was only twenty years old. A serious student of parliamentary rules and customs, she served as the parliamentarian for the Texas legislature and even wrote a popular school text on parliamentary procedure. In 1931 she ran for a seat in the Texas legislature but was defeated. In that same year, she married a former governor of Texas, William Pettus Hobby. William Hobby was the publisher of the *Houston Post* at the time, and as a consequence Oveta Culp Hobby found herself in several positions at the newspaper. It was the onset of World War II, however, that brought Hobby to prominence.

Director of the WAC

As the United States became increasingly involved with the Allies in 1941 (the United States did not officially enter the war until December of that year), Hobby took an executive position with the Department of War's public relations branch. Before long she was given the task of creating a women's auxiliary unit in the army. This she did, and in 1942 Hobby was made the director of the Women's Army Auxiliary Corps (WAAC). The WAAC had been designed to incorporate women into the war effort while segregating them from the traditional male units. The WAAC's formal institutionalization into the armed forces was increased in 1943, and the unit's name was changed

to the Women's Army Corps (WAC). Hobby was commissioned as a colonel, and she remained the director of the WAC until the war's end in 1945. She earned a Distinguished Service Medal in that year in recognition of her contributions to the war effort.

Hobby's leadership position in the WAC and her officer's commission served as milestones for women's integration into the military. Under her leadership, some 100,000 women proved themselves as capable, reliable, and professional military personnel. In subsequent years the military would become more fully integrated, and

Oveta Culp Hobby *(Library of Congress)*

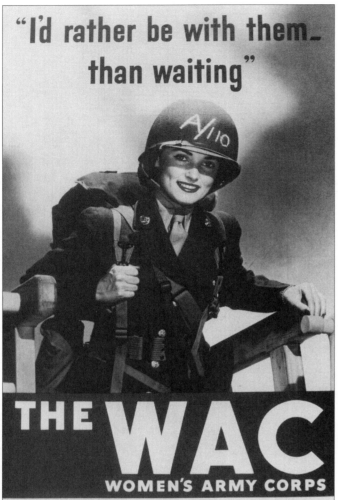

"I'd rather be with them... than waiting"

THE WAC
WOMEN'S ARMY CORPS

Apply at U.S. Army Recruiting Station or ask your local Postmaster

A World War II recruitment poster for the Women's Army Corps, directed by Oveta Culp Hobby throughout the war. *(National Archives)*

women would be assigned to almost every type of military unit, with the notable exception of combat roles.

Secretary of HEW

After the war, Hobby turned again to newspapers and politics. She became involved in General Dwight D. Eisenhower's presidential campaign, helping him secure victory in 1952. President Eisenhower appointed her to lead the Federal Security Agency, which subsequently was reorganized into the Department of Health, Education, and Welfare (HEW). As secretary of HEW, Hobby became only the second woman to hold a cabinet position in the United States (following Frances Perkins, who had been secretary of labor for President Franklin D. Roosevelt).

Hobby was influential in helping to form an identity and institutional culture for the new agency. She was an involved and active leader, at times earning praise for her activism and at times drawing criticism. She took a skeptical view of socialized medicine, which at the time was promoted by some powerful members of Congress. She also held strong anticommunist credentials, supporting Eisenhower's policies of investigation and mandatory oaths for ensuring the loyalty of government employees. Her support for the firing of more than two hundred HEW employees under

The Department of Health, Education, and Welfare

The U.S. Department of Health, Education, and Welfare (HEW) was created in 1953 under the administration of newly elected president Dwight D. Eisenhower. Oveta Culp Hobby served as its first secretary. HEW was intended to address a range of social issues and problems that had become especially salient with the population boom and industrial shifts that followed World War II. HEW was reorganized and renamed the Department of Health and Human Services in 1980.

this policy, as well as her alleged opposition to school desegregation, earned Hobby the disapproval of some liberals. However, those criticisms were often muted out of consideration for the political importance of having a woman in such an important post.

Hobby resigned her post in July, 1955, in order to care for her husband, who had fallen ill. Upon hearing of Hobby's resignation, Secretary of the Treasury George Humphrey is reported to have quipped, "What? The best man in the cabinet?" Hobby took over her husband's responsibilities as editor of the *Houston Post* and subsequently assumed various positions, including chairman of the board in 1965. The paper was sold to a Canadian firm in 1983. Hobby died on August 16, 1995, following a stroke.

Bibliography

Grahn, Elna Hilliard. *In the Company of WACs.* Manhattan, Kans.: Sunflower University Press, 1993.

Shire, Al, ed. *Oveta Culp Hobby.* Houston, Tex.: W. P. Hobby, 1997.

Spratley, Dolores R. *Women Go to War: Answering the First Call in World War II.* Columbus, Ohio: Hazelnut, 1992.

Steve D. Boilard

In 1953, when the U.S. Department of Health, Education, and Welfare was established, Oveta Culp Hobby became its first head. *(Library of Congress)*

Ho Chi Minh

Born: May 19, 1890; Kim Lien, Vietnam, French Indochina
Died: September 3, 1969; Hanoi, North Vietnam

Vietnamese anticolonial political leader, president of North Vietnam (1954-1969)

Ho Chi Minh (HOH CHEE MIHN), born Nguyen Sinh Cung (NEW-yehn SIHN KOONG), was the son of poor peasants in French Indochina. He was greatly influenced by his father, a Confucian scholar who had lost his governmental job because of his opposition to the colonial regime. In 1909, Ho graduated from the prestigious National Academy of Hue. He then taught school in several villages, while also working as an activist in behalf of Vietnamese independence.

Early Revolutionary Career

In 1911, Ho Chi Minh took a job as a kitchen helper on a French ocean liner. He did not return to Vietnam for thirty years. After living in London and the United States, he settled in Paris in 1917. Taking the name Nguyen Ai Quoc (Nguyen the Patriot), he worked with a variety of anticolonial groups. He unsuccessfully attempted to meet with President Woodrow Wilson at the Paris Peace Conference of 1919. Increasingly commit-

Vietnamese nationalist (Vietminh) leader Ho Chi Minh at a reception in Paris in 1946. *(National Archives)*

ted to the Marxist-Leninist ideology, he was a founder of the French Communist Party in 1920. By this time, Ho was convinced that anticolonial nationalism and communist revolution were inseparable goals.

In 1923, Ho moved to Moscow to study at the University of Oriental Workers. During this period he wrote an influential pamphlet, *French Colonialism on Trial.* Sent to southern China by the Communist International in 1924, he organized the Vietnam Revolutionary Youth Organization. In 1930, he successfully united several radical groups into the Indochinese Communist Party. In 1931, British authorities in Hong Kong arrested him, but they refused to turn him over to the French, who had sentenced him to death in absentia. Released the next year, he continued his revolutionary activities in Moscow and China.

North Vietnamese soldiers of the National Liberation Front in 1968. (Agence France/Archive Photos)

When the Japanese occupied Indochina during World War II, Ho cooperated with the United States, Britain, and China. Returning to Vietnam in 1941, he announced the formation of the Vietminh, a coalition of nationalistic groups. About

The French Communist Party

Ho Chi Minh lived in Paris from 1917 to 1923, and there he began his struggle for the rights of the Vietnamese people. He was also, in 1920, a founding member of the French Communist Party (PCF). Ho and French socialists, inspired by the Russian Revolution (1917), founded the party at the Socialist Congress of Tours. A majority of the delegates voted to join the Third International (the international communist organization based in Moscow). Originally the PCF was composed of diverse ideological viewpoints, but within a decade it had accepted the Leninist principles of democratic centralism and did not allow any dissent within its ranks.

During the Great Depression of the 1930's, the PCF was sympathetic with the hard-line, totalitarian approach of Soviet dictator Joseph Stalin. In the 1940's, many French workers were convinced that only the CPF represented their class interests, and the party obtained 28 percent of the French vote in 1946. Later, during the Cold War, the CPF was generally subservient to the Soviet Union, although it did oppose the Soviet invasion of Czechoslovakia in 1968. In 1981, the CPF received only 15 percent of the vote, and it continued to decline thereafter. With the fall of the Soviet Union in 1991, the CPF ceased to exercise any significant influence within French politics.

The Vietminh

Ho Chi Minh and his communist followers founded the Vietnamese Independence League (commonly known as the Vietminh) in 1941. The organization provided a united front for all nationalists opposed to colonial rule. The Vietminh was created in an attempt to emphasize guerrilla warfare and to deemphasize Marxist-Leninist ideology. General Vo Nguyen Giap was the organization's major military strategist. During World War II, the Vietminh fought the Japanese and occupied Hanoi. Beginning in 1946, the Vietminh fought for independence from France in the First Indochina War, which ended with the Geneva Agreements of 1954. Although the Vietminh was officially reconstituted into the Lien Viet Front in 1951, the term Vietminh continued to be used to designate procommunist forces in South Vietnam. When the National Liberation Front was created in 1960, the term "Vietcong" (Vietnamese Communists) became the most common designation.

this time he took the name Ho Chi Minh (He Who Enlightens). With the defeat of Japan in 1945, the Vietminh controlled a large part of northern Vietnam. On September 2, Ho proclaimed Vietnamese independence, using language taken from the American Declaration of Independence.

The First Indochina War

After France refused to recognize Vietnam's independence, Ho agreed to negotiate the terms for making Vietnam into an autonomous state within the French Union. In 1946, he traveled to France to attend the Fontainebleau Conference, but the two sides could not agree on a settlement. In November, a full-scale war began with a French naval bombardment of Haiphong.

During the war against the French, Ho had the major role in forming political policy, while most of the military strategy was left to General Vo Nguyen Giap. As the war progressed, the French tended to control the major cities, while the Vietminh was dominant in the countryside. In 1950, Ho and his followers formed the Democratic Republic of Vietnam (DRV), which was quickly recognized by most Soviet bloc countries. With the outbreak of the Korean War in 1950, the conflict in Vietnam came

Ho Chi Minh was a seasoned revolutionary and a champion of the poor; he possessed both great charm and ruthless determination. *(Archive Photos)*

to be viewed by the West as a struggle between "communism and the free world." The United States assisted the French with about $2 billion in military aid.

In 1954, the Vietminh decisively defeated French troops at Dien Bien Phu. At the Geneva Conference of that year, a compromise agreement divided Vietnam along the 17th parallel. Ho's DRV became the official government in the north, while a noncommunist regime took over in the south. The agreement called for unification based on national elections after two years, but the United States and South Vietnam refused to endorse this controversial provision.

President of North Vietnam

Ho Chi Minh's position as president of North Vietnam was established in the constitution of 1959. He was also chairman of the ruling Lao Dong (workers' party). Ho's authoritarian government punished dissidents and conducted massive land reform, so thousands of landowners and conservative Catholics fled to South Vietnam. After consolidating his control over the north, Ho began to plan an uprising in the south, In 1960, he encouraged the formation of the National Liberation Front (NLF), which was also called the Vietcong. The government of Hanoi worked closely with the NLF, and communist forces soon gained control over much of the countryside in the south.

The Vietnam War began in 1965 when the United States sent regular troops to South Vietnam. Within three years the American commitment totaled more than 500,000 troops. In response, Ho was able to obtain increased support from both the Soviet Union and China, and by 1967 an estimated twenty thousand North Vietnamese troops were streaming into the south each month. Following the Tet Offensive of 1968,

the United States gradually began to withdraw from the war. Ho's health was failing by this time, and his governmental role was primarily ceremonial when he died in 1969.

Ho's Significance

Ho Chi Minh, often called Uncle Ho, combined nationalism with Marxist-Leninist communism, and he saw no contradiction in these two positions. A seasoned revolutionary who lived very simply, he was widely revered as a champion of the poor peasants. He was a man of great charm, but he also demonstrated ruthless determination in pursuing his goals. He was a man of action with great ability for organizing and inspiring revolutionary movements. His major weaknesses included a dogmatic approach to economic theory and a general lack of concern for individual freedom. Although the unification of Vietnam in 1975 was correctly seen as a triumph of Ho's nationalism, the Vietnamese people soon discovered that the communist system could not produce prosperity.

Bibliography

Archer, Jules. *Ho Chi Minh: Legend of Hanoi*. New York: Crowell-Collier, 1971.

Fenn, Charles. *Ho Chi Minh: A Biographical Introduction*. New York: Charles Scribner's Sons, 1973.

Halberstam, David. *Ho*. New York: Random House, 1971.

Ho Chi Minh. *On Revolution: Selected Writings*. New York: Praeger, 1967.

Karnow, Stanley. *Vietnam: A History*. New York: Viking, 1991.

Lacouture, Jean. *Ho Chi Minh: A Political Biography*. New York: Vintage Books, 1968.

Thomas T. Lewis

Oliver Wendell Holmes, Jr.

Born: March 8, 1841; Boston, Massachusetts
Died: March 6, 1935; Washington, D.C.

U.S. legal scholar and Supreme Court justice (1902-1932)

Oliver Wendell Holmes, Jr. (O-lih-vur WEHN-duhl HOHLMZ JEW-nyur), was the son of a famous author and medical doctor. His mother was Amelia Lee Jackson, daughter of a justice of the Massachusetts Supreme Judicial Court. As a young man, Holmes attended Harvard University, earning a B.A. in 1861. During the Civil War, Holmes—a tall, lean man—served with distinction as an officer on the battlefield and was seriously wounded at the battles of Ball's Bluff, Antietam, and Chancellorsville.

Early Career in the Law

Holmes graduated from Harvard Law School in 1866 and was admitted to the bar in 1867. From

Oliver Wendell Holmes, Jr. *(Library of Congress)*

1870 to 1873, he edited the *American Law Review*. In 1872 he married Fanny Bowditch Dixwell, a friend of many years. During his private practice of law in Boston, he pursued his interest in the history of the law. In 1873 he published the twelfth edition of James Kent's learned yet popular *Commentaries on American Law*. In 1881 Holmes published his masterpiece, *The Common Law*, which earned for him a place in the first rank among the interpreters of America's legal heritage. The life of the law, he asserted at the beginning of his book, was not logic but experience. This maxim has had an enormous influence on American legal thought. His achievement earned him an appointment to the Massachusetts Supreme Judicial Court 1882, where he sat for twenty years. He became chief justice of the court in 1899.

Associate Justice Holmes

In 1902 President Theodore Roosevelt appointed Holmes to the U.S. Supreme Court as an associate justice. In the course of three decades on the bench, Holmes established himself as a master stylist of the English language and a magisterial interpreter of the U.S. Constitution. He was an exponent of judicial self-restraint, the position that the making of law was the job of the legislature, not the courts. In Holmes's opinion, the Constitution allowed the Congress and the state legislatures wide latitude for social experimentation.

He was also a major force among his fellow justices in interpreting the right of free speech under the First Amendment. The best test of truth, he argued, is its power to prevail in the competition of ideas in a free market. He formulated the rule of "clear and present danger" governing speech in a free society: Words could be illegal when used in such a way as to create a

---

Due Process of Law

This concept means that laws must be reasonable and be applied fairly and equally. Oliver Wendell Holmes, Jr., argued that due process is grounded in the common law. Common law is the consensus of English-speaking jurists, reached over the centuries, concerning limits on the power of a government to make or apply law that is unreasonable or arbitrary.

The Fifth Amendment to the U.S. Constitution (1791) requires the federal government to ob-

serve due process; the Fourteenth Amendment (1868) extended that restriction to state governments. The Supreme Court has understood due process to protect citizens against unreasonable or arbitrary search and seizure, self-incrimination, and cruel and unusual punishment. Due process also protects the right of persons accused of crimes to confront hostile witnesses and to have counsel and a jury trial.

"clear and present danger of the substantive evils" that Congress has a right to prevent. No one, Holmes contended, had the right to falsely shout fire in a crowded theater. Holmes has been called the great dissenter, a misleading appellation. He demonstrated his brilliance as much in concurring as in dissenting opinions. He retired from the Supreme Court on January 12, 1932.

Through his book *The Common Law* and other writings, Oliver Wendell Holmes, Jr., has influenced modern understanding of the history and philosophy of law as a living organism. As a judge seated on the highest judicial bench of his country, he eloquently applied his erudition to the thousands of cases that came before him. He played a leading part in shaping the basic constitutional doctrines of free speech and due process that define the role of American government. Finally, over an unusually long and fruitful judicial career, he served as a powerful inspiration to generations of men and women of the law who were to follow him.

Bibliography

Bowen, Catherine Drinker. *Yankee from Olympus: Justice Holmes and His Family*. Boston: Atlantic/Little, Brown, 1944.

U.S. Supreme Court justice Oliver Wendell Holmes, Jr. (right), with Chief Justice William Howard Taft at a White House reception in 1922. *(AP/Wide World Photos)*

707

Howe, Mark DeWolfe. *Justice Oliver Wendell Holmes: The Shaping Years, 1841-1870*. Cambridge, Mass.: Harvard University Press, 1957.

_____. *Justice Oliver Wendell Holmes: The Proving Years, 1870-1882*. Cambridge, Mass.: Harvard University Press, 1963.

Novick, Sheldon M. *Honorable Justice: The Life of Oliver Wendell Holmes*. Boston: Little, Brown, 1989.

White, G. Edward. *Justice Oliver Wendell Holmes: Law and the Inner Self*. New York: Oxford University Press, 1993.

Charles H. O'Brien

Harold Holt

Born: August 5, 1908; Sydney, Australia
Died: December 17, 1967; near Portsea, Victoria, Australia

Prime minister of Australia (1966-1967)

The parents of Harold Edward Holt (HEH-ruhld EHD-wurd HOHLT) had little political influence on their son. His mother died while he was a teenager, and his father was in the theater business. At the age of eleven, Harold was sent to boarding school at Wesley College in Melbourne, so did not have a close family life. Although he graduated from the University of Melbourne's Law School in 1930, he did not practice law extensively. He was elected to the federal Parliament as a member of the United Australia Party in 1935, and within five years he became minister for labour and national service. When Robert Menzies resigned as prime minister in 1966, Holt was the overwhelming choice to replace him.

Holt Becomes Prime Minister

Harold Holt's term as prime minister of Australia was cut short after only two years by a tragic accident. Consequently, he had little time to develop a distinct leadership style and continued many of the polices of Menzies, his predecessor. For most of this period he was preoccupied with issues relating to the Vietnam War. He was a great admirer and enthusiastic supporter of U.S. president Lyndon B. Johnson, and he claimed that Australia would go "all the way with LBJ" in its military commitment in Vietnam.

Because Menzies had retired in an election year, it was Holt's responsibility to lead his party into the 1966 election. President Johnson visited Australia before the election. His popularity probably contributed to Holt's victory over the Labor Party even though Labor had promised to recall Australian soldiers from Vietnam if elected. The Labor Party leader at the time, Arthur Calwell, provided uninspiring leadership for the opposition, a fact that also contributed to Holt's victory. Despite the lingering controversies over Vietnam, the Liberal-Country Party coalition won twice as many seats in the House of Representatives as the Labor Party.

Problems in Office

During 1967 several incidents embarrassed Holt and the government. In the so-called VIP affair, it was revealed that government ministers had inappropriately used Royal Australian Air Force planes for travel. Holt claimed that the incident was an honest error, but the Labor Party was quick to suggest that the occurrence implied that the government was either dishonest or incompetent. In the same year, the government

Harold Holt *(National Archives)*

709

Immigration Policy in Australia

The Immigration Restriction Act of 1901 made it very difficult for non-Caucasians to immigrate to Australia. This restrictive immigration policy, generally referred to as the White Australia policy, was designed primarily to prevent the immigration of people from Asia, and it continued well into the 1950's. Harold Holt was minister for immigration in the Robert Menzies government during the 1949-1956 period. During this time he reduced the residency requirements for Australian citizenship, although barriers limiting Asian immigration remained in place. Later, as prime minister, Holt continued the process of relaxing Australia's strict immigration laws. He traveled to Asia and visited many Asian leaders in their own countries, encouraging increased immigration from the region. Australia's small population and resulting shortage of workers was a motivation to expand immigration. Efforts were made to match immigrant skills with the jobs that were needed as the Australian economy grew in the 1960's.

reopened the *Voyager* inquiry. Some years earlier, two military ships, the *Voyager*, a destroyer, and the *Melbourne*, an aircraft carrier, had collided, with considerable loss of life. The question of human error in the accident lingered for years. Both incidents were exploited by the Labor opposition, who relentlessly pointed out the government's mistakes and weaknesses. When the charismatic Gough Whitlam replaced Calwell as opposition leader, the Labor Party gained political momentum and became a more effective political opponent for the Liberal Party. In the 1967 half-Senate election, the above factors were on the voters' minds: Holt's government lost control of the Senate, although it retained control of the House of Representatives.

Despite the problems, Holt continued to promote Australia's industrial development and encouraged increased immigration. He was admired by his colleagues and, notwithstanding a disaster at the next election, most likely would have continued as prime minister for some years. His term was tragically cut short, however, when he disappeared while swimming at Cheviot

Australian prime minister Harold Holt arriving in New York in 1966 for a meeting of the U.N. General Assembly and a discussion of the Vietnam War and other issues with U.S. president Lyndon B. Johnson. *(AP/Wide World Photos)*

Beach on the Mornington Peninsula just before Christmas in 1967. Despite a massive search, his body was never recovered and he was presumed drowned.

Bibliography

Albinski, Henry S. *Politics and Foreign Policy in Australia: The Impact of Vietnam and Conscription.* Durham, N.C.: Duke University Press, 1970.

Carrol, Brian. *From Barton to Fraser: Every Australian Prime Minister.* North Melbourne, Australia: Cassell, 1978.

Galligan, Brian. *Federal Republic: Australia's Constitutional System of Government.* Cambridge, England: Cambridge University Press, 1995.

Weller, Patrick, ed. *Menzies to Keating: The Development of the Australian Prime Ministership.* Carlton, Australia: Melbourne University Press, 1992.

Nicholas C. Thomas

Harold Holt voting in Australia's 1966 election, in which his Liberal coalition defeated the Labor Party, then led by Arthur Calwell. *(AP/Wide World Photos)*

Erich Honecker

Born: August 25, 1912; Neunkirchen, Germany
Died: May 29, 1994; Santiago, Chile

East German leader, head of East Germany's Communist Party (1971-1989)

Erich Honecker (EH-rihk HO-neh-kur) was born into a German working-class family that was active in radical politics. At the age of fourteen, Honecker became a member of the Communist Youth Movement. His experience in this organization would help prepare him for work among young people after World War II. A construction worker by trade, he joined the Communist Party of Germany (KPD) in 1929. After Adolf Hitler and the Nazis outlawed all other political parties, Honecker joined the illegal antifascist movement and organized young leftists throughout Germany. The Gestapo—Hitler's secret police—became aware of his actions. In 1935 they gave him ten years at hard labor for opposing the Nazi dictatorship.

A Rising East German Star

Freed by the Soviet Red Army at the end of World War II, Honecker soon joined returning exiled German communists. His organizational abilities allowed him to rise quickly within the Communist Party apparatus, which was sponsored by the Soviets in their zone of occupation. In 1946 he was an important founder of the Free German Youth (FDJ), which served as the youth group of the German Communists. Honecker was a rising star within the German communist world, and he was elected to the KPD Central Committee that same year. One of his most important early duties was to help organize the forced merger of the Social Democratic Party and the KPD in the east. This task, which required both strength of personality and a degree of tact, was successful, and the Socialist Unity Party (SED) was created.

Heir Apparent

By the time of the official proclamation of the German Democratic Republic (DDR), or East Germany, in 1949 from the Soviet zone of occupation, it appeared that Honecker was a key contender for higher party office, perhaps even to replace party leader Walter Ulbricht. His authority increased in 1961 when Ulbricht gave him the job of overseeing the construction of the Berlin Wall, which they built to stem the tide of refugees heading west in search of political freedom, higher wages, and more consumer goods. Honecker, who called the wall an "antifascist protective barrier," carried out this assignment with great success. For the next five years, his

East German leader Erich Honecker (right) with Soviet Communist Party head Leonid Brezhnev in the 1960's. *(Camera Press/Archive Photos)*

influence within the party and the DDR's government increased steadily as SED leaders saw Honecker as an invaluably energetic yet loyal official. His unfailing loyalty to Ulbricht and SED leadership paid off in 1967, when he was formally designated as the successor to the party leader.

Leader of East Germany

Honecker became the leader of the SED in 1971 and head of the East German government five years later. His succession to power was greeted with optimism by many who thought he would be a more tolerant and open ruler than Ulbricht had been. Honecker did open up the country to more Western trade and travel—particularly with West Germany—but he continued to run a repressive government that prevented its citizens from freely traveling outside the Soviet bloc. His rule was noted more for its emphasis on economic development than ideological campaigns. Honecker took great pride in the DDR becoming one of the top ten industrial countries in the world. The result was an undemocratic but relatively prosperous society that had a high level of social security but a low level of political freedom.

Erich Honecker in October, 1989, the month he was forced to resign as head of the East German government. *(Imapress/Archive Photos)*

Free German Youth

Founded soon after World War II, the Free German Youth (FDJ) became an important source of training and recruitment for the East German regime. Erich Honecker, as chair of the FDJ from 1946 to 1955, molded the organization to be an institution which could mobilize young East Germans at the behest of the SED. Participation in the political education of the youth group was key to later advancement within both the party and the government.

Still, many FDJ activities were social or recreational in nature, which led some people to call it a type of "red" boy scouts. Further, young people's natural curiosity about the world and taste for the exotic was satisfied by numerous international anti-imperialist solidarity campaigns. These campaigns mobilized FDJ members in defense of various victims of repression ranging from South Africans to Palestinians. A prime focus of the organization was always the struggle for peace. The terrible consequences of war were stressed, and the East German regime was touted as "the state of socialism and peace on German soil." Thus, members were urged to protest all new deployments of weapon systems in West Germany, such as the Pershing II and cruise missiles of the 1980's.

The Trial of Honecker in 1992-1993

Erich Honecker was charged with abuse of power and ordering criminal acts, and his trial raised a number of complex legal and moral issues. His lawyers argued that the West German government, which had previously welcomed him as a legitimate head of state, had no right to try him for crimes committed in another (albeit since dissolved) country. In addition, many observers believed that the trial had a vindictive aspect and pointed out that most world leaders could be charged with similar crimes. As public opinion turned against the trial, Honecker's health worsened, and the court finally released him on humanitarian grounds.

The Fall of Honecker

By the 1980's, Erich Honecker was in his seventies and increasingly gave signs of being out of touch with the people of East Germany and with the monumental changes taking place in the Soviet bloc. When confronted with pressure for internal reforms from Soviet leader Mikhail Gorbachev, Honecker seemed both rigid and uncertain. Unable to adjust to the rapidly changing political conditions, he saw his regime collapse amid massive antigovernment demonstrations. When a number of important leaders within the SED, such as the DDR's spy chief, Markus Wolff, frustrated Honecker's attempts to use force against the protesters, he was forced to resign in October, 1989.

Within a year, the DDR had merged with West Germany and ceased to exist as an independent nation. In 1992 Honecker was brought to trial for his role in political repression such as ordering the shooting of East Germans fleeing over the Berlin Wall. By this time, however, Honecker's health was fading, and he was released in 1993. He retired to Chile—many of whose officials had once received political asylum from Honecker—where he died in 1994.

Honecker's Legacy

It has been said that Erich Honecker set for himself the impossible task of building socialism in half a country. Moreover, his attempt was made without regard for the rights or desires of East Germany's citizens. During the early years of his rule, the DDR was increasingly accepted as a legitimate member of the world community, even by West Germany. There was full employment and free health care and education; almost all citizens had their basic economic needs met. Yet while he was able to lead his nation to a decent standard of living, Honecker was unable to accept the people's desire for political liberties. He prided himself on being one of the Soviet Union's most reliable allies, but when the Soviet leadership moved toward reform and greater freedom he found himself out of step.

Bibliography

Lippmann, Heinz. *Honecker and the New Politics of Europe.* New York: Macmillan, 1972.

Marcuse, Peter. *Missing Marx.* New York: Monthly Review Press, 1991.

Steele, Jonathan. *Inside East Germany: The State That Came in from the Cold.* New York: Urizen Books, 1977.

William A. Pelz

Herbert Hoover

Born: August 10, 1874; West Branch, Iowa
Died: October 20, 1964; New York, New York

President of the United States during the onset of the Great Depression (1929-1933)

Herbert Clark Hoover (HUR-burt CLAHRK HEW-vur) has been one of the most maligned presidents in American history because he had the misfortune to take office shortly before the 1929 stock market crash and the Great Depression of the 1930's. Because of his ill-timed accession to the nation's highest office, his contributions to the business environment of the United States are often overlooked. His many offices included stints as secretary of commerce, head of the World War I Office of Food Administration, and leader of the American Relief Foundation after World War I. Following his one term as president (1929-1933), he continued to contribute to the nation with studies of government efficiency and effectiveness.

Early Years

Hoover's father, Jesse Hoover, was a farm implement dealer and blacksmith; his mother, Hulda Minthorn, was a teacher. The family was Quaker and provided a religious influence that lasted throughout his life. Hoover learned early that hard work and diligence were qualities that were prized and rewarded. Hoover's father died when he was six, and his mother only two years later. He was subsequently raised by relatives, including an uncle in Oregon. While working as an office boy in his uncle's business, Hoover spent his spare time assisting the company bookkeeper and decided he wanted to pursue a career in accounting. This objective was later changed to the field of engineering when Hoover joined the initial class of students to enter Stanford University. Following graduation in 1895, he began a career that led to his recognition as a distinguished mining engineer. He worked for several mines in Australia, then moved to China in 1899,

shortly after his marriage to Lou Henry—also a geological engineering graduate of Stanford. He later worked at mines in Russia, Burma, and Japan. He was a regular contributor to mining journals. He authored a book in 1909 entitled *Principles of Mining*—a volume that combined his interests in engineering and accounting.

Because Hoover's consulting firm managed mines for numerous corporations, he was in a position to standardize the accounting and management functions. This standardization made comparability of operations and financial statements possible, which led to greater efficiency in mining operations. Hoover's philosophy throughout his mining career was "elimination of waste."

Herbert Hoover *(Library of Congress)*

A Boxer, or Chinese nationalist member of the "righteous harmonious fists." Herbert Hoover's mining company in China became caught in the middle of the struggle known as the Boxer Rebellion. *(National Archives)*

A Career Change

Hoover's mining career ended with the beginning of World War I, and he began a career in public service. By this time, his mining career had made him a wealthy man. He first held the position of administrator for Belgian relief and later the position of U.S. food administrator. In this latter job, his goals were to stabilize prices while ensuring ample supplies of wheat, meat, corn, and poultry. One author described Hoover as a "man of action" at a time when action was desperately needed. Hoover's techniques allowed the United States to weather the crisis without the food riots and hyperinflation experienced by other combatants in the war. His emphasis on efficiency of operations showed through in government as it did in mining—one commentator stated that Hoover could squeeze more out of a dollar than anyone else in Washington. From 1921 to 1928, Hoover served as secretary of commerce in the Warren G. Harding and Calvin Coolidge administrations. As secretary, Hoover preached the concept of efficiency, including emphasis on con-

Hoover and the Boxer Rebellion

In early 1900, many antiforeign disturbances erupted in northern China. Armed Chinese zealots had the objective of eliminating foreigners and their works. These militant patriots were known as Boxers because the name they adopted translated as "righteous harmonious fists." Herbert Hoover's company was attempting to acquire Chinese mining rights, and the turmoil made business difficult and dangerous. Foreigners and Chinese Christians were burned alive, and missionary churches were set on fire. Regular Chinese army units soon joined the Boxers.

In June, 1900, Hoover's mining operation was attacked by five thousand Chinese soldiers and twenty-five thousand Boxers. His settlement of

Tientsin was defended by about three thousand men, including twenty-five hundred Russian and British soldiers. Within a week, the Chinese forces had increased to 380,000. Only hostility between the Boxers and the disciplined Chinese army regulars prevented exploitation of their superiority in numbers. Despite constant shelling, the village held out for four weeks until reinforcements in the form of about two thousand Japanese troops and U.S. Marines arrived. The combined troops then attacked the disorganized Chinese, with Hoover riding along as a guide. The Chinese fled in disorder, and the ordeal was over.

Black Thursday and Black Tuesday

Thursday, October 24, 1929, is called Black Thursday because it was on this day that the stock market crash of 1929 began. Stock prices dropped $4 billion—a record decline—and the volume of trading was so great that clerks could not clear all the transactions until 5:00 A.M. the next day. On Friday, banks stepped in—particularly the House of J. P. Morgan—to buy up stocks and support the market. The following Monday, however, a panic ensued, and thousands of investors were ruined.

The next day, Tuesday, October 29, became known as Black Tuesday because that day witnessed a price drop that was even larger than that of the previous Thursday. The stampede to unload stocks resulted in a $14 billion loss. The sixteen leading stocks alone dropped nearly $3 billion. Confidence in the economy was shattered, and thus began the Great Depression that affected the world throughout the 1930's. By November 13, when stocks hit their lowest point, stock market values had declined more than $30 billion. This amount was equivalent to what the United States had spent on its involvement in World War I.

President Herbert Hoover could do nothing to stem the fall of public confidence. He bore the brunt of public anger, since it seemed that he was not addressing the problems of the unemployed. By the early 1930's, homeless people had built settlements of cardboard shacks; they came to be called "Hoovervilles."

vincing manufacturers to standardize their parts and supplies.

Hoover the President

Hoover's luck ran out shortly after he became the thirty-first U.S. president in 1929. The stock market crashed in October, 1929, and a massive worldwide depression—the Great Depression—followed. Hoover spent the last three years of his presidency attempting unsuccessfully to bring the economy back to normal. He met with industry leaders, tried to balance the government budget, and attempted to increase both production and consumption, but nothing worked. Franklin D. Roosevelt defeated him in the presidential race of 1932. Hoover spent much of the last thirty years of his life trying to defend himself against the blame leveled at him by a disheartened populace. He wrote numerous books explaining his positions.

Hoover is generally remembered as being the president in office when the stock market crashed and the Depression began, but his work in Washington before his presidency was well received. Industry as a whole benefitted from his popularization of efficiency measures and standardization of production. His contributions to the mining industry were particularly significant: His emphases on cost accounting and management efficiency took a disorganized industry and made it routinely profitable. In the late 1940's, as a Harry S Truman appointee, Hoover headed a commission (known as the Hoover Commission) to study the efficiency of the executive branch of the U.S. government. The commission's report emphasized the contributions of budgeting and accountability—factors which, when implemented, have contributed to government operations. Thus, other than his presidency, Hoover should be remembered as a contributor to efficiency and effectiveness in business and government.

Bibliography

Darling, J. N. *As Ding Saw Hoover*. Ames: Iowa State Press, 1954.

Nash, George H. *The Life of Herbert Hoover: Master of Emergencies, 1917-1918*. New York: Norton, 1996.

Smith, Richard N. *An Uncommon Man: The Triumph of Herbert Hoover*. New York: Simon & Schuster, 1984.

Sobel, Robert. *Herbert Hoover at the Onset of the Depression, 1929-1930*. Philadelphia: J. B. Lippincott, 1975.

Wilson, Joan Hoff. *Herbert Hoover: Forgotten Progressive*. Boston: Little, Brown, 1975.

Dale L. Flesher

J. Edgar Hoover

Born: January 1, 1895; Washington, D.C.
Died: May 2, 1972; Washington, D.C.

Head of the U.S. Federal Bureau of Investigation (1924-1972)

John Edgar Hoover (JON EHD-gur HEW-vur) was the son of a federal government official and a devout conservative Christian mother. From his parents, both of Swiss descent, he received a disciplined religious upbringing. In 1917, after graduating from George Washington University Law School, Hoover entered the U.S. Department of Justice, where he worked for the rest of his life. He became director of the Federal Bureau of Investigation (FBI) in 1924. He never married.

Reform of the FBI

Hoover took over an organization in need of reform. As he knew from several years working as assistant to the U.S. attorney general, it had suffered for years from the pernicious effects of political patronage. Among his first acts was to fire all corrupt and incompetent personnel. He instituted strict new hiring policies. His FBI was to be a professional agency of career civil servants appointed and promoted on merit. He required employees to be trained in accounting or law. Clear lines of authority were established, with control in the director's office, not in a politician's hands.

One of Hoover's first priorities was to establish a centralized service of identification within the bureau for the use of federal, state, and local law enforcement agencies. By the time of his death, the Identification Division had three thousand employees, a bank of 150 million fingerprints, and seven thousand contributing agencies. Another contribution he made to law enforcement was the FBI crime laboratory, established in 1932. It helped solve cases by analyzing and identifying blood, hair, firearms, paint, handwriting, typewriters, inks, and other bits of evidence. Most of the staff in the laboratory division were required to have scientific or technical training.

Also in 1932, Hoover began compiling crime statistics for the Uniform Crime Reports (UCR), a barometer of criminal activity in the United States. In 1935 he established a training school, later called the FBI National Academy. Over the following twenty years, it graduated some thirty-two hundred students, many of whom became chiefs of police and other leaders in law enforcement. Convinced of the need to engage the public in a "war on crime," Hoover enlisted the media. By the end of 1935, journalists and motion pictures had firmly established the image of the FBI as the country's leader in scientific policing.

J. Edgar Hoover *(Library of Congress)*

FBI director J. Edgar Hoover testifying before the Senate Internal Security Subcommittee in 1953. *(Archive Photos)*

Domestic Surveillance

In the mid-1930's, as war loomed in Europe and Asia, the United States felt threatened by subversion from outside and within. Hoover set the FBI to the task of policing the activities of communists, fascists, and other radicals within the country. When World War II broke out in Europe in 1939, the bureau's Intelligence Division was granted sole power to investigate and collect information concerning acts of espionage, subversion, and sabotage. From the beginning, Hoover engaged in wiretapping and employed informants for the surveillance of American citizens as well as foreigners.

In the 1950's, at the high point of the Cold War, Hoover's focus shifted mainly to investigating domestic subversion. Like his friend Senator Joseph McCarthy of Wisconsin, Hoover was convinced that the spread of communism at home and abroad was the country's greatest danger. From this perspective, he assigned a low priority to dealing with organized crime, until forced to do so by pressure from the Kennedy administration, notably attorney general Robert F. Kennedy. Hoover and Robert Kennedy bitterly disliked each other. Later in the 1960's, Hoover regarded protests against the Vietnam War as little less than treasonous.

Hoover was also distressed by agitation among minorities in the United States for an end to centuries of oppression and discrimination. Greatly magnifying their threat to national security, he targeted civil rights organizations and their leaders, whom he suspected of communist

The Federal Bureau of Investigation

In 1908 U.S. attorney general Charles J. Bonaparte organized a small group of investigators within the Department of Justice. They became known as the Bureau of Investigation, responsible for investigating all violations of federal law except those assigned to another agency. The bureau grew rapidly during World War I and the Red Scare that followed. In 1919 J. Edgar Hoover was placed in charge of the bureau's General Intelligence Division, which targeted radical aliens. By 1924 the threat of subversion had diminished. As the bureau's new director, Hoover concentrated his remarkable administrative skills on rebuilding the bureau into an elite law enforcement agency. He enforced a strict code of dress and conduct and forbade the use of intoxicants. Agents had to wear dark suits and neckties. With the exception of a few black chauffeurs, Hoover recruited only white males.

Hoover and the Politics of Deceit

J. Edgar Hoover owed some of his virtually unchallenged authority until the last decade of his life to skillful policies of deception. As head of the General Intelligence Division under Attorney General Palmer, he gladly collaborated in his boss's exaggeration of the danger of domestic subversion by foreign-born radical aliens. In the early 1930's, as part of his campaign against gangsters, he enlisted aid from the press and from Hollywood. He focused on high-profile cases, planting carefully tailored stories of FBI arrests. He also shaped the plots of numerous films depicting the bureau's agents as super cops. Hoover systematically attempted to mold the public's image of the FBI and its director as flawless.

He manipulated Congress as well as the public, escaping serious scrutiny of his practices and winning easy approval of his budgets. His public relations policies worked successfully until they were challenged in the last years of his life. Darker aspects of Hoover's practice of deception appear in his brutal, unfair, and often dishonest personal attacks on civil rights leaders, particularly Martin Luther King, Jr., in the 1960's.

sympathies. He carried on a long, bitter, personal vendetta against Martin Luther King, Jr. From 1963 to 1968 wiretaps were used to obtain information about the civil rights leader's private life in an attempt to discredit him.

Hoover had become immensely powerful. Few members of Congress were free of the fear that embarrassing or incriminating evidence against them might be tucked away in the bureau's secret files. Hoover complied with presidents who wanted information from the bureau about political opponents. On occasion, he leaked personal information to damage his enemies. (After his death in 1972, a scandalous dossier on Eleanor Roosevelt was found in his "official and confidential" files.) In the last few years of his life, he continued to be feared—no president dared dismiss him from office—but his reputation was clearly declining.

Hoover did more than any other person to develop the Federal Bureau of Investigation into a professional, effective federal law enforcement agency. Under him the FBI also applied its technical and scientific resources to lifting the level of professionalism among the nation's state and local policing agencies. For decades he also served his country as a pillar of stability and continuity.

However, Hoover had deep flaws, both personal and professional. Since his death, allegations of homosexuality, transvestism, collusion with Mafia leaders, and other hidden vices have tarnished his reputation for probity. In addition, his rabid anticommunism, his discrimination against blacks and women, and his authoritarian style of leadership weakened public support for the FBI and left it ill-prepared to carry on without him.

Bibliography

O'Reilly, Kenneth. *Hoover and the Un-Americans: The FBI, HUAC, and the Red Menace.* Philadelphia: Temple University Press, 1983.

Potter, Claire Bond. *War on Crime: Bandits, G-Men, and the Politics of Mass Culture.* New Brunswick, N.J.: Rutgers University Press, 1998.

Powers, Richard Gid. *G-Men: Hoover's FBI in American Popular Culture.* Carbondale: Southern Illinois University Press, 1983.

_____. *Secrecy and Power: The Life of J. Edgar Hoover.* New York: Free Press, 1987.

Summers, Anthony. *Official and Confidential: The Secret Life of J. Edgar Hoover.* New York: Putnams's, 1993.

Charles H. O'Brien

Félix Houphouët-Boigny

Born: October 18, 1905; Yamoussoukro, Ivory Coast
Died: December 7, 1993; Yamoussoukro, Ivory Coast

First president of the independent Ivory Coast (1960-1993)

Félix Houphouët-Boigny (fay-LEEKZ ew-FWAY bwah-NYEE) was the son of a Baule chief. He was educated in French colonial schools and graduated as a physician in 1925. He practiced medicine until 1940. He also took part in the organization of African planters who opposed French policies of forced labor and the inequities of colonial economic policy.

Houphouët-Boigny was the founder of the African Agricultural Syndicate, the Rassemblement Démocratique Africain (the RDA, also known as the African Democratic Assembly), and the Democratic Party of Côte d'Ivoire (PDCI), which was a branch of the RDA. In 1945, he began a political career that spanned nearly five decades.

Félix Houphouët-Boigny *(Library of Congress)*

He served in a number of local, territorial, and regional assemblies, as mayor of Abidjan, as a member of the French National Assembly from 1945-1959, and as a government minister prior to the achievement of independence in 1960. He was one of Africa's most notable advocates of freedom and independence even before he assumed the leadership of the Ivory Coast.

A Founding Father

Houphouët-Boigny, more than any other figure in the country's politics, may be rightly called the founding father of the Ivory Coast (in French, Côte d'Ivoire). He was the prime minister during the transition phase to independence from France, and at independence he was elected the first president of the republic. He was elected to seven successive five-year terms as president until his death in 1993. No other African leader can claim so lengthy and so successful a legacy of rule.

Although Houphouët-Boigny adopted the democratic parliamentary system of the French at his country's independence, he determined within a few years that a multiparty system would be too disruptive and inefficient, and he moved decisively to establish the PDCI as the sole national party. Although he centralized the political process, Houphouët-Boigny encouraged liberal economic development, free enterprise, and foreign investment. Coupled with the country's diverse agricultural economy, forest resources, diamonds, manganese, and modest supplies of oil, these policies encouraged spectacular economic growth during the 1960's and 1970's, leading many to refer to the "Ivoirian miracle"—an economy that contrasted vividly with the failing economic policies of many other newly independent African countries.

While the economy prospered, Houphouët-Boigny consolidated political authority to himself. The PDCI became the means through which he implemented decisions. Traditional ruling chiefs were bypassed in the political process, thus diminishing the possibility of interethnic disputes and conflicts. Houphouët-Boigny relied heavily on his ties to France to ensure the country's security and thus kept the Ivoirian army very small. This policy reduced the possibility of a *coup d'état*. The result of all these policies was a stable and reasonably popular regime despite the authoritarian nature of its political rule.

Ivory Coast president Félix Houphouët-Boigny in 1971, at the height of the country's economic growth, nicknamed the "Ivoirian miracle." *(AP/Wide World Photos)*

Calls for Reform

During the late 1970's and the 1980's, the Ivory Coast's economic growth slowed considerably, leading to growing unrest in the country and to demands for increased democratization. Criticism of Houphouët-Boigny included complaints about his penchant for large, frivolous building projects, including the world's largest basilica (church) in his birthplace of Yamoussoukro. Houphouët-Boigny, realizing that reforms would be necessary, agreed to the establishment of multiparty competition. These reforms were implemented in 1990, and he was rewarded by Ivoirians with his seventh term as president.

When the political life of a country is domi-

Economic Success in the Ivory Coast

If there is one factor that will be remembered by the people of the Ivory Coast regarding the leadership of Félix Houphouët-Boigny, it will be the spectacular economic growth his policies sparked during the first two decades of the country's existence. The Ivory Coast (Côte d'Ivoire) is the world's largest producer of cacao and the third largest producer of coffee. Exports from these sectors buoyed the Ivoirian economy. Substantial exports of a diverse agricultural sector also contributed to prosperity, as did the availability of timber, a variety of minerals, and a modest supply of oil. Although overcutting of forests and price declines for commodities led to economic retrenchment in the 1980's, Houphouët-Boigny's liberal economic policies, helped the country weather the economic storms. The Ivory Coast continues to be a favorite location for foreign investors because of its support of free enterprise and its long-standing political stability.

The African Democratic Assembly

Félix Houphouët-Boigny's advocacy of African rights and his campaign on behalf of reform of colonial policies were not merely fought on behalf of people of the Ivory Coast. His concerns extended to the other French-speaking regions of Africa. His founding of the Rassemblement Démocratique Africain (RDA), better known in English as the African Democratic Assembly, reflected his belief that Africans deserved political freedoms and independence. Houphouët-Boigny's campaign on behalf of African planters and agricultural interests had convinced him of the need for political organization. In 1944 he founded the African Agricultural Syndicate to lobby for African agricultural interests. In April of 1946 he founded the Parti Démocratique de la Côte d'Ivoire (PDCI), which would become the principal vehicle for championing Ivoirian independence.

In October of 1946, Houphouët-Boigny established the RDA as a regional body to unite french-speaking territorial parties into a wider regional and cooperative movement. The PDCI was but one branch of this larger West African movement. Thus, even before the Ivory Coast's independence in 1960, Houphouët-Boigny had distinguished himself as one of Africa's foremost statesmen, and the groundwork he laid during the late-colonial period paved the way for the independence of many West African countries.

nated by a single personality in the way Houphouët-Boigny dominated Ivory Coast politics, fears often arise about instabilities after the death of the ruler. Houphouët-Boigny understood that steps would need to be taken in order to ensure a smooth transition in leadership. After his election to his seventh and last term as president, he turned attention to the problem of succession. Upon his death on December 7, 1993, Henry Konan Bedie, whom he had groomed as his successor, became president.

Development and Peace

Houphouët-Boigny was one of Africa's best known and most successful political figures. He led his country to independence, and, although he followed an authoritarian style of rule, his policies promoted both peace and prosperity in the Ivory Coast. His country's prosperity attracted millions of neighboring West African workers. He maintained peaceful relations with neighboring states and among the factions within his own country.

He used his power and political skill deftly to guide his nation toward effective economic development and political stability, and was wise enough to adjust and reform when, toward the end of his life, political dissension arose. He laid a very stable foundation for subsequent governments to build upon, and will be remembered as his nation's most prominent patriot and one of Africa's most influential statesmen.

Bibliography

Handloff, Robert E. *Côte d'Ivoire: A Country Study*. Washington, D.C.: U.S. Government Printing Office, 1991.

Harshe, Rajen. *Pervasive Entente: France and the Ivory Coast in African Affairs*. London: Macmillan, 1984.

Mundt, R. J. *Historical Dictionary of the Ivory Coast*. Metuchen, N.J.: Scarecrow Press, 1987.

Riboud, Michelle. *Ivory Coast, 1960-1986*. San Francisco: ICS Press, 1987.

Robert F. Gorman

John Howard

Born: July 26, 1939; Sydney, New South Wales, Australia

Prime minister of Australia (took office 1996)

John Winston Howard (JON WIHN-stuhn HOW-urd) was born to middle-class parents; he attended Canterbury Boys' High, and then the University of Sydney. At the age of eighteen, Howard became active in the Australian Liberal Party (whose pro-free market tendencies would lead it to be described as "conservative" in the United States). He graduated from the university with a law degree and was a solicitor (lawyer) in several Sydney firms during the 1960's. In 1971, he married Alson Janette Parker, known as Janette; they had two sons and one daughter. In 1974, Howard was elected to Parliament as a Liberal from the Bennelong constituency.

A Mandate and Its Consequences

Howard joined the Liberal government in 1975, rising quickly to become treasurer in 1977. When the Liberals went into opposition after 1983 and then lost another election the year after, Howard became leader in 1985. After losing the 1987 election to incumbent Bob Hawke's Labor Party, however, Howard was replaced by John Hewson, a hard-line "economic rationalist." After Hewson unexpectedly lost the 1993 election, the party turned again to Howard, who in the meantime had served as opposition spokesman on a number of issues. Howard waged an energetic and broad-based campaign in 1996, and he won by a wide margin. As prime minister, Howard used his mandate to redirect many government policies.

Whereas his predecessor, Paul Keating, had stated that Australia was a multicultural nation that was part of Asia, Howard reaffirmed Australia's identity as a pro-Western nation and stressed its alliance with the United States. Howard and his treasurer, Peter Costello, advocated the privatization of Telstra, the Australian telephone company. A plan to construct more nursing homes was abandoned by Howard over fears that senior citizens would have to sell their homes to finance it.

Aboriginal land rights remained an issue in the Howard government, along with the wider issue of white Australians' need to reconcile with the indigenous population.

Howard was judged more sympathetic to the rights of white farmers than was his predecessor, an inclination that emerged after the Australian High Court handed down the Wik decision (*Wik People vs. State of Queensland*) in 1996. This decision confirmed the recognition of Aboriginal

A jubilant John Howard in 1996 after his conservative coalition won a resounding victory over Australia's Labor Party, led by Paul Keating. *(AP/Wide World Photos)*

Australian prime minister John Howard at a 1997 news conference in Jakarta, Indonesia, promising Australian willingness to participate in efforts to aid in the Indonesian financial crisis. *(Reuters/Enny Nuraheni/Archive Photos)*

land rights established in an earlier case, *Mabo and Others vs. State of Queensland* (1992). Howard sought to amend the Wik decision through enacting legislation giving more rights to pastoralists (farmers and grazers). The newly recognized land rights of the native peoples were thereby jeopardized. Parliament managed to pass compromise legislation giving some concessions to both sides, though most Aborigines remained dissatisfied with the result.

Determining Australia's Future

Although the onset of the Asian economic crisis in the fall of 1997 vindicated Howard's decision not to see Australia's future as an indubitably Asian one, it also posed a serious threat to the health of Australia's economy, which had been at the center of Howard's political agenda. At home, the Howard government was surprised by the rise of the One Nation Party, led by Pauline Hanson, a Queensland politician who openly called for an end to Asian immigration and a rollback of Aboriginal rights. Some Australians accused Howard of subtly encouraging the emergence of

The Travel Rorts Affair

The Australian civil service is supposed to be apolitical. About a year into the Howard government, however, it was plunged into controversy in what came to be called the travel rorts affair. Travel "rorts," or reimbursements for travel expenses, are a common feature of Australian political life, given the size of the country and the distance between many of its major cities and the capital, Canberra. In May, 1997, a member of the prime minister's staff, Fiona McKenna, did not inform the prime minister's aide, Grahame Morris, about reimbursements of expenses she had made to John Sharp, the transport minister. On September 26, the prime minister fired both Morris and McKenna.

Since the government had earlier dismissed many civil service employees on the grounds that they were partisans of the opposition Labor Party, the crisis took on a partisan coloration. The Howard government responded to criticism by attacking the opposition finance spokesman, Senator Nick Sherry, for making excessive reimbursement claims for trips to Tasmania to see his family. Sherry attempted suicide on October 3, 1997. This dramatic turn of events helped place the issue in perspective and caused it to fade from the headlines. However, the question of the role of the civil service in a nation with a potential change of government every three years remained challenging.

John Howard (center) touring the New York Stock Exchange in 1997. *(Reuters/Mike Segar/Archive Photos)*

Hanson's racist views by soft-pedaling the multicultural agenda of his predecessor. Most fundamentally, Howard was faced with the desire of many Australians to disestablish the British monarch as sovereign of Australia and formally proclaim a republic as a sign of Australia's coming emergence into the twenty-first century. Though Howard himself remained a staunch monarchist, many even in his own party preferred a republic, and a constitutional convention was held in March, 1998.

A Second Term

Howard called an election for October 3, 1998, in which he was challenged not only by the Labor leader, Kim Beazley, but also by Hanson. The election debate focused largely on economic is-

sues. Though the margin of the Liberals and their coalition partner, the National Party, was smaller than before, the elections resulted in a second Howard government.

Bibliography

Bunbury, Bill. *Unfinished Business: Reconciliation, the Republic and the Constitution.* Sydney: ABC Books, 1998.

Hendeson, Gerard. *A Howard Government? Inside the Coalition.* New York: HarperCollins, 1995.

_____. *Menzies' Child: The Liberal Party of Australia.* Sydney: HarperCollins, 1998.

Melleuish, Gregory. *The Packaging of Australia: Politics and Culture Wars.* Sydney: University of New South Wales Press, 1997.

Nicholas Birns

Victoriano Huerta

Born: December 23, 1854; Colotán, Jalisco, Mexico
Died: January 13, 1916; El Paso, Texas

Mexican revolutionary, provisional president of Mexico (1913-1914)

A lifelong soldier in the Mexican army, Victoriano Huerta (veek-toh-ree-AH-noh WAYR-tah) was basically a conservative who became a dictator during a critical and turbulent time. Huerta had little in common with the rebels who sought either reform or revolution during the 1910-1920 period of civil war in Mexico.

Huerta was born in a small village, and his mixed-blood father and indigenous mother provided him only a rudimentary education. Huerta attached himself to a federal general who stopped in his community. The general selected Huerta as his personal secretary, resulting in Huerta's being admitted into the Colegio Militar, the training ground of Mexican army officers. Commissioned as an officer in the corps of engineers in 1877, Huerta served on the general staff but distinguished himself as a combat officer in the field.

Civil War

When Mexico's civil war broke out in 1910, Huerta made it clear that he would not join the rebels. After the triumph of Francisco Madero, however, Huerta agreed to support the new reformist government by fighting active revolutionaries such as Emiliano Zapata. However, when Pascual Orozco revolted in March, 1912, Madero's cabinet convinced a reluctant Madero to allow Huerta to lead government forces against Orozco. Huerto triumphed, with the result that his prestige among conservatives soared. When a conservative revolt broke out in February of 1913, Huerta promised to defend President Madero but worked behind the scenes with the plotters so that he could become provisional president.

Huerta as Dictator

Once in power, Huerta jailed Madero, and circumstantial evidence points strongly to Huerta's guilt in planning the former president's murder. Huerta did not worry, because he had the strong backing of the U.S. ambassador as well as support from most European nations. When revolts broke out against him, however, Huerta feared social revolution. His response was military, and he declared that he would win at any cost. The federal army campaigned ruthlessly. Huerta also tried to militarize society. Nearly everyone had to wear a uniform, as thousands were drafted into

Victoriano Huerta *(Library of Congress)*

The 1914 U.S. Invasion of Mexico

The final blow to Victoriano Huerta's dictatorship was U.S. intervention. In April, 1914, a small landing party from the USS *Dolphin* landed in Tampico to secure gasoline. Meanwhile, Venustiano Carranza's rebels attacked the port as the U.S. sailors wandered into a restricted dock area. Mexican officials arrested the foreigners but apologized quickly. Since the boat carrying the sailors supposedly was flying the U.S. flag, President Woodrow Wilson demanded that Mexican authorities fire a twenty-one gun salute

to it. Huerta refused. Meanwhile, Wilson learned that a German ship was scheduled to arrive in Veracruz with armaments for Huerta. Wilson therefore ordered the seizure of Veracruz. U.S. Marines occupied the city after a brutal bombardment as Mexican casualties mounted into the hundreds. The public outcry was emotional, and even the rebel forces protested the U.S. intervention. Wilson's attempt to rid Mexico of Huerta nearly backfired.

the army. Schools provided military instruction, and war production increased. The government shut down critical newspapers as a vast network of secret agents spied on the population. The Huerta regime was responsible for dozens of assassinations, including a deputy and a senator. When legislators protested publicly, Huerta closed Congress and marched the lawmakers to jail. The Huerta regime endured because the military and landowners knew that they faced the loss of land and the end of the traditional military if the insurgents won. When labor groups criticized him, Huerta had them exiled.

Fiscal problems began to weaken Huerta. European banks that controlled Mexican finances were angered when Huerta seized customs revenue committed to previous loans. Printing an excessive supply of paper money that rapidly lost its value, the government operated with a

huge deficit. Meanwhile, rebels occupied key oil and cotton-producing areas. Finally, the forces of Francisco Villa, Venustiano Carranza, and Alvaro Obregón routed Huerta's army in the spring of 1914, forcing him to flee to Europe. Huerta agreed to work with the German espionage service in northern Mexico, but U.S. agents arrested him on the way to the border. He died in prison.

Bibliography
Grieb, Kenneth J. *The United States and Huerta*. Lincoln: University of Nebraska Press, 1969.
Meyer, Michael C. *Huerta: A Political Portrait*. Lincoln: University of Nebraska Press, 1972.
Sherman, William L., and Richard E. Greenleaf. *Victoriano Huerta: A Reappraisal*. Mexico City: Imprenta Aldina, 1960.

Douglas W. Richmond

Charles Evans Hughes

Born: April 11, 1862; Glens Falls, New York
Died: August 27, 1948; Osterville, Massachusetts

U.S. Supreme Court justice (1910-1916), secretary of state (1921-1925), and chief justice (1930-1941)

Charles Evans Hughes (CHAHRLZ EH-vuhnz HEWZ) was the only child of an itinerant evangelical minister and a former schoolteacher. He grew up in a home where books and learning were highly valued. After attending public schools, Hughes spent two years at Madison (now Colgate) University before transferring to Brown, where he graduated third in his class. He briefly taught school and read the law before entering Columbia Law School. After graduating in 1884, Hughes joined a New York firm and four years later married a partner's daughter, Antoinette Carter. They had one son and three daughters.

Progressive Reformer

Hughes devoted himself tirelessly to his law practice. In 1905, he was appointed to head several investigative committees that were a part of the Progressive era's efforts to regulate business and to protect consumers. Hughes chaired an examination of abuses committed by New York's utilities industry. After exposing inflated rates and adulterated gas, Hughes's committee recommended regulating, rather than breaking up, the utilities monopoly. He led a similar investigation of the insurance industry. Hughes was elected governor of New York in 1906. Although never particularly adept at partisan politics, he supported popular programs such as regulation of large industries and workmen's compensation laws during his two terms.

Supreme Court Justice

In 1910, President William Howard Taft named Hughes to the Supreme Court of the United States. During the six years he served as an associate justice, Hughes brought his progressive views about economic regulation to the Court. Hughes wrote the unanimous Supreme Court opinion in *Miller v. Wilson* (1915), which upheld a California law that provided a maximum eight-hour work day for women in industry. He also supported the authority of Congress to regulate railroad rates in *Houston, East and West Texas Railway v. United States* (1914).

Several of Hughes's opinions had implications for equal rights. In a 1914 case, *McCabe v. Atchison, Topeka, and Santa Fe Railroad*, the Supreme Court found unconstitutional the railroad's policies that provided dining and sleeping cars for white passengers only. In *Bailey v. Alabama* (1911) he wrote that labor contracts which held many poor black sharecroppers on the land were a violation of the Thirteenth Amendment, which prohibited slavery. Hughes's record during his

Charles Evans Hughes *(Library of Congress)*

first appointment to the Supreme Court was generally humane and progressive.

Presidential Candidate and Secretary of State

In 1916, Hughes was persuaded to resign from the Court and to run as the Republican Party's candidate for president against the incumbent, Woodrow Wilson. Although the United States was not yet involved militarily in World War I, which had begun in 1914, foreign policy was the major issue during the campaign. Hughes took the advice of the more belligerent Republicans and demanded stronger measures against Germany. After his defeat, Hughes returned to private law practice until he was named secretary of state by President Warren G. Harding in 1921.

There was then considerable disagreement in

U.S. secretary of state Charles Evans Hughes (center) with other State Department officials in Washington, D.C. *(Library of Congress)*

the government concerning what the United States' role in the postwar world should be. The Republicans opposed participation in the League of Nations and in most other international bod-

---

Roosevelt's Court-Packing Plan

Franklin D. Roosevelt's New Deal brought a new level of federal regulation to the Depression-era economy. During Roosevelt's first term, the Supreme Court, composed of a number of conservative justices appointed by Republicans during the 1920's, declared major New Deal laws unconstitutional. A significant setback for the administration occurred in 1935, when the Court found the National Recovery Act unconstitutional and expressed a very narrow definition of the power of Congress to regulate the economy. Roosevelt, furious at the Court for its anti-New Deal decisions, accused it of having a "horse-and-buggy" definition of commerce.

After his landslide reelection in 1936, Roosevelt decided to take action. Claiming that the older justices could not handle the Court's heavy workload, he asked Congress to allow the presi-

dent to appoint an additional justice for each one over seventy years old, up to a total of six. His goal was to appoint enough judges sympathetic to the New Deal that its programs would be held constitutional. If the legislation had passed, the Supreme Court could have been expanded from nine to fifteen members. The plan, which seemed to challenge the independence of the Court, was unpopular with Congress, the public, and the judiciary. Chief Justice Charles Evans Hughes prepared a memo for the Senate demonstrating that the Court was operating efficiently. In addition, retirements and the change of the votes of several justices led the Court, under Hughes's direction, to sustain major New Deal laws after 1937. The defeat of Roosevelt's "court-packing" law can be at least partly credited to Charles Evans Hughes.

The Washington Arms Limitation Conference

Fearing a naval race between Great Britain and Japan in the years after World War I, secretary of state Charles Evans Hughes presided over a 1921-1922 naval disarmament conference in Washington, D.C. He opened the meeting with a surprisingly candid speech that called for reducing the American navy along with the British and Japanese fleets in a ratio of 5:5:3. In return for naval cutbacks, Hughes promised the Japanese that the United States would not increase its fortifications on Guam or the Philippines. The signatories to the treaty promised to consult before taking any action in the Pacific region. The Washington Naval Treaties defused international tensions in the immediate postwar period.

ies. Hughes worked to facilitate Germany's payment of war reparations (payments for war damages that were demanded of Germany after World War I) through a system of American loans, and he attempted to discourage an arms race, especially through the Washington Arms Limitation Conference negotiations of 1921-1922. He also attempted to build better relationships with Latin American nations, removing U.S. Marines from the Dominican Republic and Nicaragua.

Chief Justice

In 1930, as the United States was sinking into the worst economic depression in its history, President Herbert Hoover appointed Hughes chief justice of the United States. During his eleven years in that post, Hughes saw the Court move into its elegant new building—and move to reinterpret the constitutionality of sweeping federal involvement in the economy. Franklin D. Roosevelt was elected president in 1932, and his New Deal legislation attempted to combat the Depression with programs to provide relief for unemployment, economic recovery, and reform. During Roosevelt's first term, the Supreme Court declared several major New Deal programs unconstitutional, generally on the basis that Congress did not have the regulatory authority to intervene in the economy.

These decisions angered Roosevelt and led to a serious conflict between him and the Court. It was resolved partly through Hughes's skillful handling of the situation. After 1937, the justices modified their interpretation of the commerce clause of the U.S. Constitution, permitting Congress wide latitude to expand the role of the federal government. Hughes is generally credited with presiding over a revolution in constitutional interpretation while maintaining the integrity of the Supreme Court. In addition, Hughes led the Court in upholding First Amendment rights of free expression against infringement by the states. Key decisions upheld the rights of citizens to demonstrate, picket, and distribute leaflets in public places against restrictive city ordinances. In general, while Hughes presided, the Supreme Court embodied the theory that the Constitution is a living document that evolves in response to the changing political and social environment. Hughes retired from the Court in 1941.

Bibliography

Glad, Betty. *Charles Evans Hughes and the Illusions of Innocence.* Urbana: University of Illinois, 1966.

Perkins, Dexter. *Charles Evans Hughes and American Democratic Statesmanship.* Boston: Little, Brown, 1956.

Pusey, Merlo J. *Charles Evans Hughes.* 2 vols. New York: Harper and Row, 1951.

Mary Welek Atwell

William Morris Hughes

Born: September 25, 1864; London, England
Died: October 28, 1952; Sydney, Australia

Prime minister of Australia (1915-1923)

William Morris Hughes (WIHL-yuhm MOH-rihs HEWZ) was born in London. The Hughes family immigrated to Australia in 1884. For his first six years in Australia, Hughes was an itinerant worker largely in rural areas. By 1890 he owned a small general store in the suburbs of Sydney.

Labor Activist

Hughes became interested in workers' rights during the early 1890's. After assuming positions in the local labor union, he became president of the Waterside Workers' Association, which included nearly all Australian longshoremen. He began to be interested in politics, founding the Labor Party in New South Wales and being elected to that state's Legislative Assembly in 1894. In 1901, the year Australia became fully self-governing, Hughes entered Parliament on the federal level. His politics were unique to their day. While a populist and an energetic defender of workers' rights, Hughes also stood for positions that later would be termed conservative. For instance, he was a strong defender of a continued role for Australia in the British Empire, and he remained loyal to Britain. He also was a believer in white racial superiority and wholly approved of the "White Australia" policy, which prohibited Asians from immigrating to Australia; he also did not disapprove of discriminating against Australia's Aborigines.

Voice for the Working Man

Short in stature but brimming with energy, Hughes soon became a popular political figure. While his acquisition of a law degree in 1904 made him more acceptable to the established elite, his brashness and informal charm endeared him to the common people. In 1914, when Australia entered World War I under the uncertain leadership of Labor Party prime minister Andrew Fisher, Hughes was strongly enthusiastic. When Fisher's ministry crumbled in 1915, Hughes was the natural candidate to take over as prime minister. Hughes assumed office in the aftermath of the Gallipoli campaign, which despite its failure on a military level had proved that the Australian soldier could be counted upon and inspired patriotism.

Conscription Controversy

By 1916, British casualties in Europe necessitated replenishment from troops from Australia

William Morris Hughes *(Library of Congress)*

Australian troops fighting against the Turks in the Dardanelles campaign in World War I. *(National Archives)*

and New Zealand. To supply these troops, the two overseas dominions were asked to institute a draft, or "conscription." Hughes visited Britain for three months in 1916. Hughes's mission was not only to promote cooperation among the various parts of the British Empire in the war effort but also to raise Australia's profile within Britain. Hughes became a popular figure in London, and

The Gallipoli Campaign in World War I

In April, 1915, the British high command decided to attack Turkey to weaken the Central Powers on their southern flank. Australian and New Zealand (Anzac) troops made up a large portion of the combatants who landed on the Gallipoli Peninsula. There was unexpectedly strong resistance from the Turks (led by Kemal Atatürk), and the scale of the fighting on the western front meant that Britain did not allocate many of its resources to the Gallipoli campaign.

The Allies' offensive quickly became bogged down well short of the city of Gallipoli itself. Allied soldiers were unable to capture the mountain of Chunuk Bair, regarded as the military key to seizing their operational objective. By January, 1916, the Anzac troops and their British comrades had been forced to evacuate. The Australian troops for the most part had expected a different, more glamorous sort of war and were not prepared for the routine trench warfare that awaited them. Despite the military defeat, the Gallipoli campaign was a "baptism by fire" not only for the Australian army but for Australia as a whole. The anniversary of the landings, April 25, is still celebrated as Anzac Day in Australia.

The Nationalist Party

The Nationalist Party was born during World War I because of a conflict over conscription (the drafting of men to serve in an army). The Labor Party, with its strong Irish and working-class base, had resentments against Britain and was not willing to commit fully to the war effort. It also feared that foreign workers would take the jobs of the conscripted Australian soldiers. Hughes was expelled from the Labor Party in September, 1916, because he continued to display pro-conscription sentiments. Hughes moved to form a "National Labor" government with Conservative support that would enable him to continue as prime minister. Shortly renamed the Nationalist Party, Hughes's coalition won a landslide victory in 1917 that enabled him to remain in office throughout the war. The consensus that had prevailed during the war crumbled, however, in the early 1920's, and Hughes was forced out of office. The United Australia Party arose shortly thereafter, which continued much of the Nationalist agenda.

his assurances of support were valued. He returned to Australia believing that conscription was a necessity. Conscription was fiercely opposed by many elements in Australian society, however, particularly Irish Catholics opposed to British domination of Ireland and thus unsympathetic to the war effort. The Catholic archbishop of Melbourne, Daniel Mannix, was a key leader of the opposition. Hughes was expelled from the Labor Party and had to reassemble his coalition under the Nationalist Party banner. Australian voters defeated conscription in October, 1916, and then again by an overwhelming majority in December, 1917. In between the two referenda, however, Hughes's coalition won a national election. The general direction of the war effort was given support, therefore, even as conscription itself was rejected.

The Little Digger

Hughes cultivated an image as a strong supporter of the Australian fighting man. He was nicknamed the Little Digger, "digger" being a term for the ordinary Australian soldier, somewhat like "G.I." in the United States. Hughes was seen as guiding Australia through the war, and his reputation took on luster when Australian participation in the Middle East theater helped win the war for the Allied side. After the war, at the Paris Peace Conference in 1919, Hughes was instrumental in securing a separate Australian representation in the League of Nations. He also bargained for Australian administration of the former German colony of Papua in New Guinea under a League of Nations mandate.

Though Hughes had long since lost Labor support, he continued as leader of the Nationalist coalition. This position involved him working with men of a far more temperamentally conservative bent than he; Hughes himself retained a sentimental allegiance to working people and to centralized control of the economy. He also remained active in international affairs. When, in 1922, it seemed that Britain and Turkey would recommence hostilities, Hughes agreed to commit Australian troops to revisit the scene of Gallipoli. The crisis, however, was averted. In February, 1923, Hughes was ousted as prime minister by Conservatives Stanley Bruce and Earle Page.

Hughes remained in Parliament for almost thirty years after his ouster. In 1937, he became foreign minister in the government of Robert Gordon Menzies. Hughes was strongly anti-Nazi, even as Menzies favored appeasement of Germany. This difference led to Hughes's resignation after he criticized Menzies's lack of awareness of the menace posed by Nazism. Hughes lived to the age of eighty-eight, surviving to give counsel to the Australian leaders during World War II.

Australia's First World Leader

Hughes was the first Australian leader to be well-known internationally. His prominence abroad also glamorized his image at home. Hughes remains one of the most admired politicians in Australian history.

Bibliography

Booker, Malcolm. *The Great Professional: A Study of W. M. Hughes*. New York: McGraw-Hill, 1980.

Fitzhardinge, L. F. *William Morris Hughes: A Political Biography*. 2 vols. Sydney: Angus and Robertson, 1964, 1979.

Horne, Donald. *In Search of Billy Hughes*. South Melbourne: Macmillan of Australia, 1979.

Kerr, Greg. *Lost Anzacs*. New York: Oxford University Press, 1998.

Nicholas Birns

Cordell Hull

Born: October 2, 1871; Overton (now Pickett) County, Tennessee
Died: July 23, 1955; Bethesda, Maryland

U.S. secretary of state (1933-1944), winner of 1945 Nobel Peace Prize

Cordell Hull (kohr-DEHL HUHL) was born in a log cabin in the foothills of the Cumberland Mountains in upper-middle Tennessee. His father was a farmer who worked hard to provide a good education for his five sons. After his early education in a variety of schools, Hull graduated in June, 1891, before his twentieth birthday, from Cumberland Law School in Lebanon, Tennessee. This fulfilled his dream of becoming a lawyer; he further hoped to be involved in politics. Following the tradition of his family, he had become a staunch Democrat.

Tennessee Politics

Hull's first political office was as a member of the Tennessee House of Representatives from 1893 to 1897. His election in 1892 was part of a state Democratic Party landslide so big that some predicted the demise of the Republican Party in Tennessee. Although he was only twenty-one years old, Hull's party loyalty and speaking ability had already won him the respect of his party's leadership. When the session opened in January, 1893, he was made the chair of the Committee on Enrolled Bills and was a member of the Judiciary Committee, the Committee on Municipal Affairs, and the Rules Committee.

Hull had no trouble being reelected to the legislature in 1894. His role in resolving the disputed gubernatorial election of that year taught him much about the democratic process of government and gained for him more praise from his party. The remainder of Hull's second term was uneventful, and he did not seek a third. He entered private law practice in Celina, Tennessee. In 1898 he served as an army captain during the Spanish-American War. From 1903 to 1907 Hull was a district circuit judge in Tennessee. During these judicial years, Hull gained a reputation as a serious and hard-working judge and attracted the attention of law-abiding and influential people in Tennessee.

U.S. Congress

Cordell Hull rose to national prominence during his twenty-four years in Congress, first in the House of Representatives (1907-1921, 1923-1931), and then in the Senate (1931-1933). His first four years in the House were, as is normal for a new

Cordell Hull *(The Nobel Foundation)*

U.S. secretary of state Cordell Hull (center) escorting Japanese emissaries to the White House in November of 1941, three weeks before Japanese war planes attacked the U.S. base at Pearl Harbor, Hawaii. *(Library of Congress)*

member of Congress, obscure years. Most of his time was spent trying to secure passage of projects favorable to his district. However, he did win the respect of liberals in the Democratic Party, which captured control of Congress in the off-year elections of 1910. When the Sixty-second Congress convened on December 4, 1911, Hull's obscurity ended. He joined a small group of House Democrats who were planning a parliamentary revolution in the new Congress that was specifically designed to curb the power of the Speaker of the House. That position had become dictatorial, especially under long-time Republican Speaker Joe Cannon. In the committee assignments for the new Congress, Hull was appointed to serve on the House Ways and Means Committee. Through the parliamentary revolution, this committee became the steering committee of the House.

Cordell Hull had earlier become a supporter of a national income tax. When the Sixteenth Amendment to the U.S. Constitution removed the major obstacle to such a tax in 1913, Hull, as a member of the Ways and Means Committee, wrote the first federal income tax law. In 1916 he

U.S. Relations with Japan, 1941

Cordell Hull had much experience with issues relating to Japan, which had been an aggressor nation in Asia since the late nineteenth century. The primary victim of that aggression had been China.

In 1934 Secretary of State Hull rejected a proposed "Japanese Monroe Doctrine" that would have given Japan a free hand in China. Nonetheless, Japan invaded China in 1937. Four years later, in the spring of 1941, Hull met for three weeks with Japanese ambassador Nomura Kichisaburo in a concentrated effort to prevent war. The major issues were Japan's China policy and her alliance with Germany and Italy. The talks produced no encouraging results. Lower-level talks continued throughout the year, but the issues were unresolved. Japan finally broke off the talks in Washington on December 7, 1941, as Japanese war planes were approaching Pearl Harbor.

The Good Neighbor Policy

The Good Neighbor Policy, designed to provide better relations between the United States and the nations of Latin America, was initiated in 1913 by President Woodrow Wilson. However, it was not until President Franklin Roosevelt took office in 1933 that significant actions were taken toward that goal. Secretary of State Cordell Hull became the major force in pursuing the Good Neighbor Policy. Another important leader was Sumner Wells, first as ambassador to Cuba, then as undersecretary of state for Latin America. The intent of the policy was to end resentment toward the United States that had resulted from earlier policies; such as the big-stick diplomacy of Theodore Roosevelt and the dollar diplomacy of William Howard Taft.

A series of Pan-American Conferences began in 1889 to work for cooperation between the American nations. The seventh conference was held in Montevideo, Uruguay, in 1933. Hull represented the United States. Attending nations agreed not to interfere in the internal affairs of the other nations. The eighth conference, in Lima, Peru, in 1938, produced the Declaration of Lima declaring that the American nations would stand together in the event of foreign attack. The high point of the Good Neighbor Policy came during the ninth Pan-American Conference in Bogota, Colombia, in 1948: the creation of the Organization of American States (OAS).

wrote a revision of that law and sponsored the federal estate tax.

Another area of Hull's influence in Congress was in support of U.S. leadership in world affairs. He shared the view of newly elected Democratic president Woodrow Wilson that the United States must become the moral leader of the world. Hull supported President Wilson's tariff-reduction legislation, which created an atmosphere for better international relations. Throughout the remainder of his time in Congress, Hull was active in foreign affairs issues.

Secretary of State

The election of President Franklin D. Roosevelt in 1932 thrust Hull into a position of world leadership. In 1933 Hull resigned his newly won seat in the Senate to accept the president's invitation to be his secretary of state. Hull held this office during the turbulent years of the 1930's and early 1940's. Because of failing health, he resigned following the 1944 presidential election. During his first eight years as secretary of state, Hull led in making reciprocal trade, financial, and defense

U.S. secretary of state Cordell Hull signing the Neutrality Proclamation in 1939. *(Anthony Potter Collection/Archive Photos)*

treaties with other nations. He was the major architect of President Roosevelt's Good Neighbor Policy with the nations of Latin America. At the Montevideo Conference in Uruguay in 1933, he won cooperation by accepting the policy of nonintervention in the internal affairs of other nations.

By 1936 Hull's diplomatic efforts were concentrated on halting aggression by Japan in Asia and preventing war in Europe. When World War II officially began in 1939, Hull believed that aiding the Allies was the best way to halt the aggression both in Asia and Europe. He also began planning a new international peacekeeping organization to take effect after the war. At the Moscow Conference of Foreign Ministers in 1943, the decision to form the United Nations was finalized, and definite plans began to be made. For his leading role in this process, Hull was called the Father of the United Nations by President Roosevelt and was awarded the 1945 Nobel Peace Prize.

Bibliography

Gellman, Irwin. *Secret Affairs: Franklin Roosevelt, Cordell Hull, and Sumner Wells*. Baltimore: Johns Hopkins University Press, 1995.

Hinton, Harold. *Cordell Hull: A Biography*. Garden City, N.Y.: Doubleday, 1942.

Hull, Cordell. *The Memoirs of Cordell Hull*. 2 vols. New York: Macmillan, 1948.

Utley, Jonathan G. *Going to War with Japan: 1937-1941*. Knoxville: University of Tennessee Press, 1985.

Glenn L. Swygart

Hubert H. Humphrey

Born: May 27, 1911; Wallace, South Dakota
Died: January 13, 1978; Waverly, Minnesota

U.S. political leader, vice president (1965-1969)

Hubert Horatio Humphrey, Jr. (HEW-burt hoh-RAY-shee-oh HUHM-free JEW-nyur), graduated from the University of Minnesota in 1939. In 1940 he earned a master's degree in political science from Louisiana State University. During the Depression he returned to South Dakota to help run the family drug store, but his goal was to complete his Ph.D. and become a college professor. Instead, he accepted a job with the War Production Administration in 1941 and would spend the rest of his life in public service. Humphrey married Muriel Buck in 1936. They had four children.

Progressive Leader

Elected mayor of Minneapolis in 1945 and reelected in 1947, Humphrey established a Council on Human Relations to review racial discrimination problems and obtained enactment of the first municipal Fair Employment Practices law in the United States. Mayor Humphrey became a national figure at the 1948 Democratic Party National Convention in Philadelphia. He argued in support of a minority plank on civil rights. His passionate speech before the convention persuaded a majority of the delegates to adopt the progressive pro-civil rights plank.

Humphrey was a key figure in uniting the Minnesota Democratic Party and the state's Farmer-Labor Party into a competitive liberal party that dominated Minnesota politics for more than twenty years. Elected to the U.S. Senate in 1948 and reelected in 1954 and 1960, Senator Humphrey's progressive ideas, especially in support of civil rights, were opposed by the Senate's conservative majority. He did, however, endear himself to the Senate majority leader, Lyndon B. Johnson, and became the one liberal in the Senate able to negotiate concessions from the relatively conservative Texan. Humphrey sought to win the Democratic Party's 1960 presidential nomination. After losing primaries in Wisconsin and West Virginia to John F. Kennedy, he dropped out of the race.

Master Legislator

In the 1960's, Humphrey achieved his major legislative successes. He was instrumental to the establishment of the U.S. Arms Control and Disarmament Agency, establishment of the Peace

Hubert H. Humphrey *(Library of Congress)*

On a Southeast Asia trip, U.S. vice president Hubert H. Humphrey (second from left) inspects a wheat crop in India. (*National Archives*)

The 1968 Presidential Campaign

The 1968 presidential election was one of the closest in American history. Republican Richard M. Nixon defeated Democrat Hubert H. Humphrey by a narrow margin. Some 13.5 percent of the votes went to independent candidate George Wallace, a southern segregationist who had left the Democratic Party. Nixon won 43.4 percent, and Humphrey won 42.7 percent. The electoral vote was Nixon 301, Humphrey 191, and Wallace 46.

President Lyndon B. Johnson had decided not to seek reelection. A Democratic primary challenge from antiwar senator Eugene McCarthy failed; Robert Kennedy's primary campaign ended shockingly when he was assassinated the night of the California primary. Humphrey won the Democratic nomination without entering a single primary. This situation so badly divided the Democratic Party that it changed its nominating rules for future elections so that delegate votes would be assigned on the basis of popular participation. Protests and violence at the Democratic Convention in Chicago, Wallace's strength among conservatives, and division over the Vietnam War all seriously eroded support for the Democratic Party. Only Humphrey's articulation of a Vietnam position independent of Johnson's made the election close.

Corps, ratification of the 1963 Nuclear Test Ban Treaty, and passage of the 1964 Civil Rights Act. Virtually every progressive legislative enactment, from nutrition programs to medical care for the elderly, bore Humphrey's mark. His record as a liberal leader and effective legislator, together with his outstanding ability as an orator, placed Humphrey at the height of his political career.

In 1964, hand-picked by President Lyndon Johnson as his running mate, Humphrey was elected vice president of the United States. A loyal vice president, Humphrey became one of the leading defenders of the president's Vietnam policy. As the Vietnam War expanded and eroded Johnson's popularity, Humphrey also suffered a loss of popularity in the liberal community, which generally opposed the war. After President Johnson withdrew from the 1968 presidential race, Humphrey defeated the anti-Vietnam War senator Eugene McCarthy in a bitterly divisive primary race (during which Robert Kennedy was assassinated). He won the Democratic nomination for the presidency but lost the 1968 election to Republican Richard M. Nixon.

After 1968, Humphrey returned to Minnesota, where he was once again elected to the Senate in 1970 and reelected in 1976. He ran for president again in 1972, this time losing the nomination to George McGovern. Recovering somewhat from his loss of popularity during the Vietnam War era, Humphrey continued to lead the liberal cause in the Senate until his death in January of 1978.

Hubert Humphrey was perhaps the most important and the most celebrated American liberal of his generation. Committed to social justice and advocating an active government to achieve it, Humphrey started his career an idealistic reformer. He learned the art of legislative compromise and emerged as the premier liberal lawmaker of his time. As orator, leader, legislator, and politician, Humphrey stands as the foremost example of progressivism in American politics.

Hubert Humphrey campaigning for the vice presidency in 1964. *(Bernard Gotfryd/Archive Photos)*

Bibliography

Garrettson, Charles Lloyd, III. *Hubert H. Humphrey: The Politics of Joy.* New Brunswick, N.J.: Transaction Publishers, 1993.

Humphrey, Hubert H. *The Education of a Public Man: My Life and Politics.* Garden City, N.Y.: Doubleday, 1976.

Mann, Robert. *The Walls of Jericho: Lyndon Johnson, Hubert Humphrey, Richard Russell, and the Struggle for Civil Rights.* New York: Harcourt Brace, 1996.

Solberg, Carl. *Hubert Humphrey.* New York: Norton, 1984.

Robert O. Schneider

Hussein I

Born: November 14, 1935; Amman, Transjordan (now Jordan)
Died: February 7, 1999; Amman, Jordan

King of Jordan (1952-1999)

Hussein ibn Talal (hoo-SAYN IHB-uhn tah-LAHL), the first-born child of Jordanian crown prince Talal and the Hashemite princess Zein, was a direct descendant of the Prophet Muhammad, the kings of the Hejaz, who traditionally guarded the Muslim holy cities of Mecca and Medina, and Abdullah, the first king of Jordan.

Prince Hussein attended the Islamic Education College in Amman, Victoria College in Alexandria, Egypt, and Harrow School in England. Hussein was with his grandfather, King Abdullah, in Jerusalem when the king was assassinated by an anti-Western fanatic on July 20, 1951. Hussein became king when the Jordanian Parliament re-

moved his father, King Talal, from the throne on August 11, 1952, because of mental illness. A regency council governed Jordan until Hussein's eighteenth birthday, permitting him to attend Britain's Sandhurst Royal Military College.

King of Jordan

King Hussein's enthronement on May 2, 1953, coincided with that of his cousin, Faisal II of Iraq. Traditionally Jordan was a tribal society. Under Hussein's guidance it emerged as a constitutional monarchy with a cabinet responsible to the king and a popularly elected Parliament (the years 1974-1984 were an exception). A majority of the kingdom's population is Palestinian, a factor which has directly involved King Hussein in numerous Arab-Israeli controversies. A poor nation, Jordan depends on the financial generosity of its Western allies and other Arab states.

Jordan's continued independence is a tribute to Hussein's shrewd political intelligence, which strategically balanced competing interests among his Bedouin and Palestinian subjects, Arab nationalists and fundamentalists, and Israelis and Arabs. Independence also meant that Hussein participated in a frequently shifting set of alliances within the Arab world. Guided by the wise counsel of Queen Mother Zein and his maternal uncle, Sherif Nasser—as well as the international support of Britain and the United States—Hussein withstood four Arab-Israeli wars, several coups, the 1958 collapse of the Arab Federation, a 1970 civil war against Palestinian organizations, and numerous assassination attempts.

Arab-Israeli Conflict

Fearing an Israeli attack in 1967, Hussein decided to join his Arab rival, Gamal Abdel Nasser

Hussein I *(Library of Congress)*

King Hussein (seated, third from right) meeting with powerful Jordanian tribal leaders in 1960. *(Archive Photos)*

The Arab Federation

The Hashemite kingdoms of Iraq and Jordan formed the Arab Federation on February 14, 1958, in direct response to Egyptian president Gamal Abdel Nasser's creation of the United Arab Republic (UAR) with Syria on February 1, 1958. Iraqi King Faisal headed the federation, with Hussein as deputy king. The prime minister of Iraq was the Arab Federation's prime minister, and the prime minister of Jordan was deputy. The capital of each nation alternated as the federation capital for six-month intervals. Foreign policy, finance, education, and diplomatic representation were to be unified. Even though Iraq was the wealthier nation and had a larger population, both Iraq and Jordan were given an equal number of representatives in the union's Parliament. The union flag of black, red, white, and green was a replica of the one used by Faisal in his 1920 entry into Damascus as king of Syria. The Arab Federation collapsed July 14, 1958, when a military coup overthrew the Iraqi monarchy and brutally murdered Faisal II and the entire Iraqi royal family. Egypt's President Nasser was suspected of supporting the takeover. Jordan's limited resources prevented Hussein from direct intervention.

Black September, 1970

The September 1, 1970, attempt to assassinate King Hussein brought Jordan to the brink of civil war. Rival Palestinian organizations within Jordan, known as the *fedayeen*, had created their own state within Jordan that challenged the king's authority. The more extreme Popular Front for the Liberation of Palestine (PFLP) conducted a series of airplane hijackings and passenger kidnappings intended to embarrass Hussein internationally. The conflict was never described as a full-scale civil war because a majority of the kingdom's Palestinian subjects remained uninvolved. Hussein was initially reluctant to take military action against fellow Arabs for fear of intervention by Iraq and Syria.

Determined to save his kingdom, however, Hussein had no choice but to unleash his army within days of the assassination attempt. A number of factors helped lead to King Hussein's ultimate success against the *fedayeen*, among them a bungled Syrian invasion of Jordan, Russian pressure on Syria, the sudden death of President Nasser of Egypt, and continued support from Britain and the United States. The *fedayeen* were rounded up and expelled from Jordan by July of 1971. However, their expulsion cost Hussein the leadership of the Palestinian people: The Arab League assigned this role to Yasir Arafat and the Palestine Liberation Organization (PLO).

of Egypt, against Israel in the Six-Day War. The move was a major gamble. The defeat of Jordan, and its loss of the West Bank of the Jordan River and East Jerusalem, resulted in a flood of new refugees into the rest of the kingdom, which was financially unprepared for such an event. On the other hand, had King Hussein not joined his fellow Arabs, Jordan's Palestinian population might have overthrown him. The loss of the West Bank hobbled Jordan's nascent capitalist economy, and the fact that Muslim holy sites in East Jerusalem were now under Israeli control weakened the king's position among Arabs.

In 1970 King Hussein expelled rival Palestinian groups threatening the stability of the kingdom. This action led to the Arab League's 1974 deci-sion to declare the Palestine Liberation Organization (PLO) the sole legitimate representative of the Palestinian people. The Arab League's action deprived Hussein of the role the Hashemite kings

King Hussein arriving in Cairo for the Arab summit of 1996. *(Reuters/Jim Hollander/Archive Photos)*

of Jordan had played since the conclusion of the first Arab-Israeli war in 1948. Nevertheless, King Hussein remained an important contributor to the public and private international discussions on the future of the Palestinian people and peace in the Middle East. He was committed to the peace process and normalized relations with Israel, recognizing the right of the Jewish state to exist.

The Royal Family

King Hussein was an avid water skier and experienced pilot and was known for his fondness for fast cars. He was married four times. The first two marriages ended in divorce. He was the devoted father of eleven children. The king's first wife was a Hashemite cousin, Dina Abdel Hamid, with whom he had a daughter, Alia. Hussein's second wife, Antoinette Gardiner (an English woman who took the name Princess Muna), had two sons, Abdullah and Faisal, and twin daughters, Zein and Aisha. Alia Baha Eddin Toukan, Hussein's third wife, died in a helicopter crash in 1977, leaving a son Ali and a daughter Haya. American-born Queen Noor, the former Lisa Halaby, married Hussein in 1978. The royal couple had four children, sons Hamzah and Hashem and daughters Iman and Rayiah. In 1998 Hussein went to the United States to receive cancer treatment, which was not successful. Two weeks before his death in February, 1999, King Hussein replaced his brother, Hassan, who had been crown prince for thirty-four years, with his own eldest son, Abdullah, as the heir to Jordan's Hashemite throne.

By the time of his death, King Hussein had held power in the Middle East longer than anyone else in the modern era. Without Hussein, Jordan would probably have ceased to exist as an independent state. The king's rule turned Jordan from a tribal desert society into a modern state. Constitutional monarchy replaced absolute rule, but no one in Jordan was unaware of the king's still powerful role. Hussein's ability to gauge the views of his people correctly and retain their approval enabled him to remain on the throne. In 1956 he was willing to reduce British influence in Jordan's Arab League by firing its British commander and replacing its British officers with Jordanians. In 1990 he sided with Iraq against the United States and its allies in the Persian Gulf War. Both actions reaffirmed the king's mission to put Jordan first. King Hussein will be remembered as the "father of modern Jordan," a key figure in Middle Eastern politics, and an international leader whose mission to secure peace and justice transcended national boundaries.

Bibliography

Hussein, King of Jordan. *My War*. New York: William Morrow, 1969.

_____. *Uneasy Lies the Head*. London: Heinemann, 1962.

Lunt, James. *Hussein of Jordan*. New York: William Morrow, 1989.

Satloff, Robert B. *From Abdullah to Hussein*. New York: Oxford University Press, 1994.

Snow, Peter. *Hussein*. Washington, D.C.: Luce, 1972.

William A. Paquette

Saddam Hussein

Born: April 28, 1937; Tikrit, Iraq

President of Iraq (installed 1979)

Saddam Hussein, full name Saddam Hussein al-Tikriti (sah-DAHM hoo-SAYN ahl-tihk-REE-tee), was born to an impoverished Sunni family on April 28, 1937. His father either died or abandoned his family when Saddam was an infant. Largely neglected and perhaps abused by his stepfather, Saddam sought to take control of his life at an early age. He insisted on receiving an education, which his stepfather eventually permitted, and became attracted to military service as a career. In 1963, he married his uncle's daughter, Sajida. The couple would have two sons later in the decade.

Early Political Activity

Hussein also became increasingly interested in politics. Iraq had gained independence in 1932, when Britain's mandate over the country ended. The fledgling Iraqi government, technically a monarchy, was both unstable and unpopular, launching oppressive policies and murderous pogroms against its own people. At age twenty, Saddam joined the Arab Ba'th Socialist Party, a radical Arab nationalist organization opposed to the government. In 1958 the monarchy was overthrown, but opposition soon materialized against the new government, which had connections with the communists. In 1959 Hussein was involved in an attempt to assassinate Iraq's prime minister. The attempt failed, and Hussein went into exile in Syria and then Egypt. In Cairo he studied law, but he never completed his studies.

After five years in exile, Hussein returned to Iraq, where the Ba'th Party had just seized power. The new regime was quickly overthrown, however, and Hussein was arrested and imprisoned. He escaped from jail in 1966.

Assumption of Power

In 1968, Hussein helped to lead a coup that successfully placed the Ba'th Party in control of the country. Hussein's uncle, Ahmed Hassan al-Bakr, became the new prime minister and commander in chief of the armed forces. Hussein became vice president of the Revolutionary Command Council. From his position in the new government, Hussein moved steadily to remove political opponents and rivals. With the political backing of his uncle, Hussein engineered personnel changes in the leadership and in various military and political offices. He also worked to head

Iraqi president Saddam Hussein waving to supporters in Baghdad in 1995. *(Reuters/Ina/Archive Photos)*

off threats to the Baʿth party and his uncle's leadership.

In 1979, the year of neighboring Iran's revolution, al-Bakr retired from the leadership, putatively for health reasons. Hussein was installed as president in July, 1979. Immediately after taking office, he declared that he had uncovered and foiled a vast foreign-supported conspiracy to overthrow the Iraqi leadership. This declaration marked Hussein's first use of a tool that he employed regularly to rally public support for his regime.

In addition to his post as Iraq's president, Hussein served as the chairman of the Baʿth Party's Revolutionary Command Council.

Saddam Hussein (right) shaking hands with U.N. secretary-general Kofi Annan. The two were meeting in February, 1998, to discuss a looming crisis over allowing U.N. weapons inspectors access to sites in Iraq. *(Reuters/INA/Archive Photos)*

Iraq Invades Kuwait

In August, 1990, Iraqi armies invaded the small country of Kuwait, claiming it as a restored "province of Iraq." The overwhelmed Kuwaiti military collapsed almost instantly, and Iraq occupied the country. The rest of the world, including many Arab countries, denounced the invasion as a violation of Kuwaiti sovereignty. The U.N. Security Council passed a resolution demanding that Iraq withdraw from Kuwait by January 15, 1991.

Economic and trade sanctions were placed on Iraq, but they seemed to have little effect. Meanwhile, the administration of U.S. president George Bush built an international coalition of military forces to remove Iraq from Kuwait by force should sanctions fail. Within twenty-four hours after the January 15 deadline passed, these forces began bombing Iraqi positions. Several weeks later, allied forces attacked the Iraqi forces by land, and within several days the Kuwaiti capital had been liberated and Iraqi forces were surrendering and retreating. A cease-fire was formally negotiated on April 6, 1991. It required that Iraq pay reparations for war damages, eliminate its weapons of mass destruction, and meet certain other conditions. Kuwaiti sovereignty was restored, but Iraq's compliance with the cease-fire resolution was repeatedly called into question in subsequent years.

The Kurds in Iraq

The country of Iraq is home to a sizable Kurdish minority; Kurds compose about one-fifth of Iraq's population. The Kurdish people, most of whom are Sunni Muslims, have a long history of oppression at the hands of the Turks, Iraqis, and others. Sensing weakness in Saddam Hussein's regime in the wake of the Gulf War, Iraqi Kurds rebelled against the government in 1991. The Kurds may also have been encouraged by implicit promises of protection from the United Nations and the Gulf War's victors, who established "safe areas" and "no-fly zones" (areas over which Iraqi planes were forbidden to fly) in Kurdish parts of Iraq.

The Kurdish rebellion was short-lived, however, as Hussein's regime quickly restored order. The government killed or jailed numerous Kurdish dissidents and sent more than a million Kurds into exile in Turkey, Iran, and northern Iraq. Kurds have continued to experience oppression in all these areas, leading to increased calls for the establishment of an independent Kurdish state.

Whatever his formal positions, Hussein had become Iraq's unquestioned dictator, working relentlessly and brutally to suppress all political opposition. Among his more notorious actions in this regard was his ordering of chemical-weapons attacks on his country's Kurdish population in the 1980's. Many observers have drawn parallels between the political tactics and cult of per-

As Iraqi troops retreated from Kuwait in early 1991, they set many of Kuwait's oil fields afire. *(U.S. Navy)*

sonality surrounding Saddam Hussein and those of Soviet leader Joseph Stalin.

Exploiting the economic potential of Iraq's enormous oil reserves, Hussein amassed the region's largest military force. In 1980 he directed this force against Iraq's rival, Iran, which had recently been taken over by Ayatollah Ruhollah Khomeini. The war took an enormous toll on Iraq's population, economy, and military strength, and it ended inconclusively in 1988. The abysmal living standards resulting from the eight-year war undercut public support for Hussein, but his regime's renewed suppression of opposition, coupled with its demonization of foreign powers such as Israel and the United States, helped to ensure Hussein's continued grip on power.

Persian Gulf War

With Iraq's military force partly recovered from the war with Iran, Hussein launched an invasion of the small neighboring country of Kuwait in 1990. The immediate territorial gains and psychological renewal brought about by the invasion quickly evaporated as the United States led an international coalition to force the Iraqi military to withdraw from oil-rich Kuwait. Condemned by the United Nations, defeated by U.S.-led armies in the 1991 Persian Gulf War, isolated by a strict trade embargo, and subject to weapons inspections, Iraq became an international pariah.

Hussein, however, did not accept this defeated status. Within a short time he was defying the United Nations by refusing to permit U.N.-led inspections of possible weapons facilities. He continued to develop weapons of mass destruction, to oppress the Kurdish and Shiite populations within Iraq, and to sponsor terrorism abroad. While these actions exacerbated Iraq's

pariah status in the West, they seemed to evoke sympathy from a number of other countries. More important for Hussein, they distracted the Iraqi population from their miserable and oppressed condition at the hands of Hussein's regime, directing blame to outside "enemies of Iraq."

To the frustration and disappointment of Western leaders, Hussein was still in power in the late 1990's. By December, 1998, the United States and Great Britain were so frustrated by Hussein's continued refusal to let U.N. inspectors visit suspected weapons sites that they launched bomb and missile strikes against numerous sites in Iraq. Allowing such inspections by the United Nations had been a condition of the Gulf War cease-fire agreement. In early 1999, a former member of the U.N. inspection team alleged that—as Hussein had long insisted—certain members of the team were actually spying for the United States' Central Intelligence Agency.

Bibliography

Henderson, Simon. *Instant Empire: Saddam Hussein's Ambition for Iraq*. San Francisco: Mercury House, 1991.

Karsh, Efraim, and Inari Rautsi. *Saddam Hussein: A Political Biography*. New York: Free Press, 1991.

Miller, Judith, and Laurie Mylroie. *Saddam Hussein and the Crisis in the Gulf*. New York: Random House, 1990.

Stefoff, Rebecca. *Saddam Hussein*. Brookfield, Conn.: Millbook Press, 1995.

Triumph Without Victory: The Unreported History of the Persian Gulf War. New York: U.S. News and World Report, 1992.

Steve D. Boilard

Hayato Ikeda

Born: December 3, 1899; Yoshina, Hiroshima Prefecture, Japan
Died: August 13, 1965; Tokyo, Japan

Premier of Japan (1960-1964)

Hayato Ikeda (hah-yah-toh ee-keh-dah) was the second son of a wealthy family of rice wine brewers. He studied law and economics at Kyoto Imperial University. Ikeda managed his own brewing business for a short time but then entered government service to begin a twenty-three year career in financial administration. Starting in the taxation offices of small cities, he worked his way steadily upward. By 1945 he was head of the National Tax Bureau.

Hayato Ikeda after his election as Japan's prime minister in 1960. *(Archive Photos)*

Bureaucrat to Politician

In the course of his bureaucratic service Ikeda developed an impressive knowledge of Japan's financial structure and its problems. Later he wrote several books on taxation, cost accounting, budgeting, and tax law. He also developed close working relationships with many of Japan's leading bankers and industrialists. During the American occupation after World War II he provided valuable assistance in fighting inflation.

In 1949 Ikeda decided to enter elective politics, winning a seat in the House of Representatives. He became close to then-Prime Minister Shigeru Yoshida, who appointed him finance minister, one of the most powerful positions in the cabinet. Ikeda continued his anti-inflation policies, won passage of a tax cut, and helped to negotiate the U.S.-Japan peace treaty along with a U.S.-Japan security treaty that placed Japan under American protection. Ikeda headed the powerful Ministry of International Trade and Industry (MITI) under Prime Minister Nobusuke Kishi.

In 1960 Kishi pushed for renewal of the security treaty in a particularly high-handed way in the face of violent demonstrations and strikes by a variety of antigovernment and pacifist groups. It was thought by many in Kishi's and Ikeda's Liberal Democratic Party (LDP) that they might lose power over this issue. It was also clear that the treaty would have to be renewed, however unpopular it might be, for the sake of maintaining good relations with the United States. The LDP decided that Kishi would have to resign, and the political turmoil would have to be calmed. On July 18, 1960, Hayato Ikeda was chosen prime minister to accomplish this difficult task.

The Income Doubling Plan

Ikeda restored harmony among LDP factions by distributing appointments equitably and by sacrificing some of his direct decision-making control. He gained support among the opposition parties by reassuring them that Japan would not be overly subservient to U.S. interests. Finally, he sought to shift the government's priorities to domestic matters in order to bring together a majority of Japanese in a new consensus built around high economic growth and widespread prosperity. In 1961, in what was called the Income Doubling Plan, Ikeda proposed that the government stimulate the economy by means of public works and central planning initiatives to an average 7.2 percent annual growth (thus doubling the gross national product in ten years). He hoped to stimulate domestic consumer demand through government expenditure. Any deficits in the government budget would be offset by increases in tax revenues from higher incomes. Wage-price inflation would be avoided by greater efficiency in output and accelerated exports.

The results of the Income Doubling Plan exceeded all expectations. Instead

Hayato Ikeda reviewing troops in Tokyo. *(Archive Photos)*

Japanese Business Comes of Age

Prime Minister Hayato Ikeda was crucial in bringing about a new era in the Japanese economy. His Income Doubling Plan introduced a model for high growth in a free-enterprise economy. The government worked closely with business by setting goals and directions to integrate corporate efforts. Government designed public works, set tax policies, utility rates, subsidies, and established social security and health care safety nets. It held down military spending and encouraged labor to move from farms into industry. Business was encouraged to create the worldwide infrastructure for marketing exports. Small business was formed into *keiretsu* (integrated supplier groupings). This was to be the shape of Japanese business for four decades.

of ten years, Japan's gross national product doubled in four years. Government spending increased tremendously, but budgets were balanced without tax increases or borrowing. Annual per-capita national income more than tripled.

Hayato Ikeda died of throat cancer less than a year after the 1964 Tokyo Olympics had showcased his new, prosperous Japan. He had gone from faceless bureaucrat to being Japan's most successful postwar politician. His formula for economic success—free enterprise in partnership with government—guided Japan for four decades. Many other Pacific Rim countries also followed this model.

Bibliography

Campbell, John C. *Contemporary Japanese Budget Politics*. Berkeley: University of California Press, 1977.

Curtis, Gerald L. *The Japanese Way of Politics*. New York: Columbia University Press, 1988.

Hayao, Kenji. *The Japanese Prime Minister and Public Power*. Pittsburgh, Pa.: University of Pittsburgh Press, 1993.

David G. Egler

İsmet İnönü

Born: September 24, 1884; Smyrna, Ottoman Empire (now İzmir, Turkey)
Died: December 25, 1973; Ankara, Turkey

President (1938-1950) and prime minister (1961-1965) of Turkey

İsmet İnönü (ihs-MEHT ih-nuh-NEW), also referred to as İsmet Pasha (ihs-MEHT pah-SHAH), was born in Smyrna, a largely Greek Ottoman city. Appropriate to the Turkish warrior tradition, İsmet (he had only the single name as a young man) was educated in military schools, graduating at the top of his class of the General Staff College. He initially pursued a military calling, becoming the youngest general in the Ottoman army. Later he turned to a political career with even greater success.

Early Influences

Early in his career, İnönü met Mustafa Kemal, later known as Atatürk (father of the Turks). Kemal was the military genius who saved the Turkish state from complete destruction after the end of World War I. Kemal was to be the guiding star of İnönü's fortunes as statesman and political leader. They met as students in military school and later served as army officers. They became involved in the Young Turk movement, a political party later called the Committee for Union and Progress (CUP). With this organization they first elaborated their vision of a Western-leaning secular Turkey. The Committee for Union and Progress realized many of its goals, in spite of resistance from the sultan, but it succeeded in establishing a Turkish republic only upon the collapse of the Ottoman Empire after World War I.

İnönü the Warrior

İsmet Pasha rapidly rose in the ranks of the Ottoman army, serving on the Third Army general staff in Edirne, then as chief of staff in Yemen. During World War I, he commanded the Fourth Army in Syria. He was undersecretary of war by the time of the Ottoman surrender in 1918. He joined Mustafa Kemal in armed resistance against the Allied occupation of Turkish Anatolia after the end of the war and won signal victories against the Greek invaders at both battles of İnönü. From this he received his surname in 1934, when Turks for the first time began to use family names.

Ironically, it was from the chaos of defeat and national humiliation that this political team of warriors eventually forged a new and stronger country. As chief of the Ottoman general staff, İnönü had seen the loss of most of the Ottoman European possessions in the Balkan Wars of 1912-

İsmet İnönü *(Express Newspapers/K893/Archive Photos)*

755

İsmet İnönü (left) with members of the Turkish military in 1960, after a military coup toppled the government of Adnan Menderes. *(Library of Congress)*

1913. In 1918, as undersecretary of war on the side of the Central Powers, he found himself on the losing side of World War I. In 1919 the Greeks invaded Anatolia in hopes of regaining some areas with Greek populations. However, Kemal, aided by his loyal deputy İnönü, drove the Greeks from Anatolia.

Statesman and Practical Politician

İnönü's political career evolved as a natural outcome of his military success. In 1920 he was elected to the Ottoman parliament as representative for Edirne. After the fall of the Ottoman state, it was İnönü's proposal that the capital of the new Turkish state be moved to Ankara. His first important job as foreign minister of the Grand National Assembly of 1922 was to head the Turkish delegation to the 1923 Lausanne Peace Conference. Here he was successful, gaining most of Turkey's objectives. Upon the proclamation of the new Republic of Turkey in October, 1923, President Atatürk appointed İnönü as prime minister. He held the post until 1937 and thereafter at intervals for much of his political career.

Throughout this period, and until Atatürk's death in 1938, the two worked together closely. Atatürk's program of westernization and secularization of the former Ottoman Empire was methodical and relentless. If Atatürk was inclined to be flamboyant, impatient, and emotional, İnönü was patient, deliberate, and cautious. Although sometimes characterized as ignorant and ruthless, İnönü was a person of wide interests and abilities, a devoted family man, and a person of integrity.

Successor to Atatürk

Upon Atatürk's death in 1938, İnönü was his natural successor as president of the Turkish Re-

The Second Turkish Army

In 1916, Colonel İsmet Pasha, later İsmet İnönü, met General Mustafa Kemal (later Atatürk), who had just been promoted to general and received the title of Pasha. He had taken over command of the Second Turkish Army in Southeastern Anatolia. This fateful meeting of two military thinkers was to begin the collaboration that resulted in the formation of the Turkish Republic, a new state built on the ruins of the Ottoman Empire. The success that İnönü and Atatürk achieved in the war of independence of 1919-1923 by using the nationalistic army to push the Greeks from Anatolia had the effect of giving the army a quasi-political role in twentieth-century Turkish life.

The Coup of 1960

The army, a pillar of the Turkish state, was expanded and modernized after World War II. Many officers distrusted the slow political processes of the emerging multiparty system as impeding rapid change. They viewed the army as more effective in achieving consensus and reform. In May, 1960, General Cemal Gürsel demanded political reforms, resigning when they were refused. His resignation was followed by a coup on May 27. Gürsel was installed as chairman of a National Unity Committee. Leaders of the Democrat Party, with whom the army had important differences, were imprisoned.

Some coup leaders believed that the army should take over political leadership for an extended period, while others saw the takeover as merely an interim measure. Those who favored the shorter tenure prevailed, sending their opposition into exile. The National Unity Committee had as its mission the destruction of the Democrat Party and the creation of a new constitution. The new military government abolished the Democrat Party in September, 1960. Leading Democrats were tried for corruption, unconstitutionality, and treason. The majority were found guilty. Three former ministers, including Prime Minister Menderes, were executed, while others faced life imprisonment. A new constitution was drawn up and submitted to the National Unity Committee. It was then redrawn, presented to a Constituent Assembly in January, 1961, and approved by voters in July. It established a two-chamber parliament, proportional representation, and presidential election by the Senate and National Assembly. After the first elections of October, 1961, the army withdrew from direct political involvement.

public and chairman of the Republican People's Party. One of his most significant achievements as president lay in maintaining Turkish neutrality during World War II in spite of pressure to enter the fray on the side of Germany. After the war, İnönü was instrumental in encouraging multiparty democracy in Turkey even though this meant losing his leading role. In the 1950 election, his Republican People's Party was defeated by the new Democrat Party. İnönü then assumed the role of loyal opposition, defending the importance of secularization and westernization against extremist views from either side. This role became difficult under the regime of President Celal Bayar and Prime Minister Menderes. However, their rule was curtailed by the military coup of 1960. In twentieth-century Turkish politics the military has often acted as the watchdog of politics and has felt empowered to intervene in cases of perceived abuse. The new Turkish President, Cemal Gürsel, asked İnönü to form a coalition government. Several coalitions were formed, none with outstanding success. After the failure of the third coalition and the outbreak of the 1964 Cyprus crisis, İnönü resigned as prime minister, although he remained active as a member of his party until his death.

Bibliography

Ahmad, Feroz. *The Making of Modern Turkey*. London: Routledge, 1993.

Heper, Metin. *İsmet İnönü: The Making of a Turkish Statesman*. Boston: Brill, 1998.

Lewis, Bernard. *The Emergence of Modern Turkey*. 2d ed. London: Oxford University Press, 1968.

Schick, İrvin Cemal, and Ertugrul Ahmet Tonak, eds. *Turkey in Transition: New Perspectives*. New York: Oxford University Press, 1987.

Gloria Fulton

Itō Hirobumi

Born: September 2, 1841; Tsukari Village, Chōshū, Japan
Died: October 26, 1909; Harbin, Manchuria, China

Four-time prime minister of Japan between 1885 and 1891, drafted the Meiji Constitution (1885)

Itō Hirobumi (ee-toh hee-roh-bew-mee) was born into the farmer class in a remote village in Chōshū but became a samurai through his father's adoption as heir to the samurai family house of Itō. The families of Chōshū held a domain on the main island of Japan. This domain was fiercely loyal to the emperor, but Japan was ruled at this time by the Tokugawa shogun, the supreme warlord in Edo (Tokyo). The emperor was in reality only a symbol of leadership with no real governing powers. Also at this time, Western powers, led by Admiral Matthew Perry of the United States, had forcibly opened Japan (beginning in 1853) from its self-imposed isolation from the world, causing tremendous social unrest in Japan.

"Expel the Barbarians"

Itō was trained as a samurai and a scholar by Yoshida Shōin, who was later executed for rebellion against the shogun. He was one of the brightest students of the prestigious academy and quickly rose to the top of his class. Although fearful of the influence of the Western powers on Japanese society, Itō and several others were fascinated by their weapons and ships and studied Western technology. Feelings against foreigners and the shogun, who pursued a policy of appeasement, were increasing. Itō and several of his associates participated in attacks against foreign delegations under the slogan, "Honor the Emperor, Expel the Barbarians!" One such occurrence was a dramatic attack in 1862 on the British delegation near Edo. A year later, Itō convinced four prominent Chōshū men to take him with them on a trip to England to learn about modern navies and conditions in enemy countries.

Conflict and Reform

While on this trip, Itō became convinced that resistance to the military might of the West was futile; he saw the powerful armaments of the Western armies and navies. During his stay in England, his party received word that hostilities had broken out between Britain and Satsuma, another province in Japan that was in opposition to the ruling shogun. British warships bombarded and destroyed the Satsuma capital city of Kagoshima. Later, Itō heard news that Chōshū

Itō Hirobumi *(Library of Congress)*

artillery had attacked foreign shipping. Convinced that Japan was heading down a path of certain destruction, the party quickly prepared to leave England. They arrived in Japan in time to see warships from the United States, England, France, and Holland leave for Chōshū. The ships bombarded the Chōshū capital and soundly defeated the Chōshū forces.

These events proved to be a major turning point in the history of Japan. The Satsuma and Chōshū provinces joined forces against the military government of the shogun and in 1866 defeated the shogun by using weapons and tactics borrowed from the West. They forced his resignation in 1867. This event led to the assumption of power by seventeen-year-old Emperor Meiji. Itō was placed in a high

Itō Hirobumi was named resident general of Korea after Japan occupied it in 1904. Here Japanese police execute three Korean farmers who protested Japanese land policies. *(Korea Society, Los Angeles)*

position in foreign affairs under the leaders of the Meiji Restoration, Kido, Ōkubo and Saigō. These leaders undertook a major reformation of Japanese society. They instituted land reforms, indus-

---

The Sino-Japanese War

After Japan emerged from isolation (beginning in the 1850's), it almost immediately began to contend with China for control of the Korean peninsula. In 1894, local revolts by traditionalists in Korea broke out, and the Korean king called for help from China. China sent troops to quell the rebellion.

Viewing the increase in Chinese influence, Itō Hirobumi sent troops to protect Japanese interests in Korea and to force a confrontation with China. In June, 1894, Japan demanded that China send no more troops to Korea and that the Korean government implement an extensive list

of reforms. Japanese troops occupied the Korean royal palace, and war was declared in August. To the surprise of the world, in only one month Japanese forces had captured most of Korea and controlled the Yellow Sea. By February, 1895, Japan occupied Manchuria to the north and the southern approaches to Beijing from the sea. China was forced to surrender. China paid an indemnity, ceded the island of Taiwan and the Liaotung Peninsula, and signed a commercial treaty recognizing Japan on an equal level to the Western powers.

The Meiji Constitution

The Meiji Constitution, drafted in 1885, followed the German model, wherein the emperor was "a cornerstone, secure in his grasp of sovereign power." The emperor reigned but did not directly rule the government. The government was a "social monarchy" designed to arbitrate the competing interests of different groups in society within the context of Confucian thought and national strength. Most power was reserved to the emperor: the power to declare war, treaty power, and the power to call or dissolve the national assembly (the Diet). The emperor was also the supreme commander of the armed forces. In reality the emperor did not govern directly but was established as a symbol of imperial lineage in a line of emperors going back to "ages eternal." Most of the real power lay with the Executive Council and the Privy Council, composed of the emperor's senior political advisers. These leaders ruled through the government cabinet and bureaucracy. The legislature included an upper house and a lower house. The upper house consisted of noblemen and appointees of the emperor. The lower house was elected by males twenty-five years old and older. Many civil rights were guaranteed by the constitution, but they were subject to limitation by the government. The Meiji Constitution was officially redrawn in 1947, after World War II.

trialization, and modernization of the military. They looked to the West to learn the most effective practices of the modern world.

In 1871, a mission was sent to Europe and the United States to gain diplomatic recognition and to renegotiate unequal treaties that had been signed by the shogun. Itō was invited to accompany the leaders of the delegation and became close friends with Ōkubo, a prominent leader. The mission was divided into three groups, one to study Western law, another to study trade and industry, and the third to study education. All members of the mission were also to study the military. The mission visited the United States, Britain, France, Belgium, Holland, and Germany.

Upon their return to Japan, a great controversy arose concerning the prospect of war with Korea. Ōkubo and his allies persuaded the government to avoid war causing many in the pro-war faction to resign from the government. Itō was placed as minister of public works and was one of Ōkubo's most loyal allies. Ōkubo was assassinated in 1878 and was replaced by Itō as a councillor to the emperor and home minister.

Father of the Meiji Constitution

Under pressure, the emperor assigned Itō to draft a constitution for approval by the government. In 1882 Itō embarked on another trip to the West, this time to find constitutional models to meet Japan's political and cultural needs. After Itō's return to Japan, he was appointed Japan's first prime minister in 1885, and the drafting of the constitution commenced. In 1892, he was called upon once again to serve as prime minister and was successful in negotiating changes in some of the unequal treaties with the West. He also waged a successful war with China. Itō resigned as prime minister in 1896 after the West forced Japan to return the Liaotung Peninsula to China. He returned again as prime minister in 1898. In 1890, he established a political party that he used to win a fourth and final election as prime minister, but this cabinet lasted only seven months.

In 1901, tensions in Korea flared up again when Russia showed signs of expanding its influence over the Korean peninsula. Japan formed an alliance with Britain, and events led to war with Russia in 1904. Japan won decisive victories on land and destroyed the Russian fleet at sea. Japan occupied Korea as a protectorate, and Itō was appointed resident general of Korea. In the fall of 1909, while on an inspection tour of Manchuria, Itō was assassinated by a Korean nationalist.

Bibliography

Beasley, W. G. *The Rise of Modern Japan*. 2d ed. New York: St. Martin's Press, 1995.

Hall, Josef Washington. *Eminent Asians*. New York: D. Appleton, 1929.

Hamada Kengi. *Prince Ito*. Washington, D.C.: University Publications of America, 1979.

Oka Yoshitake. *Five Political Leaders of Modern Japan*, Tokyo: University of Tokyo Press, 1986.

Tsunoda, Ryusaku, William Theodore De Bary, and Donald Keene. *Sources of Japanese Tradition*. Vol. 2. New York: Columbia University Press, 1958.

W. David Patton

Jesse Jackson

Born: October 8, 1941; Greenville, South Carolina

U.S. political and civil rights leader, founder of PUSH (1971)

Jesse Louis Jackson (JEH-see LEW-ihs JAK-suhn) was born the son of Helen Burns Jackson and his adoptive father, Charles Henry Jackson, a post office maintenance worker. Reared in Greenville, South Carolina, he attended the University of Illinois for one year, and then transferred to North Carolina A&T State, graduating in 1963 with a bachelor's degree in sociology. He attended the Chicago Theological Seminary, leaving in the spring of 1965 to join Dr. Martin Luther King, Jr., in the drive for voting rights in Selma,

Jesse Jackson *(Library of Congress)*

Alabama. The school later conferred an honorary doctor's degree on him. Jackson was ordained a Baptist minister in 1968.

Early Civil Rights Campaigns

As a college student in Greensboro, North Carolina, Jackson became active in civil rights demonstrations and was arrested for leading a sit-in in front of a municipal building. He also supported civil rights during his years in Chicago. After the voter drive in Selma, Alabama, Jackson became a field director for the Congress of Racial Equality (CORE). In 1967 King named Jackson the national director of Operation Breadbasket of the Southern Christian Leadership Conference (SCLC). Operation Breadbasket was a program to secure more jobs for African Americans in bakeries, milk companies, and other such industries that had many African American customers.

King's assassination in 1968 thrust Jackson into the forefront of civil rights activity. In 1971 SCLC's board of directors suspended him as director of Operation Breadbasket for failing to get its permission to organize trade fairs for African American businessmen. Jackson started a new organization known as People United to Save Humanity (PUSH) to boost minority employment and to assist minority-owned businesses. He led it until he announced his candidacy for president of the United States in 1984.

Presidential Campaigns

Jackson's campaign highlighted three aspects of African American political life at the time. First, there was disagreement over what constituted leadership among African Americans. Second, there was increasing division between the poor and the middle class within the community.

Third, there was dissatisfaction with the Democratic Party concerning its move to the Right in response to the popularity of Republican President Ronald Reagan. Jackson won 21 percent of the votes in Democratic primaries and caucuses, but only 11 percent of the delegates to the convention.

During the 1984 campaign Jackson spoke of a diverse constituency supporting his candidacy. After the election he founded the National Rainbow Coalition as a vehicle to work for social and economic justice. The coalition also provided Jackson a platform for his next run for the presidency. In 1988, after a fourth-place finish in the Iowa caucus, Jackson won thirteen primary or caucus victories and placed second in twenty-three, taking a total of twelve hundred delegates. Despite Jackson's second-place finish, however, Michael Dukakis, the nominee of the Democratic Party, named Texas senator Lloyd Bentsen as his running mate.

Jesse Jackson, second from left, on a Memphis, Tennessee, motel balcony with Hosea Williams, Martin Luther King, Jr., and Ralph Abernathy on April 3, 1968. King was assassinated on the balcony the next day. *(AP/Wide World Photos)*

Jackson's Efforts After 1988

Jackson continued to be active in civil rights issues through the 1990's. In 1996 he became the chief executive officer of the combined organization Rainbow/PUSH Action Network, and in February of 1997 he was arrested during a protest over the firing of a minority-owned firm doing

The Rainbow Coalition

The National Rainbow Coalition was founded on November 10, 1984, by the Reverend Jesse Jackson as a political organization, based in Washington, D.C., that would attempt to build a coalition of racial minorities, the poor of all races, and sympathetic whites. This was, in general, the constituency that Jackson attracted in his bid for the 1984 presidential nomination of the Democratic Party. The Rainbow Coalition established groups in all fifty states with the purpose of working toward economic justice, national and world peace, human rights, and dignity for all persons. It emphasized civil rights, government policy, labor relations, equality of education, minority businesses, the environment, and the distribution of health care.

Jesse Jackson in 1998, speaking at a United Nations conference as a "special envoy" of the U.S. president and secretary of state. *(AP/Wide World Photos)*

construction work at the Museum of Science and History in Chicago. In August, 1997, he and San Francisco mayor Willie Brown led a group of marchers across the Golden Gate Bridge in opposition to new anti-affirmative action laws.

Jackson's political ambitions also remained alive. In 1990 he was elected as a "statehood senator" for Washington, D.C.: His task was to lobby for statehood for the district. President Bill Clinton named Jackson a coleader of a presidential mission to the African-American summit in Zimbabwe and then a presidential envoy for the promotion of democracy in Africa. In May, 1998, Jackson raised the possibility of running for president in the year 2000, but he later announced that he would not run. In May of 1999, Jackson led a delegation of religious leaders to war-torn Yugoslavia and secured the release of three U.S. soldiers being held by Yugoslavia as prisoners of war.

Bibliography

Cohen, Elizabeth O. *The Jackson Phenomenon: The Man, the Power, the Message.* New York: Doubleday, 1989.

Frady, Marshall. *Jesse: The Life and Pilgrimage of Jesse Jackson.* New York: Random House, 1996.

Reed, Adolph L., Jr. *The Jesse Jackson Phenomenon: The Crisis of Purpose in Afro-American Politics.* New Haven, Conn.: Yale University Press, 1986.

Paul L. Redditt

Cheddi Jagan

Born: March 22, 1918; Plantation Port Mourant, British Guiana (now Guyana)
Died: March 6, 1997; Washington, D.C.

Leader of Guyana independence movement, president of Guyana (1992-1997)

Cheddi Berret Jagan (CHEH-dee BAH-raht JAY-guhn) was a leader in the independence movement of British Guiana (called Guyana after independence in 1966), the only colony of Great Britain in South America. He was also a controversial Marxist, founding the People's Progressive Party (PPP). He was born to sugar-cane growers descended from immigrants from India. The population of Guyana is composed primarily of people of African descent, followed by those of Indian descent. There is antagonism between these groups because of the influence of the latter in business.

Early Career

Jagan studied dentistry in the United States, where he met Janet Rosenberg, a nursing student and radical political activist. The two were married. Returning to British Guiana in 1943, Jagan established a dental practice in the capital, Georgetown, and entered politics. He won a seat in the colonial legislature in 1947. He sought the independence of Guiana and its establishment as a socialist state. To these ends he founded the People's Progressive Party (PPP) in 1950. Three years later, this party won a legislative majority (eighteen of twenty-four seats), and Jagan became chief minister in the colonial government.

Immediately acting to put his leftist agenda into effect, Jagan alarmed the British government, then headed by Winston Churchill. Supported by the United States, the British alleged that Jagan intended to establish a communist state. British troops and warships were sent to the colony and Jagan removed from office. In 1954 he and his wife led a civil-disobedience campaign against the colonial regime. They were briefly arrested. The British government revised the colony's constitution so that in future elections Jagan and his party would be kept in a minority role.

Politics of Controversy

After the elections of 1957, Jagan became minister of trade and industry and cooperated with the British colonial government to improve economic conditions. However, he also made overtures to Soviet-bloc countries and to Fidel Castro's Cuba. In 1961 the British granted Guiana internal self-government but, to Jagan's chagrin, not complete independence. In the new government Jagan was elected premier. He inaugurated an austerity program that provoked riots in which blacks looted the stores of Indian owners.

Cheddi Jagan *(Library of Congress)*

The People's Progressive Party

The People's Progressive Party (PPP) was founded in 1950 by Cheddi Jagan, a leader in British Guiana's Indian community, and Forbes Burnham, a lawyer in the African community. Janet Jagan, Jagan's wife, served as secretary. The PPP was Guyana's first modern political party. Its power base was the labor unions, and its ideology Marxist.

The party advocated land reform and the creation of new land through reclamation projects. It called for the independence of the colony, universal suffrage, and political reform. Further, it demanded that the government of an independent Guyana take a strong role in developing agriculture, business, and industry for the new country. Because of the radical ideology of the Jagans, Burnham left to found a more moderate independence party in 1955, the People's National Congress (PNC). The PNC received significant U.S. and British support. The PPP remained a major political force in Guyana, but over time it has considerably moderated its original radical views.

Jagan was forced to call in British troops to put down the turmoil.

In 1966 Guyana achieved independence and became a member of the Commonwealth of Nations. Four years later it became a republic. The new country's boundaries with neighboring Venezuela and Suriname were not clear, and truces and troop removals had to be negotiated with them. With American support and an alliance with a small third party, Forbes Burnham became president. The People's National Congress (PNC) dominated Guyanese politics for the next generation. Jagan was leader of the opposition. Presiding over a corrupt regime, Burnham died in office in 1985. He was followed by another PNC president, Desmond Hoyt.

With the end of the Cold War, Jagan was elected president in 1992. The economies of South America improved in the global expansion of the 1990's, and Jagan's radical ideology was now much softened. He sought foreign investment and supported privatization of state industries. Suffering a heart attack in 1997, he died in office and was succeeded by Janet Jagan.

Cheddi Jagan, as prime minister of British Guiana, lecturing in New York in 1961. *(Library of Congress)*

Bibliography

"Cheddi (Berret) Jagan." *Current Biography,* April, 1963, pp. 206-208.

Hope, Kempe R. *Guyana: Politics and Development in an Emergent Socialist State.* Oakville, Ontario, Canada: Flatiron Book Distributors, 1985.

Spinner, Thomas J., Jr. *A Political and Social History of Guyana, 1945-1983.* Boulder, Colo.: Westview Press, 1984.

Edward A. Riedinger

Jiang Qing

Born: 1914; Zhucheng, Shandong, China
Died: May 14, 1991; Beijing, China

Chinese political leader, wife of Mao Zedong, and member of the Gang of Four

Jiang Qing (JYONG CHIHNG), also spelled Chiang Ch'ing, was born Li Shumeng, the daughter of a concubine living in the household of a small-town landowner. She was raised by her grandfather and was renamed Li Yunhe after she became an orphan. By her early teens she had joined a touring theatrical group and become interested in leftist politics. In 1933, she secretly joined the Chinese Communist Party. She was arrested and jailed for her communist political activities. After her release she went to Shanghai, where she acted successfully in various roles under the stage name Lan Ping (blue apple). After the Japanese invasion, Jiang Qing fled to the city of Chongqing (Chungking) and later crossed the Nationalist lines to travel to the Communists' stronghold at Yan'an to teach drama. There she first met Mao Zedong. Captivated with her, Mao eventually gave her the name Jiang Qing (azure river) and expressed a desire to marry her. However, other Communist leaders were suspicious of Jiang Qing and were upset over Mao's treatment of his third wife. Eventually an agreement was reached, and the two were permitted to marry in 1939 with the proviso that she abstain from political activity in the future.

Little is known about the activities of Jiang Qing during the 1950's. She remained in the background, appearing at official events and serving as a member of a number of cultural committees. Despite her promise not to participate in politics, in 1963 Jiang Qing publicly entered Chinese political life when she led a move to modernize traditional Beijing Opera in an attempt to rid it of so-called counter-revolutionary influences.

The Cultural Revolution

In an attempt to revitalize the revolution and eliminate political enemies, Mao Zedong proclaimed the Great Proletarian Cultural Revolution in 1966. In marked contrast to her more traditional role in the 1950's, Jiang Qing became a powerful political force. She directed the so-called Red Guards to attack physically bureaucrats, academics, artists, and others she deemed enemies of the revolution. At the height of the excesses of the Cultural Revolution, Jiang Qing was perhaps the most visible and enthusiastic supporter of the Cultural Revolution. In raucous speeches she denounced individuals and institutions at will—often with disastrous consequences for thousands of people. During this

Jiang Qing *(Archive Photos/Archive France)*

The Gang of Four

The Gang of Four, or the Shanghai Four, was a group of individuals who were accused of acts of murder, torture, and political terror during the years of the Cultural Revolution. While their 1980 trial and convictions reminded some observers of the show trials of the Soviet Union's Joseph Stalin era, the trial did serve as a catharsis to millions of Chinese terrorized by Mao's Red Guards. Along with Jiang Qing, the Gang of Four included Zhang Chunqiao (an army official), Yao Wenyuan (a Shanghai journalist), and Wang Hongwen (a Shanghai textile worker). Wang Hongwen's radicalism had propelled him to the position of vice chairman of the Communist Party at the age of thirty-seven.

The intense political fervor of the Cultural Revolution in the 1960's led to untold numbers of arrests, persecutions, and deaths in China. *(Archive Photos)*

period, she was one of the few advisers that Mao trusted. He appointed her to the Politburo (the Communist Party's policy-making committee), and she assumed the role of ideological censor of all of China's art, music, literature, and theater.

Downfall

As the Cultural Revolution's millions of deaths, beatings, and persecutions began to tear at the fabric of Chinese society, many in the leadership began to back away from the revolutionary fanaticism championed by Jiang Qing. As Mao's health rapidly deteriorated, Jiang Qing moved quickly to prepare for the leadership struggle that would follow his death. Her candidate, Hua Guofeng, proved inexperienced and ill-equipped to take over the leadership after the death of Mao in 1976. Within a month of Mao's death, Jiang Qing was arrested, and in 1980 she was put on trial and charged with complicity in thirty-four thousand deaths and 700,000 persecutions. Despite confessions from others,

Jiang Qing remained defiant during the nationally televised trial. While never offering regrets, she explained that "I was Mao's dog; what he said to bite, I bit." To millions of Chinese, she was the "white-boned demon" whose actions were guided by a plan to succeed Mao. She was sentenced to death, a sentence that contained a two-year reprieve during which it was hoped she would confess her crimes. She remained defiant, and the sentence was commuted to life imprisonment in 1983. She remained in custody until she committed suicide in May, 1991.

Bibliography

Bosania, David. *Verdict in Peking: The Trial of the Gang of Four*. New York: G. P. Putnam, 1984.

MacFarquhar, Roderick. *The Origins of the Cultural Revolution: Volume Three, the Coming of the Cataclysm*. New York: Columbia University Press, 1997.

Terrill, Ross. *The White-Boned Demon: A Biography of Madam Mao Zedong*. New York: Simon and Schuster, 1992.

Lawrence Clark

Jiang Zemin

Born: August 17, 1926; Yangzhou, Jiangsu Province, China

General secretary of Chinese Communist Party (took office 1989); president of China (took office 1993)

Jiang Zemin (JYONG DZEH-MIHN), also written Chiang Tse-min, grew up in a small Chinese city on the banks of the Chang River west of Shanghai. In 1946, Jiang joined the Chinese Communist Party (CCP); in 1947, he graduated from the electrical machinery department of Jiaotong University in Shanghai. After the Communists gained power in China in 1949, Jiang served in several position in Shanghai, including deputy director of a foodstuff factory and a soap factory. In 1955, Jiang was sent to the Soviet Union for training at an automobile factory in Moscow. After returning to China in 1956, he worked in the Changchun automobile plant, the Shanghai Electrical Equipment Research Institute, the Wuhan Power Machinery Institute, and the First Ministry of Machine-Building.

Jiang Zemin *(Reuters/Archive Photos)*

Industrial Administration

From 1971 to 1979, Jiang was the deputy director and then director of the Foreign Affairs Bureau under the Machine-Building Ministry. In 1978, Jiang was appointed vice president of the Society of Mechanical Engineering. Between 1980 and 1982, he worked as the vice minister of the Administrative Commission for Import and Export Affairs. In addition, Jiang was named vice minister of the Foreign Investment Commission in 1981, and in 1982 he was appointed vice minister of the Ministry of Electronics and then minister in 1983. Jiang was elected a member of the CCP Central Committee in 1982 at the twelfth Party Congress. In September, 1984, Jiang was named the deputy head of the Leading Group for the Electronics Industry under the State Council.

Political Moves

Jiang's political career was ignited in 1985 when he returned to Shanghai as its Communist Party deputy secretary, then secretary, and later mayor. Serving as the mayor of Shanghai from 1985 to 1988, Jiang proved to be a very effective administrator, making progress in developing the economic potential and resolving serious infrastructure problems in Shanghai. Under Jiang's direction, Shanghai was the first city in China to auction land-use rights, even though such a procedure violated communist policy. Entering the Politburo (the party's executive committee) at the thirteenth CCP Congress in 1987, Jiang was appointed party general secretary in Shanghai in 1988, a policy-making post superior to that of mayor.

In 1989, Chinese students and other citizens were involved in large demonstrations demanding democratic reforms in China. As the demand for democratic reforms grew, Jiang took the side of the conservatives. In June, after the Beijing massacre of demonstrators at Tiananmen Square, Chinese leader Deng Xiaoping chose Jiang as the general secretary of the CCP to replace Zhao Ziyang, who was dismissed for supporting the pro-democracy movement. In addition, in November of 1989, Jiang took over as chairman of the Central Military Commission when Deng stepped down.

High-rise buildings on Hong Kong's harbor. Chinese president Jiang Zemin presided over the return of Hong Kong to China on July 1, 1997. *(Japan Air Lines)*

Party General Secretary

As Communist Party general secretary, Jiang followed the party line; being a moderate, he did not ruffle political feathers at a sensitive time in Beijing. With his unauthoritarian style and the allegiance of China's military establishment, Jiang managed to achieve a balance among the interests of the CCP's major factions. Jiang put a renewed emphasis on communist philosophies in selecting and promoting party officials and frequently spoke out against the

The Return of Hong Kong

In the early 1980's, China and Great Britain began negotiations on an agreement to transfer Hong Kong back to China in 1997, after 156 years of British colonial rule. The agreement signed in 1984 concluded that Hong Kong would become a special administrative region (SAR) of China on July 1, 1997. In 1985, committees were established to prepare the framework for Hong Kong's government administration, known as the Basic Law. At midnight on July 1, 1997, with newly chosen Hong Kong chief executive Tung Chee-hwa and Chinese president Jiang Zemin officiating, Hong Kong reverted to Chinese sovereignty, and its new Beijing-appointed legislature was sworn in.

Under the terms of the 1984 agreement, Hong Kong would maintain its free-enterprise (capitalist) economy for at least fifty years after 1997. According to the Basic Law, Hong Kong's social, economic, and political systems would remain distinct from those of China, with China assuming responsibility for the defense and foreign policy of Hong Kong. After the transition citizens of Hong Kong continued to enjoy considerable freedom of speech, movement, and religion. Although several civil liberties were reduced, such as the right to protest and freedom of press, Jiang pledged to respect Hong Kong's autonomy and its tradition of free enterprise. Most Hong Kong residents remained hopeful about the future.

Freedom of the Press in China

Although the Chinese constitution states that freedom of the press is a fundamental right of all citizens, the government interprets the Communist Party's leading role as superior to these rights. The government does not permit citizens to publish criticism of senior leaders or to publish opinions that contradict basic Communist Party doctrine. The party and government tightly control the press, using it to propagate current communist ideologies. More than ten thousand distributed publications, including twenty-two hundred newspapers, are under explicit orders to follow Communist Party directives and guide public opinion as directed by political authorities. In January, 1997, the State Council issued new regulations governing the publishing industry. The regulations stated that people could express their views on state affairs and could publish academic and literary works, but they stipulated that people could not publish any material contrary to the constitution or which might reveal state secrets, endanger the national security, or harm China in any way.

Jiang Zemin in 1997 addressing the opening of the fifteenth Communist Party congress in Beijing. *(Reuters/ Will Burgess/Archive Photos)*

decadent ideas and lifestyle of the Western capitalist world. In 1993, he was appointed to the largely ceremonial government position of president.

Despite Jiang's leadership, a class gap was widening in China, and constant inflation became a serious problem. In the early 1990's, more than a million social disturbances were reported in rural villages, leading to more than eight thousand deaths that created ill feelings between farmers and the government. Urban areas experienced increased crime, and revolutionary groups grew in number. Widespread reports of human rights abuses strained relations with China and the rest of the world.

In 1996, Jiang initiated an anticrime drive that was well received by the Chinese. In July of 1997, he officially reclaimed Hong Kong, which had been a British colony, and he continued to campaign for the return of Taiwan, the island where Chinese Nationalists set up their own government in 1949, to mainland communist China. In October 1997, Jiang became the first Chinese head of state to visit Washington, D.C., in twelve years. He met with President Bill Clinton and discussed nonproliferation of nuclear arms, human rights, military cooperation, law enforcement, trade relations, and energy and environmental issues.

Receiving the military's unequivocal support and having the ability to generate consensus within the Chinese hierarchy, Jiang maintained stability in the face of many challenging circumstances. Through his unauthoritarian style of leadership, Jiang kept his potential rivals reasonably content. He also enjoyed a high profile internationally at a time when the United States and other Western governments sought to engage China with respect to human rights and other issues. Jiang was successful in reducing crime, fighting illegal drug problems, and promoting economic reforms. In 1997, he was one of the officiators in the smooth handover of Hong Kong to China and in a successful fifteenth CCP Congress. Because of his efforts, relations with the United States and the Western world improved.

Bibliography

Chao, Linda. *The First Chinese Democracy*. Baltimore: The Johns Hopkins University Press, 1998.

Feigon, Lee. *China Rising: The Meaning of Tiananmen*. Chicago: I. R. Dee, 1990.

Nathan, Andrew J. *China's Transition*. New York: Columbia University Press, 1997.

Thompson, Mark V. *Crisis at Tiananmen: Reform and Reality in Modern China*. San Francisco: China Books and Periodicals, 1990.

Yu-lin, Yu. *Communist China's Political and Economic Situation Under the Leadership of Jiang Zemin*. Taipei World League for Freedom and Democracy, 1992.

Alvin K. Benson

Mohammed Ali Jinnah

Born: December 25, 1876; Karachi, India (now Pakistan)
Died: September 11, 1948; Karachi, Pakistan

Indian Muslim activist, first governor-general of Pakistan (1947-1948)

Mohammed Ali Jinnah (moo-HAH-muhd ah-LEE JIH-nah) was the son of a hide merchant. The family belonged to a Shiite Muslim sect, the Khojas. After an early education in his native language, Gujerati, he received his high school education in English. In 1892 he was sent to England to work in business but decided to study law instead. He was called to the bar in London in 1896. On his return to India he settled in Bombay, where he became very successful and wealthy; he entered politics.

Early Political Career

Jinnah served in the Imperial Legislative Council, 1910-1919, and in the Indian Legislative Assembly, 1924-1930 and 1935-1947, as a repre-

Mohammed Ali Jinnah *(Archive Photos)*

sentative of the Muslims of Bombay. In the early stage of his career he was a member of both the All-India National Congress party (founded in 1885) and the All-India Muslim League party (founded in 1906). He espoused a secularist view of politics and often spoke about the necessity of cooperation between Hindus and Muslims. He was so famous for this that in 1916 he was called the "ambassador of Hindu-Muslim unity." However, Jinnah also believed that Mahatma (Mohandas) Gandhi was turning the Congress into an exclusively Hindu party. Consequently, during the 1920's, he became increasingly alienated from it.

Political Career, 1919-1934

In 1919 the British passed legislation (one of the Government of India Acts) that established a new constitution. The ensuing elections further divided the Hindu and the Muslim communities by revealing that Hindus had voted for Hindus and Muslims for Muslims. The attempts to devise a constitution acceptable to both Hindus and Muslims also divided the two groups. In 1929 Jinnah produced his own constitution, called the "Fourteen Points." During the 1920's and the early 1930's Jinnah sought a compromise with the Congress, but by the mid-1930's he had moved to a position diametrically opposed to compromise.

All discussions between Jinnah, other Muslim leaders, and the Hindus ended in a stalemate and led to more bitterness between the two communities. In 1930 Jinnah went to London to represent the Muslims at the Round Table Conferences, organized to reach agreement about a future constitution between the British and the Indians. The conference failed, and Jinnah was so disenchanted with the political situation that he remained in London to practice law. He did so for the next four years and only returned to India permanently in 1934 after a number of influential Muslims asked him to return and assume the leadership of the Muslims of India.

The Sole Spokesman

Between 1935 and 1936 Jinnah reorganized the All-India Muslim League to contest the general elections that were to be held in India in late 1936 and early 1937 as a result of the passage of the Government of India Act of 1935. Now completely separated from the Congress and vehemently opposed to its policy of noncooperation, Jinnah became the permanent president of the All-India Muslim League and its "sole

Hundreds of Muslim refugees crowd aboard a train leaving New Delhi for Pakistan in September, 1947, after the August partition of India and Pakistan. *(AP/Wide World Photos)*

spokesman." The league called him Quaid-i-Azam (great leader). After the general elections of 1936-1937, Congress assumed the government in seven of the provinces of India and over the

The All-India Muslim League

The All-India Muslim League was founded in Dacca on December 30, 1906. It was created in response to the founding of the Indian National Congress in 1885 and to the constitutional reforms which the British were introducing into India. The Muslims wished to make sure their interests were represented in the new constitution. In the first thirty years of its existence, the league was not a very active organization. It held an annual meeting at which various prominent Muslims gave speeches about the conditions of Muslim life in India. Membership of the party was small, with few people bothering to pay their annual membership dues. In 1930 the re-nowned poet Muhammad Iqbal called for the creation of Muslim states in the northwest part of India. In 1936 Mohammed Ali Jinnah assumed the permanent presidency of the league and reorganized the party. On March 23, 1940, the party put forward the Pakistan Resolution, which demanded a separate state for the Muslims of India. In the general elections of 1945-1946 the All-India Muslim League won a resounding victory, fulfilling its claim that it represented the Muslims of India and that they wanted the creation of Pakistan. Both Congress and the British reluctantly agreed. On August 14, 1947, Pakistan was created.

Pakistan

Pakistan was created at midnight on August 14, 1947, as a state for the Muslims of South Asia. Mohammed Ali Jinnah is considered the creator of the nation. In 1947 Pakistan consisted of East and West Pakistan, but in 1971 East Pakistan seceded and became a separate state, Bangladesh, with a capital at Dacca. The capital of Pakistan is Islamabad. Islam is the official religion, the rupee is the currency, and Urdu is the official language. Baluchistan, the North-West Frontier Province, Punjab, and Sind are the four provinces of Pakistan, although there is also a semiautonomous tribal area in the north. Pakistan was under civilian rule until the military coup of October 7, 1958. Since then the army has dominated the political life of Pakistan even if civilians run the government. Most of Pakistan's budget is spent on the military. In 1998 Pakistan tested its first nuclear devices.

next two years enacted a number of laws that Jinnah argued were destroying the Muslim way of life in India. This was especially true in the United Provinces—the "heartland of Islam"—from which a number of influential Muslims joined his side and became strong supporters. On March 23, 1940, Jinnah's All-India Muslim League put forth the "Pakistan Resolution," which demanded separate Muslim states for the Muslims of India.

The Campaign for Pakistan

Between 1940 and 1947, Jinnah led the campaign to create the new state of Pakistan. He started a newspaper, *Dawn,* and through the pages of the newspaper he and his followers developed a strong propaganda campaign in favor of the creation of Pakistan. Jinnah also organized conferences at which the All-India Muslim League argued for Pakistan. He also focused on regional Muslim parties and tried to bring all of their members into the league. Muslim students throughout India were also organized to work for the league. This campaign was aimed at persuading the British that when independence came India should be divided. In negotiations with the British, Jinnah was immovable in his demand for Pakistan. The result of the league's constant campaigning and organizational work was that in the general elections held in 1945 and 1946 the league won almost all of the Muslim seats. By 1947 Jinnah could claim that Muslims had voted overwhelmingly for Pakistan.

Pakistan's First Governor-General

In negotiations with the British from 1945 to 1947 in New Delhi, in Simla, and in London Jinnah continued to voice the demand for Pakistan. In the end, both the Congress party and the British agreed that when independence was granted Pakistan should be created. From August 15, 1947, when Pakistan was established, until his death, on September 11, 1948, Jinnah was Pakistan's first governor-general. His birthplace, Karachi, was selected as Pakistan's first capital, and Jinnah's mausoleum can be found there.

Bibliography

Jalal, Ayesha. *The Sole Spokesman: Jinnah, the Muslim League and the Demand for Pakistan.* Cambridge, England: Cambridge University Press, 1985.

Mujahid, Sharif al. *Quaid-i-Azam Jinnah: Studies in Interpretation.* Karachi, Pakistan: Quaid-i-Azam Academy, 1981.

Wolpert, Stanley. *Jinnah of Pakistan.* New York: Oxford University Press, 1984.

Roger D. Long

Joseph-Jacques-Césaire Joffre

Born: January 12, 1852; Rivesaltes, Roussillon, France
Died: January 3, 1931; Paris, France

French military commander, victor of 1914 Battle of the Marne

Joseph-Jacques-Césaire Joffre (zhoh-SEHF ZHOK say-ZAYR ZHO-fruh) was the son of a Catalan barrel maker. He grew up speaking Catalan at home and French at school. Taciturn and methodical even in youth, the boy Joffre showed talent for mathematics, science, and drawing at his primary school in Perpignan. He entered the prestigious Lycée Charlemagne in Paris in 1868, and a year later was the youngest student, at seventeen, admitted to the École Polytechnique in Paris, where he studied engineering. Called to military service at the outbreak of the Franco-Prussian War (1870-1871), he joined an artillery unit at Vincennes. He was promoted to lieutenant shortly after and served in artillery regiments until war's end.

Career Officer

Returning to school after the war, Joffre graduated with an engineering degree but gave up civil engineering for a career in the military. He rose to the rank of captain in 1876 and was assigned to constructing forts. His talents for building were recognized when he was posted to the Pyrenees during tensions with Spain; in Villefranche, he expertly constructed ramparts to protect France's border. In 1884 Joffre entered the colonial service when he joined Admiral Courbet's staff in Vietnam during the Tonkin War. He built a line of fortifications across the island of Formosa to deter Chinese forces contesting France's entry into Indochina. Courbet awarded him the Cross of the Legion of Honor in 1885.

Trench Warfare

In a local revolt at Ba Dinh, Vietnam, in 1887, Joffre built a series of trenches and routed the enemy by setting fire to the bamboo fields. Trench warfare would become the dominant military strategy of World War I. On his return to Paris, Joffre was attaché to the War Ministry and in 1891, professor of fortifications at the École Militaire at Fontainebleau. He left a year later for the Sudan, where his conquest of Timbuktu (in central Mali) in 1893 made him famous. Other achievements included fortifying Madagascar during tensions with the British.

His rise to the top echelons of the French military was rapid in the next decade. In 1905 he was named commander in chief of the Sixth Infantry and Third Army, and he was made a member of the high command in 1910. The following year

World War I French military commander Joseph-Jacques-Césaire Joffre (right) with U.S. general John J. Pershing in the Governor's Gardens in Paris. *(Archive Photos)*

The Battles of the Marne

There were two World War I battles fought at the Marne River, which lies some 30 miles (48 kilometers) north of Paris, at which German forces were stopped from attacking Paris. The first occurred in September, 1914, the second in July, 1918. In the 1914 battle, the Germans were unopposed in their march through Belgium and across the Marne. General Joseph-Jacques-Césaire Joffre attacked first and drove back the first German army under General von Kluck, thus saving Paris.

Other German forces arrived soon after but were unable to push south, so they retreated. The second Marne battle was the turning point of the war that led to Germany's defeat. This battle occurred July 15-August 2, 1918. German forces were again marching on Paris from the Marne, but they were halted by French general Ferdinand Foch commanding an Allied force that included several American divisions. The Americans won their first important victory there, at Chateau-Thierry.

War Minister Adolphe Messing appointed him major general of the army.

An aloof, practical man known for his brilliant analytic powers, Joffre triumphed over an equally brilliant German strategist, Alfred von Schlieffen, in his first major battle of World War I (1914-1918). Von Schlieffen had conceived the

British soldiers in a front-line trench during World War I. Joseph-Jacques-Césaire Joffre had used trench warfare in 1887 in Vietnam, and it became a standard form of warfare in World War I. *(Archive Photos)*

plan to attack Paris with the right wing of a large invading force, while a left wing invaded Russia. It was this crucial decision to split the main force in two that gave Joffre his greatest military victory at the first battle of the Marne (September 6-9, 1914). Joffre followed two principles in war: to be always on the offensive, and to surround the enemy. In attacking first he saved Paris from almost certain conquest.

However, trench warfare soon made further advances difficult. After his first victory, Joffre was unable to move his armies effectively, as all sides of the conflict burrowed into trenches for the duration of the war. After the French suffered heavy losses on different fronts, General Nivelle replaced Joffre as commander in chief; he was removed from office in December, 1917, and assigned to the École Militaire. He was later named marshal of France. In 1918 he was honored by election to the French Academy.

Bibliography

Joffre, Joseph. *My March to Timbucktoo*. New York: Duffield, 1950.

Kahn, Alexander. *The Life of General Joffre*. New York: Frederick A. Stokes, 1950.

Recouly, Ramon. *General Joffre and His Battles*. New York: Charles Scribner's Sons, 1960.

Paul Christensen

John XXIII

Born: November 25, 1881; Sotto il Monte, Italy
Died: June 3, 1963; Vatican, Rome, Italy

Pope of the Roman Catholic Church (1958-1963)

John XXIII (JON thuh TWEHN-tee THURD was the 262d supreme pontiff, or pope, of the Roman Catholic Church. During his leadership, from 1958 to 1963, he was regarded as a liberal pope. He is best known for calling the Second Vatican Council (Vatican II), which led to reform throughout the church, and for writing the encyclical *Pacem in terris* (*Peace on Earth*).

John XXIII was born Angelo Giuseppe Roncalli (AHN-jay-loh jew-ZEH-pay rohn-KAH-lee) at Sotto il Monte, near Bergamo, in northern Italy. He was the eldest son and the third of thirteen children born to a farming family. He decided at a young age to become a priest, studying at the seminary in Bergamo. Later he won a scholarship to the Pontifical Seminary in Rome. On August 10, 1904, he was ordained a priest and said his first mass at St. Peter's Basilica in Rome. His early life in a small village—and a large family—had developed his diplomatic skills. These skills were called on in his various foreign appointments and would later serve him in his office as pope. Though holding the highest office within the Roman Catholic Church, John XXIII never forgot his roots as a peasant farmer's son and treated all those he met with dignity, respect, and friendship.

Rising Through the Ranks

Young Father Roncalli was sent to Bergamo to serve as secretary to the bishop. He also taught church history at the Bergamo seminary, where he had begun his own studies for priesthood. World War I interrupted this career, however, and Father Roncalli became First Sergeant Roncalli of the medical corps and later Lieutenant Roncalli of the chaplains' corps in the Italian army. After the war he was made an archbishop. Pope Pius XI sent him to a tough diplomatic post in Bulgaria and later to Greece and Turkey.

During the German occupation of Greece from 1941 to 1944, Roncalli took great risks to save as many people as possible from the Nazis. After World War II, the next pope, Pius XII, named Archbishop Roncalli nuncio to France, where he served for eight years. While there he became the Vatican's first observer in the United Nations

Pope John XXIII (center) addressing reporters covering the Ecumenical Council at the Vatican in 1962. *(Library of Congress)*

Educational, Scientific, and Cultural Organization (UNESCO). He found himself respected and loved because of his sincere, unassuming, and pleasant demeanor, according to biographer Frederick Franck.

In 1952, at the age of seventy-one, Archbishop Roncalli was awarded the red biretta of cardinal as well as the grand cross of the Legion of Honor by Pope Pius XII. During the forty-eight years Cardinal Roncalli had spent in the clergy, very little of it had been under the direct influence of Rome. Having served in foreign countries, he saw all people as his spiritual responsibility, regardless of whether they were Catholic or even Christian.

Making Changes

When Pope Pius XII died on October 9, 1958, Cardinal Roncalli traveled to Rome. He was one of the fifty-one cardinals in the Vatican conclave, the gathering which elects the next pope. Never assuming that he would be chosen—he had purchased a round-trip ticket—Roncalli took the name John XXIII when elected to succeed Pope Pius XII. Because of his advanced age, John XXIII was expected to be a short-term pope—someone to occupy the papal seat while the next pope was groomed. His five-year term

was longer than expected and was filled with changes.

He broke with tradition in small ways, but the changes were big enough to upset his advisers. For instance, his first papal blessing was televised. When he was crowned on November 4, 1958, he preached at the mass. He opened the gardens to visitors during the times he himself was enjoying them. The greatest change, however, was in announcing, in 1959, the Second Vatican Council. His advisers were against convening the council because the church was not in crisis. John XXIII, however, felt that the Catholic Church needed help to meet the needs of modern society. When his advisers insisted that the necessary preparation would not allow the council to open by 1963, John XXIII is said to have responded with: "Then we shall convene in 1962."

Writing the Encyclical

The first session of Vatican II began in October, 1962. John XXIII would not live to see its conclusion. Very ill with stomach cancer, he worked on an encyclical, or open letter to the bishops, "Peace on Earth." It was intended to unite the "human family" through justice, love, and freedom. Franck describes "Peace on Earth" as "the first time a Pope had addressed himself not just to

---

Vatican II

On January 25, 1959, Pope John XXIII summoned a council at the Vatican. Because it was the second such council ever held in the history of the church, it was called the Second Vatican Council, or Vatican II. The previous council had been called to address a crisis in the church, but John XXIII's purpose for Vatican II was *aggiornamento*, renewal or updating, of the Catholic Church. Meeting the needs of modern society and reuniting all Christians were his goals. After two years of preparation, the first of four sessions opened on Octo-

ber 12, 1962. Twenty-four hundred bishops from around the globe attended, as did observers from other religions. Vatican II closed on December 8, 1965. It was one of the most talked-about events of the decade, captivating Catholic and non-Catholic alike. Vatican II led to many changes within and without the Catholic Church. For instance, Latin was dropped from the mass in favor of the local language. Laypeople (nonclergy) were given greater participation in the mass. Interactions with other religious faiths were also improved.

Ecumenism

The unity of all Christian religions is known as ecumenism. Differences in both doctrine and religious practice exist among the various Christian religions. They change as these religions evolve. From the time of the Reformation in 1517, when Martin Luther, a German monk, broke from the Catholic Church and began Protestantism, new beliefs have led to the formation of new Christian sects. An ecumenical movement began in the early 1900's that sought to unite all Christian faiths. It focused on the Protestant religions until the 1960's, when the Catholic Church became more involved. Vatican II endorsed the ecumenical movement. In addition to efforts to unite all Christians as much as possible, the Catholic Church works to unite the Eastern Orthodox churches with the Roman Catholic Church.

Catholics, but to all men." This encyclical insisted that human rights and responsibility are the foundation for world peace. It ensured that Vatican II would remain focused as John XXIII had intended. His successor, Paul VI, saw the council through to completion.

Ironically, John XXIII was more appreciated by people outside the Catholic Church than by those within it. He received the Balzan Foundation Peace Prize in 1962. After his death on June 3, 1963, *Time* magazine named him Man of the Year. He was also awarded the U.S. Presidential Medal of Freedom.

Bibliography

Franck, Frederick. *"I Love Life!" Said Pope John XXIII*. New York: St. Martin's Press, 1967.

Hebblethwaite, Peter. *Pope John XXIII: Shepherd of the Modern World*. New York: Doubleday, 1985.

Johnson, Paul. "Kitchen Pope, Warrior Pope." *Time*, December 26, 1994, p. 79.

McBrien, Richard P. *Lives of the Popes: The Pontiffs from St. Peter to John Paul II*. San Francisco: Harper, 1997.

Walch, Timothy. *Pope John XXIII*. New York: Chelsea House, 1987.

Lisa A. Wroble

John Paul II

Born: May 18, 1920; Wadowice, Poland

Pope of the Roman Catholic Church (elected 1978)

Karol Jozef Wotyła (KAH-rohl YEW-sehf voy-TIH-wah), later Pope John Paul II (JON PAWL thuh SEH-kuhnd), was born into a tragedy-stricken family during the year in which modern Poland was reborn. He lost his mother, Emilia, at the age of six, his elder brother Edmund at age fourteen, and his father, Karol, at twenty-one. A superlative student and promising actor, Wotyła worked under the brutal Nazi occupation in a rock quarry and factory. In 1942 he entered an underground seminary and was ordained on November 1, 1946. Wotyła studied for two years in Rome and returned to Poland for parish assignments. He lectured at Jogiellonian University and taught ethics and philosophy in Lublin. He was named a bishop by Pius XII in 1958, and shortly thereafter he was summoned to Rome by John XXIII to participate in the Second Vatican Council

(Vatican II). In 1963, Wotyła was named archbishop of Krakow and under Paul VI became a cardinal in 1966. He collaborated with Paul VI in drafting *Humanae Vitae*, which forbade the use of artificial contraception by Catholics. After the brief pontificate of John Paul I, Cardinal Wotyła was elected to the papal seat on October 16, 1978, becoming the first Polish pope and the first non-Italian pope since 1523.

Confronting Communism

John Paul II faced two major challenges as he assumed the papacy. The first was protecting the rights of the Catholic Church and its believers who lived in communist countries through guarantees of human rights and religious freedom. Second, he had to restore order within the Church, which had been badly divided over post-Vatican II disputes in liturgy, dogma, and moral theology.

Although he consistently pursued both challenges, the first phase of his papacy was highlighted by the struggle with communism and his assertion of human rights for all. His trip to Poland in 1979 stimulated processes of reform that reverberated throughout the communist world and eventually contributed to the fall of the communist regime in Poland ten years later. In rapid succession, other communist states also collapsed.

John Paul II, who traveled widely during the 1980's, became an important figure not only in the political life of Poland, but also in the wider global

Pope John Paul II on his historic 1998 visit to Cuba, being greeted by Cuban premier Fidel Castro. *(AP/Wide World Photos)*

arena. In the first six years of his papacy alone he traveled to thirty-seven countries. By the end of the 1990's he had made more than eighty apostolic visits throughout the world. His message to governments everywhere concerned issues of social and economic justice and human rights. He met with leaders throughout the world to bring these messages to them personally. In 1998 John Paul made history by visiting the island nation of Cuba, a communist country ruled by Fidel Castro. The church had long been suppressed in Cuba, yet the pope's popular support and personal diplomacy won several concessions from the government. Castro

Pope John Paul II before holding a mass at a World War II monument in Rio de Janeiro, Brazil, in 1997. *(AP/Wide World Photos)*

himself greeted the pope. To the people who thronged by the millions to see and hear him, his message was to respect life and the moral teachings of the Gospels and the Church.

John Paul II's Trip to Poland

On June 2, 1979, Pope John Paul II landed at Warsaw airport to begin a nostalgic and historic visit to his homeland of Poland. In thousands of churches throughout Poland, which is overwhelmingly Catholic, church bells rang as the pope's plane landed. He had strong words against the communist government of Poland and words of consolation and hope for the Polish people. He called for the opening of frontiers, for religious freedom, and for justice and peace. Throughout his tour, huge throngs greeted him at public appearances and masses. The pope visited national shrines. In a visit to the site of the World War II Nazi concentration camp at Auschwitz, he prayed for reconciliation with the Jewish community.

Nearly a third of the Polish nation saw him in person during his visit.

Relations with the communist leaders of Poland were quite tense during the visit, as he rejected the Marxist view of the working class as nonspiritual instruments of production. The pope successfully challenged the legitimacy of the government, but he did not want to provoke a rebellion. Instead he hoped for peaceful change. Ten years later, after much turmoil and instability, his hope materialized: The communist government lost elections to Lech Wałęsa's Solidarity Party, and Poland embarked on the difficult road to political and economic reform.

Evangelium Vitae

John Paul II issued the encyclical *Evangelium Vitae* (gospel of life) in 1995 to clarify Catholic Church teachings concerning abortion, euthanasia, and the death penalty. In the document he stresses that the dignity of the individual calls foremost for the respect of life as a gift of God. No other right has meaning unless life itself is preserved. Hence all forms of killing people must be resisted. According to *Evangelium Vitae*, those people who are most vulnerable, such as the unborn and the aged, most need society's protection. However, even the guilty criminal should be spared except in the most extreme cases—where harm to society can be prevented only by capital punishment. When society loses its sense of the sacredness of life, the pope asserts, it begins to promote a culture of death and of personal convenience over genuine charity and justice.

Confronting Modernism

With the fall of communism in the early 1990's, John Paul II discerned new threats to the dignity of humankind in the form of Western commercialism, liberalism, materialism, secularism, and hedonism. He redoubled efforts in the 1990's to confront those who called for relaxation of norms regarding the use of birth control, the practices of abortion and euthanasia, priestly celibacy, and the ordination of women. He disciplined those clergy and theologians who challenged the Catholic Church's teaching authority. John Paul II's critics, while acknowledging his personal charisma and wide popularity—and praising his positions on human rights, peace, and social justice—opposed him on specific moral and dogmatic issues; among these are his opposition to abortion, contraception, capital punishment, and euthanasia. They asserted that he too rigidly adheres to outmoded moral norms that alienate modern people. John Paul II's defenders pointed out that he is consistent in his message, whether on social or moral issues, and that as pope he is required to preach the teachings of Christ without compromise. To John Paul II, the modern person must conform to the timeless moral law.

In his effort to impose greater order in the Church, John Paul II issued a new *Catechism of the Catholic Church* (1993). He also issued many encyclicals, including *Veritatis Splendor* (1993) and *Evangelium Vitae* (1995), which explicate his personalist philosophy, attack modern theories of morality, and affirm the culture of life over the "culture of death." John Paul II canonized more saints than any other pope in history. His devotion to the Virgin Mary and his belief in the Fatima prophecies were deepened during his brush with death by assassination in 1981.

Bibliography

Bernstein, Carl, and Marco Politi. *His Holiness: John Paul II and the Hidden History of Our Time.* New York: Doubleday, 1996.

John Paul II. *Crossing the Threshold of Hope.* New York: Alfred A. Knopf, 1994.

Kwitny, Jonathan. *Man of the Century: The Life and Times of Pope John Paul II.* New York: Henry Holt, 1997.

Szulc, Tad. *Pope John Paul II: The Biography.* New York: Scribner, 1995.

Robert F. Gorman

Lyndon B. Johnson

Born: August 27, 1908; near Stonewall, Gillespie County, Texas
Died: January 22, 1973; en route to San Antonio, Texas

President of the United States (1963-1969)

Lyndon Baines Johnson (LIHN-duhn BAYNZ JON-suhn) was the son of a Texas state legislator from the state's Hill Country and an ambitious, educated mother. Lyndon graduated from Southwest Texas State Teacher's College in 1930 and became an aide to a congressman in 1931. In 1934 he married Claudia Alta Taylor, who was thereafter known by her nickname, Lady Bird. They had two daughters, Lynda and Luci. In 1935 Johnson was named as the Texas director of the National Youth Administration (NYA). Two years later he ran for Congress from the tenth district and was elected.

Road to the White House

A strong supporter of Franklin D. Roosevelt and the New Deal, Johnson moved rightward during the 1940's as Texas became more conservative. He lost a race for the U.S. Senate in 1941. During World War II, he served briefly in the Navy and received the Silver Star for bravery on a hazardous bombing mission. In 1948 he won the Democratic primary for the U.S. Senate by only eighty-seven votes. The closeness of the result and the charges of fraud that swirled around the campaign won him the ironic nickname "Landslide Lyndon." Investments in radio stations provided the basis for his ample fortune.

In the Senate, Johnson rose rapidly to become the majority leader in 1955. Surviving a severe heart attack that same year, he began to seek the presidency. He supported the Civil Rights Act of 1957 as a way of showing that he could move beyond his southern base. His run for the Democratic nomination in 1960 failed, but John F. Kennedy asked him to become the vice presidential nominee. Johnson's presence on the ticket helped carry the South and put Kennedy in the White House. The vice presidential years were difficult ones for Johnson. He felt excluded from the decision making of the administration and knew that members of the Kennedy circle regarded him with contempt. Everything changed on November 22, 1963, when President Kennedy was assassinated during a trip to Dallas, Texas. Lyndon Johnson became president and pledged to the nation that he would carry forward Kennedy's legacy.

A Dynamic Beginning

Johnson's first year in office was a success in every respect. He persuaded Congress to pass the

Lyndon B. Johnson *(Library of Congress)*

785

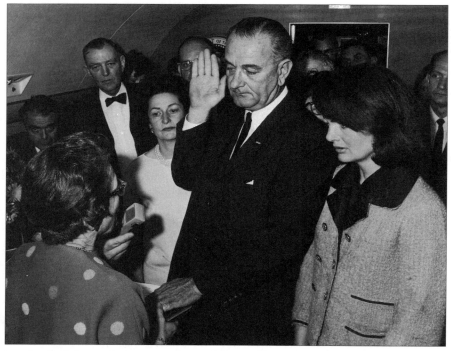

Lyndon B. Johnson being sworn in as U.S. president aboard Air Force 1 while Lady Bird Johnson and John F. Kennedy's widow, Jacqueline (right), look on. *(Lyndon Baines Johnson Library)*

landmark Civil Rights Act of 1964, which gave Americans of all races access to public accommodations. The new president proclaimed the goal of "the Great Society" as something for which the nation should strive, and he declared a "War on Poverty." With the economy booming, the nation at peace around the world, and Johnson in charge, he won the Democratic nomination and faced the challenge of the Republicans, led by Senator Barry Goldwater of Arizona. Johnson trounced the conservative Goldwater with 61 percent of

The Great Society

In May, 1964, President Lyndon B. Johnson told an audience at the University of Michigan that the United States should seek to become "the Great Society." A liberal nationalist, Johnson believed that the federal government could eliminate poverty, improve the environment, provide Medicare to the elderly, support education, and rebuild the nation's cities, among other programs. After his election in 1964, Johnson persuaded Congress to enact many of these laws. In the process, the term "Great Society" became associated with Johnson's expansive view of national power and his ambition to be a great president in the mold of Franklin D. Roosevelt.

However, the war in Vietnam, congressional opposition, and racial divisions wounded John-

son's political standing and reduced his ability to implement his Great Society vision in the 1960's.

Some of the specific programs, such as the War on Poverty, were badly administered. By the time he left the White House in 1969, the term "Great Society" had become identified with large, wasteful government programs. Although large sums were indeed spent on these programs, with the exception of Medicare they never composed a significant percentage of the federal budget. Many of the central elements of Johnson's agenda, such as Medicare, have remained popular with the American people. Thus, while the concept of the Great Society was abandoned, its historical legacy is still apparent.

Containment

To respond to the threat of an expansionist Soviet Union after World War II, American policy makers devised the doctrine of containment. The policy involved resisting the growth of communist power through economic, diplomatic, and military means so that over time the internal weaknesses of the Soviet Union would be exposed and its threat would be blunted. In shaping American strategy in the Vietnam War, Lyndon B. Johnson and his aides were much influenced by their perception that North Vietnam was part of a larger communist threat that had to be resisted as an episode in the implementation of containment. Critics charged that Johnson misread the Vietnam situation, erroneously linking it to the Soviet threat.

the popular vote and a margin of 486 to 52 in the electoral college.

Once elected in his own right, Johnson pressed forward to implement his vision of the Great Society. A flood of legislation ensued in 1965 as the Democrats in Congress passed bill after bill. These included the Voting Rights Act of 1965, Medicare, the Immigration Act, the Highway

U.S. president Lyndon Baines Johnson signs into law the landmark Civil Rights Act of 1964. *(National Archives)*

Beautification Act, Head Start, and many more. By the end of the year, however, support for such legislation ebbed in Congress as voters turned away from the president's programs. Urban riots in major cities and an upsurge of African American militance produced a white backlash against and within the Democratic Party.

The Vietnam War

Adding to the president's political difficulties was the war in Vietnam. During 1964 Johnson had told the American people that the conflict against North Vietnam and communist insurgents in South Vietnam would not be expanded. As the U.S.-supported regime in Saigon seemed close to collapse in 1965, however, the administration began bombing strikes against the North designed to force negotiations. To protect air bases, significant numbers of ground troops were deemed necessary. By July, 1965, Johnson and his administration had embarked on ground offensives to achieve their diplomatic objectives.

Over the next two and a half years, Johnson escalated the war. Soon protests arose on both the Left and the Right over the conduct of the war, and the resulting social turmoil was blamed on the president. Johnson could neither win victory quickly nor convince his constituents to accept a longer war. His secretive style eroded public confidence, and his political base collapsed. The Republicans made large gains in the 1966 congressional elections. During 1967 it became apparent that the Vietnam War was stalemated, and strong opposition to Johnson's renomination in 1968 surfaced within the Democratic Party.

The unexpected Tet Offensive by the Viet Cong in early 1968 completed Johnson's downfall. After he barely defeated an antiwar candidate, Senator Eugene McCarthy, in the New Hampshire primary, Johnson announced his withdrawal from politics on March 31, 1968. Last-minute negotiations during his final months in office failed to produce a peace settlement, and his vice president, Hubert Humphrey, lost the 1968 election to Richard M. Nixon. Johnson left office on January 20, 1969, a repudiated president. He returned home to Texas, where he died of a heart attack near his birthplace four years later.

A Failed Presidency

Despite his impressive political skills and string of legislative successes, Lyndon Johnson did not achieve the record of presidential greatness that he sought. His most important domestic legacy was his contribution to the civil rights revolution through the landmark laws that he championed. The failure of his Vietnam policy overshadowed his accomplishments in the White House. The devious manner in which he implemented the strategy of escalation and his lack of candor with the American people produced a disillusionment with mainstream politicians that some consider his most important legacy. Yet he remains one of the most interesting and controversial of all modern presidents.

Bibliography

Conkin, Paul. *Big Daddy from the Pedernales: Lyndon Baines Johnson*. Boston: Twayne, 1986.

Dallek, Robert. *Lone Star Rising: Lyndon Johnson and His Times, 1908-1960*. New York: Oxford University Press, 1991.

_____. *Flawed Giant: Lyndon Johnson and His Times, 1961-1973*. New York: Oxford University Press, 1998.

Johnson, Lady Bird. *A White House Diary*. New York: Holt, Rinehart and Winston, 1971.

Johnson, Lyndon. *The Vantage Point: Perspectives on the Presidency*. New York: Holt, Rinehart and Winston, 1971.

Lewis L. Gould

Barbara Jordan

Born: February 21, 1936: Houston, Texas
Died: January 17, 1996; Austin, Texas

U.S. congresswoman (1973-1979)

Barbara Charline Jordan (BAHR-bah-rah shahr-LEEN JOHR-duhn) was the daughter of Ben and Arlyne Patten Jordan. Her father was a minister and warehouse worker; she was one of three children born to the couple. Her early education began in the segregated inner-city schools of Houston, ending with graduation from Phillis Wheatley High School in 1952. Attending Texas Southern University, taking a B.A. in political science and history, she graduated magna cum laude in 1956. Completing law studies at Boston University, she took the bar examinations and was admitted to the Massachusetts and Texas bars in 1959. She began her practice in Houston in 1960.

Achievements

Jordan's life was a series of firsts. From the prizes won in high school to her award of the Presidential Medal of Freedom, she demonstrated how gender and ethnic barriers could be overturned. After two failures to win election to the Texas Senate (in 1962 and 1964), she won her district in 1966. In 1972, although it was only for a day, she became the acting governor of the state of Texas. In that same year, she was elected to the House of Representatives and assigned to the Committee on Government Operations and the Judiciary Committee.

During the summer of 1974, Jordan achieved national acclaim for her defense of the Constitution during the Watergate hearings concerning Richard M. Nixon's involvement in a coverup of illegal activities by White House figures. Her speech advocating impeachment of Nixon was widely considered oratorically brilliant. Jordan was involved in congressional efforts to extend the Voting Rights Act of 1965. She was also involved in the passage of the Consumer Pricing Act, a bill repealing antitrust exemptions that kept certain prices at artificially high levels. Her next moment in the public spotlight came when she gave the keynote speech at the Democratic National Convention on July 12, 1976. She spoke of the philosophies of the party and its meaning for democracy. However, these achievements, recognitions, and acclaims were all shaded

Barbara Jordan *(Library of Congress)*

789

Former Texas representative Barbara Jordan acknowledging cheers during her keynote address at the 1992 Democratic convention. *(Reuters/Ray Stubblebine/Archive Photos)*

Barbara Jordan's 1976 Democratic Convention Speech

Barbara Jordan's keynote speech at the Democratic National Convention on July 12, 1976, was entitled "Who Then Will Speak for the Common Good?" The speech affirmed the philosophies and visions of the Democratic Party. It urged listeners to recognize the realities of contemporary life in America, but it also voiced the hope that America become a nation that would not be destroyed by loss of a "common national endeavor." While recognizing that the task would be difficult, she stressed that all Americans must remember that they "share a common destiny," urging in conclusion that Americans find "new ways to implement that system and realize our destiny."

by her awareness of the neurological condition, multiple sclerosis, that would eventually affect, then end, her career in government service.

Career in Education

Jordan's withdrawal from public service—her service in Congress ended in 1979—did not mean abandonment of her lifelong concerns with people or government. Jordan's staunch beliefs in the worth of the individual and the U.S. Constitution appeared in her final projects as well. She began teaching public policy at the University of Texas at Austin, assuming the Lyndon B. Johnson Chair of National Policy in 1982. Her public appearances were few but meaningful. She was a participant in the debate over the nomination of Robert Bork to the Supreme Court, speaking against the candidate; she gave one of the nominating speeches for Lloyd Bentsen at the Democratic Convention in 1988. By then she spoke from a wheelchair because of the effects of multiple sclerosis. In 1992 she again delivered the keynote address to the Democrats at their national convention.

Awards

Jordan received many awards, each reflecting the philosophies that guided her life. Among them were the Eleanor Roosevelt Val-Kill Medal, the Nelson Mandela Award for Health and Human Rights, and the Presidential Medal of Freedom. She was an inductee into the African American Hall of Fame and the National Women's Hall of Fame. President Bill Clinton appointed her chairwoman of the Committee on Immigration Reform.

Bibliography

Browne, Ray B. *Contemporary Heroes and Heroines*. Detroit, Mich.: Gale Research, 1990.

Jordan, Barbara, and Shelby Hearn. *Barbara Jordan: A Self-Portrait*. Garden City, N.Y.: Doubleday, 1979.

Ries, Paula, and Anne J. Stone, eds. *The American Woman, 1992-93*. New York: W. W. Norton, 1992.

Maude M. Jennings

Juan Carlos I

Born: January 5, 1938; Rome, Italy

King of Spain (from 1975)

Juan Carlos Alfonso Víctor María de Borbón y Borbón (WAWN KAHR-lohs ahl-FOHN-soh VEEK-tohr mah-REE-ah thay bohr-BOHN ee bohr-BOHN) was born the first son of Don Juan de Borbón y Battenberg and Doña María de las Mercedes de Borbón y Orleáns. On his father's side, he descended from King Alfonso XIII of Spain and Queen Victoria of England. Relatives on his mother's side include Don Carlos de Borbón. The two dynastic branches—those of Isabel II and the Carlists—that were separated upon the death of Ferdinand VII in 1833 came together again in Juan Carlos.

Prince Juan Carlos, the future Spanish king, in his naval uniform. *(Archive Photos/Camera Press)*

Early Life

In 1942 Juan Carlos moved with his parents to Switzerland, where he pursued elementary studies at Rolle and then at Ville Saint-Jean, a boarding school at Fribourg run by Marian Fathers. He joined his parents in Estoril, Portugal, in 1947 and then set foot on Spanish soil for the first time on September 9, 1948, to continue his education and to prepare for leading Spain. After he passed his *bachillerato* (school-leaving examination), it was Spanish dictator Francisco Franco's idea that Juan Carlos would spend two years at the Zaragoza Military Academy, followed by a year each in the naval and air force academies. He earned the rank of lieutenant in each of the services. From 1961 to 1962, Juan Carlos undertook a special program of studies at Madrid University that included study tours throughout Spain. From 1963 to 1968, he was on temporary assignments to various ministries.

On May 14, 1962, Juan Carlos married Princess Sophia of Greece in Athens; she converted to Catholicism afterward. Their three children, Elena (born in 1963), Cristina (1965), and Felipe (1968), were all born in Madrid. The royal family took up residence at the Zarzuela Palace, just outside Madrid in an area of low woodlands. The Palace of Marivent in Palma de Mallorca became their summer home.

Independent Successor to Franco

One of Franco's greatest problems as dictator of Spain (1939-1975) was the designation of his successor as head of state. Juan Carlos' father, Don Juan, had considered himself the heir to the Spanish throne since Alfonso XIII abdicated shortly before dying in 1941. However, by 1962, Franco indicated that he preferred Juan Carlos to reign in the future. By virtue of the Law of Succession (1947) and the Organic Law of the State (1969), Prince Juan Carlos was designated successor as king on July 22, 1969. Although the prince had to affirm his allegiance to Franco and Franco's constitution and political system, Juan Carlos was firmly committed to democratic change by 1969.

Juan Carlos I (WAWN KAHR-lohs thuh FURST) took the throne on November 22, 1975, two days after Franco died. The king immediately lent the authority of his office to helping to democratize the Spanish political system. He was particularly important in maintaining military support for democratic reforms and in winning the support of Catalonia, a region in northeastern Spain, for the new Spanish government by restoring its Generalitat (government). The defining moment of the king's reign came on February 23, 1981, when Lieutenant-Colonel Antonio Tejero of the Civil Guard burst into the Congress of Deputies with several hundred guardsmen to prevent the investiture of a new civilian

Spanish king Juan Carlos I (second from right) and wife Sofia watch a military parade in 1996 with visiting Portuguese president Jorge Dampiaio and his wife Jose Rita. *(Reuters/Sergio Perez/Archive Photos)*

The Spanish Democratic Monarchy

Even before assuming the throne in 1975, Juan Carlos wanted a democratic monarchy. He knew from his travels that this system was what most Spaniards wanted. He correctly believed that it would allow him to moderate and arbitrate the activities of government, and he realized that only a democratic Spain would be fully integrated into Europe. Democracy was established rapidly: The first democratic elections since 1936 were held on June 15, 1977, and a new constitution was ap-

proved on October 31, 1978. The king, who vowed never to leave Spain nor to abdicate, worked assiduously to consolidate the monarchy as an institution. King Juan Carlos I chose not to have a royal court and instead established a reputation for mixing easily with commoners, with whom he achieved popularity. The upbringing of his son, Felipe, included careful preparation for his own assumption of the Spanish crown.

government and to return Spain to Franco's principles. The king never flinched, and he convinced rebellious army units to return to their barracks. Other major accomplishments of the king include reconciling Spaniards to a plural, multicultural Spain by defending the regional languages (Catalan, Basque, and Galician) in their respective autonomous communities and forging special relationships with many other heads of state, which facilitated the foreign-policy initiatives of Spain's premiers.

Bibliography

Anderson, Jon L. "The Reign in Spain." *The New Yorker*, April 27/May 4, 1998.

Gilmour, David. *The Transformation of Spain: From Franco to the Constitutional Democracy*. London: Quartet Books, 1985.

Powell, Charles. *Juan Carlos of Spain: Self-Made Monarch*. New York: Macmillan, 1966.

Vilallonga, José Luis de. *The King: A Life of King Juan Carlos of Spain*. Translated by Anthea Bell. London: Weidenfeld & Nicolson, 1994.

Steven L. Driever

János Kádár

Born: May 26, 1912; Fiume, Austro-Hungarian Empire (now Rijeka, Croatia)
Died: July 6, 1989; Budapest, Hungary

Premier (1956-1958; 1961-1965) and first secretary (1965-1988) of Hungary

János Kádár (YAH-nohsh KAH-dahr) was born János Jozsef Czermanik (YAH-nohsh YOH-zhehf CHEHR-mah-nyeek). He joined the Communist Party (then illegal) in 1932 and became a member of the Hungarian underground during World War II. He then served in a succession of posts in communist governments. His career culminated in the period between 1965 and 1988, when as first secretary of the Central Committee he pursued economic reforms while remaining loyal to the Soviet Union.

Rise to Power

When the communists took power in Hungary in 1948, Kádár was made minister for home affairs. He pursued a program of reform and liberalism similar to that of Josip Tito in Yugoslavia. Stalinists within Hungary—that is, members of the Communist Party who submitted to the authority of the Soviet Union—drove Kádár from power and imprisoned him in 1951. He was one of a generation of communist leaders in Eastern Europe who were purged because they seemed insufficiently loyal to the Communist Party. His fate reflected the plight of Communist Parties that deemed their very survival dependent on backing from the Soviet Union. These parties did not rely on popular support; on the other hand, they also feared direct Soviet occupation, which would deprive their countries of even a modest amount of independence.

After three years of imprisonment, Kádár returned to power in 1956 in the anti-Stalinist government of Imre Nagy. This government was a short-lived attempt to re-create an autonomous Hungary. However, the Soviet army and its Eastern European allies invaded Hungary to overthrow Nagy (battling the rebellious Hungarians in the streets). Kádár decided to switch sides—he became a Stalinist and established a government slavishly beholden to Moscow.

Premier and First Secretary

In 1958, Kádár had Nagy and other anti-Stalinists tried and executed. He served as premier of Hungary from 1961 to 1965, when he relinquished his position but remained first secretary of the Central Committee. In 1962, Kádár rid the government of several old-line Stalinists, and gradually his regime relaxed its restric-

János Kádár *(Reuters/B. Smith/Archive Photos)*

Hungarian premier János Kádár (left) at the Warsaw train station, arriving for a Warsaw Pact summit. *(Library of Congress)*

der Soviet control until 1988, when Kádár was forced from office. On May 8, 1989, shortly before he died, he was expelled from the Central Committee because of his close association with the Soviet Union.

Other than Yugoslavia's Tito, Kádár was perhaps the most successful leader of the post-Stalinist era. He continued to support Soviet foreign policy, including Moscow's invasion of Czechoslovakia in 1968, but he nevertheless enacted reforms that changed the character of communism in his country. Inevitably, under his leadership, the evolution of a quasi-capitalist system also meant greater latitude for individuals, who could develop their own lives so long as they did not directly challenge the ideology of the government. When the wave of liberation movements in Eastern Europe in the late 1980's began, Hungary was already well along in its own transformation.

tions—especially on economic life—becoming a model for communist countries wishing to experiment with market economies. In 1977, Kádár introduced a measure of free speech—but only for Communist Party members. Civil liberties were still curtailed, and Hungary remained un-

Hungarian Resistance During World War II

During World War II (1939-1945), Hungary was allied with fascist Italy and Germany. The country's authoritarian leaders preserved the power of the upper classes, opposed land reform and the redistribution of wealth advocated by the Communist Party, and pursued a policy of anti-Semitism. János Kádár, like other communists, joined the resistance movement against Germany and Italy. Because of the many communists in the ranks, Hungarian resistance in World War II encompassed not merely opposition to a foreign aggressor but also a fundamental antagonism to the Hungarian government, which had declared

war on the Soviet Union in 1941.

Therefore, many in the resistance considered the Soviet Union's invasion of Hungary in 1944 an act of liberation, because it overthrew a fascist-oriented Hungarian government. Most Hungarians, however, including most in the resistance, were not communists. In postwar elections, the Communist Party received less than one-fifth of the vote. It was included in a coalition government. The Communist Party destroyed this government in 1948, when Kádár and his allies seized control of the country through his post in the Home Affairs office.

A Soviet tank patrolling Budapest, Hungary, in 1956, after the Soviet invasion. After the invasion, János Kádár established a Stalinist government in Hungary. *(National Archives)*

Nevertheless, Kádár's legacy is a troubled one. He seems to have bargained away freedoms for Hungarians in order to solidify his own political position, yet his position kept moving away from the very masters who had put him in power. His policies were called "pragmatic revision," a term which suggests that any leader in Hungary during this period could attempt only those reforms that did not arouse Soviet suspicions. Bolder leaders such as Nagy, lost not only their power but also their lives.

Bibliography

Felkay, Andrew. *Hungary and the USSR, 1956-1988: Kádár's Political Leadership.* New York: Greenwood Press, 1989.

Gati, Charles. *Hungary and the Soviet Bloc.* Durham, N.C.: Duke University Press, 1986.

Shawcross, William. *Crime and Compromise: Janos Kádár and the Politics of Hungary Since Revolution.* New York: Dutton, 1974.

Carl Rollyson

Constantine Karamanlis

Born: March 8, 1907; Küpköy (now Próti), Macedonia
Died: April 23, 1998; Athens, Greece

Two-time prime minister (1955-1963, 1974-1980) and president (1980-1955, 1990-1995) of Greece

Constantine Karamanlis (KON-stahn-teen kah-rah-mahn-LIHS), prominent twentieth-century Greek statesman, was prime minister from 1955 to 1963 and from 1974 to 1980. He was twice president between 1980 and 1995. He prevented the Cyprus crisis from turning into all-out war, but he was not able to resolve underlying problems.

Early Influences and Career

Karamanlis grew up in Greek Macedonia, the eldest of seven children. His father, a teacher, was active in the troubled political environment of early twentieth-century Macedonia, and he ran

Constantine Karamanlis in London in 1959. *(Express Newspapers/Archive Photos)*

afoul of both Turkish authorities and Bulgarians for his nationalist activities. He urged his son to stay out of politics, but to no avail. Constantine received a law degree from the University of Athens in 1932 and practiced law in Athens. He soon became active in the Populist Party and was elected to Parliament in 1935.

During the Ioannis Metaxas dictatorship, from 1936 to 1941, and the Axis occupation of Greece during World War II, Karamanlis avoided politics. After the war he was reelected to Parliament in 1946 and named labor minister. As minister of social welfare during the Greek civil war, he helped 750,000 displaced farmers who had fled the countryside to escape the fighting. In 1952 he became minister of public works under Alexandros Papagos, and he held five cabinet positions between 1946 and 1955. In 1955, on Papagos's death, he was chosen by King Paul to be prime minister.

Prime Minister

Karamanlis formed his own party, the conservative National Radical Union (ERE), which won parliamentary majorities in five elections. His ministry improved Greek relations with Yugoslavia, but the situation on the island of Cyprus was causing difficulties with neighboring Turkey. At this time Cyprus was a British protectorate. Relations between the Greek and Turkish communities on the island were uneasy. Karamanlis helped establish an independent republic there in concert with Turkey and Great Britain in 1960.

In June, 1963, he resigned as prime minister after King Paul rejected his advice to postpone a state visit to London because of probable demonstrations. Karamanlis lived in exile in Paris between 1963 and 1974, refusing to discuss the

Independence for Cyprus

Cyprus, a large island off the coast of Turkey, has a Greek majority population but a long history of Ottoman control. For centuries there had been conflict between the Greeks and Turks who shared the island. In 1959, Greek prime minister Constantine Karamanlis and his Turkish counterpart, Adnan Menderes, agreed to establish an independent republic of Cyprus in which Greeks and Turks would share power. The Republic of Cyprus was formed in August, 1960, with Greek archbishop Makarios (Makarios III) as president and Fazil Kutchuk, representing Turkey, as vice president. This seemingly workable solution was beset by ethnic disagreements, and eventually it was destroyed by Greek and Turkish nationalists unwilling to compromise.

The situation worsened after a military junta seized power in Greece in 1967. It reached crisis proportions in July, 1974, when the Greek national guard launched a coup in Cyprus, hoping to assassinate Makarios and unite the island with Greece. The attempt failed, and five days later Turkish forces landed. Then Greece's junta fell, and Karamanlis was recalled from exile to form a democratic government. Three guarantor powers, Britain, Greece, and Turkey, met in Geneva. However, the Turks continued their military preparations and gained control of northern Cyprus. In December, 1974, Makarios returned to the Cyprus presidency. The Turks did not relinquish control of the northern part, however, and eventually proclaimed it a separate country. In spite of U.N. and European Union attempts to intervene, Cyprus became a land divided.

Greek situation. New elections brought George Papandreou's Center Union Party to power. However, Papandreou also clashed with the monarchy and was forced from office. After some weak coalition governments, a junta led by army colonels seized power in April, 1967, and ruled Greece repressively for seven years.

When the junta attempted a coup in 1974 against Archbishop Makarios (Makarios III) of Cyprus, Turkey invaded and occupied north Cyprus to protect the Turkish minority. As the junta fell apart, with Greece on the brink of war with Turkey, Karamanlis was summoned home to be prime minister. He insisted that the armed forces be subordinated to civilian authority. He also avoided war with Turkey over Cyprus, which would have no doubt ended disastrously for Greece. In parliamentary elections that year, his New Democracy Party won 220 of 300 seats. He legalized the long-banned Communist Party and conducted the referendum in 1974, which abolished Greece's monarchy, re-placing it with a republic and a new constitution.

In May, 1980, Karamanlis resigned as prime minister and was elected president. Among his most important contributions was his responsible fiscal policy and Greece's acceptance of full membership in the European Community (EC) in 1981. When in March, 1985, Socialist prime minister Andreas Papandreou withdrew his party's support for Karamanlis's reelection, Karamanlis resigned from the presidency. He served a second term as president, however, from 1990 to 1995.

Bibliography

Clogg, Richard. *A Concise History of Greece*. Cambridge, England: Cambridge University Press, 1992.

Genevoix, Maurice. *The Greece of Karamanlis*. London: Doric Publications, 1973.

Woodhouse, C. M. *Karamanlis: The Restorer of Greek Democracy*. Oxford, England: Clarendon Press, 1982.

Gloria Fulton

Rashid Karami

Born: December 30, 1921; Tripoli, Lebanon
Died: June 1, 1987; aboard a helicopter traveling from Tripoli to Beirut, Lebanon

Ten-time prime minister of Lebanon between 1955 and 1987

Rashid Karami (ra-SHEED KAH-rah-mee) was raised a wealthy Sunni Muslim during the 1921-1941 French mandate for Syria and Lebanon. He received a French education at the College des Freres at Tripoli, in northern Lebanon, before attending the Faculty of Law at the University of Cairo, Egypt. Karami practiced law for four years after obtaining his license in 1947. His 1951 election as deputy in the Lebanese Parliament gave him the position of his late father, mufti Abdul-Hamid Karami.

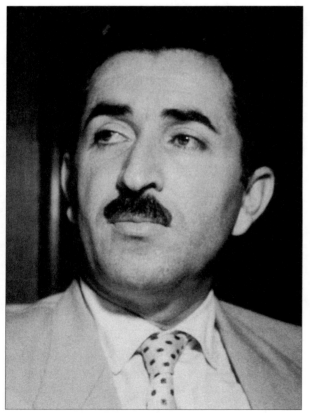

Rashid Karami *(Library of Congress)*

Establishing His Reputation

Karami served ten nonconsecutive terms as prime minister of Lebanon, beginning in 1955. An Arab nationalist, he pursued solidarity for pan-Arab causes. Karami was first noted internationally during the 1956 Suez Crisis, when he supported Egypt's Gamal Abdel Nasser's vision of nationalizing the Suez Canal. He quickly established himself as Lebanon's preeminent Sunni politician. Following the 1958 collapse of the Lebanese political system, Karami and General Fuad Chehab restored civil order using the slogan "No victor, no vanquished."

Following the 1967 Arab-Israeli War and the December, 1968, Israeli raid on Beirut International Airport, Karami committed the Lebanese government to recognizing what he called the "legitimate right of the Palestinian people to struggle for the liberation of their homeland." He also promulgated the concept of *tansiq*, or coordination, to preserve Lebanese independence from the Palestine Liberation Organization (PLO) in the 1969 Cairo Accord.

The 1980's

In May, 1983, Karami joined a diverse group of Lebanese political figures to form the National Salvation Front. Their intent was to resist implementation of the May, 1983, agreement between Israel and Lebanon that followed Israel's 1982 invasion of Lebanon. In 1985, in his last attempt to reach a comprehensive settlement of Lebanon's complex problems, Karami brokered the 1985 Tripartite Agreement between Lebanese forces, the Shia Amal militia, the Druze community, and his own Popular Socialist Party militia.

The Lebanese Civil War

The fierce and bloody Lebanese civil war, which began in April, 1975, caused political instability and devastated the country's infrastructure and economy. President Suleiman Franjieh called on Rashid Karami in May, 1975, to resume his former post as prime minister, making him the central Lebanese political figure seeking to mediate the conflict. Retaining command of the army while appointing political rival and former president Camille Chamoun as interior minister, Karami initially refused to order military intervention. He wanted to avoid forcing the army to take sides, thus splitting it along partisan lines. This split eventually occurred.

Karami set up his headquarters in the old Ottoman Serail government house in downtown Beirut in October, 1975, and began negotiations with other political leaders. A seventeen-point constitutional charter was produced in February, 1976. It included the adoption of a fifty-fifty formula for Christian and Muslim representation in Parliament, replacing the previous six-to-five ratio that favored the Christians. A cease-fire agreement between new Lebanese president Elias Sarkis, Palestine Liberation Organization (PLO) chairman Yasir Arafat, and leaders of Syria, Saudi Arabia, Kuwait, and Egypt was produced in October, 1976. However, the major issues that had initiated the fighting were not resolved. The truce included enforcement of the peace via a thirty-thousand-member Arab Deterrent Force, composed of mostly Syrian soldiers, and a commitment by Arafat to refrain from further interference in Lebanese domestic affairs.

While Rashid Karami was Lebanese prime minister in 1982, Israel invaded Lebanon. These U.S. Marines are part of a multinational peacekeeping force that came to Lebanon later that year. *(U.S. Navy)*

Karami's Final Year

Two years later, a May 21, 1987, vote in the Lebanese Parliament formally abrogated both the 1983 Israel-Lebanon agreement and the 1969 Cairo Accord. Karami, as prime minister, refused to sign the bill. Karami was killed in June, 1987, by an explosive device placed under his seat in a military helicopter. His murder damaged the future prospects of a political resolution to ongoing Lebanese conflicts. Salim al-Huss was appointed acting prime minister, and he immediately signed the bill that Karami had adamantly opposed. Samir Geagea, head of the banned Lebanese Forces Militia, and fifteen other suspects were charged with Karami's assassination.

Bibliography

Deeb, Marius. *The Lebanese Civil War*. New York: Praeger, 1980.

Fisk, Robert. *Pity the Nation: Lebanon at War*. London: Andre Deutsch, 1990.

Hiro, Dilip. *Lebanon—Fire and Embers: A History of the Lebanese Civil War*. London: Weidenfeld and Nicolson, 1993.

Khalaf, Samir. *Lebanon's Predicament*. New York: Columbia University Press, 1987.

Daniel G. Graetzer

Kenneth Kaunda

Born: April 28, 1924; Lubwa, Northern Rhodesia (now Zambia)

Prime minister (1962-1964) and first president of Zambia (1964-1991)

Kenneth David Kaunda (KEH-nehth DAY-vihd kah-EWN-dah) was born at a mission at Lubwa, in Northern Rhodesia (Zambia), which was at the time a British protectorate. His father was a Church of Scotland minister, and his mother was one of the few black women teachers in southern Africa. When only eight, Kenneth was forced to do odd jobs to help support the family because his father died. Nonetheless, he persevered and entered the Munali Secondary School in 1941, where he was an outstanding student and athlete. In 1943 he returned to the Lubwa mission as a teacher and headmaster, positions he held until 1947. During this period he met and married Betty Banda; they would have nine children.

Nationalist Politics

After working for a year in Southern Rhodesia (Zimbabwe), where he witnessed severe racial discrimination, Kaunda returned to Northern Rhodesia and worked at another boarding school. There he encountered more racism. In 1949, he committed himself to a career in politics in order to help gain equal rights for blacks. That year he and some colleagues formed the Northern Rhodesia African National Congress (ANC), a nationalist organization founded to pursue equality for blacks and independence from England.

Kaunda quickly moved up the ladder, and by 1953 he was the secretary-general of the Northern Rhodesian ANC, second in command to Harry Nkumbula. He held the post for five years. During that period he was once imprisoned for possession of banned literature. Also while secretary-general, Kaunda visited India and became a firm advocate of Mahatma Gandhi's philosophy of nonviolence. In 1958 Kaunda split with Nkumbula and formed the Zambia African National Congress in order to take a stronger stand for black political equality. Although Kaunda advocated nonviolence, his organization was judged a threat by the white power structure. In 1959 Kaunda organized a boycott of elections. He was arrested and sent to a prison in Southern Rhodesia. He was freed in January of 1960 and returned to the struggle in Northern Rhodesia.

Independent Zambia

The early 1960's witnessed decolonization across Africa, and the British were planning to

Kenneth Kaunda *(Library of Congress)*

Zambian president Kenneth Kaunda (left) meeting U.N. secretary-general U Thant in New York. *(Agence France/Archive Photos)*

the British proposed a new constitution for Northern Rhodesia that would allow blacks to achieve a slim majority in parliament. In elections that October, Kaunda won a seat in Parliament. He was named minister of social welfare in the new coalition government.

In 1963 the British enacted further reforms of the constitution that allowed more extensive control of Parliament by blacks. In elections held in January, 1964, the United National Independence Party was triumphant. Kaunda, at age thirty-nine, became the youngest prime minister in the British Commonwealth. Shortly thereafter, the British announced

grant independence to Northern Rhodesia. Kaunda, as the foremost black nationalist in the country, was in the middle of the negotiations. He gained international stature, visiting U.S. president John F. Kennedy at the White House. In 1962, that Northern Rhodesia would be officially independent as of October, 1964. At the joyous celebration, Zambia became Africa's thirty-sixth independent nation. Sworn in for a five-year term as Zambia's first president, Kaunda announced

The Central African Federation

In 1953 the British government established the Central African Federation, also known as the Federation of Rhodesia and Nyasaland. It included the colony of Southern Rhodesia (later Zimbabwe) and the protectorates of Nyasaland (later Malawi) and Northern Rhodesia (later Zambia). Much of the enthusiasm for the project came from white politicians in Southern Rhodesia such as Roy Welensky, and whites dominated the government of the federation. The primary reason that Southern Rhodesians wanted to join with Northern Rhodesia was to reap some of the profits from the rich deposits of copper there. The one

concrete accomplishment of the federation years, the Kariba dam and hydroelectric project, was built primarily to power those mining operations. The racial philosophy of the federation government was supposed to be one of partnership, but it was immediately apparent to black nationalists that racial discrimination and white domination were not going away. Independence movements in Nyasaland led by Hastings Banda and in Northern Rhodesia led by Kenneth Kaunda convinced the British in the early 1960's that the federation must be dissolved. The end came in December, 1963.

The Politics of Copper

Throughout the recent history of Zambia, politics and copper have been intertwined. In 1953 Northern Rhodesia was made part of the Central African Federation because whites in Southern Rhodesia wanted a share of the north's copper wealth. Shortly after Zambia gained independence in 1964, Southern Rhodesia blocked Zambian access to oil. Desire to keep the copper mines operating convinced the British government to lead an airlift of fuel into Zambia. A few years later, in 1969, Kenneth Kaunda's government seized 51 percent of the country's copper mines. Zambia was the world's third largest supplier of copper, and the economy prospered. In 1974, however, copper prices plummeted, and Zambia was soon wracked by debt and unemployment. The ongoing crisis caused by copper's collapse finally ended Kaunda's long reign in 1991.

that his nation would not align itself with any of the world's powerful nations.

Despite his hope of staying out of international conflict, Kaunda's new nation of Zambia very quickly became caught up in turmoil that enveloped southern Africa. In 1965 Ian Smith and his white government of Southern Rhodesia declared independence from Britain. Britain responded by establishing economic sanctions against the illegal regime. Kaunda supported the sanctions. Smith soon closed off the rail links between Zambia and the sea (the rail line passed through Southern Rhodesia), thereby blocking the imports of coal and oil necessary to fuel the excavation of copper, Zambia's primary export. The British and American governments came to the aid of Zambia, airlifting in the necessary fuel until new roads and rails could be completed.

Although Zambia's fuel crisis passed, the conflict in neighboring Southern Rhodesia escalated in the early 1970's into a major war. A liberation army of black southern Rhodesians led by Joshua Nkomo established bases in Zambia. As a result, the fighting often spilled across the border and into the Zambian capital, Lusaka. During the years of fighting, Kaunda expended considerable effort to broker a peace. He met regularly with leaders and diplomats from around the world, and he hosted U.S. secretary of state Henry Kissinger during his diplomatic intervention in

1976. Ultimately, Kaunda and other black presidents played a key role in forging the final settlement that brought peace and an independent Zimbabwe (the new name of Southern Rhodesia) in 1980.

Challenges to Kaunda

The economy of Zambia collapsed in the 1970's when the price of copper plummeted, and from then on Kaunda struggled to retain control of the government. Unable to quell dissent, he established a one-party system. As his critics gained strength in the 1980's, Kaunda had many arrested for supposed assassination plots or alleged drug-trading activity. His most formidable opposition came from the labor movement. After a coup attempt in 1990, Kaunda agreed to multiparty elections. With labor union support, Frederick Chiluba defeated Kaunda in 1991. During the next few years, two of Kaunda's sons were accused of attempting to overthrow Chiluba and jailed. On Christmas Day, 1997, Kaunda himself was jailed on similar charges; he was not released until July, 1998.

Kaunda's legacy is a mixed one. He was one of the great leaders of the African nationalist movement in the 1950's and 1960's. Intelligent and charismatic, he wrote several books and was a talented musician. His mediation skills helped bring peace to Zimbabwe. Faced with the daunting economic challenges of the 1970's, however, he turned away from open democracy and tried to stifle opposition. Nonetheless, his contribution to southern African freedom and independence is a great one.

Bibliography

Chan, Stephen. *Kaunda and Southern Africa: Image and Reality in Foreign Policy*. New York: British Academic Press, 1992.

Chisala, Beatwell S. *The Downfall of President Kaunda*. Lusaka, Zambia: B. S. Chisala, 1994.

Hall, Richard. *Kaunda: Founder of Zambia*. London: Longman's, 1964.

Kaunda, Kenneth. *Zambia Shall Be Free*. London: Heinemann, 1962.

Macpherson, Fergus. *Kenneth Kaunda of Zambia*. London: Oxford University Press, 1974.

Andy DeRoche

Karl Kautsky

Born: October 16, 1854; Prague, Austro-Hungarian Empire
Died: October 17, 1938; Amsterdam, the Netherlands

Austrian-born Marxist theoretician and author

Karl Kautsky (KAHRL KOWT-skee) joined the Austrian Social Democratic Party while he was a student in Vienna, Austria. In 1880 he moved to Zurich, Switzerland, to work on the German socialist periodical *Der Sozialdemokrat* under the direction of Eduard Bernstein. The following year he visited London, where he met Karl Marx and Friedrich Engels before returning to Vienna. In 1882 Kautsky moved to Stuttgart, where he joined the left-wing publishing house Dietz Verlag. He created a new socialist journal, *Die Neue Zeit* (the new age), but was forced by the antisocialist laws to return to Zurich in 1883. From 1895 until 1890, he edited his journal from London under the supervision of Engels.

Leader of European Socialism

With the end of the antisocialist laws in 1891, Kautsky returned to Germany, where he quickly became a leading theoretician of the German Social Democratic Party (SPD). It was his intellectual authority that was largely responsible for the radical, Marxist tone of the party's Erfurt program of that year. In the two decades that followed, Kautsky became the most important popularizer of Marxism in Europe. He wrote countless essays and many influential books, such as *The Agrarian Question* (1899), *The Social Revolution* (1902), and *The Road to Power* (1909).

Taking an active role in internal SPD affairs, he attacked his former mentor Bernstein as having forsaken revolution in favor of reforms. On the other hand, he later criticized his former collaborator, Rosa Luxemburg, for being too radical. As Europe moved toward World War I, Kautsky was widely called, not without a touch of irony, "the pope of European socialism."

War and Revolution

When World War I broke out in August, 1914, Kautsky, despite misgivings, agreed to support the imperial German government. However, his doubts about the defensive nature of the war grew until he was convinced that socialists should no longer unconditionally support their government. To press for peace, Kautsky helped establish a new Independent Social Democratic Party (USPD), which demanded an end to the war. The USPD was a major player in the German revolution of November, 1918, which overthrew Kaiser

Karl Kautsky *(Library of Congress)*

The Mensheviks

The Russian socialist movement split into rival factions a decade before World War I. The more radical group was called the Bolsheviks, and the more gradualist faction the Mensheviks or Menshevists. This rivalry became bitter after the Russian Revolution of 1917, with Mensheviks being arrested as counter-revolutionaries by the new Bolshevik government. Karl Kautsky sided with the more gradualist and, to his mind, more democratic Mensheviks. The Mensheviks, like Kautsky, did not believe that Russia had the material basis for a socialist society and thought it would have to go through a period of capitalist development first. From that time on, Soviet writers denounced Kautsky as a Menshevist, often ignoring his other writings completely.

William II's imperial German government and established the democratic Weimar Republic.

While many socialists, such as Rosa Luxemburg, welcomed the triumph of Vladimir Lenin, Leon Trotsky, and the radical Russian Bolsheviks

Marxist revolutionary Rosa Luxemburg, whom Karl Kautsky eventually criticized as being too radical. *(Archive Photos)*

in the fall of 1917, Kautsky was critical at an early point. He argued that what the Bolsheviks were building was not socialism but a new form of class society based on political terror. Kautsky wrote many anti-Bolshevik books that sharply contrasted his vision of socialism with Russian practices. In 1920, when most of the USPD voted to unite with the German Communists, Kautsky refused and later rejoined the SPD.

In 1924 Kautsky returned to Vienna to concentrate on his writings and renew ties with the Austrian Social Democrats. For the next ten years he wrote extensively, although his prestige never returned to its prewar glory. With the rise of Nazism, he fled first to Prague in 1934 and then, on the eve of Adolf Hitler's invasion of Czechoslovakia, emigrated to Holland, where he died soon after in 1938. In terms of both sheer volume and intellectual quality, Karl Kautsky was one of the most important Marxist writers of his time. His works influenced a generation of European socialists—even those who, like Lenin, later became his enemies. With the split in the world socialist movement into pro-Russian and anti-Russian factions, his contributions as a thinker and organizer were often forgotten, as many lauded or denounced Kautsky simply for his view of the Bolsheviks.

Bibliography

Donald, Moira. *Marxism and Revolution: Karl Kautsky and the Russian Marxists, 1900-1924.* New Haven, Conn.: Yale University Press, 1993.

Geary, Dick. *Karl Kautsky.* Manchester, England: Manchester University Press, 1987.

Kautsky, Karl. *Karl Kautsky: Selected Political Writings.* Edited by Patrick Goode. New York: St. Martin's Press, 1983.

Salvadori, Massimo. *Karl Kautsky and the Socialist Revolution, 1880-1938.* London: New Left Books, 1979.

William A. Pelz

Paul Keating

Born: January 18, 1944; Sydney, New South Wales, Australia

Prime minister of Australia (1993-1996)

Paul John Keating (PAWL JON KEE-tihng) was born into a working-class Irish Catholic family in Bankstown, a suburb of Sydney. He attended school in Bankstown, but left at fifteen. He completed his degree by taking evening classes at Belmore Technical College and Sydney Technical College. Keating held various clerical jobs and even briefly managed a rock group called the Ramrods. In 1975, he married Anna Johanna Maria von Iersel, known as Annita, a European flight attendant whom he met on an overseas trip.

Paul Keating *(Popperfoto/Archive Photos)*

A Career in Politics

Keating became involved with the Australian Labor Party (ALP) while still a teenager. In 1968 he became an official with the Federated Municipal and Shire Council Employees' Union. From this step, he entered the House of Representatives in 1969 at the age of twenty-five as ALP member for the seat of Blaxland, which he held until his retirement from Parliament in 1996.

For a brief period in 1975, toward the end of Gough Whitlam's period as prime minister, Keating was minister for northern development. He was president of the New South Wales Labor Party from 1979 to 1983 and federal treasurer from March, 1983, to June, 1991, in the government led by prime minister Robert Hawke. When the Hawke government took office, the Australian economy was in recession, caused in part by an unaffordable explosion in wages at the start of the 1980's. Hawke and Keating responded with important structural changes to the Australian economy, including the decision to float the Australian dollar in December, 1983. At the same time, they maintained an alliance with the trade union movement aimed at restraining wage demands and sustaining economic growth. By 1986 the recession had passed, but Keating pressed on with further reforms to deal with weaknesses in the economy.

From Treasurer to Prime Minister

During the 1980's the reforms made by Hawke and Keating were largely successful. Keating became unpopular with the public, however, which perceived him as arrogant and ruthless. The government won elections in 1984 and 1987, but by the 1990 election the economy was troubled by high interest rates, which made home loans expensive. The government won another election in March, 1990, but the nation entered a recession later in the year. In 1991 Keating twice challenged Hawke for leadership of the ALP, losing in June but winning in December. Many in the party believed that Hawke had become a weak leader and that Keating's flair, aggressive instincts, and mastery of economic issues gave the ALP its best chance of obtaining an electoral victory in harsh circumstances.

Australian prime minister Paul Keating, campaigning for a second term in 1996, is surrounded by schoolgirls in Sydney. *(AP/Wide World Photos)*

The 1993 and 1996 Elections

Despite the nation's economic problems, Keating won a victory in the federal election of March, 1993, defeating Liberal Party leader John Hewson. The election was dominated by Hewson's radical "Fightback!" package of radical economic policies and Keating's response to it, "One Nation." Keating ran an aggressive campaign based on fears about the Liberals' proposed goods and services tax.

As prime minister, Keating supported land rights for Australian Aborigines, stronger ties with Asia, and a move for Australia to become a republic. His supporters were excited by his leadership on these issues, but he remained unpopular with the wider public. At the next election, in 1996, the Liberal Party under John Howard conducted a cautious campaign and won an easy

One Nation

In November, 1991, the Liberal opposition leader, John Hewson, presented his comprehensive "Fightback!" policy. It was dominated by radical economic reforms, including a 15 percent goods and services tax. When Paul Keating deposed Labor Party leader Robert Hawke and became prime minister, he replied to it with an equally comprehensive policy document, "One Nation," which was released in February, 1992. The "One Nation" policy was intended to combat the recession that Australia had entered in 1990's.

It contained a four-year plan of reform that included two installments of personal tax cuts and measures aimed at economic growth. However, following Keating's victory over Hewson in the 1993 election, the second installment of tax cuts was abandoned. In 1997 the name One Nation was adopted by a new political party with racist overtones founded by Pauline Hanson. Hanson was a former Liberal who had been elected in 1996 as the Independent member for the seat of Oxley.

Paul Keating (left) speaking at a joint news conference with Singapore's prime minister, Goh Chok Tong, in 1995. As Australian prime minister, Keating advocated stronger ties with Asian countries. *(AP/Wide World Photos)*

victory. Shortly afterward, Keating quit politics, taking up business and academic interests.

Bibliography

Carew, Edna. *Paul Keating: Prime Minister*. Sydney, Australia: Allen & Unwin, 1992.

Edwards, John. *Keating: The Inside Story*. Melbourne, Australia: Penguin, 1996.

Kelly, Paul. *The End of Certainty: Power, Politics, and Business in Australia*. Rev. ed. Sydney, Australia: Allen & Unwin, 1994.

Russell Blackford

Frank B. Kellogg

Born: December 22, 1856; Potsdam, New York
Died: December 21, 1937; St. Paul, Minnesota

U.S. secretary of state (1925-1929), winner of 1929 Nobel Peace Prize

Frank Billings Kellogg (FRANK BIH-lihngz KEH-log), the son of a farmer who moved his family to Minnesota in 1865, had little formal education. Nonetheless, he studied law and passed the Minnesota bar exam in 1877. For the next ten years, Kellogg struggled to make a living as a lawyer and held a variety of minor political offices. In 1886 he married Clara M. Cook. They had no children.

Success in the Law

In 1887 an important lawyer hired Kellogg, allowing him the opportunity to establish important legal and political contacts. In the first decade of the twentieth century, Kellogg was involved in three major court cases that brought him to national prominence. All three cases were aimed at breaking corporate monopolies. His victories in these cases earned him the position of president of the American Bar Association in 1912. Kellogg was also active in the Republican Party, serving on the Republican National Committee from 1904 to 1912. In 1916 the voters of Minnesota elected Kellogg to the U.S. Senate. During Senate debate over whether to ratify the Treaty of Versailles (the treaty drawn up in 1919 after World War I), Kellogg initially took the position of a "mild reservationist"—those who called for passage with some revisions. He ultimately opposed the treaty, however. Following a failed reelection bid in 1922, Kellogg served briefly as President Calvin Coolidge's ambassador to Great Britain. In late 1924, Coolidge asked Kellogg to serve as his secretary of state. Kellogg accepted and took office in March, 1925.

Secretary of State

Kellogg was not a dynamic secretary of state. For most of the 1920's the United States experi-

enced an economic boom, and domestic affairs took precedence over international concerns. Moreover, many Americans harbored bitter feelings about American participation in World War I and opposed any involvement in foreign political or military affairs. Kellogg accepted the prevailing notions of his time. American reluctance to take a leadership role was evidenced by the 1928 multinational treaty that bears the secretary's name. Signed by sixty-four nations, the Kellogg-Briand Pact denounced war. Lacking any mechanisms for enforcement, the pact was largely meaningless. Nevertheless, Kellogg considered

Frank B. Kellogg *(The Nobel Foundation)*

813

the pact, which kept the United States from any political commitments, to be one of the great successes of his administration.

Kellogg did face two important foreign policy issues during his tenure as secretary. When growing tensions with Mexico threatened war, Kellogg declared that Bolsheviks, or communists, were behind the troubles. Members of Congress treated the claim with scorn. Seeking to calm the turmoil, Kellogg moderated his comments and permitted the ambassador to Mexico to reach an agreement with the Mexican government. Kellogg showed better judgment in his dealings with China, which was struggling to end international restrictions on its sovereignty. He agreed to renegotiate tariff rates, but he was unable to resolve the debate over extraterritoriality, which exempted foreigners residing in China from prosecution under Chinese law. Kellogg maintained a moderate stance even when Japan and Great Brit-

U.S. president Calvin Coolidge signing the Kellogg-Briand Pact in 1928. Seated at the table are Coolidge (left) and Secretary of State Frank B. Kellogg. *(Library of Congress)*

ain called for stricter sanctions against China for an incident involving the death of foreigners.

Kellogg did not retire from public life when he left the State Department in March, 1929. For his efforts at promoting peace, specifically the Kellogg-Briand Pact, he was awarded the Nobel Peace Prize in 1930. From 1930 to 1935 he served

Antitrust Legislation

At the beginning of the twentieth century, many Americans feared the growth of giant corporations which held monopolies on certain industries. Known as trusts, these corporations could set high prices because they had no competition. Prior to 1903, the Sherman Anti-Trust Act of 1887 had been used successfully only twice in efforts to "bust," or break up, trusts. After President Theodore Roosevelt took office in 1901, the federal government became more aggressive in its prose-

cution of trusts. Frank B. Kellogg earned renown as a trust-buster when he prosecuted three antitrust cases. The most celebrated case involved Standard Oil, a company that controlled most of the United States' petroleum marketing and refining. The company was worth an estimated $600 million in 1910. In 1909 and again on appeal in 1911, Kellogg successfully argued before the U.S. Supreme Court that Standard Oil was in violation of antitrust laws.

on the Permanent Court of International Justice (commonly known as the World Court) even though the United States was not a member.

Bibliography

Ellis, L. Ethan. *Frank B. Kellogg and American Foreign Relations, 1925-1929*. New Brunswick, N.J.: Rutgers University Press, 1961.

_____. *Republican Foreign Policy, 1921-1933*. New Brunswick, N.J.: Rutgers University Press, 1968.

Ferrell, Robert H. *Frank B. Kellogg/Henry L. Stimson*. Vol. 11 of *The American Secretaries of State and Their Diplomacy*, edited by Robert H. Ferrell. New York: Cooper Square, 1963.

Thomas Clarkin

U.S. secretary of state Frank B. Kellogg (left) in front of the U.S. State Department. *(Library of Congress)*

George F. Kennan

Born: February 16, 1904; Milwaukee, Wisconsin

U.S. diplomat, historian, and expert on Russia

The father of George Frost Kennan (JOHRJ FROST KEH-nuhn), Kossuth Kennan, was the son of a poor Wisconsin frontier family who became both a lawyer and an engineer. Kennan's mother, the former Florence James, died during George's infancy. Upon graduation from Princeton University in 1925, George Kennan applied to the U.S. Foreign Service. Because he anticipated a growing importance in relationships between the Soviet Union and the United States, he chose specialized training in the Russian language and Russian affairs.

George F. Kennan *(National Archives)*

Early Assignments

Kennan served in Geneva, Hamburg, Berlin, and the Baltic states from 1927 to 1933. During this time he married a young Norwegian woman, Annelise Soerensen (subsequently the mother of their two daughters). He was then appointed aide and interpreter to William C. Bullitt, the American ambassador to the Soviet Union. During this first assignment in Moscow, he developed a distrust of the Soviet leaders and disdain for idealistic Americans who, in the early Depression years, saw communism as a possible source of a more equitable world order. He did not, however, particularly fear any Soviet military threat to the West, and he favored limited agreements between the United States and the Soviet Union.

After holding several consular and secretarial posts in Moscow, Kennan spent a year in Washington, D.C., at the Soviet desk of the State Department. He was then sent to Prague and Berlin. Kennan was in Berlin upon the United States' entrance into World War II. He was confined for several months at Bad Nauheim, Germany, but eventually returned to the United States. After wartime assignments in Lisbon and London, he served from 1944 to 1946 as chargé d'affaires in Moscow. There he observed the conduct of the Soviet regime at war's end and the beginning of what came to be called the Cold War.

Years of Influence

Back in Washington as a policy planner in 1947, Kennan contributed an anonymous and controversial article to the journal *Foreign Affairs* in defense of the policy of "containment" of the Soviet Union. President Harry S Truman appointed him ambassador to the Soviet Union in 1952, but his imprudent comparison of the Soviet

Union to Nazi Germany (to a reporter in Berlin) destroyed his credibility in Moscow and led to his recall. When Dwight D. Eisenhower became president, Kennan retired from the Foreign Service. While he was a faculty member at the Princeton University Institute for Advanced Study, his Reith Lectures in 1957 urged the United States to take the initiative to end both the partitioning of postwar Europe and the proliferation of nuclear weapons. The lectures were broadcast by the British Broadcasting Corporation (BBC). The controversy arising from these proposals established Kennan as a major critic of Cold War policies.

George F. Kennan (right) with Soviet officials in Moscow in 1952, as the new U.S. ambassador to the Soviet Union. *(AP/Wide World Photos)*

He returned to diplomatic life from 1961 to 1963 as President John F. Kennedy's ambassador to Yugoslavia, but congressional opposition to his attempts to foster President Josip Broz Tito's independence from Moscow hampered his effectiveness. Thereafter Kennan wrote and lectured extensively, and in 1975 he founded the Kennan Institute for Advanced Russian Studies in Washington, D.C.

Kennan's Accomplishments

His lifelong study of Russian and Soviet affairs, together with his service in the Soviet Union and other sensitive areas, made George F. Kennan a leading Russian expert. Long a provocative

---

Russia Leaves the War

Of the many books written by George F. Kennan, *Russia Leaves the War* (1956), the first volume of his *Soviet-American Relations, 1917-1920*, was the first of two to win Pulitzer Prizes. It is a highly specialized history covering events in Russia from the Bolsheviks' seizure of power in November, 1917, to March, 1918, when the revolutionary Russian government concluded a separate piece treaty with Germany and took the country out of World War I. Furthermore, the book focuses only on those developments that involved the United States. The narrow focus of the book enabled Kennan to develop in absorbing detail the issues and personalities involved and to explain the complexities of the situation that faced President Woodrow Wilson's administration. Kennan brought to the book insights gained from his own Foreign Service career, much of it spent in the later Soviet Union and in analyzing U.S.-Soviet relations.

George F. Kennan (left) in New York, talking with architect Romaldo Giurgola. *(Archive Photos)*

thinker, he exerted the influence of an intellectual gadfly, unafraid to challenge the prevailing wisdom in international politics. His forcefully expressed convictions that the West could place limited trust in the Soviet Union and that the United States should take the lead in ending the nuclear arms race did much to focus discussion and stimulate foreign-policy planning in the dangerous decades of the Cold War.

Bibliography

Kennan, George F. *Memoirs: 1925-1950*. Boston: Little, Brown, 1967.

_____. *Memoirs: 1950-1963*. New York: Pantheon, 1983.

Mayers, David. *George Kennan and the Dilemmas of U.S. Foreign Policy*. New York: Oxford University Press, 1988.

Miscamble, Wilson D. *George F. Kennan and the Making of American Foreign Policy, 1947-1950*. Princeton, N.J.: Princeton University Press, 1992.

Polley, Michael. *A Biography of George F. Kennan: The Education of a Realist*. Lewiston, N.Y.: E. Mellen Press, 1990.

Robert P. Ellis

John F. Kennedy

Born: May 29, 1917; Brookline, Massachusetts
Died: November 22, 1963; Dallas, Texas

President of the United States (1961-1963)

John Fitzgerald Kennedy (JON fihtz-JEH-ruhld KEH-neh-dee), one of nine children born to Joseph and Rose (Fitzgerald) Kennedy, was the first Roman Catholic elected president of the United States. His father, a millionaire by age thirty-five, served as U.S. ambassador to England before World War II. In 1940 Kennedy graduated from Harvard University. His senior thesis, *Why England Slept*, was published as a book and helped start him on a brief career as a journalist. He married Jacqueline Bouvier in 1953. Only two of the couple's children, Caroline and John, survived infancy.

Pursuit of Power

Scarlet fever, diphtheria, and back problems were among Kennedy's many childhood health ailments. He also suffered from Addison's disease as an adult. Nevertheless, Kennedy served in the Navy as commanding officer of a torpedo patrol boat in the Pacific during World War II. In 1943 a Japanese destroyer sliced his PT-109 in half. His courageous leadership of his men until their rescue distinguished him as a war hero. With support from his father, Kennedy's postwar ambitions turned to politics.

In 1946 John F. Kennedy was elected to the U.S. House of Representatives. By 1952 he had defeated Henry Cabot Lodge for a seat in the U.S. Senate. As a congressional Democrat, Kennedy was a moderate on most issues. He emphasized pragmatism over idealism. Considered bright and attractive, he presented a rational style designed to build his career toward its ultimate objective, the presidency.

Running for President

A bid for the vice presidential nomination at the 1956 Democratic Convention, while unsuccessful, brought Kennedy to the favorable attention of party leaders. He later gained additional favorable exposure in the Senate's investigation into allegations of racketeering and corruption in labor unions. By 1960 Kennedy was a frontrunner for the Democratic presidential nomination. He won it easily, but not before competing in several state primaries, where he demonstrated that his youth and his Catholicism would not harm his chances for victory.

In 1960, at age forty-three, John F. Kennedy was elected president by a narrow popular-vote margin and an electoral college majority of 303-219.

John F. Kennedy *(Library of Congress)*

U.S. president John F. Kennedy conferring with top Air Force officers during the tense days of the Cuban Missile Crisis of October, 1963. *(National Archives)*

himself more effectively than a tired and rough-looking Nixon, won this first political battle of the television age. The youngest elected American president, Kennedy gained popularity while he was in office. Together with his young family, as the first true television-era president, he projected a sense of grace and charm that the nation embraced.

Years of Crisis

Kennedy's presidency coincided with a dangerous period of the Cold War, and foreign-policy concerns dominated his presidency. In Berlin, Germany, tensions between the United States and Soviet Union over the divided city resulted in a showdown which led to the Berlin crisis of 1961 and the building of the Berlin Wall by East Germany.

He defeated Republican vice president Richard M. Nixon. The 1960 election featured the first televised debates between presidential candidates. Kennedy, who looked better and projected

The Berlin Crisis

From 1945 to 1948, in the aftermath of World War II, Germany was governed by joint Allied (American, English, French, and Russian) commissions. In 1948 the Soviet Union withdrew from the joint commissions. A Soviet effort to blockade Berlin was defeated by a massive Allied airlift of supplies. The nation of Germany and the city of Berlin was divided into communist (East German) and democratic (West German) sections.

In 1961, with an increasing number of East German refugees fleeing to West Germany through Berlin, the Soviets acted again. At a June summit in Vienna between President John F. Kennedy and Nikita Khrushchev, the Soviet leader threatened to sign a treaty with East Germany calling for the removal of Western support for West Berlin.

Khrushchev threatened military force to enforce the treaty. Kennedy responded by warning of severe reprisals, possibly war.

As the United States responded to the Soviet threat with new military spending and troop call-ups, the Soviets decided on a less dangerous course of action. On August 13, 1961, construction began on the Berlin Wall, dividing East and West Berlin. Designed to cut off the flow of East German refugees to West Germany, the wall did not represent an attack upon the West. Kennedy concluded that access to West Berlin and the security of West Germany could be preserved without a war. The Berlin Wall, the most powerful symbol of its era, remained until its peaceful removal and the reunification of Germany at the end of the Cold War.

The Kennedy Assassination

A 12:30 P.M. on November 22, 1963, President John F. Kennedy was assassinated as his open limousine drove slowly through a motorcade in downtown Dallas, Texas. Kennedy, mortally wounded in the head and neck, died almost instantly. The U.S. government's official investigation conducted by a special commission headed by Chief Justice Earl Warren, concluded that the shooting was the work of a lone sniper named Lee Harvey Oswald. Oswald, a former U.S. Marine, was captured a few hours after Kennedy died. Oswald himself was shot and killed two days later by Jack Ruby, a Dallas nightclub owner with known ties to organized crime. Controversies abound with respect to the evidence in Kennedy's assassination. Critics of the Warren Commission report have argued that Oswald did not act alone, if he was involved at all, and numerous conspiracy theories (generally involving the government or organized crime) have been promulgated.

Berlin became a symbolic justification for expanding Cold War policies. Massive increases in defense spending, increases in foreign aid, and a major commitment to the space program were among the measures that Kennedy promoted.

In Southeast Asia, governments backed by the United States were losing ground to communist movements. Kennedy decided to make a stand in South Vietnam. He increased the number of U.S. military advisers (to more than seventeen thousand by 1963) and increased the level of U.S. commitment to South Vietnam's government. He was uncomfortable with the notion of deploying massive U.S. forces in Vietnam, and evidence is mixed on whether Kennedy would have allowed U.S. troops to assume a major combat role, as President Lyndon Johnson did later.

In Cuba, Kennedy backed a Central Intelligence Agency (CIA) plan to use Cuban refugees in an invasion to overthrow communist dictator Fidel Castro. The dismal failure of this April, 1961, invasion at Cuba's Bay of Pigs represented Kennedy's worst setback. In 1962 Cuba was at the

John F. Kennedy on a tower beside the Berlin Wall. The wall surrounding West Berlin was built by East Germany to keep East Germans from fleeing to the West. *(John F. Kennedy Library)*

center of another crisis, one that very nearly led to nuclear war. The Soviet Union, in part to deter another invasion of Cuba, attempted to place short-range offensive nuclear missiles in Cuba. Kennedy, made aware of missile sites by spy-plane photographs, insisted that the sites be removed. A blockade of Cuba implemented by U.S. naval forces halted Soviet shipments into Cuba. After tense days, diplomatic measures prevailed: The Soviets agreed to dismantle the missile sites. Following the Cuban Missile Crisis, Kennedy and Soviet leader Nikita Khrushchev sought to negotiate a reduction in tensions. The result was the 1963 Nuclear Test-Ban Treaty, a limited treaty that was the first arms agreement between the two superpowers.

Civil Rights

The issue of civil rights represented the greatest domestic crisis of the early 1960's. Fearful that support for strong civil rights legislation would cost needed political support from a conservative majority in Congress, Kennedy initially advised caution in the pursuit of equal rights. Liberal critics found this unacceptable. By 1963 events had moved the nation and Kennedy to embrace a more dynamic course. He proposed a civil rights bill in 1963 (passed after his death, in 1964) to combat segregation in public accommodations. He also placed his presidency more squarely behind the cause of civil rights as a moral matter. Kennedy's tax, welfare, education, and domestic proposals became bogged down in Congress as a result.

The assassination of John F. Kennedy on November 22, 1963, leaves the assessment of his presidency very much open to debate. His appeal embodied the experiences of his generation. Supporters argue that, having led the nation through crises, he exhibited a capacity to grow and a potential for greatness. Critics claim that he was an ambition-driven political pragmatist who traveled the safe middle ground. That this debate continues is, perhaps, evidence of how compelling a figure he was in his time.

Bibliography

Beschloss, Michael R. *The Crisis Years: Kennedy and Khrushchev 1960-63*. New York: HarperCollins, 1991.

Kern, Montague, et al. *The Kennedy Crises*. Chapel Hill: University of North Carolina Press, 1983.

Martin, Ralph. *A Hero for Our Time*. New York: Ballantine, 1983.

Reeves, Richard. *President Kennedy: A Profile in Power*. New York: Simon and Schuster, 1993.

Schlesinger, Arthur M., Jr. *A Thousand Days: John F. Kennedy in the White House*. Boston: Houghton Mifflin, 1965.

Robert O. Schneider

Robert F. Kennedy

Born: November 20, 1925; Brookline, Massachusetts
Died: June 6, 1968; Los Angeles, California

U.S. attorney general (1961-1963) and senator (1965-1968)

Robert Francis Kennedy (RO-burt FRAN-sihs KEH-neh-dee) was the third of four sons and the seventh of nine children of Joseph Patrick Kennedy and Rose Fitzgerald, both members of second-generation Irish Catholic families that wielded power in politics and finance. Kennedy attended public schools in Bronxville, New York, transferred to the Gibbs School in London while his father was ambassador to Great Britain, and completed his college preparatory work at Milton Academy. His service in the Naval Reserve during World War II temporarily interrupted his Harvard University undergraduate education, which he completed in 1948. He married Edith Skakel in 1950 and graduated from the University of Virginia Law School in 1951.

Political Career

In 1952 Kennedy left a position in the criminal division of the Department of Justice to serve as campaign manager for his brother John's campaign for the U.S. Senate from Massachusetts. Following his brother's election, he worked briefly for Senator Joseph McCarthy's Senate Subcommittee on Investigations but resigned in 1953. After 1954 he served as counsel for the Senate Democratic minority and wrote a report which criticized McCarthy's investigation of the army.

Kennedy continued his work as legal counsel and investigator throughout the 1950's until he was again drafted by his brother—this time to run his 1960 presidential campaign. After John F. Kennedy's narrow victory over Richard Nixon, Robert Kennedy reportedly had to be convinced by his brother and father to accept the position of attorney general in the new cabinet. Kennedy's three years as attorney general included a number of notable accomplishments. For example, he refocused Federal Bureau of investigation (FBI) attention away from the pursuit of communists to investigating organized crime, and he supporting the forces of racial justice and change—from civil rights Freedom Riders to access to higher education to voting rights.

However, Kennedy's most lasting legacy as an attorney general probably lies in the advice and counsel he provided for his brother. Robert Kennedy's wisdom and moderation are legendary in

Robert F. Kennedy *(Library of Congress)*

823

U.S. attorney general Robert F. Kennedy (left) conferring at the White House with civil rights leaders Martin Luther King, Jr., Roy Wilkins, and A. Philip Randolph in 1963. *(National Archives)*

tation when he convinced his brother to respond to Soviet premier Nikita Khrushchev's first, rather than his second, message.

John F. Kennedy's assassination in 1963 ultimately led to Robert Kennedy's resignation as attorney general early in 1964 in order to run for U.S. Senate from New York. Although Kennedy had spent part of his childhood in Bronxville and Riverdale, he was criticized by his opponents as a Massachusetts carpetbagger. However, he defeated incumbent Kenneth Keating and served with distinction in the U.S. Senate, his first and only elected political position, from 1964 until his death in 1968.

his well-documented opinions during the Cuban Missile Crisis. While other cabinet members counselled President Kennedy to invade or bomb the island, Robert Kennedy proposed a naval blockade. He later helped avoid nuclear confron-

Social Legacy

Kennedy is remembered not only as an antiwar and anti-Johnson administration Democrat but also as one of the first national politicians to

The Kennedys and the Mob

Robert F. Kennedy's work in Washington, D.C., during the 1950's as a legal counsel and investigator included work in 1954 on the John McClellan Committee of the U.S. Senate, charged with investigating organized crime. His work in this area culminated in 1957 when he became chief counsel of the Senate Select Committee on Improper Activities in the Labor or Management Field (also called the Rackets Committee). The committee was concerned about the influence and control that organized crime seemed to be exerting in the

election procedures and in management operations of various trade unions. Kennedy's cross-examination of Teamsters' Union president Jimmy Hoffa made national figures of both men. It also started a feud which ended only with Kennedy's death in 1968 and Hoffa's disappearance in 1976. Although conspiracy theories continue to surface to connect either or both of the two Kennedy assassinations to "the Mob," evidence in this area remains conjectural at best.

The 1968 Presidential Primaries

As a Democratic senator from New York, Robert F. Kennedy became one of the leading spokesmen opposing the war in Vietnam and Johnson administration policies in general. However, it was Senator Eugene McCarthy who first challenged Lyndon Johnson in the New Hampshire primary in February of 1968. Although Johnson won a plurality in the primary, McCarthy's winning 30 percent of the vote is thought to have been a factor in Kennedy's mid-March announcement that he was running for the presidency. When Johnson decided at the end of March not to run for re-election, the Democratic race became a contest between McCarthy, Kennedy, and Vice President Hubert Humphrey. In May, Kennedy defeated McCarthy in Indiana and Nebraska but lost to McCarthy in Oregon at the end of the month. On June 4, Kennedy defeated Humphrey in South Dakota and McCarthy in the pivotal California race. That night Kennedy was at his California headquarters at the Ambassador Hotel in Los Angeles. He did not delivery his victory speech until after midnight. In the early morning hours of June 5, he was shot by Sirhan Sirhan shortly after leaving the stage. He died the following day.

identify with and to articulate the needs of marginalized and disfranchised Americans: African Americans and Latinos living in the ghettos and barrios of urban America, Native Americans, both on and off reservations, Chicano farmworkers in California, migrant workers from Oregon to Michigan to upstate New York, and families of all backgrounds living in vermin-infested slum housing.

Kennedy's strident righteousness in his legal investigations of the 1950's logically gave way to his concern for social equality in the 1960's. His public record attests tangible advances, such as the Labor Reform Act of 1959 and the Civil Rights Act of 1964, neither of which would have passed in the same form without his input. However, Kennedy's most enduring legacy is without doubt his ability to inspire Americans to serve and to sacrifice for their fellow citizens. He provided a vision of hope and possibility in an era of great change.

The last speech Kennedy ever gave was his California primary victory speech, delivered in the early morning hours of June 5, 1968; he was assassinated in a hotel hallway after delivering the speech. In the speech Kennedy noted the significance of winning the South Dakota and

U.S. senator and presidential candidate Robert F. Kennedy campaigning in the California primary in Sacramento, California, in 1968. He was assassinated in Los Angeles three weeks later. *(AP/Wide World Photos)*

California primaries on the same day—one state rural, the other heavily urbanized. Kennedy clearly saw himself as the leader of a new, multi-cultural American vision of the future. Even decades after his death, his name and his words are invoked by politicians and leaders of all political persuasions as a shorthand way to affirm a moral, purposeful view of a democratic society.

Bibliography

Beran, Michael Knox. *The Last Patrician: Bobby Kennedy and the End of American Aristocracy*. New York: St. Martin's Press, 1998.

Dooley, Brian. *Robert Kennedy: The Final Years*. New York: St. Martin's Press, 1996.

Halberstam, David. *The Unfinished Odyssey of Robert Kennedy*. New York: Random House, 1969.

Heymann, C. David. *RFK: A Candid Biography of Robert F. Kennedy*. New York: Dutton, 1998.

Klagsbrun, Francine, and David C. Whitney, eds. *Assassination: Robert F. Kennedy, 1925-1968*. New York: Cowles, 1968.

Newfield, Jack. *Robert Kennedy: A Memoir*. New York: Dutton, 1969.

Schlesinger, Arthur M. *Robert Kennedy and His Times*. Boston: Houghton Mifflin, 1978.

Sorensen, Theodore C. *The Kennedy Legacy*. New York: Macmillan, 1969.

Richard Sax

Jomo Kenyatta

Born: c. 1894; Ichaweri, near Nairobi, British East Africa (now Kenya)
Died: August 22, 1978; Mombasa, Kenya

First president of independent Kenya (1964-1978)

Jomo Kenyatta (JOH-moh kehn-YAH-tah) was a member of the Kikuyu tribe, the most westernized tribe in Kenya. He was born near Nairobi; there is no record of the exact date of his birth. His early education was at the hands of missionaries of the Church of Scotland. He developed a strong sense of his identity as an African and of the necessity of leading his people to self-rule.

Colonization of Kenya

Kenyatta was a leader in the African nationalistic movement from the 1920's. In 1922 he joined the East African Association (EAA), led by a fellow Kikuyu, Harry Thuku. The EAA's primary purpose was to seek the return of lands lost by African tribes to European settlers. This problem was a particular sore spot for the Kikuyu, because they had lost land partly through a cultural misunderstanding. Among the Kikuyu, land was traditionally held privately by families, but the British colonial leaders interpreted their references to "our land" as meaning a quasi-feudal system in which the tribal governments held the land. Therefore, the British regarded the beginning of colonialism as transferring title to the British government, who could then distribute it to the settlers. This situation led to serious economic dislocation for Africans, who were often reduced to working for others or for the white settlers when they could no longer farm their own land.

Nationalist Leader

The EAA later reorganized as the Kikuyu Central Association (KCA), and in 1928 it named Kenyatta its general secretary. Kenyatta founded a monthly newspaper written in Kikuyu, *Mwigithania*, which was intended to create a sense of Kikuyu unity and educate the Kikuyu about the political situation. In 1929 the KCA sent Kenyatta to London to fight for Kikuyu rights in the White Highlands, a mountainous area where a large number of European settlers owned extensive holdings. Two years later he returned to England to take a degree in economics at the London School of Economics. There he wrote a thesis entitled *Facing Mount Kenya*, an extensive ethnographic study of the Kikuyu that he would publish as a book in 1938. It remains one of the best sources for information on Kikuyu tribal life prior to the Mau-Mau Uprising. Kenyatta also traveled extensively in Europe during that period and visited the Soviet Union. In 1945 he

Jomo Kenyatta *(Archive Photos)*

827

Jomo Kenyatta in Nairobi, Kenya, after being sworn in as premier in 1963. *(AP/Wide World Photos)*

organized the fifth Pan-African Congress in Manchester. The event was intended to serve as a way of bringing African leaders together to discuss common problems and the ultimate goals of African self-rule.

In 1946 Kenyatta returned to Kenya to take an active role in politics. Following the Mau-Mau Uprising he was imprisoned and convicted of taking an active part in the violent rebellion, although he maintained his innocence of those charges for the rest of his life. He was imprisoned until 1961, at which time he was released under the stipulation that he remove himself to a remote area. For the next three years he was exiled into the countryside, forbidden to enter the capital of Nairobi or the surrounding area. Even while in exile, Kenyatta remained a leader of the independence movement. In 1960 he was elected president in absentia of the Kenya African National Union (KANU).

Leader of Independent Kenya

In 1963 Kenya attained its independence, and the edict banning Kenyatta from Nairobi was

Kenyan Independence

Before independence, Kenya had been under direct British colonial rule since 1895, following the financial failure of a Crown corporation that had been operating in the area. In the period after World War II, a new generation of African Kenyans educated by European missionaries developed a growing sense of nationalism. They began demanding the right of self-determination. After the Mau-Mau Uprising, British suppression of the opposition produced only further riots and fighting. In 1957, even with very restricted voting rights, Africans elected eight representatives to the colonial legislature.

In response to this, the British government drafted a new colonial policy in 1960. Kenya was

to be governed by Africans. The 1961 elections brought an African majority into the legislature. However, the Kenya African National Union (KANU) refused to form a government as long as Jomo Kenyatta remained imprisoned. Thus the opposition party, the Kenya African Democratic Union (KADU), formed a government, paving the way for full independence. In 1963, KANU secured a victory, and Kenyatta became the first prime minister of a self-governing Kenya. Later that year, Kenya became a fully independent monarchy within the British Commonwealth. The following year, Kenya was declared a republic, and Kenyatta became its first president.

The Mau-Mau

In the late 1940's, a secret movement within the Kenya African Union (KAU) sought to unite Kenya's Africans to demand that the British change their colonial policies to improve the lives of Africans. This group was known as the Mau-Mau. When their requests through normal political channels failed to produce the desired response, the movement turned terroristic. In 1952 the British colonial government took military action against the Mau-Mau rebels and jailed thousands. Instead of quelling the revolt, this action led to massive fighting that lasted until 1956. The struggle ultimately convinced the British that keeping Kenya was counterproductive.

rescinded. He was subsequently elected president of Kenya in 1964 when it became a republic. He held this position for the rest of his life. Kenyatta was forgiving toward the white inhabitants of newly independent Kenya. He not only permitted them to remain and keep their vast estates but also permitted them to become citizens on an equal footing with African Kenyans. He wanted

Kenyan premier Jomo Kenyatta (left) welcomes U.S. federal judge (and future Supreme Court justice) Thurgood Marshall to Nairobi in 1963. *(Library of Congress)*

to create a nonracial society and bring an end to all forms of discrimination. He did not want to replace one kind of discrimination with its mirror image.

Although Kenyatta often talked about "African socialism," in practice he regarded communism as another form of colonialism and allied firmly with the West. He followed the principles of a private-enterprise, free-market system. His practices led to substantial economic growth, but wealth was not equally distributed among all Kenya's tribes. The heavily westernized Kikuyu, the best-educated tribe, were poised to take the best advantage of the changes. Because Kenyatta himself was a Kikuyu, members of other tribes often accused him of favoring his own. However, it could reasonably be argued that the difference was that the Kikuyu were best equipped to use the new opportunities open to them. Feelings that the government treated tribes unfairly proved to be divisive and led to considerable resentment and ethnic tension among tribes. Kenyatta was not without his opponents, and many criticized him harshly, but he generally did not respond with repressive tactics. When he died in 1978, Kenyatta left his country with a tradition of stability, democracy, and personal freedom unusual in sub-Saharan Africa.

Bibliography

Delf, George. *Jomo Kenyatta: Towards Truth About "the Light of Kenya."* Westport, Conn.: Greenwood, 1975.

Kenyatta, Jomo. *Facing Mount Kenya.* New York: Random House, 1962.

Malhotra, Veena. *Kenya Under Kenyatta.* Columbia, Mo.: South Asia Books, 1990.

Leigh Husband Kimmel

Aleksandr Fyodorovich Kerensky

Born: May 2, 1881; Simbirsk (now Ulyanovsk), Russia
Died: June 11, 1970; New York, New York

Russian revolutionary and provisional prime minister (1917)

Aleksandr Fyodorovich Kerensky (uh-lyihk-SAN-dur FYOH-duh-roh-vyihch kyeh-RYEHN-skoo-ih) was born in the central Volga River town of Simbirsk, which was also the birthplace of Vladimir Lenin. The city was composed mostly of conservative landowners who opposed the liberal reforms of Czar Alexander II, who was assassinated two months before Kerensky was born. Simbirsk also had a small elite of teachers, doctors, lawyers, and judges who were more liberal and strongly supported the reforms. Kerensky, whose father was a teacher and school administrator, belonged to this group. As a six-year-old boy, Kerensky was aware of the arrest of Alexander Ulyanov, Lenin's older brother, for revolutionary activities. Later, while studying law at the University of St. Petersburg, he developed his own revolutionary ideas.

Early Revolutionary

After graduating with a law degree in 1904, Kerensky became a lawyer in St. Petersburg. He often defended revolutionaries charged with political crimes. He was a sympathetic bystander to the events of Bloody Sunday (January 20, 1905) and the revolution of 1905. Later that year he secretly joined the Socialist Revolutionary Party, which was officially banned by the government of Czar Nicholas II. Publicly, Kerensky declared himself a member of the Group of Toil, a legal political party with a moderate platform supporting the rights of laborers. In 1912 he was elected as a delegate from that party to the fourth duma, the consultative assembly granted by Czar Nicholas after the revolution of 1905. He soon gained a reputation as a dynamic speaker and as an advocate of moderate socialist ideas. Kerensky later became identified with the Men-

sheviks, the moderate branch of the Social Democrats, an earlier revolutionary party that split in 1905. The radical branch of that party became the Bolsheviks and was led by Kerensky's former townsman, Vladimir Lenin.

In 1914, unlike the radical socialists such as Lenin, Kerensky supported Russia's entry into World War I. He saw the war as a chance for Russia to secure its rightful place of leadership in European affairs. Kerensky soon blamed Russia's poor performance and heavy losses in the war on the czarist government, which was becoming increasingly corrupt under the influence of individuals such as Grigori Rasputin. When the

Aleksandr Fyodorovich Kerensky *(Library of Congress)*

831

Artist's rendition of the Bloody Sunday massacre of protesters by the czar's troops outside the Winter Palace in St. Petersburg, January 22, 1905. *(Library of Congress)*

March revolution began in 1917, Kerensky stepped to the forefront and supported the dissolution of the monarchy.

Events of 1917

After the abdication of Czar Nicholas II, two organizations took control of Russia's destiny. One of these was the provisional government set up by the Duma. In this government Kerensky was made the minister of justice. The other organization was the Petrograd (St. Petersburg) Soviet of Workers' and Soldiers' Deputies, which strongly advocated socialist reforms. In this organization Kerensky became vice chairperson.

The Provisional Government

The abdication of Czar Nicholas II in March, 1917, put the destiny of Russia into the hands of two organizations. The Petrograd Soviet spoke for the people, and the provisional government spoke for the elite revolutionaries. For the revolution to produce democracy in Russia, this dual-power arrangement of self-constituted bodies with no electoral mandates had to function. In its earliest days, the provisional government was composed mostly of bourgeois liberals. In May, it became more of a coalition of liberals and socialists, with Aleksandr Kerensky emerging as the major leader. By July, the dual-power arrangement was falling apart, and the pendulum was swinging toward the Petrograd Soviet. The Kornilov Mutiny in September sealed the doom of the provisional government. It was dissolved on November 7 by Vladimir Lenin.

The Socialist Revolutionary Party

About 1900 the radical revolutionaries in Russia formed two major political parties. One was called the Social Democrats (SD). Appearing in 1898, it was the first Marxist party in Russia. The other party was the Socialist Revolutionary (SR) Party, founded in 1901, primarily by Victor Chernov. Although influenced by Marxism, the Socialist Revolutionaries engaged in a running debate with the Social Democrats about the nature and future of Russian society. Whereas the Social Democrats were an elite party exclusively representing the workers, the Social Revolutionaries claimed to represent the vast Russian peasantry. Both groups gained large followings among students and professionals. In 1905 Aleksandr Kerensky secretly joined the Social Revolutionaries, although later he joined a branch of the Social Democrats called the Mensheviks.

Both parties were involved in terrorism. For the Socialist Revolutionaries, terrorism was the primary method of operation. They sought to stir the peasants to action by example. Many bombings and assassinations were carried out between 1901 and 1905. Following the revolution of 1905, the party boycotted the attempts at reform by the czarist government. In March, 1917, following the abdication of the czar, the party reemerged as the "March SRs" and had the largest group of delegates in the Petrograd Soviet of Workers' and Soldiers' Deputies. Following the Bolshevik Revolution in November, 1917, the Socialist Revolutionaries and similar groups were outlawed as counterrevolutionaries.

As the only person to hold positions in both organizations, Kerensky became a liaison between them and the recognized leader of the government. His popularity with the people grew when he instituted the civil liberties that had long been in demand.

In May, 1917, the provisional government, with Kerensky's approval, issued a statement of war aims for the continuation of Russia's role in World War I. However, the people of Russia had suffered greatly during the war and had hoped for a decrease, if not an end, to Russia's participation. The uproar over the war aims forced several ministers of the government to resign and led to Kerensky being transferred to the positions of minister of war and of the navy. He was still the dominant figure in the government.

As the military leader of Russia, Kerensky soon planned a major offensive against Germany and Austria. His hope was that such a move would hasten a victorious end to Russia's participation and would alleviate the discontent of the people.

Part of the preparation for the offensive involved Kerensky touring the Russian front lines and using his oratorical skill to rally the discouraged soldiers. However, by this time discipline had completely broken down in the army, and the June offensive was a failure. Large numbers of soldiers simply left their posts and returned to their homes. The government was again reorganized, and Kerensky emerged as the provisional prime minister.

Rise of Bolshevik Power

The first real manifestation of Bolshevik power was a brief uprising by soldiers in July in St. Petersburg. The government was able to crush the uprising and begin suppression of the Bolshevik Party. Lenin fled to Finland, and Leon Trotsky was arrested. Kerensky also faced right-wing opposition. In September the commander in chief of the army, General Larv Kornilov, attempted to march on St. Petersburg, supposedly to save the provisional government. His dismissal by Kerensky did not stop his march. Kerensky was forced to legalize the Red Guard under Trotsky to end the Kornilov mutiny.

The Bolshevik overthrow of the provisional government was completed on November 7, 1917. Kerensky escaped from St. Petersburg in an automobile provided by the U.S. embassy. His attempt to rally the troops at the front failed, and he was forced into hiding. In May, 1918, Kerensky fled to Paris. In 1940 he moved to the United States, where he lived until his death in 1970. His last years were spent lecturing and writing books. Among his books were *Russia and History's Turning Point* (1965), which is partly autobiographical, and *The Murder of the Romanovs* (1935), which he coauthored with Paul Bulygin.

Bibliography

Abraham, Richard. *Alexander Kerensky: The First Love of the Revolution*. New York: Columbia University Press, 1987.

Katkov, George. *The Kornilov Affair*. New York: Longman, 1980.

Kerensky, Alexander. *Russia and History's Turning Point*. New York: Duell, Sloan and Pearce, 1965.

Glenn L. Swygart

Albert Kesselring

Born: November 20, 1885; Marktstedt, Bavaria, Germany
Died: July 16, 1960; Bad Nauheim, West Germany

German commander of southern forces during World War II

Albert Kesselring (AL-burt KEH-sehl-rihng), the son of a town education officer, joined the German army in 1904. He married Pauline Keyssler in 1910, and they had one adopted son. Kesselring served Germany as an artillery captain during the early years of World War I and received a promotion to the General Staff before the end of the conflict. After the war he remained in the army, transferring to the Luftwaffe (air force) in 1935. He became chief of the Luftwaffe General Staff in 1936.

Early Years of World War II

At the outbreak of World War II, Kesselring advocated a high degree of cooperation and coordination among the air, armored, artillery, and infantry forces—a position counter to traditional German military thinking. Kesselring's position eventually prevailed with the General Staff, and it resulted in the sudden, overwhelming Blitzkrieg (lightning war) attacks that led to quick German victories in Poland (1939) and France (1940). For his efforts in these campaigns, Kesselring was promoted to field marshal in 1940. His leadership of the Luftwaffe during the Battle of Britain (1940–1941), however, was not nearly so successful. He apparently concurred with Hermann Göring's decision to redirect bombing raids to civilian rather than military targets. This decision proved to be a fatal mistake, as it gave the British air forces time to rebuild enough strength to eventually defeat the Luftwaffe offensive. In the summer of 1941, Germany ended the British campaign and launched a new offensive against the Soviet Union. Kesselring played a significant role in helping to coordinate a new round of Blitzkrieg attacks.

Command of Southern Axis Forces

In late 1941 Kesselring was named commander in chief of all southern Italian and German forces. With Erwin Rommel, he directed the African campaign (1941-1943). After initial success, it eventually succumbed to the overwhelming numerical advantage of Allied forces. During this campaign, Kesselring was burdened with an antagonistic relationship with Rommel and difficult interactions with his Italian allies. The fall of Africa and then Sicily in the summer of 1943 marked a transition in Kesselring's career; he

Albert Kesselring *(Library of Congress)*

835

The Italian Retreat, 1943-1945

The Allies began their invasion of southern Italy in September of 1943, and when Italy switched sides and declared war on Germany in October, a quick and easy victory seemed assured. However, German forces under Albert Kesselring established a strong defensive position in central Italy—the Gustav Line—that stopped the Allied advance for the remainder of 1943.

An Allied landing at Anzio, north of the Gustav Line, in January of 1944 was contained by Kesselring and failed to improve Allied fortunes. It was not until May that overwhelming air superiority enabled the Allies to breach the Gustav Line. Kesselring's forces were not routed, however, and a second strong defensive position, the Gothic Line, was established in northern Italy. This line held until April, 1945, when thinned German forces collapsed under Allied attack. German forces surrendered on April 29, ending a campaign that probably prolonged the war by keeping large Allied forces from German borders.

went from an innovative offensive strategist to a brilliant defensive commander.

Kesselring's skill in establishing strong defensive positions prevented what the Allies hoped would be a quick and easy victory in Italy. His first defensive position, the Gustav Line, delayed the Allied advance for nearly a year, and his second defensive line, the Gothic Line, held firm until the waning days of the war. Kesselring was recalled from Italy in March of 1945 and appointed commander of western forces. The rapidly deteriorating German position in the west was untenable, however, and there was little that Kesselring could do to stem the Allied advance. He surrendered the southern half of German troops on May 7, 1945.

Later Life

In 1947 a British military court tried and convicted Kesselring of war crimes—in particular, of ordering the killing of 335 Italian civilians in reprisal for an attack on German soldiers. He was sentenced to death, but the sentence was later commuted to life in prison. Pardoned and freed in 1952, he wrote his memoirs, *Soldier Up to the Last Day* (1953) and became the leader of German veterans' groups. A brilliant strategist, versatile commander, and man of great diplomatic skill, Kesselring is widely regarded as one of the most capable military leaders of World War II.

Bibliography

Botjer, George, F. *Sideshow War: The Italian Campaign, 1943-1945*. College Station: Texas A&M University Press, 1996.

Kesselring, Robert. *The Memoirs of Field-Marshal Kesselring*. Mechanicsburg, Pa.: Stackpole Books, 1997.

Macksey, Kenneth. *Kesselring: German Master Strategist of the Second World War*. Mechanicsburg, Pa.: Stackpole Books, 1996.

Paul J. Chara, Jr.

John Maynard Keynes

Born: June 5, 1883; Cambridge, England
Died: April 21, 1946; Tilton, Sussex, England

English political economist

John Maynard Keynes (JON MAY-nurd KAYNZ) was the son of the esteemed British economist and university administrator John Neville Keynes and Florence Ada (Brown). After his graduation from the prestigious Eton school, Keynes returned to King's College, Cambridge, where he studied mathematics and philosophy. At Cambridge the celebrated economist Alfred Marshall mentored Keynes and influenced him to pursue economics and politics.

Early Career

Keynes was the eldest child in a fairly prosperous academic family, and he followed a traditional educational path. At Eton and Cambridge he excelled both socially and in his studies. He was looked upon as an intellectual prodigy, and he developed a number of long-lasting and meaningful friendships with writers and artists. The varied intellectual interests and friendships that Keynes formed in his days as a student influenced him throughout his life. As a result of his Cambridge friendships, Keynes became connected with the celebrated circle of bohemian writers and artists known as the Bloomsbury Group. Throughout his adult life, Keynes moved in, and was influential in, the world of public policy as well as in academic and literary circles.

Keynes took a degree in mathematics in 1905 but remained at Cambridge for another year to study economics with Alfred Marshall and Arthur Cecil Pigou. In 1906 he left Cambridge to become a civil servant in the British India Office, though he returned to Cambridge in 1908 as a lecturer in economics. His first book, *Indian Currency and Finance* (1913), was an analysis of the gold-exchange standard. This book led to his participation in public policy as a member of the Royal Commission on Indian Finance and Currency (1913-1914).

World War and the Great Depression

In 1915, after the outbreak of hostilities in World War I in 1914, Keynes took a leave of absence from Cambridge to work at the Treasury. He distinguished himself with his involvement with the economic management of the war and issues of foreign currency exchange. At the end of the war, at the Paris Peace Conference, he accompanied the British prime minister, David

John Maynard Keynes *(Library of Congress)*

An unemployed man selling apples on a New York street during the Great Depression. John Maynard Keynes offered a revolutionary explanation for the Depression. *(AP/Wide World Photos)*

Lloyd George, as an economic adviser. He was the Treasury's principal representative at the conference. His strong disagreements with the economic clauses of the peace treaty caused him great personal hardship and led him to resign his position. Ultimately they led to the publication of his book *The Economic Consequences of the Peace* (1919), in which he denounced the economic provisions of the treaty. This book was widely circulated, and it transformed Keynes into an international public policy figure.

Throughout the 1920's Keynes remained influential in several areas. His reputation as Britain's—and arguably the world's—most prominent and well-known economist was helped by his writings as a journalist for such publications as *The Times* (of London), the *Manchester Guardian*, and the *New Statesman*. His professional influence was heightened by the publication of significant scholarly works on monetary economics and his position as editor of Britain's foremost scholarly journal, *The Economic Journal*. In 1925 he publicly opposed Britain's return to the gold standard at the prewar price ratio. He increasingly found himself at odds with public policies.

The Bloomsbury Group

The Bloomsbury Group was an influential circle of free-thinking intellectuals, writers, and artists who gathered at members' homes around the residential and academic area of Bloomsbury Square. The early members of the group were generally allied with Cambridge University. The group met regularly from around 1904 into the 1930's. The group was an informal literary and philosophical society that examined aesthetic and philosophical issues but disdained discussion of politics and commerce. They were generally bohemian, agnostic, and irreverent toward customary or late Victorian-era morals and tra-

ditional wisdom. The "Bloomsberries" (as they became labeled) clearly had an impact on British culture. They were not without their critics. The English writer D. H. Lawrence for instance, considered much of the work of the "Bloomsberries" to be elitist and simple-minded. Members of the Bloomsbury circle included philosopher G. E. Moore, economist John Maynard Keynes, historian G. Lowes Dickinson, art critics Roger Fry and Clive Bell, biographer and literary critic Lytton Strachey, painters Duncan Grant and Vanessa Bell, and novelists E. M. Forster and Virginia Woolf.

Keynes's General Theory of Employment

Published in 1936 in the midst of the Great Depression, John Maynard Keynes's most enduring and influential book is *The General Theory of Employment, Interest, and Money*. The Great Depression was a time of extraordinary economic misery. The depth and duration of this economic decline was so severe that it crushed individual and collected confidence in the fundamental stability of economic and social institutions. Keynes's book challenged the traditional wisdom that economic depression is only a temporary departure from full employment. The continuing economic depression of the 1930's plainly contradicted traditional wisdom. For that reason Keynes in *The General Theory of Employment, Interest, and Money* put forth an alternative explanation of how an economy operates. He held that an economy need not be inherently stable and that long-term departures from full employment are possible. Moreover, since an economy might be unable to correct itself even in the long run, a more activist and interventionist approach to economic problems would be appropriate. The publication of this book generated a new school of economic thought and a new field of study: macroeconomics. Prior to its publication, economists had concentrated on microeconomics, the study of the economic decisions made by individuals. With macroeconomics they now also analyzed the operation of an economy as a whole.

The intensity of the economic downturn of the 1930's—the Great Depression—throughout the industrialized world left many economists and policy makers dazed and perplexed. It became increasingly obvious that conventional explanations and remedies were inadequate to resolve the enduring crisis. Keynes's classic book, *The General Theory of Employment, Interest, and Money* (1936), offered an alternative explanation for the persistence of unemployment and advocated spending policies as a means to remedy economic downturns. Keynes had in essence stood conventional economic doctrine on its head. He unleashed what has become known in economic reasoning as the Keynesian revolution.

Despite being in poor health, Keynes played a prominent role at the Bretton Woods Conference, begun in 1944 in New Hampshire. The World Bank and the International Monetary Fund (IMF) grew out of the conference. The conference prepared the industrial world (Europe and the United States) for the arduous task of reconstruction after so many years of economic depression and war.

John Maynard Keynes with his wife, Russian ballerina Lydia Lopokova; they were married in August, 1925. *(Archive Photos/Popperfoto)*

839

Intellectual and Political Importance

John Maynard Keynes is nearly universally acclaimed as the most influential and important political economist of the twentieth century. He changed the way economists think about the world. Economists began to debate the inherent stability of an economic system. Keynes and his supporters held that an economy would not necessarily correct itself and thus could require more direct and active interventionist policies. Critics of Keynes offer their own alternative views and explanations of how an economy works. Issues such as the creation of jobs and the capacity or incapacity of an economy to adjust in times of economic and political crisis remain at the heart of many heated public policy debates. The intensity of these debates plainly reflects the continued significance of these issues.

Bibliography

Harrod, Roy F. *The Life of John Maynard Keynes*. New York: W. W. Norton, 1951.

Johnson, Elizabeth, and Harry G. Johnson. *The Shadow of Keynes: Understanding Keynes, Cambridge, and Keynesian Economics*. Chicago: University of Chicago Press, 1978.

Keynes, John Maynard. *The Economic Consequences of the Peace*. New York: Harcourt, Brace and Howe, 1920.

————. *The General Theory of Employment, Interest, and Money*. New York: Harcourt, Brace & World, 1936.

Skidelsky, Robert. *John Maynard Keynes: Hopes Betrayed, 1883-1920*. New York: Viking Penguin, 1983.

————. *John Maynard Keynes: The Economist as Savior, 1920-1937*. New York: Viking Penguin, 1992.

Timothy E. Sullivan

Ruhollah Khomeini

Born: November 9, 1902; Khomein, Iran
Died: June 3, 1989; Tehran, Iran

Political and religious leader of Iran (1979-1989)

Ruhollah Khomeini (ruh-HO-lah koh-MAY-nee), often called by his clerical title, Ayatollah Khomeini, was born into a family that had produced many Islamic religious leaders. His father was murdered when Ruhollah was five, and he lost his mother and aunt when he was fifteen. As a boy he studied at a Qur'anic school, then at Qom, where he later became an instructor. In 1944 he published his first book, *Secrets Revealed*, which criticized Iranian leader Reza Shah Pahlavi's (shah since 1941) introduction of Western secular ideas and policies. Khomeini's reputation at Qom grew as both a scholar and a legal arbiter. In 1960 he published a book of rulings on Islamic behavior and rose to the highest rank in Shia Islam, that of ayatollah.

Early Political History

Throughout the 1940's and 1950's, Khomeini pursued his political beliefs in his writings. His book of rulings argued that Iran needed a leader who would rule according to Islamic law. In 1963, a series of events in the Iranian government further politicized Khomeini's ideology; he began to speak out and build his reputation as a political leader. The first event was a decree establishing women's suffrage as well as the freedom to use any holy book, not only the Qur'an, for oath-taking ceremonies. The second was the White Revolution, a program that included land reform. The third was the granting of diplomatic immunity to U.S. military personnel in Iran.

On June 3, 1963, Khomeini publicly denounced the shah and called on Iranians to protest against the monarchy. The shah sent troops to quell the protesters, thousands of people were killed, and Khomeini spent a brief period in jail. Khomeini was exiled to Turkey in 1964 for a short time and then to Iraq, where he spent almost fifteen years.

The events of 1963 were crucial in turning people toward the clergy—and to Khomeini in particular—for leadership. Khomeini possessed great charisma and commitment to Islam, and he was an impassioned speaker. From Iraq, he reached the masses by means of the clergy's grassroots political work. Groups of students (in Iran and abroad) helped spread Khomeini's message. His sermons were broadcast over radio, and audiocassettes were distributed throughout Iran and among Iranians living overseas. Islamic or-

Ruhollah Khomeini in 1988. *(AP/Wide World Photos)*

Iranian demonstrators outside the U.S. embassy in Tehran in December, 1979, a month after it was seized by radical students and ten months after Iran's Islamic revolution. *(Library of Congress)*

ganizations established banks that provided businesspeople with loans, and they built mosques and hospitals. In a society in which people were tired of the shah's corruptness and the cultural values of the pro-Western program he championed, Khomeini's message appealed to moderate, conservative, and militant Iranians alike.

Tensions mounted in Iran during the late 1970's. Khomeini's followers grew in number daily. The shah attempted to lessen Khomeini's power by pressuring Iraqi leader Saddam Hussein to force him out of Iraq. Ironically, Khomeini's move to France improved his position

The Islamic Revolution in Iran

Between 1977 and 1979, the Ayatollah Ruhollah Khomeini consolidated his support for an Islamic revolution into a strong popular movement against Iran's ruling shah. In January, 1979, the shah left the country for what was called an "extended vacation." He transferred power to Shapur Bakhtiar. Khomeini returned to Iran from France, arriving on February 1, 1979, to a huge reception of cheering crowds. Bakhtiar soon fled the country. Khomeini established a provisional government. The Islamic Republic was officially declared, following a public referendum, on April 1, 1979. Later that year, a new constitution was passed. It provided for the Majles (parliament), a president, and the granting of supreme authority to the *faqih* (the supreme jurisprudent, or Khomeini himself).

The Islamic revolution radically changed the lives of everyday Iranians. The government attempted to force public morality to conform with Shia Islam's strict standards. Enforcement was carried out by various government-sanctioned groups, including the Office of Propagation of Virtues and Prevention of Vice. Women, previously accustomed to wearing Western-style clothing, now had to don the *chador*, a heavy black veil. Women's rights became severely limited, and gender segregation was enforced in school and public places. The traditional themes of Persian art were replaced by Islamic images. Newspapers, radio, and schools similarly focused on Islam. In universities, the curriculum was transformed. Anyone deviating from the government's standards could face arrest.

The Iran-Iraq War

After the fall of Iran's shah in 1979 and the subsequent Islamic revolution, relations between Iran and neighboring Iraq grew increasingly tense. In Iraq, the government feared that Ruhollah Khomeini's criticism of Iraq's ruling party could spark a repeat of the Iranian revolution there. In September, 1980, Iraqi leader Saddam Hussein invaded the Shatt al Arab waterway, Iran's largest oil-producing region.

During the first year of the war, Iraqi forces captured a number of key towns. Control of the war switched hands several times. Neither side would grant concessions. In the spring of 1988, newly reinforced Iraqi troops, bolstered by international help, retook areas Iran had previously captured. Khomeini's forces were greatly diminished. Iranian president Ali Akbar Hashemi Rafsanjani played a key role in influencing a reluctant Khomeini to accept an cease-fire, which occurred in August, 1988.

The war resulted in heavy damages and expenses for both sides. Iranian boys as young as thirteen were sent to battle, and the country's casualties were estimated at about 750,000 people. Iran's military costs were more than $80 billion, and damage to the oil industry and oil revenues was about $50 billion. Most world governments blamed Iran for the war, increasing Iran's diplomatic isolation. The war also resulted in various Arab countries banding together for common protection in case of attack.

by bringing him into increased contact with the international press and giving him international telephone access. Inside Iran, anti-shah demonstrations and the deaths of hundreds of citizens at the hands of the shah's military brought more Iranians to the Islamic side and worsened the shah's already precarious hold on the nation. The shah lost ground quickly as soldiers left the military, the rich fled Iran with millions of dollars of capital, workers went on strike, and arms circulated among militant Islamic groups.

The Islamic Revolution

After the shah stepped down in January, 1979, Khomeini returned to Iran in February, 1979. The revolution happened soon afterward. Khomeini sought to change all of Iranian society. He faced many obstacles. The government and banks were cash-poor. Moreover, revolutionary forces represented a wide range of ideologies. Khomeini and his followers managed to push out competing groups until Shia Muslims formed a majority and he became supreme ruler. A major event shortly

The Ayatollah Ruhollah Khomeini holding a press conference in February, 1979, shortly after his return to Iran. *(AP/Wide World Photos)*

after the revolution was the takeover of the U.S. embassy in Tehran by Iranian students. They held fifty-two American hostages in the embassy for 444 days. Iran became even more isolated in 1989, after Khomeini placed a fatwa (a religious decree to kill) on British writer Salman Rushdie, whose 1988 novel *The Satanic Verses* criticized fundamentalist Islam.

Khomeini's Legacy

The Islamic Iran that Khomeini created was beset by functional problems. Primary among these was the fact that Khomeini was presiding over two ideological factions within the ruling clergy. One was more concerned with the country's national interests, while the other was more concerned with maintaining religious ideology. Khomeini dealt with this by siding alternately with each faction. He received the respect from clergy necessary to act as final arbiter, and he managed to keep disparate factions united as a ruling body. Khomeini transformed Iranian society into a conservative culture in which Islam alone dictated cultural heritage and practices.

Bibliography

Dorraj, Manochehr. *From Zarathustra to Khomeini: Populism and Dissent in Iran*. Boulder, Colo.: Lynne Rienner, 1990.

Gordon, Matthew. *Ayatollah Khomeini*. New York: Chelsea House, 1987.

Mackey, Sandra. *The Iranians: Persia, Islam, and the Soul of a Nation*. New York: Penguin Books, 1998.

Xiomara Garcia de la Cadena

Nikita S. Khrushchev

Born: April 17, 1894; Kalinovka, Kursk region, Russia
Died: September 11, 1971; Moscow, U.S.S.R.

Premier of the Soviet Union (1958-1964)

Nikita Sergeyevich Khrushchev (nyih-KYEE-tah syihr-GYAY-yeh-vyihch kroosh-CHOF) was the son of a miner in Ukraine, which during his youth was part of Czar Nicholas II's Russian Empire. As a young man Khrushchev participated in the 1917 Russian Revolution, joined the Communist Party, and enlisted in the Red Army. He helped fight for Vladimir Lenin's fledgling communist government in the subsequent civil war. Khrushchev rapidly rose through party ranks, establishing himself as an agricultural specialist. He became a full member of the highest Communist Party body, the Politburo, during the reign of Josef Stalin (1928-1953). With Stalin's death in 1953, Khrushchev was one of three primary Soviet leaders. Within a few years he had established himself as the first secretary of the Communist Party and the leader of the Soviet government.

Domestic Policies

Khrushchev was a political and economic reformer. The country he inherited from Stalin suffered from an alienated society, a totalitarian government, and an inefficient, state-dominated economy. Khrushchev sought to ameliorate these conditions through a series of reform programs in the late 1950's and early 1960's. The most significant and notable aspect of Khrushchev's domestic reforms was his "de-Stalinization" program. In effect, Khrushchev denounced the systematic oppression, political corruption, and paranoia of Stalin's regime. He also purged the worst of Stalin's political henchmen from party and government positions, and he released millions from Stalin's prison camp system.

Seeking to improve his country's industrial capacity to keep up with the United States in the Cold War, Khrushchev introduced a variety of economic reforms, including a partial decentralization of the government's economic planning apparatus. In addition, he sought to boost the production of housing and consumer goods in an effort to regain the confidence and cooperation of Soviet citizens.

In agriculture, Khrushchev pushed a major campaign to bring vast new areas of the Soviet Union under cultivation. He ordered the deployment of hundreds of thousands of new tractors, the relo-

Nikita S. Khrushchev *(Archive Photos)*

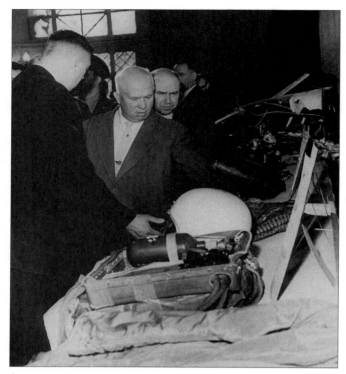

Soviet premier Nikita S. Khrushchev inspecting wreckage from the American U2 spy plane shot down over the Soviet Union in May, 1960. *(Library of Congress)*

cation of large populations, and the construction of massive irrigation projects to create new agricultural operations on the Soviet Union's vast "virgin lands." The program did not produce the harvests envisioned and was especially disappointing in the light of its enormous cost and effort.

Foreign Policy

Khrushchev led the Soviet Union during some of the most critical years of the Cold War. He made some important symbolic revisions to Soviet foreign policy doctrine, such as recognizing that war with the United States was not inevitable and calling for "peaceful coexistence" with the West. At the same time, Khrushchev placed a high priority on the development of nuclear weapons that could reach the United States, an effort that overlapped with the Soviet space program. The Soviet Union experienced a number of successes during Khrushchev's reign in both areas, including the deployment of intermediate-range nu-

Khruschev and De-Stalinization

Although Nikita Khrushchev had been a highly placed official within Joseph Stalin's regime, Khrushchev made "de-Stalinization" a central part of his reform program after succeeding Stalin. In 1956, Khrushchev delivered a long speech that was highly critical of Stalin's programs and personality. Although this "secret speech" at the Twentieth Congress of the Soviet Union's Communist Party was not formally made public, it soon became common knowledge. Khrushchev became strongly associated with the process of de-Stalinization.

De-Stalinization amounted to an effort to stabilize a society that had been terrorized by Stalin's arbitrary and fearsome secret police.

Khrushchev relaxed constraints on artistic and academic expression, decentralized certain political and economic structures, and subjected the secret police to new political oversight and other reforms. He released millions of prisoners from the "gulag" prison-camp system established by Stalin. He attempted to provide new civil protections and to increase living standards for the Soviet citizenry. Khrushchev's de-Stalinization was only partly successful, for while he renounced the worst excesses of Stalin's tyranny, he remained committed to the core principles of Soviet communism, which patently rejected liberal democracy and economic freedom.

The U-2 Incident

On May 1, 1960, the Soviet Union shot down an American U-2 spy plane flying through Soviet airspace. Believing that the pilot had been killed or had committed suicide per established procedures, the United States denied that the plane had been on a spying mission. However, the pilot, Francis Gary Powers, had been captured alive and admitted to Soviet authorities that he had been spying. He was subsequently convicted of spying at a Soviet trial.

The U-2 incident exacerbated Cold War tensions between the United States and the Soviet Union. Khrushchev threatened to bomb American U-2 bases, and the United States went on a nuclear alert. Khrushchev also canceled a planned visit by President Dwight D. Eisenhower to Moscow. The incident colored subsequent crises during Khrushchev's rule, including that caused by the U.S.-backed Bay of Pigs invasion of Cuba and the Cuban Missile Crisis.

clear missiles, the launching of the world's first satellite (Sputnik) atop a ballistic missile, and the sending of animals and humans into space.

Because of his behavior in the United Nations and other international meetings, Khrushchev was sometimes ridiculed as uncouth, unsophisticated, and boorish. Yet as the leader of one of the world's two superpowers, Khrushchev's diplomacy carried enormous weight. His famous statement about the Soviet Union's ability to "bury" the West caused both anger and fear in the United States, feeding the anticommunist paranoia that often infused American policy and public debate. Khrushchev's famous "kitchen debate" with U.S. vice president Richard M. Nixon in 1959 encapsulated many of the feelings between the two countries, each trying to position itself as the champion of a superior social and economic system.

The competition of the Cold War reached its peak during the Cuban Missile Crisis in October of 1962.

Khrushchev had ordered the placement in Cuba of Soviet nuclear missiles with the capacity to strike the United States. When privately confronted by American diplomats about the weapons, Khrushchev and his spokesmen denied that they were offensive missiles. President John F. Kennedy went public with the information and demanded their immediate removal. Khrushchev was severely tested by the crisis, which simultaneously confronted him with the possi-

Nikita S. Khruschev addressing the Supreme Soviet in 1956. Khrushchev criticized the policies of his predecessor, Joseph Stalin. *(National Archives)*

bility of a nuclear strike from the United States and the possibility of suffering a humiliating diplomatic defeat on the world stage. The latter took place. Within two weeks after the crisis erupted, Khrushchev had reluctantly agreed to remove the missiles.

Loss of Power

Partly as a result of his botched plan to place missiles in Cuba, and partly because of his alienation of Communist Party conservatives and military leaders with his reforms, Khrushchev was forced from power in 1964. It was significant, however, that Khrushchev was permitted to live out the rest of his natural life as a pensioner. Without a formal mechanism for succession of the top leadership, the Soviet Union had never before experienced a peaceful transfer of power from one living leader to another. Indeed, the previous thousand years of Russian history was marked with violent and duplicitous seizures of power within the monarchy.

Khrushchev died in 1971 at the age of seventy-seven. His successor, Leonid Brezhnev, reversed various aspects of de-Stalinization and other of Khrushchev's reforms. However, in the mid-1980's Soviet leader Mikhail Gorbachev followed to a large extent in the tradition of Khrushchev, instituting sweeping reforms.

Bibliography

Fursenko, Aleksandr, and Timothy Naftali. *One Hell of a Gamble: Khrushchev, Castro, and Kennedy, 1958-1964*. New York: Norton, 1997.

Khrushchev, Nikita S. *Khrushchev Remembers: The Glasnost Tapes*. Boston: Little, Brown, 1990.

Khrushchev, Sergei. *Khrushchev on Khrushchev: An Inside Account of the Man and His Era*. Boston: Little, Brown, 1990.

McCauley, Martin. *The Khrushchev Era: 1953-1964*. New York: Longman, 1995.

Tompson, William J. *Khrushchev: A Political Life*. Oxford, England: Macmillan, 1995.

Zubok, V. M. *Inside the Kremlin's Cold War: From Stalin to Khrushchev*. Cambridge, Mass.: Harvard University Press, 1996.

Steve D. Boilard

Kim Il Sung

Born: April 15, 1912; Man'gyondae, near P'yongyang, Korea (now North Korea)
Died: July 8, 1994; P'yongyang, North Korea

Premier of North Korea (1948-1994)

Chairman of the Korean Workers' Party and president of the Democratic Republic of Korea, Kim Il Sung (KEEM EEL SUHNG) was the undisputed leader of North Korea for a half century. Kim was born Kim Song Ju in a village near P'yongyang. His father, Kim Hyong Jik, was a teacher. The Kim family moved to China's Jilin Province in 1919, where Kim completed his primary education. In 1927, Kim Song Ju began to attend Yuwen Middle School in the city of Jilin. In 1929 he was arrested by local police for anti-Japanese activities and jailed for several months.

Early Political Activities

In 1931, Kim Song Ju joined the Communist Youth League. He soon organized a small guerrilla force, which became part of the Communist Northeast Anti-Japanese United Democratic Armies (the NEAJUDA). In 1935, Kim created the Korea Recovery Society and became the organization's president. From this position he laid out the ten principles for Korea's independence. For years, Kim and his guerrilla force continued activities in the mountains in Manchuria and northern Korea. In 1941, after a major setback, Kim fled to the Soviet Union, where he studied at a military academy and joined the Red Army.

After World War II, Kim returned to Korea from the Soviet Union. In February, 1946, he became the chairman of the North Korean Provisional People's Committee. In July he was named vice chairman of the North Korean Workers' Party which had merged with the Communist Party and the New People's Party. In September, 1948, after the establishment of the Korean People's Democratic Republic in northern Korea, Kim became the first premier. Around this time he began to use the name Kim Il Sung, reputedly after a martyred uncle. In 1949, Kim became the chairman of the Workers' Party.

War for Korean Unification

An intense patriot, Kim took the unification of the Korean peninsula as his ultimate goal. Between 1948 and 1950, he built a formidable armed force with Soviet assistance while leading the country in postwar reconstruction. He also provided support to communist guerrillas in the south of Korea. The U.S. occupation of the south stood in his way, however. In August, 1948, the Republic of Korea (South Korea) was pronounced,

Kim Il Sung in 1962. *(National Archives)*

Kim Il Sung (right), premier of North Korea from 1948 to 1994, fostered a "cult of personality" centered on himself. He turned North Korea into a highly regimented, militaristic society. *(National Archives)*

Guerrilla Warfare Against the Japanese

After the annexation of Korea by Japan in 1910, many Korean patriots fled their country to the Manchuria region of China. There they continued anti-Japanese activities. Between September, 1931, and February, 1932, the Japanese Kwangtung Army occupied all of Manchuria and established a puppet state. While the Chinese government in Nanjing pursued a policy of nonresistance by withdrawing its troops to the south of the Great Wall, thousands of Chinese and Korean exiles organized themselves into anti-Japanese guerrilla bands. Kim Il Sung organized a small guerrilla band of about thirty Korean expatriates.

In 1935, the Chinese Communist Party brought various anti-Japanese forces into the Northeast Anti-Japanese Democratic United Armies (NEAJDUA). The NEAJDUA conducted guerrilla warfare against the Japanese occupation force. It had established three war zones by the end of 1937. The Japanese responded by sending in large number of troops and employing the infamous "Three All" policy—burn all, kill all, and loot all—against the resistance. The Japanese campaigns inflicted serious casualties on the NEAJDUA and forced its main force to retreat across the Sino-Soviet border. While some NEAJDUA units remained in Manchuria, others established bases in the Soviet Union. From there they continued their raids into Manchuria.

North Korea's Invasion of the South

In March, 1950, Kim Il Sung visited Moscow. He stopped in Beijing on his way home, seeking support for his war for Korean unification. While both Joseph Stalin of the Soviet Union and China's Mao Zedong were sympathetic, neither showed great enthusiasm for Kim's plan. Not to be discouraged, Kim went ahead on his own with preparations for the unification of his country. On June 25, hostilities broke out along the 38th parallel, which divided the North and

South. The next day, Kim called for general mobilization, and North Korean troops moved southward across the parallel en masse. In three days, North Korean troops had captured Seoul, the capital of the Republic of Korea. The invasion not only signified the beginning of what Kim called the Fatherland Liberation War but also launched a bitter struggle that involved eighteen countries and cost more than two million lives before the Korean War ended.

with Syngman Rhee as president, and it was recognized by the United Nations (U.N.). To Kim, this represented an attempt by the hostile West to make the separation of the Korean nation permanent. He responded by establishing the People's Democratic Republic of Korea in September.

In June, 1950, Kim put his plan for national unification into action. Troops from North Korea crossed the 38th parallel, which divided North and South Korea. Contrary to Kim's anticipation, the U.S. government reacted to the civil war in Korea immediately and forcefully. On June 27, President Harry S Truman authorized the use of U.S. military forces in the Korean conflict. On July 7, a U.N. resolution led to an intervention force composed of troops from fifteen U.N. member nations in addition to the United States.

Within a few weeks, North Korean troops had demolished the defense of the South and pushed the small allied force to a tiny area around Pusan. The tide turned in mid-September, however, when U.N. forces successfully landed near Inchon. In October, when U.N. forces pushed toward the Sino-Korean border, the Chinese government responded by sending troops to Korea. The Korean War dragged on for two years. Eventually, after difficult negotiations, a truce was arranged in 1953.

The Postwar Years

After the war, Kim Il Sung led his country in reconstruction, with generous assistance from the Soviet Union and China. His economic policy focused on industrialization and collectivization of agriculture. He strengthened his position in the government by purging his major rivals in a series of trials. Kim managed to inspire the confidence of the Korean people in his Chullima (flying horse) Movement, which emphasized rapid economic reconstruction through self-reliance. Korea achieved economic self-sufficiency, even though first the Soviet Union and then China withdrew assistance.

Kim also managed to keep Korea independent of both China and the Soviet Union. In 1986, he discovered and crushed a coup led by his own wife. In his last years, he successfully promoted his son, Kim Jong Il, as his successor. However, his hard-line policy made North Korea one of the most isolated countries in the world; this was true even though the country maintained diplomatic ties with more than 130 countries. His economic policy, after its initial success, faltered badly and suffered from administrative inflexibility. In a time of rapid change and globalization, the North Korean government seemed to hang on to the status quo. As a result, the government became increasingly rigid, and the economy inefficient. In the 1990's, the situation was bad enough that serious food shortages occurred. Kim was an absolute ruler who fostered what is often termed a "cult of personality" as part of his propaganda system. He molded Korea into a highly regimented, even militaristic, society.

In the early 1970's, Kim endorsed a campaign centered on the Three Revolutions—technological, ideological, and cultural. It was led by his son, Kim Jong Il. The campaign was intended to reenergize the ruling party and streamline the bureaucracy. It was not particularly successful; campaigns such as this did not help North Korea end its diplomatic isolation or its economic stagnation. In his last few years, Kim seemed to have softened his position on the issue of national unification. In the 1980's, with the support of both China and the United States, the North and South started negotiations for peaceful unification. In an agreement in 1991, the North and South Korean governments pledged not to attack each other. Kim Il Sung died in July, 1994, and was succeeded by his son, Kim Jong Il.

Bibliography

"Kim Il Sung." *Current Biography* 55 (Sept., 1994): 59-60.

Macdonald, Donald S. *The Koreans: Contemporary Politics and Society*. Boulder, Colo.: Westview Press, 1990.

Savada, Andrea Matles, ed. *North Korea: A Country Study*. Washington, D.C.: U.S. Government Printing Office, 1994.

Peng Deng

Ernest Joseph King

Born: November 23, 1878; Lorain, Ohio
Died: June 25, 1956; Portsmouth, New Hampshire

U.S. chief of naval operations during World War II

Ernest Joseph King (UR-nehst JOH-sehf KIHNG) learned about the sea from a former sailor who lived in his landlocked home town. While still a boy, he tried to run away to sea, but he was apparently dissuaded by a neighbor's cooking. He then waited until he graduated from high school and received an appointment to the U.S. Naval Academy in Annapolis. His father, a railroad mechanic, gave him a round-trip ticket in case he changed his mind. He kept the return portion for many years as a memento.

Early Career

While still in the academy, King briefly served as a naval cadet aboard the USS *San Francisco* during the Spanish-American War. He subsequently graduated with distinction and served the two years then required before being commissioned as an ensign. He served on a number of ships before being sent ashore to serve as an instructor in ordinance and gunnery at the Naval Academy. He gained a reputation as a strict but fair duty officer. Over the next several years King alternated between sea and shore postings. Shortly after World War I he received a series of assignments that acquainted him with submarine operations. In 1925 he commanded the salvage of the USS *S-51*, a submarine that sank off the Rhode Island coast.

Having gained experience with both surface ships and submarines, King next began his career in naval aviation. In 1927 he reported to the Naval Air Station at Pensacola for flight training and was designated a naval aviator. Shortly thereafter he was involved in the salvage of another submarine, *S-4*. Over the next several years, King held steadily more responsible positions. In February, 1941, he was made commander in chief of the Atlantic Fleet, a position he held until the United States entered World War II in 1941.

Head of the Navy

After the Japanese attacked Pearl Harbor on December 7, 1941, the Navy made major changes in its command structure. King was given the position of commander in chief of the U.S. fleet, which gave him overall operational command of American naval forces. In March of 1942 he was

Ernest Joseph King *(Library of Congress)*

853

The Joint Chiefs of Staff

The United States' armed forces have long recognized the importance of coordinating the activities of the different service branches. However, early joint boards had no effective power and could only offer advice. This situation changed during World War II. The growing complexity of modern warfare made coordination essential. After the Japanese attack on Pearl Harbor, U.S. president Franklin D. Roosevelt and British prime minister Winston Churchill created the Combined Chiefs of Staff to coordinate U.S. and British military efforts. However, the U.S. military lacked an agency to provide input to this body.

In 1942 Roosevelt created the U.S. Joint Chiefs of Staff without any formal legislative mandate. It consisted of the senior commanders of each branch of the military: General George C. Marshall, chief of staff of the Army; Admiral Ernest J. King, chief of naval operations; and General Henry H. Arnold, deputy Army chief of staff for air and chief of the Army Air Force. The president added his own military adviser, Admiral William D. Leahy, who filled a function analagous to that of the chairman of the joint chiefs in the formalized postwar organization of the Joint Chiefs of Staff.

Admiral Ernest Joseph King, commander in chief of the U.S. fleet during World War II, speaks to reporters in his office in December, 1941, three weeks after the Japanese attack on Pearl Harbor. *(AP/Wide World Photos)*

also made chief of naval operations; he held the two positions concurrently.

Throughout the war, King was involved in naval strategy at the highest levels. He was a member of the Joint Chiefs of Staff from the time that body was created. He attended the various conferences in which President Franklin D. Roosevelt met with other Allied leaders. King was somewhat controversial for his resistance to cooperating with British naval leaders. On December 17, 1944, he was advanced to the rank of fleet admiral, a rank that was created to enable senior American commanders to work as equals with British senior commanders. In December of 1945 Chester Nimitz replaced King as chief of naval operations. Subsequently King

At the Chinese embassy in Washington, D.C., a Chinese official presents U.S. admiral Ernest Joseph King with China's highest military medal in honor of his service in World War II. *(AP/Wide World Photos)*

served as an adviser to the secretary of the Navy, then as president of the Naval Historical Foundation.

Bibliography

Buell, Thomas B. *Master of Sea Power: A Biography of Fleet Admiral Ernest J. King*. Boston: Little, Brown, 1980.

Dallek, Robert. *Franklin D. Roosevelt and American Foreign Policy, 1932-1945*. New York: Oxford University Press, 1979.

King, Ernest J., and Walter Muir Whitehill. *Fleet Admiral King: A Naval Record*. New York: W. W. Norton, 1952.

Leigh Husband Kimmel

Martin Luther King, Jr.

Born: January 15, 1929; Atlanta, Georgia
Died: April 4, 1968; Memphis, Tennessee

U.S. civil rights leader, winner of 1964 Nobel Peace Prize

Martin Luther King, Jr. (MAHR-tihn LEW-thur KIHNG JEW-nyur), was born in Atlanta, Georgia, the son of the Reverend Martin Luther King, Sr., a civil rights leader and pastor of the Ebenezer Baptist Church. King graduated from Morehouse College in 1948. Later he received a divinity degree from Crozer Theological Seminary in Pennsylvania and a doctorate in theology from Boston University. In 1953 he married Coretta Scott.

The Montgomery Bus Boycott

In October, 1954, Martin Luther King, Jr., was ordained pastor of the Dexter Avenue Baptist

Martin Luther King, Jr. *(Library of Congress)*

Church in Montgomery, Alabama. In December, 1955, a woman named Rosa Parks was arrested for refusing to obey the segregated seating laws on Montgomery's buses. Shortly thereafter, African Americans decided to boycott the city buses. They created the Montgomery Improvement Association and elected King as president. This event marked the emergence of King as a spokesperson for civil rights. The boycott continued for 381 days until the U.S. Supreme Court declared Alabama's segregation laws unconstitutional in December, 1956.

Southern Christian Leadership Conference

The Southern Christian Leadership Conference (SCLC) was an outgrowth of the Montgomery bus boycott movement. In 1957 King met with other southern black ministers and founded the organization. King was selected as president of the SCLC, a position he held until his death in 1968. In 1959 King moved to Atlanta, where the headquarters of the Southern Christian Leadership Conference was located. Prior to 1960, King and the SCLC had focused on the goal of voting rights for African Americans. In 1958 King published *Stride Toward Freedom: The Montgomery Story*. A year later he visited India, where he became well versed in Mahatma Gandhi's tactics of nonviolent resistance.

In 1960 African American college students in the South began a sit-in movement in Greensboro, North Carolina, to protest segregated dining facilities. This movement spread throughout the South and led to the creation of the Student Nonviolent Coordinating Committee (SNCC) in 1960. At first the SNCC had ties to the Southern Christian Leadership Conference; however, it soon became an independent civil rights organization. For the next five years, SNCC and the SCLC had both a cooperative and a competitive relationship.

During the first half of the 1960's, Martin Luther King, Jr., emerged as the major spokesperson for civil rights; however, other organizations, most notably the Student Nonviolent Coordinating Committee and the Congress of Racial Equality (CORE) were also significant forces in the movement for equality. Increasingly, King found his policy of nonviolence conflicting with the approach of the more militant students. In 1961 King and the SCLC became involved in desegregation efforts in Albany, Georgia. While these efforts were largely unsuccessful, King learned from this movement the importance of a strong local base, a clear chain of command, and a coherent strategy. He applied these lessons in 1963 when the SCLC used mass demonstrations to desegregate facilities in Birmingham, Alabama. The Birmingham success, combined with his famous "I Have a Dream" speech at the March on Washington in August of 1963, catapulted King to national and international prominence. In January, 1964, *Time* magazine named him man of the year. When President Lyndon B. Johnson signed the Civil Rights Act of 1964 into law on July 2, King was

Martin Luther King, Jr. (right), with Ralph Abernathy in Montgomery, Alabama, during the 1955-1956 bus boycott. *(AP/Wide World Photos)*

The Black Panther Party

The Black Panther Party was organized in Oakland, California, by Huey Newton and Bobby Seale in the fall of 1966. In contrast to Martin Luther King, Jr.'s nonviolent philosophy, the Black Panther Party took a more militant approach to civil rights. At first the Black Panthers armed themselves and followed police officers around the city of Oakland to observe the arrest of African Americans. Later the Black Panther Party, under the leadership of Eldridge Cleaver, advocated armed revolution in order to liberate blacks from white oppression. Eventually, the Black Panther Party came under the leadership of Elaine Brown, who emphasized the need to work within the political system to achieve change. At its peak the Black Panther Party had no more than two thousand active members; however, its militant approach gave it national publicity and significant support among ghetto youth in the late 1960's and early 1970's. By the late 1970's the party had ceased to exist.

The March on Washington

On August 28, 1963, the March on Washington for Jobs and Freedom occurred. The march drew support from all the major civil rights groups as well as many civic, labor, and religious organizations, including the American Jewish Congress, the National Conference of Catholics for Interracial Justice, the National Council of Churches, and the AFL-CIO, the country's largest organization of labor unions. More than 200,000 people from all over the United States attended the largest demonstration in the history of Washington, D.C. At the Lincoln Memorial a variety of civil rights leaders addressed the audience. The highlight of the day was Martin Luther King, Jr.'s "I Have a Dream" speech. King's address clearly established him as the dominant figure of the Civil Rights movement and provided an impetus for the passage of the Civil Rights Act of 1964.

Martin Luther King, Jr., preparing to deliver his famous "I Have a Dream" speech in Washington, D.C., in 1963. *(AP/Wide World Photos)*

present. In December, 1964, King, at the age of thirty-five, was awarded the Nobel Peace Prize in Oslo, Norway.

The last major campaign of the southern Civil Rights movement occurred in Selma, Alabama. In the spring of 1965, King initiated a voting rights campaign. While conflicts continued to occur between the ministers of the SCLC and the members of SNCC and CORE, the campaign successfully culminated with the Selma to Montgomery march. In August of that year the Voting Rights Act was signed into law, and African Americans were guaranteed participation in the political process. Within ten years African American voter registration in the South increased from 2 million to 3.8 million.

The Post-Civil Rights Era

Urban rioting across the United States in the mid-1960's resulted in King developing a national agenda in the years following the passage of the Voting Rights Act. King initiated a movement in Chicago for open housing, and he publicly opposed the Vietnam War. He also began to address the problems of poverty, an issue which had not been a part of the earlier Civil Rights movement. In 1968 he initiated the Poor Peoples Campaign. In April of that year King went to Memphis, Tennessee, to support a strike by sanitation workers. There he was assassinated on April 4, 1963.

An Assessment

During his lifetime Martin Luther King, Jr., was a controversial figure, but he was the most prominent figure of the Civil Rights movement. Recognition of his role occurred in 1986, when King's birthday became a national holiday. While he was criticized by some whites as being too militant and by some blacks as being too passive, the efforts of King and the Southern Christian Leadership Conference resulted in the passage of the Civil Rights Act of 1964 and the Voting Rights Act of 1965. This legislation marked the end of legal segregation in the South and brought African Americans into the political arena as voters.

Bibliography

Fairclough, Adam. *Martin Luther King, Jr.* Athens: University of Georgia Press, 1995.

Lewis, David L. *King: A Bibliography*. Urbana: University of Illinois Press, 1978.

Lischer, Richard. *The Preacher King: Martin Luther King, Jr., and the Word That Moved America*. New York: Oxford University Press, 1995.

Oates, Stephen B. *Let the Trumpet Sound: A Life of Martin Luther King, Jr.* New York: HarperCollins, 1994.

Schulke, Flip. *He Had a Drive: Martin Luther King, Jr., and the Civil Rights Movement*. New York: Norton, 1995.

William V. Moore

William Lyon Mackenzie King

Born: December 17, 1874; Berlin (now Kitchener), Ontario, Canada
Died: July 22, 1950; Kingsmere, Quebec, Canada

Three-time prime minister of Canada (1921-1926, 1926-1930, 1935-1948)

William Lyon Mackenzie King (WIHL-yuhm LI-uhn muh-KEHN-zee KIHNG) was born into a family famous for its connection to the founding of Canada: His grandfather, William Lyon Mackenzie, had led the 1837 revolt against the British colonial government in Upper Canada. Throughout his life King felt a sense of destiny and sought to walk in the liberal reformist shoes of his illustrious ancestor.

William Lyon Mackenzie King *(Library of Congress)*

Early in his life King was forced to choose between a life in the university as a teacher and scholar or a life in government and politics. He graduated with honors from the University of Toronto in 1895 and attained an LL.B. in 1897 and an M.A. degree the following year. He then pursued studies at the University of Chicago and at Harvard, obtaining an M.A. from the latter in 1898. King moved on to the London School of Economics and was waiting to hear whether he would gain a position at Harvard when he was offered a civil service position in Canada's newly created Department of Labour. King accepted the position, and within months he was Canada's first deputy minister of labour and editor of the *Labour Gazette.* Asked by Prime Minister Wilfred Laurier to run for Parliament as a Liberal Party candidate in the 1908 election, King's victory signaled the beginning of a political career that would last through the next four decades and would make him Canada's longest-serving prime minister.

Ascent to Power

King was appointed to the cabinet as minister of labour in 1909. His academic and civil service expertise in labor relations and conciliation, coupled with his reformist ideas and his temperament as a compromiser, well suited him for the position. The Liberal Party lost the 1911 election and was again defeated in 1917 because of the party's unpopular stand against conscripting soldiers to fight in World War I. King supported Laurier on this issue, and he failed to win his own seat in the election. His opposition to conscription paid off, however, when the French Canadian wing of the party strongly supported him at the Liberal leadership convention in 1919. Strong

The *Labour Gazette*

Mackenzie King's academic background in political economy and labor conciliation made him an ideal choice as Canada's first deputy minister of labour. King was brought in to help establish the new department in 1900, and it was in this role that he founded and edited the *Labour Gazette*. The purpose of the *Labour Gazette* was to compile statistics and provide a record of labor conditions, strikes, and industrial relations throughout Canada. It also was to provide impartial and objective information on labor conditions, and the government was to take on a greater role as conciliator in labor disputes. The *Labour Gazette* proved significant in moving the government toward the role of mediating the conflicts between business and labor rather than simply taking the side of business against the working classes.

electoral support from French Canada made it possible for the Liberal Party to form a minority government in 1921, and King was subsequently able to reunite a badly split party. As a result, King would remain in office for all but six of the next twenty-seven years, and the Liberal Party would dominate Canadian politics for most of the twentieth century.

Minority Government

When King assumed the office of prime minister in 1921, Canada was a country still suffering greatly from the economic and political aftermath of World War I. English Canadians were bitter over the failure of French Canadians to support conscription. There was high unemployment and a huge debt incurred because of the war, and the country was badly split over whether trade tariffs protecting Canadian industry were fair. Those living in western Canada were generally opposed to the tariffs; those living in the rest of the country were generally in favor. King's government was unable to satisfy the western provinces' demands for tariff reform, and as a result the Liberal Party came out of the 1925 election with only 99 of 245 seats in the House of Commons. Unable to sustain his minority government, King offered his resignation to Governor-General Julian Byng, requesting him to dissolve Parliament and hold another election. The governor-general, as was

his prerogative, refused and asked the Conservatives to form a government. It lasted only a short time; a new election was then called. King made the governor-general's refusal—which has come to be known as the "King-Byng affair"—an election issue, and he won a majority victory in 1926. King's attitude toward the government of Great Britain was at best an ambivalent one. He was determined that Canada be formally recognized as autonomous, and he helped to lay the groundwork for this event at the Imperial Conferences of 1923 and 1926.

World War II and National Unity

The Conservative Party won the election of 1930. As a result, they were blamed for the economic catastrophe of the Great Depression, and the Liberals under King were back in office by 1935. King maintained his government in office until he retired in 1948. Under his leadership, the country's economy was slowly rebuilt. Progressive reforms in taxation and managing unemployment became government policy. Throughout the next thirteen years, King's leadership was guided by the overriding objective of national unity: He sought to reduce conflict among classes and regions, and especially between French and English.

When World War II came, the question of Canada's willingness to fight on the side of the Allied

The Imperial Conference of 1926

In the years following World War I there was no longer agreement among Britain's former colonies on their role in the British Empire. South Africa and Ireland wanted complete independence, Australia and New Zealand took a more conservative view, and Canada stood in the middle. Mackenzie King's attributes as a conciliator played an important role at the 1926 Imperial Conference, at which a new relationship between Great Britain and the dominions was conceived. The conference led to the creation of the British Commonwealth—a voluntary association of the dominions as "autonomous communities." In each dominion the governor-general would no longer be an agent of the British government but instead merely a representative of the Crown. Canada and the other dominions shared an equal status with Great Britain in the Commonwealth. As a result, diplomatic relations between Canada and Great Britain became formally a relationship between equals.

powers was never in doubt. The memory of World War I's conscription crisis remained, however, and King promised there would be no conscription. As the war dragged on, it became clear that voluntary military service would not be adequate. King delayed for as long as possible and then sought the approval of Canadians by way of a nationwide vote on the issue. French Canadians voted against; English Canadians were mainly in favor. Nonetheless, King managed to avoid a complete rift between French and English Canadians, and there was no repeat of the conscription crisis.

King's Legacy

Mackenzie King was Canada's most politically successful prime minister, leaving behind a legacy of progressive social reforms. He led the country through some of its most trying years with a policy of compromise and pragmatism. In a country characterized by deep regional and cultural divisions since its founding, King's style of politics has been characterized as having divided the country least.

Bibliography

Bliss, Michael. *Right Honourable Men: The Descent of Canadian Politics from Macdonald to Mulroney*. Toronto: HarperCollins, 1994.

Dawson, R. M. *William Lyon Mackenzie King: A Political Biography*. Toronto: Macmillan, 1958.

Granatstein, J. L. *Mackenzie King: His Life and World*. Toronto: McGraw-Hill Ryerson, 1977.

Patrick Malcolmson

Jeane Kirkpatrick

Born: November 19, 1926; Duncan, Oklahoma

First woman to be appointed U.S. ambassador to the United Nations (1981-1985)

Jeane Duane Jordan Kirkpatrick (JEEN DWAYN JOHR-duhn kurk-PAT-rihk) was born in Oklahoma and raised in Illinois; she went to Stephens College in Columbia, Missouri, and Barnard College in New York. She earned her M.A. and Ph.D. from Columbia University. Her career included academic research and writing, journalism, politics, and diplomacy. In 1955 she married Evron Kirkpatrick, with whom she had three sons. She was the first woman to be appointed U.S. ambassador to the United Nations (U.N.).

Refusing to Choose

After earning her master's degree, Kirkpatrick moved to Washington, D.C., and began working at the State Department, where she met her future husband. A George Washington University research position enabled her to explore Chinese communism, and she won a fellowship to study communism in France. Based on her motto, "refuse to choose," Kirkpatrick combined motherhood with career, continuing her academic work from home when she began having children. During the 1960's Kirkpatrick taught part-time at Trinity College, wrote her first book, *The Strategy of Deception: A Study in World-Wide Communist Tactics* (1963), and completed her Ph.D. She then began teaching at Georgetown University, becoming the second woman to win tenure there.

The Kirkpatrick Doctrine

Although Kirkpatrick had been an active Democrat, in the late 1960's she began supporting Republican politicians. She supported President Richard M. Nixon based on his advocacy of traditional moral values and his fervent anticommunism. Her studies led her to develop a policy of support for right-wing authoritarian regimes if that support would weaken left-wing totalitarianism. That perspective came to be known as the Kirkpatrick doctrine, and it was adopted by the Reagan administration in the 1980's.

The 1970's

Kirkpatrick's opposition to communism, belief in a strong military, and liberal views on some social issues linked her with the neoconservative movement. An advocate of improvements in women's status, she wrote the first major American book about women in government. Published in 1974, *Political Woman* enhanced Kirkpa-

Jeane Kirkpatrick *(Library of Congress)*

U.S. delegate to the United Nations Jeane Kirkpatrick in the Security Council chamber. *(Bernard Gotfryd/Archive Photos)*

an invitation to join the American Enterprise Institute. She became the first woman to serve as a senior scholar in that Washington think tank.

During the Jimmy Carter administration (1977-1981) Kirkpatrick wrote a *Commentary* magazine article that won for her the admiration of 1980 presidential candidate Ronald Reagan. "Dictatorships and Double Standards" criticized Carter's foreign policies and earned Kirkpatrick an appointment as Reagan's foreign policy adviser during his presidential campaign. It also led to her appointment as the nation's first woman to serve as ambassador to the United Nations after Reagan won the election.

trick's reputation and helped legitimize the emerging field of women's studies. She represented the United States at the 1975 International Women's Year conference held in West Africa. Kirkpatrick's 1976 book *The New Presidential Elite: Men and Women in National Politics* earned for her

U.N. Ambassador

At the United Nations, Kirkpatrick earned a reputation as a capable negotiator. She was not

---

The Coalition for a Democratic Majority

In 1972 Jeane Kirkpatrick and other Democrats organized the Coalition for a Democratic Majority. Members of the coalition believed that, since the 1960's Civil Rights movement, the Democratic Party had become too radical on some issues. While the coalition continued to advocate a fairly liberal social agenda, its perspectives on foreign policy were more compatible with those held by the Republican Party. They advocated aggressive anticommunist policies and urged the nation's leaders, including President Jimmy

Carter, to develop a stronger position against Soviet communism. They also argued for a stronger national defense. Their combination of progressive positions on social issues with avid anticommunism came to be known as neoconservatism. By the early 1980's, Kirkpatrick and some other coalition members had switched their allegiances to the Republican Party. Other members of the coalition included Daniel Patrick Moynihan, Norman Podhoretz, Midge Decter, Henry Jackson, and Michael Novak.

always popular, however, partly because of anti-American attitudes at the United Nations and partly because she was a woman working in a man's world. During her four years at the United Nations, Kirkpatrick worked to strengthen the United States' standing in the world organization and focused on the dangers of communism in Central and Latin America.

In 1985 Kirkpatrick resigned her U.N. position to return to family and scholarly responsibilities. She continued her association with Georgetown University and the American Enterprise Institute, resuming a heavy schedule of writing that included books, articles, and a syndicated *Los Angeles Times* column. She assumed positions with various foreign-policy related associations, including the Defense Policy Review Board and the Council on Foreign Relations.

Jeane Kirkpatrick in 1985 announcing her move from the Democratic to the Republican Party. *(AP/Wide World Photos)*

Bibliography

Gerson, Allan. *The Kirkpatrick Mission—Diplomacy Without Apology: America at the United Nations, 1981-1985.* New York: Free Press, 1991.

Harrison, Patricia. *Jeane Kirkpatrick, Diplomat.* New York: Chelsea House, 1991.

Kirkpatrick, Jeane J. *Political Woman.* New York: Basic Books, 1974.

Susan MacFarland

Henry A. Kissinger

Born: May 27, 1923; Furth, Germany

U.S. secretary of state (1973-1977), winner of 1973 Nobel Peace Prize

Henry (Heinz) Alfred Kissinger (HEHN-ree HINTZ AL-frehd KIH-sihn-jur), renowned scholar of international relations and dominant American statesman and diplomat of his era, was the first child of Louis and Paula Kissinger. They were Orthodox Jews. The rise of the Nazi political party and growing anti-Semitism made them realize that there was no safe future for their family in Germany, so in 1938 they fled to the United States and settled in New York. The first name given Kissinger at birth, Heinz, was changed to the Anglicized version, Henry.

Henry A. Kissinger *(The Nobel Foundation)*

Early Life

While in high school, Kissinger began working during the day at a factory to help support his family. He attended school at night. After graduating, he was accepted into the City College of New York, which provided free higher education to gifted students. Shortly after his nineteenth birthday, at the beginning of World War II, Kissinger was drafted into the U.S. Army. He was made a citizen of the United States, as were all new immigrant recruits. Kissinger's academic ability landed him in the Counter-Intelligence Corps. Germany was defeated in May, 1945, and occupied by the Allies. In June, 1945, Kissinger was assigned to command a new counterintelligence detachment whose job was to restore order in a section of Germany. Kissinger had to work with the German officials and at the same time uncover dangerous Nazis among them.

After completing his military service, Kissinger enrolled at Harvard University on a scholarship and with other financial aid. He chose government and philosophy as his main fields of study. He graduated summa cum laude (with highest honors) three years later. His academic achievements produced an additional scholarship; two years later he had earned his M.A., and two years following that, his Ph.D. His Ph.D. thesis made him more widely known in intellectual and editorial circles. It was entitled *A World Restored: Castlereagh, Metternich, and the Restoration of Peace, 1812-1822* (1957). While researching this analysis, Kissinger developed many of the ideas that shaped his future policies.

The Dawning of Power

By July, 1959, Kissinger had achieved tenure as a Harvard professor and had published books and articles on foreign policy. He also had served the government in various consulting jobs. His route to real power was opened in December, 1968, when President-elect Richard M. Nixon appointed him to be his assistant for national security affairs. The new president wanted to run U.S. foreign policy from the White House. He and Kissinger had character traits in common, and they thought alike in many ways. Kissinger soon became one of Nixon's closest advisers and contributed significantly to foreign policy achievements during Nixon's administration: opening the door to China,

Henry A. Kissinger with Chinese prime minister Zhou Enlai in 1971 at the Chinese government guest house in Beijing. *(National Archives/Nixon Project)*

Ping-Pong Diplomacy

When Henry Kissinger took office as Richard Nixon's assistant for national security affairs, the United States had not recognized the communist government of China for more than twenty years. One of Kissinger's first foreign-policy goals was to change that situation. By 1969, China had resumed contacts with many other nations and was interested in establishing trade relations with them. In April, 1971, the U.S. State Department reported to President Nixon that Zhou Enlai, China's premier, had indicated to a neutral diplomat that dramatic improvement might be possible in relations with the United States. The State Department's report also noted that China had sent its table tennis team to Japan to participate in the thirty-first *World Table Tennis Championship* in April. The U.S. table tennis team was also competing in that tournament.

One of the young American players rode on a bus with the Chinese players on an outing during the tournament, and he became friendly with the Chinese team captain. The next day they exchanged gifts. A few days later, the Chinese captain invited the American team to visit China, and the U.S. government assented. The U.S. players were given a warm welcome in China and were even received by Zhou Enlai himself. They, in turn, invited the Chinese team to visit the United States. Encouraged by the opening, Kissinger made a secret visit to China in July, 1971, for talks with Zhou. He returned with an invitation for Nixon to visit China. The historic "first"—the first time a U.S. president had visited the mainland of China—occurred on February 21, 1972.

U.S. Middle East Policy, 1973-1974

After the founding of the state of Israel in 1948, U.S. policy in the Middle East was based on the U.S. desire to support the survival of Israel while maintaining relations with the oil-rich Arab states. In 1973, Arab-Israeli relations became particularly hostile. In October of that year, Egypt and Syria attacked Israel, using newly acquired Russian military equipment. Israel requested immediate U.S. military aid. After the United States resupplied the Israeli army, Israel counterattacked and pushed back the Arab forces. At this point, U.S. secretary of state Henry Kissinger's primary problem was to convince Israel not to press its advantage and make the situation even more dangerous and destructive. Shuttling back and forth between the two camps (they refused to meet face-to-face), he was able to create a less hostile environment, assuring both the continued existence of Israel and U.S. access to Middle East oil.

signing a treaty with the Soviet Union to limit the manufacture of nuclear weapons, drafting the Vietnam peace agreement, and reducing tensions in the Arab-Israeli territorial conflicts.

U.S. secretary of state Henry Kissinger (right) with Soviet leader Leonid Brezhnev. *(Archive Photos/London Daily Express)*

Secretary of State

In September, 1973, Nixon appointed Kissinger secretary of state. Millions of Americans admired and respected Kissinger, but not all felt that way. Many remembered his part in the secret bombing and invasion of Cambodia and the Christmas Day bombing of the North Vietnamese capital, Hanoi. His reputation was also tainted by his involvement in the White House's clandestine use of wiretaps between 1969 and 1971, purportedly to reveal who was leaking national security information to the press.

A month after Kissinger was named secretary of state, he and Le Duc Tho, North Vietnam's participant in the Vietnam peace talks, were jointly awarded the Nobel Peace Prize for the Vietnam peace accords. Tho rejected the prize, saying that "peace has not yet been established in South Vietnam." Kissinger sent the American ambassador to Norway to accept his prize, and he donated his share of the money to a scholarship fund for children of servicemen killed in Vietnam.

Kissinger's career survived Nixon's August, 1974, fall in the Watergate scandal, and he was asked by Nixon's successor, Gerald R. Ford, to continue serving as secretary of state. Ford and Kissinger proved to be a relaxed, trusting team. Diplomatic challenges and accomplishments lay ahead, including Kissinger's laying the groundwork for moderates in a number of African nations to rule their countries and to thwart Soviet influence in Africa.

Five years after leaving public service, Kissinger established a highly successful consulting firm with offices in New York and Washington, D.C., offering his foreign-policy expertise to private corporations. He brought in several others who had had high-profile government careers in diplomacy. In addition to his consulting business, Kissinger served on various corporate boards.

Kissinger's opening of U.S.-China relations after twenty years of mutual distrust had a lasting impact on the world's political and economic structures. Under President Nixon, Kissinger established the National Security Council (NSC) as the primary executor of U.S. foreign policy. The council continued to fill this role in succeeding presidencies.

Bibliography

Bundy, William. *A Tangled Web: The Making of Foreign Policy in the Nixon Presidency*. New York: Hill and Wang, 1998.

Isaacson, Walter. *Kissinger: A Biography*. New York: Simon & Schuster, 1992.

Kalb, Bernard, and Marvin Kalb. *Kissinger*. Boston: Little, Brown, 1974.

Kissinger, Henry. *Henry Kissinger: White House Years*. Boston: Little, Brown, 1979.

Ollie Shuman

Horatio Herbert Kitchener

Born: June 24, 1850; near Listowel, County Kerry, Ireland
Died: June 5, 1916; off the Orkney Islands, Scotland

British military leader, secretary of war (1914-1916)

Horatio Herbert Kitchener (hoh-RAY-shee-oh HUR-burt KIHT-cheh-nur) was the son of a lieutenant colonel who retired from the military because of his wife's ill health. Significantly for the future general, his father instilled in him a sense of discipline and honor as well as a belief in British superiority. Only when the boy was thirteen did he attend a formal school, where he excelled in mathematics. In 1868 he entered the Royal Military Academy at Woolwich, England, and was commissioned in the Royal Engineers three years later.

Horatio Herbert Kitchener *(Library of Congress)*

Early Military Career

Kitchener spent most of the next twenty-five years at various postings throughout the Middle East. As an engineer, he was part of teams that surveyed Palestine, Cyprus, and the Sinai Peninsula. He served as an adviser to the Egyptian army and saw action against the Sudanese. Fascinated by the cultures of the Middle East, he learned Arabic in order to work more effectively with local governments. He even disguised himself as a native to obtain intelligence and to gain a better understanding of native culture and customs. He also became a loner who rarely took others into his confidence, a characteristic he retained for the rest of his life.

In 1892 Kitchener was appointed commander in chief of the Egyptian army. When French interests appeared to focus on the upper Nile, the British government ordered Kitchener to invade the Sudan, capture Khartoum, and advance southward to claim the entire Nile River for Great Britain. In 1898 British forces destroyed the Sudanese army at Omdurman, ending the River War. Kitchener pushed southward to Fashoda, where the French had established an outpost. The French agreed to withdraw from the Nile for territorial considerations elsewhere, and the Sudan was added to the British Empire. Kitchener was created Baron Kitchener of Khartoum and was appointed governor-general of the Sudan.

South Africa

Events in South Africa soon led to another imperial war for Great Britain. British pressures on two small Boer (Dutch South African) republics led to a Boer attack on British South Africa in 1899. With a total manpower potential of only eighty-three thousand, the Boers declared war on

The Battle of Omdurman

Omdurman lies on the western bank of the Nile near the confluence of the Blue and White Niles. In 1885 Sudanese Muslim dervishes, under the guidance of their spiritual leader, the Mahdi, captured Khartoum, across the Nile from Omdurman. They wiped out a British garrison. In 1896 Horatio Herbert Kitchener was ordered into the Sudan to establish British control of the upper Nile. He advanced his army of twenty-six thousand men cautiously, building a railroad as he went to guarantee his supply lines. On Sep-

tember 2, 1898, a force of forty thousand dervishes attacked his entrenched and well-equipped army. Dervish bravery was no match for artillery and machine guns, and few Sudanese reached British lines. More than ten thousand Mahdists were killed, and five thousand were captured. British casualties were limited to five hundred. Kitchener became a national hero, and his victory at Omdurman guaranteed British control of Sudan.

the greatest empire in the world. The Boers were initially successful, and British counterattacks ended in disaster. Field Marshall Sir F. S. Roberts was appointed commander in chief, with Kitchener as his chief of staff. Within a year the conventional Boer armies were defeated, largely because of Kitchener's reorganization of the supply system. Roberts returned to London, leaving Kitchener to finish the war. Despite being beaten in the field, the Boers refused to accept defeat. Relying upon their mobility, Boers developed a guerrilla strategy which Kitchener defeated only at great cost to the Boers. The Peace of Vereeniging in May, 1902, made Kitchener a national hero in Great Britain.

World War I

Kitchener was awarded a viscountcy for his South African success and was posted to India. He reorganized the Indian army and was promoted to field marshall in 1909. He then returned to Egypt, where he served until the outbreak of World War I. In 1914 Kitchener was appointed secretary of state for war. He believed that the war would be a protracted one, an opinion that was unpopular with the politicians running the war. His tendency to oversee everything and to hold his own counsel did not blend well with the

civilian control of the war effort. Moreover, despite knowing what needed doing, he was unable to delegate in order to get things done. By 1915 he no longer controlled war production, and he was removed from strategic planning in 1916. On June 5, 1916, on his way to Russia, his ship struck a German mine and sank. Kitchener was presumed drowned.

Kitchener was one of the great builders of the British Empire during the Victorian age. He fought and won colonial wars and administered colonial possessions in the best imperial style. He saw his duty as building a better British world. During World War I it was his visage on recruiting posters that called on young Britons to volunteer for service for King and country. Kitchener's system, when carried through by others, provided Britain with a global capability for fighting a total war. Sadly for his legacy, the horrors of trench warfare, as well as attacks on his reputation by those seeking a scapegoat, tarnished his image. His memory became a reminder more of national sacrifice than of national heroism. The later loss of empire also eroded his reputation, for symbols of imperial greatness were discarded as the empire crumbled. Still, Kitchener's life offers significant insight into the dynamics of late nineteenth-century imperial Britain.

Guerrilla Warfare in South Africa

When the conventional forces of the Boers were defeated in mid-1900, Boer leaders reverted to their traditional style of warfare. Using highly mobile cavalry commandos, Boers hit British units and then vanished, only to reappear elsewhere to harass British positions. Horatio Herbert Kitchener believed that war against the guerrillas could be won only by denying them supplies and support. With the Boer republics surrounded by British possessions, no outside aid to the Boers was possible. To limit Boer mobility, a series of defensive blockhouses was constructed along supply lines. These were later connected by fences in lines across the veldt, further limiting Boer movement. Kitchener eliminated local support by ordering the destruction of Boer farms and by removing some 120,000 Boer women and children to secure areas policed by British troops. More than 20,000 died from disease in these crowded and unsanitary "concentration camps," as they were called. Military trains were protected by forcing Boer civilians to ride on flat cars in front of engines. Special mounted units, called "flying columns," were also created. Operating as their prey did, they pursued Boer commandos mercilessly, never allowing them respite. By 1902 more than 500,000 British troops from throughout the empire were in South Africa. Finally, after eighteen months of bitter and ugly warfare, Boer guerrilla leaders capitulated.

Bibliography

Cassar, George H. *Kitchener: Architect of Victory*. London: William Kimber, 1977.

Churchill, Winston. *The River War*. 2 vols. London: Longmans, Green, 1899.

English, John. *Kitchener: An Illustrated History*. Waterloo, Ontario, Canada: Wilfrid Laurier University Press, 1983.

Magnus, Philip. *Kitchener: Portrait of an Imperialist*. New York: E. P. Dutton, 1958.

Royle, Trevor. *The Kitchener Enigma*. London: Michael Joseph, 1985.

Smithers, A. J. *The Fighting Nation: Lord Kitchener and His Armies*. London: L. Cooper, 1994.

Spies, S. B. *Methods of Barbarism? Roberts and Kitchener and Civilians in the Boer Republics, January 1900–May 1902*. Capetown, South Africa: Human and Rousseau, 1977.

Warner, Philip. *Kitchener: The Man Behind the Legend*. London: Hamish Hamilton, 1985.

William S. Brockington, Jr.

Ralph Klein

Born: November 1, 1942; Calgary, Alberta, Canada

Canadian political leader, premier of Alberta (elected 1993)

Born in 1942, Ralph Klein (RALF KLIN) would achieve both acclaim and notoriety as a municipal and provincial politician in the Canadian province of Alberta. Klein grew up in his place of birth, Calgary, Alberta. He worked in public relations for charitable organizations before becoming a full-time journalist—a reporter for a Calgary television station—from 1969 to 1980. Part of his responsibility was covering civic affairs, and it was in this capacity that Klein became well known to the citizens of Calgary.

Early Political Career

In 1980 Klein was elected mayor of Calgary. He was reelected in 1983 and 1986 with the largest margins of victory in the city's history. Although only a civic politician, Klein gained national attention during the energy crisis of the early 1980's when he publicly complained about eastern Canadians moving to Calgary to find jobs in Alberta's booming oil industry. In 1988 Klein again received national attention when his city successfully hosted that year's Winter Olympic Games.

Provincial Politics and Premier

After gaining prominence at the municipal level, Klein moved into provincial politics as a member of the party that had held power since the early 1970's, the Progressive Conservatives. Winning a Calgary-area seat in the provincial legislature in the 1989 election, Klein was quickly appointed to the cabinet as minister of the environment by Alberta premier Don Getty. In 1992, a year before an election needed to be called, Getty decided to leave politics. A leadership convention was called, and Klein announced his decision to seek the position. He won a difficult fight for the leadership and became the new premier of the province. He called an election in 1993 and proceeded to win a large majority. He proved personally popular, having traveled around the province with his wife, Colleen, campaigning from a mobile home.

Radical Change

Once in office, Klein instituted a series of changes that collectively became known as the Klein revolution. Essentially, these changes involved massive budgetary cuts, including layoffs in the civil service, in an effort to reduce the

Alberta premier Ralph Klein (right) with Canadian prime minister Brian Mulroney in 1992. *(Corbis/Reuters)*

The Progressive Conservative Party in Alberta

The Progressive Conservative Party in Alberta began as the Conservative Party in nineteenth-century Canada. It gained the prefix "Progressive" in the 1940's, when the remnants of a party by that name officially joined the Conservatives. The party was more successful at the provincial level than it was nationally. One exception prior to the 1970's was the province of Alberta, where the Progressive Conservatives (also simply called the Conservatives) had never won an election. This situation changed in 1971, when under the leadership of Peter Lougheed the party captured power. Lougheed instituted a series of reforms that involved considerable government intervention in the economy. The party proceeded to win every election for many years, usually by massive majorities. Lougheed's successors were Don Getty, who proved unpopular, and then the much more popular Ralph Klein. Klein instituted a series of radical fiscal reforms much at odds with Conservative policy of the 1970's.

province's budgetary deficit. Raising taxes was not an option in Alberta, a province which (unlike every other province in Canada) did not have a sales tax. Klein's cuts proved controversial in many quarters, especially in the capital city of Edmonton. Edmonton lost so many civil service jobs that both the city's population and its property values declined. Welfare payments were cut so much that Alberta's neighboring province, British Columbia, complained that Albertans on welfare were moving to British Columbia. Despite the changes, both Klein's personal popularity and support for his government remained high. The support was aided by the news that the fiscal belt-tightening had led to the elimination of the deficit and to a budgetary surplus.

Seeking a Second Mandate

The true test of the popularity of Klein's policies would come only in the form of a provincial election campaign. After nearly four years in power, Klein called an election in 1997. Although his government won fewer seats than it had in 1993, Klein and the Progressive Conservatives easily recaptured power for another four years. In the aftermath of the election, the Klein government began to put money back into some of the programs that had previously been cut. Klein's fiscal policies became a model followed by other provinces and even by the government of Canada. His popularity in Alberta led to speculation that he would move on to the federal level, but Klein ruled out such a move, citing the resistance of his wife, Colleen.

Bibliography

Dabbs, Frank. *Ralph Klein: A Maverick Life*. Vancouver: Greystone Books, 1995.

Lisac, Mark. *The Klein Revolution*. Edmonton: NeWest Press, 1995.

Taft, Kevin. *Shredding the Public Interest: Ralph Klein and Twenty-five Years of One-Party Government*. Edmonton: University of Alberta Press, 1997.

Steve Hewitt

Helmut Kohl

Born: April 3, 1930; Ludwigshafen am Rhein, Germany

Chancellor of West Germany, then of a reunited Germany, for sixteen years (1982-1998)

Born in 1930 in the Palatinate region of Germany, Helmut Michael Kohl (HEHL-mewt MIH-kah-ehl KOHL) studied law, history, and social and political science at the Universities of Frankfurt and Heidelberg; at Heidelberg he earned a Ph.D. in history in 1958.

Road to the Chancellorship

Kohl entered politics while still in high school, when he founded the Christian Democratic Union's (CDU) youth organization in his hometown. While a student, he was elected to the executive board of the CDU in the Palatinate. Kohl's rise in the party hierarchy was swift. Elected to the Rhineland Palatinate state legislature in 1959, he was elected prime minister of Rhineland Palatinate in 1969 and reelected in 1971 and 1975. Kohl presided over a well-run state government that initiated a number of needed reforms.

In the federal election of 1969, the CDU lost power to the Social Democratic Party (SPD) after twenty years of governing the country. Consequently, the CDU engaged in a search for a new standard-bearer. When the Christian Democrats lost a second national election to the Social Democrats in 1973, Kohl was elected CDU party chairperson. He became the opposition leader in the Bundestag, West Germany's lower house. Kohl be-came chancellor in 1982, in the middle of the legislative term. This occurred because the SPD's minor coalition partner, the Free Democrats, switched alliances, thus toppling SPD chancellor Helmut Schmidt. Kohl called for federal elections in 1983 to obtain the electorate's endorsement. Kohl held the chancellorship for the next sixteen years.

German Unification

Kohl's main contributions to politics came in foreign affairs: He was the architect of Germany's unification in 1990 and was one of the chief engineers of the further integration of Europe through a common European currency. Germany had been divided into West Germany and communist East Germany since the end of World War II. After the fall of the Berlin Wall on November 9, 1989, and the end of the communist government of East Germany, Kohl at once negotiated unification of Germany. He was able to obtain the approval of the United States, Britain, France, and the Soviet Union for German unification.

Helmut Kohl *(CNP/Archive Photos)*

German chancellor Helmut Kohl (right) greets NATO secretary-general Javier Solana at a reception for the Trilateral Commission's annual meeting in Berlin in 1998. *(AP/Wide World Photos)*

His promise to keep Germany in the North Atlantic Treaty Organization (NATO) won the support of the United States and Britain, and his pledge to integrate Germany further into the European Union (EU) won over a reluctant France. Finally, Kohl's offer to reduce the German army by one-third and to pay repatriation costs for the Soviet army gained approval from the Soviet Union's Mikhail Gorbachev. The Western allies helped persuade Gorbachev that the united Germany should remain in NATO.

After the Berlin Wall fell, East Germans held their first free election in 1989. Kohl negotiated terms of unification with this democratically elected government and was rewarded by a stunning electoral victory in the first free all-German elections (1990). Kohl held to his pledge of closer integration of Germany into Europe. In cooperation with France, Germany became the leading proponent of the Maastricht Treaty, which called for the replacement of European national currencies with a new European currency. The aim was to

European Integration: The Maastricht Treaty

In December, 1991, leaders of the member countries of the European Community (the EC, or European Common Market) met in Maastricht, the Netherlands, to draft a treaty for closer economic cooperation. The Maastricht Treaty called for a new European currency—the euro— to replace the national currencies of European countries. The German deutsche mark was the most solid and least inflationary of European currencies, and many Germans feared devaluation of their money in the conversion to the new currency. Helmut Kohl, however, was more interested in the near-certainty that a common currency would weaken the sovereignty of the national states and would lead to greater European interdependence.

Kohl's sacrifice of the deutsche mark to facilitate European unity led to the breakthrough needed for the establishment of the European Union (EU) as the successor organization to the EC. The EU went into effect late in 1993. The new euro currency was to be introduced between 1999 and 2002. The Maastricht Treaty was a quantum leap toward a united Europe. In helping lead the way, Kohl fulfilled the pledges he made during Germany's unification that a united Germany embedded in a united Europe would prevent a renewal of German nationalism and hegemony.

"The Footsteps of God in History"

Otto von Bismarck, chancellor of Germany from 1871 to 1890, played the major role in the original unification of Germany in 1871. In reference to his part in the unification, Bismarck wrote in his memoirs that when a statesman can hear the footsteps of God in history, he must try to grab the corner of God's mantle and let himself be swept along by it. Chancellor Helmut Kohl, like Bismarck, seized a historic moment: In Kohl's case, it came after the fall of the Berlin Wall, which had separated East and West Berlin, in 1989. Kohl immediately sought the reunification of Germany. Germany's Social Democratic Party opposed immediate unification; it argued for the continuance of the German Democratic Republic, at least for a time, or a German confederation. Kohl, however, prevailed. Employing great diplomatic skill and an uncanny sense of timing, he persuaded the countries of Western Europe to grant full sovereignty to a reunited Germany. These were the same countries that had defeated Germany in World War II. Kohl convinced them that anchoring and integrating a sovereign, united Germany into both the North Atlantic Treaty Organization (NATO) and the European Union (EU) was the way to prevent a resurgence of dangerous German nationalism.

make the economic—and, by extension, political—integration of Europe virtually irreversible.

Leaving Office

Kohl managed to remain in office through many domestic crises. After gaining his party's leadership in 1976, he tightly controlled the party's apparatus and defeated all challengers to his position. A consequence of this domination was the failure to groom a successor and cultivate younger party leadership. During his last term of office, a gridlock between the lower and upper houses of the legislature made it nearly impossible to introduce several overdue structural reforms. The integration of bankrupt East Germany with the West German economy, gridlock on reforms, and an economic recession resulted in more than four million people being unemployed. Germans blamed this economic setback on a lack of leadership by Kohl. Kohl, at sixty-eight, insisted on running for a fifth term in September, 1998. The challenger, Gerhard

Helmut Kohl campaigning at a Christian Democratic Party rally in July, 1998. The banner in the background protests, "We've had enough of Kohl. Thanks for the great job." *(Reuters/Fabrizio Bensch/Archive Photos)*

Schröder, campaigned on a reform pledge to revive the economy. As the polls predicted, Schröder and the SPD, in coalition with the Green Party, won the election. Kohl's CDU garnered only 35 percent of the vote.

Place in History

By the time of his defeat, in terms of longevity as German chancellor, Kohl occupied second place only to Otto von Bismarck, the unifier of Germany in the late nineteenth century (1871-1890). Kohl's place in history will be alongside such chancellors as Bismarck and Konrad Adenauer, postwar chancellor from 1949 to 1963. When Kohl left office, he had completed Adenauer's unfinished post-World War II agenda for Germany: a unified, democratic, and free-enterprise Germany, rooted in the West and integrated with Europe. Bismarck had unified Germany in 1871; Kohl unified Germany in 1990. Bismarck had dominated European diplomacy in his day (sometimes called the Age of Bismarck); Kohl in the 1990's was the driving force behind European integration.

Bibliography

Ardagh, John. *Germany and the Germans*. 3d ed. New York: Penguin Books, 1995.

Bernstein, Jerry. *The Wall Came Tumbling Down*. New York: Outlet, 1990.

Prettie, Terrence. *Velvet Chancellors: A History of Post War Germany*. New Haven, Conn.: Yale University Press, 1987.

Herbert Luft

Juscelino Kubitschek

Born: September 12, 1902; Diamantina, Brazil
Died: August 22, 1976; Near Resende, Brazil

President of Brazil (1956-1961)

Juscelino Kubitschek de Oliveira (zhew-seh-LEE-new KEW-bih-chehk thee oh-lee-VAY-ee-rah), president of Brazil and builder of Brasília, was born in the state of Minas Gerais, a stark, mountainous region in the Brazilian interior. He was the son of a widowed mother who eked out a meager income for her children as a school-teacher. His father was the descendant of a Czech immigrant to Brazil.

Early Career

Resolving to rise in life, he decided to become a doctor, working as a telegraph operator and studying at the medical school in Belo Horizonte (a planned modern city, built as the new capital of Minas Gerais at the end of the nineteenth century. He developed his skills as a surgeon through study in France. Upon his return to Brazil he married into a socially prominent family and established a thriving practice in Belo Horizonte.

Coming to the attention of the local political establishment, he was named mayor of Belo Horizonte in 1940. Minas Gerais benefited financially from increased world demand for minerals during World War II. Kubitschek used revenue from exports to enhance the physical infrastructure of his city by improving roads, electricity, and sewage. He also inaugurated a modernist architectural complex in the city, bringing together the leading Brazilian architects, landscape designers, and painters.

Kubitschek was elected governor of Minas Gerais in 1950. He expanded the number of roads, bridges, hydroelectric plants, schools, and clinics. Improvements in transportation and energy were fundamental in order for the state to achieve economic development and modernization.

President of Brazil

Kubitschek resolved to run for the presidency of Brazil in 1955. He based his appeal on an alliance with populist political forces and upon a program of national economic development that outlined a sequence of goals that his government would achieve. He promised that during his five-year presidential term there would be "fifty years of progress in five." He further promised that he would move the federal capital from Rio de Janeiro to a new city in the central highlands, to be named Brasília.

Kubitschek won election to the presidency and began to put his program of national development into effect. Moreover, he began construction of Brasília, which was completed in 1960, the year

Juscelino Kubitschek (left) meets with President Kennedy at the White House in 1961. *(Library of Congress)*

Brasília and National Development

Historically Brazil's population has been concentrated along the coast. Brasília was built in the central highlands of Brazil in order to transfer the center of power and population to the interior of the country. Inaugurated in 1960, Brasília is today a metropolis of more than a million people. The building of Brasília highlighted Jascelino Kubitschek's effort to modernize the country. The construction of the futuristic city brought together the country's chief architects, planners, painters, sculptors, and landscape designers. It was a symbol of Kubitschek's goals for national economic development and modernization. His plan for economic expansion concentrated on the development of industry and physical infrastructure. The Kubitschek government had as its goals specific increases in the production of iron, steel, automobiles, roads, electricity, and so on. It achieved dramatic increases in production together with a wider distribution of national income. These accomplishments made of Kubitschek a symbol of successful, democratic civilian government in Brazil.

before he left office. Although his presidency was successful in terms of achieving its industrialization goals, it spurred a cycle of inflation that burdened the Brazilian economy to the end of the twentieth century. Moreover, he was scorned by conservative and military forces for his political alliance with populist and radical elements and for the alleged corruption of his administration.

Kubitschek campaigned again for the presidency in 1964. However, his ambitions were cut short when the armed forces overthrew the government and set up a military regime that lasted until 1985. Kubitschek's political rights were denied, and he went into exile in Europe and the United States. Upon returning to Brazil he became an investment banking executive. He died in 1976 in an automobile accident between São Paulo and Rio de Janeiro, near the town of Resende. Some have alleged that his death may have been the result of an assassination plot.

Bibliography

Alexander, Robert J. *Juscelino Kubitschek and the Development of Brazil.* Athens: Ohio University Center for International Studies, 1991.

Medaglia, Francisco. *Juscelino Kubitschek, President of Brazil: The Life of a Self-Made Man.* New York: 1959.

Riedinger, Edward A. "The Making of the President, Brazil, 1955: The Campaign of Juscelino Kubitschek." Dissertation, University of Chicago, 1978.

Edward A. Riedinger

Juscelino Kubitschek launched the construction of Brasília, the new city inaugurated as capital of Brazil in 1960. *(Archive Photos)*

Robert M. La Follette, Jr.

Born: February 6, 1895; Madison, Wisconsin
Died: February 24, 1953; Washington, D.C.

U.S. senator (1925-1946)

Robert Marion La Follette, Jr. (RO-burt MEH-ree-uhn lah FOL-eht JEW-nyur), was the son of U.S. senator Robert Marion La Follette, Sr., from Wisconsin and Belle La Follette, the first woman to graduate from the University of Wisconsin School of Law. After attending the University of Wisconsin for three years, La Follette dropped out because of illness. A year later he became his father's personal secretary in Washington, D.C. In 1930 he married Rachel Wilson Young. They had two sons, Joseph Oden and Bronson Cutting. A progressive crusader by virtue of his reform-minded upbringing, La Follette served with distinction as the U.S. senator from Wisconsin.

Controversial Campaigns

La Follette, Jr., also known as Young Bob, inherited the family political mantle in June, 1925, when his father, U.S. senator "Fighting Bob" La Follette, died. Young Bob was selected to replace his father in the Senate. He had just turned thirty years of age, the minimum age requirement to serve as a senator. La Follette had run his father's presidential campaign the previous year and had developed expertise in understanding tax laws and private monopolies. Although his father lost the presidential election to Calvin Coolidge, Young Bob came away from that election with a better understanding of both state and national politics. Reelected in 1928, La Follette became a transitional figure in the history of the twentieth-century reform movement. He linked progressivism with urban liberalism, which took hold in the 1920's and flourished in the 1930's and beyond.

La Follette developed a national following during the 1930's. He was one of the first public figures to identify a lack of "purchasing power" as the root cause of the Great Depression. Formu-

lating a prosaic plan for combating the Depression, he suggested that the federal government help the unemployed by the massive expansion of public works, a review of economic planning,

Robert M. La Follette, Jr. *(Library of Congress)*

The 1924 Presidential Election

In 1924 conservatives dominated both major political parties. Wisconsin senator Robert M. La Follette, Sr., a nominal Republican, broke from the party when Calvin Coolidge was nominated for president. La Follette served as a leader of the Senate insurgents. He was author of several resolutions calling for investigation of the Teapot Dome and other oil leases.

At the invitation of the Conference for Progressive Political Action, La Follette accepted the presidential nomination of a new Progressive Party, which was backed by the Committee of Forty-eight, the Socialist Party, the railroad unions, and the American Federation of Labor. La Follette's platform denounced the control of industry and government by private monopolies. It favored public ownership of water, power, and railroads. The platform also addressed farm-relief considerations, including the lowering of taxes for people with moderate incomes and other legislation to aid the less privileged.

La Follette's presidential race started off well but almost immediately fell on hard times. The senator managed to raise only $200,000 for his campaign, compared with Democratic candidate John Davis's $1 million and Calvin Coolidge's $4 million. During the campaign Davis and Coolidge largely ignored each other and attacked La Follette. Coolidge won a landslide victory. La Follette was able to carry only Wisconsin, but he did come in second in twelve western states. He received nearly 5 million votes, 17 percent of the votes cast.

and total tax reform. La Follette was a major critic of the Republican president, Herbert Hoover, and became a supporter of President Franklin D. Roosevelt's New Deal. Yet he was also one of the New Deal's critics. As chairman of the Senate Civil Liberties Committee in the late 1930's, La Follette reached the height of his national prominence. He helped expose the way many employers tried to prevent their workers from organizing by using brutal force to keep them from signing up with unions.

The World War II Years

Prior to December 7, 1941, and Japan's surprise attack on the U.S. naval base at Pearl Harbor, La Follette was a staunch isolationist who wanted the United States to remain uninvolved in the general affairs of Europe. Having served as a secretary to his father during World War I, he was well aware of war profiteering and the social upheaval that occurs during crisis situations. The senator supported Roosevelt's administration of the war. He went along with the monetary conduct of the war but tried, as his father had, to devise taxes that would pay the war costs from war profits. During and after World War II, La Follette became a cautious internationalist who urged the United States to use its influence and power to keep the Soviet Union and communism in check so that their expansion would be limited.

World War II was La Follette's most troubling time. During his political career he had developed a well-established progressive philosophy that sustained him through much of his adult life. However, the complex issues and diverse problems brought about by the war caused La Follette to look inward and reevaluate his ideas. At the war's end the state of Wisconsin was probably the most isolationist of the forty-eight states, and it may have been the most liberal. The La Follette tradition was alive and well. Farmers and organized labor were at odds with La Follette, however, because they felt that he had not supported their causes sufficiently during the war. He had inadvertently alienated important segments of these two groups and thereby weakened his base of electoral support.

La Follette had one more legislative success in his twenty-one-year career as U.S. senator. Congress had lost much of the prestige and power it had before World War II, because during the war much power had shifted to the presidency. To return prestige and power to Congress, La Follette authored and guided through the Congress the Legislative Reorganization Act of 1946.

La Follette's Limitations

Despite La Follette's success as a senator, he possessed limitations as a political leader. In 1934 he abandoned the Republican Party to help create the Progressive Party of Wisconsin with his brother Philip. Philip ran successfully for governor of Wisconsin. Robert never gave the party the consistent, firm leadership required for it to survive and grow. He also began to devote less and less time

Robert La Follette greeting women supporters affiliated with the Progressive movement in 1924. *(Library of Congress)*

to the specific issues that concerned the people of Wisconsin. He was defeated by Joseph R. McCarthy in the autumn elections of 1946, a defeat largely attributable to neglect on his part.

La Follette was a complex man who was never comfortable in front of the masses. He regarded public life as something that was to be endured

Progressivism

Progressivism, or the Progressive movement, embodied a reform spirit that sought improvements in social justice, an increase in political democracy, and an end to business monopolies. In the first half of the twentieth century, both organizations and individuals were involved in preaching the progressive themes of reforming social institutions, controlling abusive power, and improving scientific efficiency. Concern existed at all levels of society, but the vanguard pressing for reform was rooted in the middle class. Many progressives were motivated by personal indignation at corporate abuses of power and political corruption. This indignation expressed itself in general opposition to the two major political parties. Many progressives stepped back from party politics but not from the government. They realized that they needed the government to obtain the leverage necessary to implement reforms.

rather than enjoyed. After he was defeated in 1946 he was offered many public positions by president Harry S Truman, but he turned them all down in order to remain in the private sector. Evidently La Follette became increasingly unhappy, and at age fifty-eight, in February of 1953, he committed suicide.

Bibliography

Johnson, Roger T. *Robert M. La Follette, Jr., and the Decline of the Progressive Party in Wisconsin.* Madison: State Historical Society of Wisconsin for the Department of History, University of Wisconsin, 1964.

La Follette, Philip Fox. *Adventure in Politics: The Memoirs of Philip La Follette.* Edited by Donald Young. New York: Holt, Rinehart, and Winston, 1970.

La Follette, Robert M. *La Follette's Autobiography.* Madison: University of Wisconsin Press, 1960.

Maney, Patrick J. *"Young Bob" La Follette: A Biography of Robert M. La Follette, Jr., 1895-1953.* Columbia: University of Missouri Press, 1978.

Thelen, David P. *Robert M. La Follette and the Insurgent Spirit.* Madison: University of Wisconsin Press, 1985.

Earl R. Andresen

Henri-Marie La Fontaine

Born: April 22, 1854; Brussels, Belgium
Died: May 14, 1943; Brussels, Belgium

Belgian jurist and peace activist, winner of 1913 Nobel Peace Prize

At age twenty-three, Henri-Marie La Fontaine (o-REE mah-REE lah-fo-TEHN) became counsel at the Brussels Court of Appeal after having studied law at the Free University of Brussels. Over the next sixteen years, he became one of Belgium's leading jurists, writing several legal works.

Energetic Reformer

Appointed secretary of a women's school in 1878, La Fontaine became an advocate for women's rights. He joined the European peace movement when British pacifist Hodgson Pratt

Henri-Marie La Fontaine *(The Nobel Foundation)*

visited Belgium in the 1880's. Becoming secretary-general of the Belgian Society for Arbitration and Peace in 1889, he participated in virtually all peace congresses held over the next twenty-five years. In 1907, he became president of the International Peace Bureau, based in Bern, Switzerland.

His reforming zeal led him into politics. Elected to Belgium's Senate as a moderate Social Democrat, he represented several constituencies over a thirty-six-year period, was the Senate's secretary for thirteen years, and was one of its vice presidents for fourteen years. Throughout his career, he showed great interest in education, labor, and foreign affairs. He introduced bills reforming primary education and mine inspection and supported the 1926 adoption of the eight-hour work day. He spoke out to demand arbitration in the Boer War, to affirm a 1911 arbitration treaty with Italy, and later, to support the League of Nations, economic union with Luxembourg, and disarmament. From 1893 to 1940, he occupied a chair of international law at the Free University of Brussels.

Visionary in Difficult Times

La Fontaine joined the Interparliamentary Union, which had been established in 1889 by parliamentarians from various nations to discuss international issues and encourage the arbitration of disputes. To him, the union was a precursor to world government. An enthusiastic member, he was chairman of its Juridical Committee and served on commissions preparing a model world parliament and arbitration treaty. In 1895, La Fontaine and Paul Otlet established the International Bibliographical Institute, a scheme to document everything noteworthy published

Arbitration

Arbitration is the peaceful settlement of disputes by the legally binding judgment of a third party, chosen by the parties of the dispute. In international law, the parties decide to submit to an agreement or compromise, hearings are held, and a judge or tribunal issues a decision known as an award. The concept of arbitration is ancient. However, modern arbitration has its roots in the 1794 Jay Treaty between Britain and the United States, which provided mixed commissions to solve disputes. In 1907, the establishment of the Permanent Court of Arbitration, later replaced by the Permanent Court of International Justice (the World Court) in The Hague, enhanced international arbitration processes. Arbitration tribunals have solved disputes over borders, maritime resources, and commercial practices.

anywhere in the world. This organization developed a methodology of universal classification. In 1907, La Fontaine and Otlet founded the Union of International Associations, devoted to documenting and promoting international organizations.

La Fontaine published several important works. The 1894 Antwerp International Peace Congress adopted his manual of peace law. In 1902, he published a reference on arbitration, including agreements, procedural rules, and case decisions. A complementary work examined the history of arbitration from 1794 to 1900. His 1904 bibliography of peace and arbitration contained more than two thousand entries. *The Great Solution: Magnissima Charta* (1916) sketched a "constitution" embodying institutions necessary for preventing wars. In 1913 La Fontaine was awarded the Nobel Peace Prize. Following the 1914 German invasion of Belgium after the outbreak of World War I, he fled to Washington, D.C., via England. In 1915 he outlined the essentials for a world court, but he now believed that world government lay many years away.

After the War

Advocating uncompromising internationalism, La Fontaine was a Belgian delegate to the 1919 Paris Peace Conference and to the First Assembly of the League of Nations in 1920-1921. Some league-affiliated bodies, such as the Institute of Intellectual Cooperation, were influenced by his plan for a world intellectual union. He also proposed the creation of an international university, library, parliament, court, bank, and clearinghouses for labor, trade, immigration, and statistical information.

La Fontaine had many talents and interests: He wrote on mountain climbing, Wagnerian opera, American libraries, and the status of American women. He taught adult education classes on modern artistic movements, served on Brussels' City Council, and produced a volume of poetry. He saw his native Belgium invaded by the Nazis but died in 1943 before it was liberated. Having outstanding administrative abilities, he contributed much to the practical organization of international bodies and to the framing of international law, particularly law related to arbitration.

Bibliography

La Fontaine, Henri. *The Great Solution: Magnissima Charta*. Boston: World Peace Foundation, 1916.

Lipsky, Mortimer. *The Quest for Peace: The Story of the Nobel Award*. New York: Barnes, 1966.

Rappard, William E. *The Quest for Peace Since the World War*. Cambridge, Mass.: Harvard University Press, 1940.

Randall Fegley

Fiorello Henry La Guardia

Born: December 11, 1882; New York, New York
Died: September 20, 1947; New York, New York

Longtime mayor of New York City (1934-1945)

Fiorello Henry La Guardia (fee-oh-REH-loh HEHN-ree lah GWAHR-dee-ah) was a congressman and, later, mayor of New York City. He was born to Italian immigrants in lower Manhattan, but he grew up in the West. After his father's death, he moved with his family to Budapest, Hungary, where he worked in the U.S. consulate and became fluent in six languages. He later secured employment at Ellis Island, the entry point for millions of European immigrants to the United States. There he was an interpreter for the U.S. Immigration and Naturalization Service; he also took night classes in law at New York University. La Guardia was admitted to the bar in 1910.

Early Political Career

La Guardia entered politics as a progressive Republican and in 1914 ran for Congress. He was unsuccessful but drew a significant portion of votes away from Tammany Hall, the dominant New York City Democratic Party organization. In 1916 he ran for Congress again and was elected; he was the first Italian-American to be elected to Congress. He served in World War I; then, in 1922, he again ran for Congress and was reelected a total of four times. La Guardia switched political affiliations to the Progressive Party, one of the most liberal political groups of the time. In 1932 he cowrote the Norris-La Guardia Act, which limited the courts' power to stop labor disputes.

Mayor of New York City

In 1929 La Guardia unsuccessfully ran for New York City mayor against Tammany Hall Democrat James J. Walker. Federal investigations exposed Tammany Hall's corruption, however, and forced Walker from office in 1932. In 1933 La Guardia was elected. He served two more terms, remaining mayor from 1934 to 1945.

La Guardia was renowned for his commitment to honesty and reform. He broke down the city's political divisions, creating a centralized government and eliminating unnecessary bureaucratic offices. He renounced loyalty to the Fusion Party and instead became a unique political force, using aggressive and progressive leadership. He fought to uproot organized crime and corrupt politicians. La Guardia improved police and fire

Fiorello Henry La Guardia *(Library of Congress)*

department service, created new low-cost housing projects, and razed older slums. He drove gangsters out of the public markets and brought more sanitary conditions and opportunity to the city's many pushcart vendors. He created the City Center for performing arts and was a patron of the arts himself.

La Guardia was nicknamed "the Little Flower," a translation of his first name as well as a reference to his small stature. He was popular with New Yorkers; aside from his political achievements, he was highly visible, viewing fires and other disaster sites. During a newspaper delivery strike, he read the comics to New York's children over the radio. La Guardia was sometimes seen as antagonistic and temperamental, and he had what some called a puritanical streak. His commitment to the city was tireless; he spent long hours at work and shunned

During his first term as New York City's mayor, Fiorello La Guardia goes to the country to address the Oneida County Fair on the fair's "La Guardia Day." *(AP/Wide World Photos)*

the wealthy lifestyle of past mayors. He maintained close contact with all city departments, requiring each to report to him personally. He appointed competent department heads, bring-

New York City in the 1930's

At the time of Fiorello La Guardia's election as mayor, the largely Irish Democratic Party organization known as Tammany Hall controlled many sectors of city politics through corrupt means. The city was also suffering the effects of the Depression, which had terminated the economic boom of the 1920's. More than 200,000 New Yorkers were unemployed, and 16 percent of the city's population was receiving relief aid. The city's financial woes were many: A low credit rating prevented it from receiving federal money, and city debt was more than $30 million.

Housing, transit, schools, and other social services were in disarray. La Guardia did much to mend these economic and social woes during his twelve years as mayor. As the first stop for most European immigrants, and often their destination of choice, New York was shaped by the influences of its various ethnic groups. New York was the manufacturing, cultural, and economic center of the United States; no other city of the time carried such influence on trends throughout the United States.

ing many previously unrepresented people into these appointments.

Unlike his predecessors, La Guardia worked closely with the federal government, securing support from President Franklin D. Roosevelt for bridges, highways, parks, schools, sewer systems, health centers, and airports. The city finally boasted a unified transit system and adequate and affordable housing for the underprivileged. Roosevelt appointed La Guardia as director of the Office of Civilian Defense in 1941, a position he held concurrently with the mayorship for about a year.

Effects of La Guardia's Mayorship

La Guardia turned the city's government around, making it an honest organization concerned with the needs of its constituents. He did much to restore citizens' faith in local govern-ment and provided an example of aggressive politics that included working with the federal government to obtain funds. His progressive actions carried a large price tag, however; the cost of social benefits resulted in a large city debt and high maintenance costs with which following mayors had to cope. In his last years, La Guardia served as director of the United Nations Relief and Rehabilitation Administration.

Bibliography

Berrol, Selma Cantor. *The Empire City: New York and Its People, 1924-1996*. Westport, Conn.: Praeger, 1997.

Elliot, Lawrence. *Little Flower*. New York: William Morrow, 1983.

La Guardia, Fiorello. *The Making of an Insurgent*. New York: J. B. Lippincott, 1948.

Michelle C. K. McKowen

New York City in the early 1940's. *(Archive Photos)*

Christian Lous Lange

Born: September 17, 1869; Stavanger, Norway
Died: December 11, 1938; Oslo, Norway

Norwegian historian, secretary-general of the Interparliamentary Union (1909-1933), winner of 1921 Nobel Peace Prize

The father of Christian Lous Lange (KRIHS-tyahn LEWS LAHNG-eh) was an engineer in the Norwegian armed services. In 1887, Lange attended the University of Oslo and studied history, French, and English, earning his master's degree in 1893. Thereafter, Christian taught in the secondary schools of Oslo for many years. In 1919, he earned his Ph.D. degree from the University of Oslo.

Christian Lous Lange *(The Nobel Foundation)*

Interparliamentary Union

In 1899, Lange became involved with internationalism when he was appointed as a secretary for the Conference of the Interparliamentary Union in Oslo. In 1900, he was appointed secretary to the Norwegian Parliament's Nobel Committee and to the planned Norwegian Nobel Institute. Lange resigned from that position in 1909 but continued as an adviser to the institute until 1933, serving on the Nobel Committee from 1934 to 1938.

In 1909, Lange was appointed secretary-general of the Interparliamentary Union and held that office until 1933. He administered the affairs of the Interparliamentary Bureau and tried to promote good personal relations among the world's legislators, to strengthen democratic institutions throughout the world, and to encourage worldwide peace by using arbitration and mediation instead of force in resolving international conflicts. Lange met with parliamentary groups in many countries, formulated the agenda for annual union meetings, edited the official publications of the union, raised money, and kept the union visible by lecturing and publishing about it.

Lange supervised the reorganization of the Interparliamentary Bureau when it moved from Bern, Switzerland, to Brussels, Belgium, in 1909. When Germany overran Belgium in 1914 in the early stages of World War I, he established the office in his own home in Oslo. After World War I, Lange convened the Council of the Union in Geneva, Switzerland, in 1919 and moved the union's headquarters to Geneva so that it would be close to the League of Nations and its array of international activities.

The Nobel Institute

The Norwegian Nobel Institute was established in 1904, and it moved into its present building in Oslo in 1905. Christian Lous Lange, who helped plan the institute's building, served as the first secretary of the Nobel Institute. The principal duty of the institute is to assist the Nobel Committee in the task of selecting the winner of the Nobel Peace Prize. Because of the Peace Prize's nature, the selection of the recipients for the Nobel Peace Prize has been exposed to the most criticism. On recommendation of the institute, the Peace Prize has been the most frequently reserved (that is, not awarded in a given year) Nobel Prize.

The Nobel Institute has its own research department and a 150,000-volume library, with the books mainly devoted to works on peace, international law, economics, and modern political history. In addition to holding Nobel Symposia for the exchange of views and information that invite specialists from around the world, the institute arranges a variety of meetings, seminars, and lectures.

International Activities and a Nobel Prize

Lange represented Norway at the Hague Peace Conference in 1907, and by 1915, he was active in the work of the Central Organization for Lasting Peace. From 1916 to 1929, Lange served as a special correspondent for the Carnegie Endowment for International Peace. At their invitation, he prepared a report on conditions in warring countries in 1917. From the opening of the League of Nations until his death, Lange served as a special adviser and as a delegate from Norway. In 1932, he headed the league's Assembly committee on political questions. In 1933, he headed the Assembly committee to keep the League of Nations informed about the Sino-Japanese situation, and in 1938, he served on the Assembly's committee on armament problems. Because of his dedicated efforts in internationalism and his peace efforts in his capacity as secretary-general of the Interparliamentary Union, Lange was awarded the Nobel Peace Prize in 1921, which he shared with Swedish prime minister Karl H. Branting.

Pioneer of Peace

Christian Lange is best remembered as one of the world's foremost advocates of the theory and practice of internationalism and pacifism. From his college days until his death, Lange's career focused on international affairs and the promotion of worldwide peace. He was known as an expert on the complicated subjects of arbitration, mediation, and control of armaments, and he made significant contributions to the preparation and development of the League of Nations. An international defender of democracy, Lange promoted free speech, free trade, universal suffrage, labor mobility, and workers' right to organize.

Bibliography

Holl, Karl, and Anne C. Kjelling, eds. *The Nobel Peace Prize and the Laureates*. Frankfurt: Peter Lange, 1994.

Landheer, Bartholomeus. *A Desirable World*. The Hague: Martinus Nijhoff, 1974.

Wehberg, Hans. *The Limitations of Armaments*. Washington, D.C.: The Endowment, 1921.

Alvin K. Benson

Julia C. Lathrop

Born: June 29, 1858; Rockford, Illinois
Died: April 15, 1932; Rockford, Illinois

U.S. social-service worker, leader of U.S. Children's Bureau (1912-1921)

Julia Clifford Lathrop (JEW-lyah KLIH-furd LAY-thruhp) was the oldest child of a lawyer who served in the Illinois legislature and later in Congress. Her mother, valedictorian of Rockford Seminary's first graduating class, participated in the women's suffrage movement. Following high school, Lathrop followed in her mother's footsteps, attending Rockford Seminary for a year before transferring to Vassar College. She earned a degree in 1880 and went to work as a secretary in her father's law office. She shared her parents' concern for social issues such as women's rights, the treatment of the mentally ill, and civil service reform and demonstrated her commitment to others when she moved to Chicago and joined the staff of Hull House in 1890.

Lathrop's Years at Hull House

Hull House, founded by Jane Addams in 1889, became Lathrop's home for more than twenty years. Like her middle-class associates at Hull House, she was committed to improving the lives of others, particularly immigrants, by living among them and providing instruction on "proper" American ways. During her tenure at Hull House, Lathrop formed close friendships with prominent reformers such as Addams, Grace and Edith Abbott, and Florence Kelley. In 1893 Lathrop accepted an appointment to the Illinois State Board of Charities. She encouraged state institutions to be more selective in their hiring, but she recognized that this could not happen until a larger supply of trained social workers existed. With this in mind, she developed

courses at the Chicago School of Civics and Philanthropy, where she was a trustee, and where she frequently lectured. Lathrop also devoted a great deal of attention to juvenile delinquency and immigration policy. She was instrumental in

Julia C. Lathrop *(Library of Congress)*

892

establishing the first juvenile court in the United States in 1899, and in 1908 she established the Illinois Immigrants' Protective League.

Children's Bureau Chief

The time Lathrop spent at Hull House and the friendships she formed with other female reformers prepared her to become the leader of the first government agency devoted to protecting mothers and children. Her sustained commitment to child welfare issues impressed President William Howard Taft, and he appointed her chief of the U.S. Children's Bureau in 1912. Lathrop had lofty goals, but she was hindered by a limited budget and a small staff of only fifteen. Despite these challenges, she orchestrated not only the survival of her organization but also its expansion. By 1921, when Lathrop turned over control of the bureau to Grace Abbott, her friend and hand-selected successor, the staff numbered more than two hundred.

Lathrop's Legacy

Under Lathrop's leadership, the U.S. Children's Bureau drew the nation's attention to the problem of maternal and infant mortality. American women, influenced by studies conducted by the Children's Bureau, began to mobilize. They demanded respect for motherhood and greater concern for children's health. Lathrop was also instrumental in securing the passage of the Sheppard-Towner Act. This act, signed into law in 1921, provided matching federal funds to states that established prenatal and child health care programs. Finally, Lathrop deserves credit for protecting the sovereignty of the Children's Bureau. She prevented its work from being taken over by the Office of Education and by the U.S. Public Health Service; consequently, she helped pave the way for other women to become involved in government service.

Bibliography

Addams, Jane. *My Friend, Julia Lathrop*. Reprint. New York: Arno Press, 1974.

Ladd-Taylor, Molly. *Mother-Work: Women, Child Welfare, and the State, 1890-1930*. Urbana: University of Illinois Press, 1994.

Muncy, Robin. *Creating a Female Dominion in American Reform, 1890-1935*. Oxford, England: Oxford University Press, 1991.

Melanie Beals Goan

The U.S. Children's Bureau

Florence Kelly and Lillian Wald proposed a national children's bureau in 1903. One day at breakfast they saw a newspaper story detailing the government's attempts to eliminate the boll weevil. Finding it ironic that the government undertook such a campaign while it did nothing to prevent the deaths of 300,000 babies each year, they developed a plan. After lobbying for almost nine years, they finally convinced President William Howard Taft to create the Children's Bureau by signing it into law in 1912. The primary goals of the bureau were to improve children's health and to eliminate child labor. The bureau conducted birth and death surveys and distributed pamphlets to mothers throughout the nation. Organizers originally designed the Children's Bureau simply to compile and disseminate information, but these activities soon prompted more drastic changes. The bureau inspired women across the nation to demand improved care for themselves and their families, and it provided an early place for women such as Julia Lathrop, its first chief, in government.

Wilfrid Laurier

Born: November 20, 1841; St. Lin, Canada East (now Quebec, Canada)
Died: February 17, 1919; Ottawa, Ontario, Canada

Prime minister of Canada (1896-1911)

Henri Charles Wilfrid Laurier (o-REE CHAHRL weel-FREED law-ree-AY) was born into a rural French Canadian family. Speaking both French and English from early childhood, he was prepared early for a professional career. After attending McGill University, he began to practice law in Montreal in 1864. Health problems and an increasing interest in government led him to transfer his efforts from law to politics, and when Canada achieved confederation in 1867, Laurier was a prominent Liberal. Although Laurier was a strong advocate for his fellow French Canadians, he concluded early in his career that French Canadians could be content within a Canadian confederation, a sentiment at times vocally opposed by his Quebec contemporaries such as Henri Bourassa.

Wilfred Laurier *(Library of Congress)*

A First for French Canadians

In 1874, Laurier was elected to the federal parliament in Ottawa. For the next thirteen years, he became the best-known French Canadian politician. Laurier so impressed his colleagues that in 1887 he was named national leader of the Liberal Party, even though most of the party was English-speaking. The choice of Laurier was facilitated by his deep admiration of British traditions, particularly the sense of liberal reformism which most English Canadians had inherited from Britain. Laurier was therefore popular among both English and French Canadians. After spending ten years in opposition, Laurier became prime minister in 1896. He was the first French Canadian ever to hold that position.

Linguistic Divisions

The Laurier government was confronted with a divisive cultural and linguistic issue. Catholics (mostly French-speaking) living in Manitoba wanted their children to go to separate Catholic, French-speaking schools, and they wanted these schools to be supported by public tax money. Drawing on the advantages he possessed by virtue of his French-speaking background, Laurier resolved the situation by permitting some religious element to be attached to the school curriculum after formal instruction had ceased for the day. This achievement won Laurier a reputation as a person who could bring Canadians together.

Trade with the United States

Laurier was next confronted with problems in foreign relations. The Laurier era saw, for the first time, foreign relations becoming important in Canadian politics. Canada still possessed many symbolic and constitutional ties to Great Britain,

Canada and the Boer War

The Boer War (1899-1902) was the first major conflict fought by Britain after Canada had become a self-ruling dominion, and Laurier was faced with deciding his nation's policy in the war effort. Most French Canadians, sympathetic with any opponents of the British, were against participation in the war, and at one point there were fierce antiwar riots in Montreal. Public sentiment in the English Canadian community was, however, overwhelmingly in favor of participating in the war. By late 1899, seven thousand Canadian soldiers had been sent to South Africa.

The Canadian troops, schooled in fighting in harsh terrain, were an effective counterpoise to the Boer armies at the battles of Paardeberg, Leliefontain, and Hart River. Canadian deaths in the war numbered 244; of those who survived, many were seriously injured, yet many survivors emerged as Canada's leaders in the next generation. Many Canadian soldiers were decorated. The war strengthened Canada's sense of solidarity with Britain and its fellow dominions, while further underscoring the difference between French and English speakers within Canada.

including the same head of state. Yet Canada was in effect self-governing. Moreover, Canada's long border with the United States made the United States at least as important to Canada as Britain was. Himself a supporter of free trade (also known as "unrestricted reciprocity") with the United States, Laurier had to mollify a substantial degree of dissent among Liberals. More popular was the idea of "imperial preference" in trade. Under this scheme, Canada would give preference in trade to Britain and to fellow British dominions.

Empire or Dominion?

Laurier also had to deal with such foreign-policy issues as Canadian participation alongside the British in the Boer War. In a way, this was a domestic issue as well, because many Canadians still felt themselves to be psychologically part of Britain. Yet Laurier always held back from proposed schemes of imperial federation, under which Canada would grow closer politically to the other Britain-derived countries. He recognized that, in the long run, the process was running the other way—toward greater Canadian independence and national self-reliance. French

Canadians certainly did not want to be merely one cog in a world-girdling, interdependent British Empire.

Industry and Immigration

The Laurier era was one of unprecedented prosperity. Canada shifted from being a primarily agricultural economy to being a primarily industrial one. Many Canadians left farms and homesteads to find work in the cities. Canada's vast reserves of natural resources became of substantial value in the world economy. Canadian wheat, produce, minerals, and precious metals brought a sizable inflow of investment. Canadian territory reached from the Atlantic to the Pacific, and now the population did as well. This fact made it increasingly unlikely that parts of Canada would ever be annexed by the United States. It also moved the axis of Canadian politics partially away from the long-standing rivalry between English-speaking Ontario and French-speaking Quebec. Since, however, the new western provinces were overwhelmingly English-speaking, the sense of alienation on the part of the French-speaking population began to increase.

The Grand Trunk

The Laurier years saw a huge population explosion in the prairie provinces of Manitoba, Saskatchewan, and Alberta, the last two of which joined the confederation under Laurier's government. The Laurier government crucially assisted this expansion by promoting the construction of the Grand Trunk Pacific. As the western spur of the Grand Trunk Railway, it amounted to a transcontinental rail link.

The railroad provided the transportation backbone to the prairie economy and made possible easy trade and communication across the continental expanse. It facilitated the settlement of many immigrants from eastern and central Europe, who contributed to the unique ethnic mix of the prairie population. The Grand Trunk also helped ensure that western Canada did not fall into economic dependence on the United States. A merchant in Winnipeg with raw materials to ship would now look eastward to Ontario or Quebec rather than south to Minnesota. Thus the railroad helped cement Canadian economic and national unity.

Improvements in transportation such as the Grand Trunk Railway made Canada feel less threatened by the United States, so Laurier felt that he had another opportunity to make the argument for free trade. In 1910, Laurier wanted Parliament to approve a reciprocity treaty with the United States guaranteeing unrestrained trade. Laurier took his case to the people, but the vehemence of the opposition by Canadian mercantile interests managed to sway a majority of the electorate. Laurier's party was defeated on September 21, 1911, ending his career in office.

Reconciliation

Laurier's years after holding office were unusually productive ones for a former politician. When Canada entered World War I in 1914, Laurier favored participation on the British and French side, but he opposed conscription—the drafting of nonvolunteers into the Canadian army. This position was important for Laurier's legacy among French Canadians, who were strongly opposed to conscription. It showed he was not a simple tool of pro-British interests. To the end, Laurier sought reconciliation between Canada's various peoples. He was never more popular than at the time of his death in 1919.

Bibliography

Clippingdale, Richard. *Laurier: His Life and World*. Toronto: McGraw Hill, 1979.

Dafoe, John W. *Laurier: A Study in Canadian Politics*. Toronto: McClelland and Stewart, 1964.

LaPierre, Laurier L. *Sir Wilfrid Laurier and the Romance of Canada*. Toronto: Stoddart, 1996.

Neatby, H. Blair. *Laurier and a Liberal Quebec*. Toronto: McClelland and Stewart, 1973.

Schull, Joseph. *Laurier: The First Canadian*. Toronto: Macmillan, 1965.

Nicholas Birns

Pierre Laval

Born: June 28, 1883; Châteldon, France
Died: October 15, 1945; Paris, France

French political leader, premier of Vichy regime (1942-1944)

Pierre Laval (pee-AYR lah-VAHL) was born in the mountainous Auvergne region, the fourth child of an innkeeper-butcher who also served as local postman. Although trained to follow in his father's businesses, Pierre went on to a legal education. He was admitted to the Paris bar in 1909, the same year he married the daughter of the mayor of Châteldon. Two years later a daughter, the couple's only child, was born. Laval's law practice focused on defending trade unionists and fellow socialists. Laval was soon a rising star in the Socialist Party, and he won election to Parliament in May, 1914, to represent the working-class Paris suburb of Aubervilliers.

During World War I (1914-1918), Laval worked hard in Parliament to bring about a negotiated peace to a war he detested. At the end of the war he voted against the Treaty of Versailles as being too harsh on Germany. As postwar French politics drifted to the Right, Laval became an independent politician. By April, 1925, he was appointed to his first cabinet post as minister of public works. One year later he was appointed minister of justice, and in 1927 he was elected to the Senate, representing the Department (district) of the Seine. In 1930 he became minister of labor for the conservative André Tardieu government, gaining fame for passage of a social insurance law. By 1931 he had climbed to the top rungs of French political power; he was named premier.

In and Out of Power

As premier of France, Laval gained notoriety as the first French premier to visit either Berlin or Washington, D.C., on official business. He failed to bring about any policy changes, however. In February, 1932, André Tardieu replaced Laval as premier but kept him as minister of labor. For the

next two years Laval was shuffled into various cabinet positions. In October, 1934, following the assassination of Foreign Minister Jean-Louis Barthou, Laval took his place. In 1935 he completed Barthou's major project, the Franco-Soviet Pact of Mutual Assistance. Yet Laval's version was much watered down from that proposed by Barthou.

In June, 1935, Laval again became premier. In foreign policy, he tried to move France closer to an alliance with fascist Italy. The end result was

Pierre Laval *(Library of Congress)*

897

the disastrous Hoare-Laval Agreement, which caused Laval's fall from power. From 1936 to 1940, an embittered Laval remained a member of the Senate but had no role in any major affairs. With the outbreak of World War II he remained steadfast in his opposition to a declaration of war on Germany. Then, as France was falling to Adolf Hitler's forces, he vehemently opposed continuing the war.

The Vichy Regime

The fall of France to the Nazis resurrected Laval's political career. He was convinced that France should collaborate with Germany and seek the best terms possible for a partnership in a new world order. In 1940 the Germans established a new French government based at Vichy, in central France. The elderly Philippe Pétain was made premier, with Laval as his deputy. The problem was that Hitler

Pierre Laval, president of Vichy France, and Philippe Pétain inspecting French troops at Vichy in 1942. *(Archive Photos)*

had little interest in collaboration or in making concessions. Hitler's meeting with Pétain in October, 1940, arranged by Laval, only provided publicity for the German propaganda machine.

The 1935 Hoare-Laval Pact

Italian fascist leader Benito Mussolini's invasion of Ethiopia in 1935 caused the League of Nations to brand Italy an aggressor and to implement economic sanctions against Italy. However, Italy was pivotal in Pierre Laval's scheme to block Adolf Hitler's ambitions and to bring about a Franco-German rapprochement from a position of strength. Consequently, Laval invited the British foreign secretary, Samuel Hoare, to Paris. There a pact was concocted to give Mussolini two-thirds of Ethiopia if he would please

the League of Nations by terminating the invasion of Ethiopia. This agreement was leaked to the press, producing a public outcry. When the British government disassociated itself from Hoare's work, a humiliated Laval saw his cabinet collapse. He never forgave the British government for its role in this foreign-policy disaster. Mussolini went on to conquer Ethiopia in the subsequent six months. By 1936 Hitler and Mussolini were collaborating in the effort to bring about a fascist takeover of Republican Spain.

The Execution of Laval

Pierre Laval had predicted, "If I succeed, there will be not enough stones in this country to raise up statues to me. If I fail, I shall be shot." He was right: On October 15, 1945, he stood before a firing squad in the Fresne prison yard in Paris, barely alive.

That morning, shortly before the wardens entered his cell, Laval had swallowed cyanide powder. His suicide, like most ventures in his career, was botched. The charges were read to him, amid his vomiting and an insatiable thirst caused by the cyanide. A van took Laval to a post, to which he was tied. Laval's last words to one of his three lawyers, a Resistance member, were, "My love for my country was as great as yours." As the command "Aim!" was given, Laval managed to shout, "Vive la France!"

Laval's failure to gain concessions, and Pétain's general dislike of the former pacifist, caused Pétain to dismiss Laval on December 13, 1940.

On April 27, 1942, at Hitler's insistence, Laval was named premier of the Vichy government. Given German military setbacks. Laval incorrectly assumed that French collaboration would now be of utmost value to Hitler, thus giving Laval needed leverage to gain concessions. Knowing Germany's need for factory workers, Laval negotiated an agreement for the return of one French prisoner of war for each three workers sent to Germany. Failure to get volunteers to work in Germany ultimately caused Laval to conscript workers. No single act did more to drive French people to join the Resistance. In June, 1942, Hitler demanded that France participate in the Final Solution and surrender all Jews in the country. Laval first resisted, but then he agreed to turn over all foreign Jews residing in France. In all, more than seventy-six thousand Jews in France were rounded up by French police and delivered for extermination. Although Laval resisted military participation in the war, he did everything else to show his support for the German war effort. In his famous radio speech of June, 1942, he told the French people that "to avoid communism establishing itself everywhere, I wish for a German victory."

Laval's Fall

By 1944 it was evident that Germany would not win the war. In August, 1944, the Germans decided to transport Laval to Innsbruck, Austria. Then, on May 2, 1945, he was flown by a German aircraft to Barcelona, Spain, where Spanish fascist dictator Francisco Franco decided to arrest him. In July Laval was returned to the French provisional government. He was tried before three hostile judges and even more hostile jurors, who hurled invectives at him when he spoke. A guilty verdict was returned and a death sentence imposed. The policy of collaborationism, which he came to symbolize, was also condemned.

Historians are still debating whether Laval should be given some credit for saving three-quarters of France's 300,000 Jews or condemned for sending 76,000 to their death. Moreover, should he be praised for bringing home French prisoners of war or castigated for sending so many French workers to an uncertain future in Germany? Did his collaborationist machinations protect France from harsher treatment by Germany or did they add to its suffering? Was he the creator of, or the scapegoat for, the policies of the Vichy government?

What is clear is that Laval's adherence to Germany until the last days of the war indicates that above all other concerns, his own career and livelihood stood paramount. It is also quite evident that he greatly overrated his powers of persuasiveness and the importance of his own participation in shaping important matters.

Bibliography

Cole, Hubert. *Laval: A Biography*. London: Heinemann, 1963.

Laval, Pierre. *The Unpublished Diary of Pierre Laval*. London: Falcon Press, 1948.

Paxton, Robert. *Vichy France: Old Guard and New Order*. New York: Knopf, 1972.

Thomson, David. *Two Frenchmen: Pierre Laval and Charles de Gaulle*. Reprint. Westport, Conn.: Greenwood Press, 1975.

Warner, Geoffrey. *Pierre Laval and the Eclipse of France*. London: Eyre and Spottiswoode, 1968.

Irwin Halfond

Bonar Law

Born: September 16, 1858; Kingston, New Brunswick, Canada
Died: October 30, 1923; London, England

Prime minister of Great Britain (1922-1923)

Andrew Bonar Law (AN-drew BO-nur LAW) was the son of a Presbyterian minister who emigrated from Ulster in northern Ireland to Nova Scotia. He was the youngest of four brothers and a sister. His mother, the daughter of an iron merchant in Glasgow, Scotland, died when the boy was two. When he was twelve, he went to Glasgow to work as an apprentice in merchant banking. In 1885 he became a partner in an ironworks

Bonar Law *(Library of Congress)*

firm and was a very successful businessman. In 1891 he married Annie Pitcairn Robley, with whom he had six children. He was active in the local Conservative Party and participated in political debates in Glasgow.

Early Political Career

In 1900 Law was elected to the House of Commons as a Conservative Party representative. He strongly supported the introduction of tariffs to protect British industries from unfair foreign competition. The issue split the party, and the Liberal Party won a landslide victory in 1906. For five years the Conservative Party used the House of Lords to block Liberal Party legislation, a tactic that resulted in the Parliament Act of 1911.

Law was elected Conservative Party leader in the House of Commons in 1911. When the Liberal Party introduced the Irish home rule bill in 1912, Law allied Conservatives (also called Unionists) with the Ulster Protestants, who vehemently opposed home rule. For two years he used an array of parliamentary tactics to defeat the Liberals and their bill. He also supported a paramilitary group in Ulster that promised revolution if home rule became law. Only the outbreak of World War I in August of 1914 prevented overt hostilities between Protestants and Catholics in Ireland.

World War I and Aftermath

When war came, Bonar Law immediately placed the use of needs of his country first. After ten months, when many Conservatives voiced dissatisfaction with the conduct of the war by Prime Minister H. H. Asquith, Law demanded a coalition government. He placed harmony above his personal interests and accepted the modest

The General Election of 1922

Bonar Law's retirement from politics in 1921 was attributable to the stress of six years of war and its aftermath. He was coaxed from retirement by Conservatives angry with David Lloyd George's settlement with Ireland and imperial policy, as well as other issues. When the Conservative Party reelected Law as party leader, Lloyd George resigned and Law became prime minister. In the election held on November 22, Law's platform was based on "tranquillity and stability." The Liberal split between H. H. Asquith and Lloyd George allowed the Labour Party to become the second major party in Britain. Since 1922, Conservatives and Labour have either shared power or been in opposition, with Liberals being a smaller third party.

position of secretary for the colonies. In December, 1916, he worked with David Lloyd George to force the resignation of Asquith as prime minister. In the new government, Lloyd George directed the war effort while Law served as chancellor of the Exchequer and as leader of the House of Commons. Under his financial management, Great Britain was better able to arrange credit for fighting the war. His public appeals for war support were especially effective as two of his sons were killed in action.

At war's end a general election (the Coupon Election) was held, and Law continued to support Lloyd George. For two years he managed the domestic issues of demobilization and Ireland while the prime minister dealt with the Versailles peace treaty and other foreign affairs. Law retired from public life in March of 1921 but returned in October, 1922, when prominent Conservative Party members asked him to lead their withdrawal from Lloyd George's coalition government. Law was then asked by the king to form a new government, and the general election of 1922 confirmed his leadership. Because

of a terminal illness, he was to serve for only seven months as prime minister.

At Law's funeral in Westminster Abbey, Asquith referred to him as the Unknown Prime Minister. While not meant as a compliment, it was appropriate. Bonar Law's legacy was substantial but, with the exception of the fight over Ulster, he avoided the limelight. He was a businessman who created the modern Conservative Party. He was also a great wartime leader, although Lloyd George received the publicity. Law served his country quietly and capably in a time of great stress and turmoil.

Bibliography

Blake, Robert. *Unrepentant Tory: The Life and Times of Andrew Bonar Law, 1858-1923.* New York: St. Martin's Press, 1956.

Gilbert, Bentley B. *David Lloyd George: A Political Life.* Columbus: Ohio State University Press, 1987.

Taylor, A. J. P. *Beaverbrook.* New York: Simon and Schuster, 1972.

William S. Brockington, Jr.

T. E. Lawrence

Born: August 16, 1888; Tremadoc, Caernarvonshire, Wales
Died: May 19, 1935; Bovington, near Clonds Hill, Dorset, England

British military leader and writer, nicknamed Lawrence of Arabia

Thomas Edward Lawrence (TO-muhs EHD-wurd LO-rehntz) was the illegitimate son—the second of five brothers—of Sarah Madden and Thomas Robert Chapman, who changed their name to Lawrence. During his infancy the family moved frequently, living in Scotland, Jersey, the Isle of Man, France, and the New Forest before settling in Oxford when Ned (as Lawrence was called in the family) was eight years old. After Oxford High School for Boys, he attended Jesus College, Oxford, from 1907 to 1910. After graduation he traveled extensively—often alone—in the Middle East and was a member of several excavations and surveys. At the beginning of World War I, Lawrence was posted as an intelligence officer in Cairo, Egypt. Two years later he joined Emir Feisal's guerrilla forces behind Turkish lines, where he helped to foster the Desert Revolt.

After the war Lawrence went to the Paris Peace Conference as an adviser to Feisal, and he lobbied for Arab independence. He became a fellow of All Souls College, Oxford, and between 1919 and 1922 he drafted several versions of his most famous book, *Seven Pillars of Wisdom* (1922). After a brief time at the Colonial Office under Winston Churchill, he served (using assumed names) in the Royal Air Force and the Royal Tank Corps from 1922 to his retirement in 1935. He died from complications of a motorcycle accident at the military hospital at Bovington in Dorset on May 19, 1935.

Lawrence and the Middle East

Lawrence developed an interest in the Middle East as a schoolboy and had already read widely on the subject before he entered Oxford to study the history, literature, and languages of the region formally. He researched his undergraduate thesis

T. E. Lawrence, "Lawrence of Arabia," in desert garb. *(Library of Congress)*

903

on medieval crusader castles by cycling around France during his holidays. In 1911 he joined the archaeological excavations at Carchemish in Syria, and he later coauthored two books about the digs. With C. Leonard Wolley, Lawrence helped to survey and prepare maps for large areas of the desert, maps that were later used by the British army in their conduct of the eastern military campaigns against the Ottoman Turks.

Because of his vast knowledge of the habits and customs of the Arabs and the geography of the Middle East, at the outbreak of World War I Lawrence was posted to Cairo as an intelligence officer, eventually with the Arab Bureau. Even as a young lieutenant he impressed his superiors with his leadership and diplomatic skills. Although he was never formally trained as a field officer, Lawrence was given a leading role in organizing and coordinating British efforts with the various elements of the Arab army under the general leadership of Prince Feisal. These collective efforts became known as the Arab Revolt. In his writings, both during the war and after, Lawrence commented knowledgeably about strategy and the tactics of insurgent forces. His role in helping to defeat the armies of the Ottoman Empire was considerable.

T. E. Lawrence *(Archive Photos)*

The Arab Revolt

During World War I, various Middle Eastern tribes, under the eventual leadership of Prince Feisal, rose up against the Turkish (Ottoman) army, which occupied vast areas of the Middle East. At the outbreak of the 1914-1918 war, Turkey joined the forces of Germany and the Austro-Hungarian Empire to fight against France, Great Britain, and Russia. Although initially the Arabs remained neutral, the threat to their holy city of Mecca encouraged their mobilization. In June, 1916, a group of inexperienced and half-armed tribesmen attacked Turkish army garrisons.

At first the Arabs were defeated by the superior and better-equipped Ottoman forces. As Arab resistance increased, however, the British came to realize that having a guerrilla force behind enemy lines would aid their advance toward Damascus. T. E. Lawrence took command in the field and helped to funnel British equipment and money to the insurgents. He helped to train and organize an army from the various Arab tribes. The exploits of this irregular army proved extremely helpful to British military efforts, especially by destroying the Turkish supply lines along the Hejaz railway that linked Medina with Damascus. It was through coverage of the war by a Chicago newspaperman, Lowell Thomas, and Thomas's subsequent illustrated speaking tour about his experiences, that T. E. Lawrence became known as Lawrence of Arabia.

"J. H. Ross" and "T. E. Shaw"

T. E. Lawrence never adapted well to the loss of privacy that resulted from the enormous fame he received as Lawrence of Arabia. So in August, 1922, in an attempt to escape from the intrusive publicity, Lawrence joined the Royal Air Force under the assumed name of John Hume Ross. However, his escape from the public eye was short-lived. After the newspapers discovered his ruse, he was discharged in January, 1923, after only six months' service.

The next month he enlisted in the army with the Royal Tank Corps, this time using the name T. E. Shaw, perhaps choosing it because of his friendship with the author George Bernard Shaw and his wife. Like his father before him, Lawrence eventually changed his name legally—to Shaw. He served in the Tank Corps, and was even posted to India, until his transfer back into the Royal Air Force in 1925. He remained in this service, working in various capacities, until his retirement in 1935. On May 19 of that year he died in the military hospital of the Royal Tank Corps at Bovington Camp not far from his home at Clonds Hill.

Arab Independence

Lawrence felt strongly that the Arab peoples should have independence from colonial control. Even though he knew about the Allies' plans to partition the Middle East after the war, he encouraged Feisel's participation in the Arab Revolt by the promise of independence. He hoped that eventually he could influence the course of the peace. After the war, the final outcome of the Treaty of Versailles parceled out the lands of the region to French and British control. This decision was profoundly disappointing for Lawrence, and guilt over his failure to achieve Arab independence haunted him for the rest of his life.

Lawrence as an Author

T. E. Lawrence will probably be best remembered in history as the author of the monumental *Seven Pillars of Wisdom*. Part travelogue, part autobiography, part military history, this often mystical book has come to be considered a major work of early twentieth-century literature. Lawrence also published books about his archaeological experiences at the dig at Carchemish (with others), *The Wilderness of Zin* (with C. Leonard Wolley), his undergraduate study on Crusader castles, and his study of conditions in the Royal Air Force, *The Mint*, which was considered so critical of the British military establishment that it was not published in a general edition until 1955. He also wrote a more popular version of his military exploits, *Revolt in the Desert*. Many other volumes of his writing, including his voluminous correspondence and diaries, were edited by others and published after his death.

Bibliography

Knightly, Philip, and Colin Simpson. *The Secret Lives of Lawrence of Arabia*. London: Nelson, 1969.

Lawrence, A. W., ed. *T. E. Lawrence by His Friends*. London: Jonathan Cape, 1937.

Thomas, Lowell. *With Lawrence in Arabia*. New York: Century, 1924.

Villars, Jean Béraud. *T. E. Lawrence: Or, The Search for the Absolute*. London: Sidgwick & Jackson, 1958.

Wilson, Jeremy. *Lawrence of Arabia: The Authorized Biography of T. E. Lawrence*. London: William Heinemann, 1998.

Charles L. P. Silet

Le Duc Tho

Born: October 14, 1911; Nam Ha Province, Tonkin (now Vietnam)
Died: October 13, 1990; Hanoi, Vietnam

Vietnamese revolutionary and North Vietnam's representative at the Paris Peace Talks, declined 1973 Nobel Peace Prize

When Le Duc Tho (LAY DUHK TOH) was born, Vietnam was a French colony. Le Duc Tho's father served as a functionary for the French colonial government. Although Le Duc Tho was educated at French schools, he soon joined the growing resistance to French rule. The goal of the movement was to rid Vietnam of the French. In 1930 Le Duc Tho helped found the Indochinese Commu-

nist Party. Consequently, he was arrested by the French and thrown into prison.

The Wars in Vietnam

Le Duc Tho was also a charter member of the Vietminh, the Vietnam Independence League. Starting in 1941, the Vietminh led a guerrilla war against the French. In the 1950's, revolutionary

Le Duc Tho preparing to appear on the television program *Nightline* in 1985; he called for normalization of relations between Vietnam and the United States. *(Reuters/Pat Benic/Archive Photos)*

leader Ho Chi Minh appointed Le Duc Tho chief Vietminh commissar in the southern part of Vietnam. He directed the insurgency movement against the French from hidden jungle bases.

When the Americans took up the war after the defeat of the French, Le Duc Tho again assumed

control of the insurgency movement in the south, this time through the National Liberation Front (NLF), or Viet Cong. By this time, Vietnam had been divided into two sections: North Vietnam, controlled by communists under Ho Chi Minh, and South Vietnam, allied with the United States.

Meanwhile, Le Duc Tho had been elected to the Politburo, the ruling body of the Vietnamese Communist Party. He continued to rise through the ranks of the Communist Party for the next three decades.

The Paris Peace Talks

On March 31, 1968, U.S. president Lyndon B. Johnson delivered a speech emphasizing peace and calling for a partial halt to the American bombing of North Vietnam. Surprising many American officials, North Vietnam responded positively to the speech. Peace talks were opened in Paris on May 13, 1968. Xuan Thuy began as the chief negotiator for the North Vietnamese; however, Le

U.S. soldiers on their way home from Vietnam in 1973 as a result of the peace talks in Paris. Le Duc Tho was a primary participant in the talks. *(Library of Congress)*

The 1973 Cease-Fire Agreement

Le Duc Tho was the chief North Vietnamese negotiator at the peace talks in Paris that led to the 1973 cease-fire. On January 27, 1973, representatives of the United States, the Democratic Republic of Vietnam (North Vietnam), the Republic of Vietnam (South Vietnam), and the Provisional Revolutionary Government of the Republic of South Vietnam (the Viet Cong) signed the Paris Peace Accords. The agreement called for a cease-fire to begin on January 27, 1973, the complete withdrawal of American troops from South Vietnam, and the return of prisoners. It

also recognized the rights of the South Vietnamese to self-determination of their political future and called for the reunification of North and South Vietnam. Although the agreement did not end the fighting in Vietnam, it did enable the United States to end its involvement in the war. On March 29, 1973, the last American troops left Vietnam. In January of 1974, South Vietnamese president Nguyen Van Thieu announced that the war had begun again. On April 30, 1975, North Vietnamese troops overran Saigon, ending the war with a communist victory.

Duc Tho soon arrived and took over the position.

For two years, the talks were stalled. In February, 1970, American negotiator Henry Kissinger began meeting secretly with Le Duc Tho in an attempt to hammer out an agreement. In October of 1972, Le Duc Tho presented Kissinger with a nine-point plan. After several months of further negotiations, the Americans and the North Vietnamese reached a cease-fire agreement, which they signed in January, 1973. South Vietnamese President Nguyen Van Thieu signed with reluctance. Henry Kissinger and Le Duc Tho were awarded the Nobel Peace Prize for their efforts; however, Le Duc Tho declined to accept the award because there was not a genuine peace in Vietnam at that time. The cease-fire led the way to the removal of American troops from Vietnam. However, the peace accords did not last long after the American withdrawal. In 1975 Le Duc Tho returned to South Vietnam as the chief strategist behind the final attack on Saigon.

Contributions to Vietnam

Le Duc Tho served on the Politburo until 1986, when he resigned, claiming ill health and advancing age as his reasons. He died in October, 1990. Stanley Karnow notes in *Vietnam: A History* (1983) that Le Duc Tho's career was "largely a mystery" to those outside Vietnam. Nonetheless, Le Duc Tho's contributions to the communist cause in Vietnam are clear. As party founder, war strategist, and peace negotiator, he helped shape postwar Vietnam.

Bibliography

Dillard, Walter Scott. *Sixty Days to Peace*. Washington, D.C.: National Defenses University, 1982.

Kissinger, Henry. *Years of Upheaval*. Boston: Little, Brown, 1982.

Nguyen Tien Hung and Jerrold L. Schecter. *The Palace File*. New York: Harper and Row, 1986.

Young, Marilyn B. *The Vietnam Wars: 1945-1990*. New York: HarperCollins, 1991.

Diane Andrews Henningfeld

Lee Kuan Yew

Born: September 16, 1923; Singapore

First prime minister of modern Singapore (1959-1990)

Lee Kuan Yew (LEE KWAHN YEW) is generally known as the father of the state of Singapore. He served as its prime minister from 1959 to 1990. Born into a well-to-do Chinese family, Lee grew up in a Singapore that was a British colony. English was his first language; later he learned Chinese (Mandarin), Malay, and Tamil.

Early Career

After World War II, Lee studied economics at the London School of Economics and law at Cambridge University, graduating with honors and special distinction. While studying in England, he was drawn to socialism. Returning home in 1950, Lee married Kwa Geok Choo, also a lawyer. Lee soon gained fame as an attorney for the union of postal workers, which achieved a major victory after a strike in 1952. He entered politics and began his rise to power with the aid of a close group of like-minded patriots who sought Singapore's independence from Britain. They formed the People's Action Party (PAP) in 1954, and Lee was its first secretary-general.

The Road to Independence

Great Britain granted an increasing measure of self-rule to its colony during the 1950's, and Singaporean elections were held in 1959. Largely as a result of Lee's eloquent campaign oratory, the PAP won a majority of seats in Parliament, and Lee became prime minister. He announced a five-year plan that included industrializing, building new housing, and improving education. He also appointed intelligent Singaporeans, dedicated to modernizing the country, to key posts.

In 1963 Singapore joined the new Federation of Malaysia. Two years later, however, Lee took Chinese PAP candidates into Malaysian elections, and racial tensions between Malays and Chinese were quickly ignited. Singapore was forced to withdraw from Malaysia in 1965 and establish itself as a tiny, independent country surrounded by powerful neighbors.

National Security and Economic Development

To establish national security, Lee and his associates traveled the world seeking alliances and cultivating friendships. He convinced the West that he was a staunch anticommunist; the United States, fighting in Vietnam and fearful of commu-

Lee Kuan Yew *(Popperfoto/Archive Photos)*

The Federation of Malaysia

Britain conferred independence upon the Federation of Malaya in 1957 and internal self-rule upon Singapore in 1959. However, Lee Kuan Yew of Singapore envisioned a merger of the two states, along with British Borneo, into the Federation of Malaysia. He successfully gained British support for the idea, which came to fruition in 1963. The federation consisted of Singapore, the Borneo territories of Sabah and Sarawak, and the states that had formerly composed Malaya. Because Lee wanted Malaysia to abolish special privileges for the indigenous Malay population, he annoyed the leaders of the former Malaya, who were of Malay ancestry. Singapore was expelled from the federation in 1965.

nism's spread, supported his government. Lee also built a well-trained Singaporean army, requiring service by all able-bodied males.

Lee's policy of allowing foreign corporations to operate with few regulations is often credited with enabling Singapore to become the world's tenth most prosperous country in per capita income by the end of the twentieth century. His government both improved social welfare services and exerted strong influence on citizens, urging cooperation and discipline. It stratified the education system to give special attention to the most gifted students. Schools taught ethics and imbued students with respect for law and order.

Lee rewarded talent by elevating loyal and able civil servants and politicians to positions of responsibility. If those he appointed proved dilatory in implementing the sweeping changes he envisioned, he discharged them. Lee's leadership brought Singaporeans stability and a very high standard of living. The trade-off involved living under a government that closely regulated society and that sometimes censored critical views and put opponents under surveillance.

Lee resigned as prime minister in 1990, becoming senior minister of Singapore, a cabinet

Singapore prime minister Lee Kuan Yew speaking to a crowd in 1964, asking for an end to racial violence. *(Library of Congress)*

Lee Kuan Yew takes the oath of office as senior cabinet minister in 1990; his hand-picked choice as Singapore's new prime minister, Goh Chok Tong, is at left. *(Reuters/Dominic Wong/Archive Photos)*

position. Lee's pace slowed considerably in the late 1990's because of health problems, but he still occasionally traveled abroad to give speeches and to advise world leaders.

Bibliography

Haas, Michael. *The Singapore Puzzle*. Westport, Conn.: Praeger, 1999.

Han Fook Kwang, Warren Fernandez, and Sumiko Tan. *Lee Kuan Yew: The Man and His Ideas.* Singapore: Times Editions, 1998.

Josey, Alex. *Lee Kuan Yew*. 2 vols. Singapore: Times Editions, 1968, 1980.

Lee Kuan Yew. *The Singapore Story: Memoirs of Lee Kuan Yew*. Singapore: Times Editions and New York: Prentice Hall, 1998.

Minchin, James. *No Man Is an Island: A Study of Lee Kuan Yew's Singapore*. Boston: Allen & Unwin, 1986.

Michael Haas; McCrea Adams

Vladimir Ilich Lenin

Born: April 22, 1870; Simbirsk, Russia
Died: January 21, 1924; Gorki, U.S.S.R.

Russian Bolshevik revolutionary leader and first leader of the Soviet Union (formed 1922)

Vladimir Ilich Lenin (vluh-DYEE-myihr ihl-YEECH LYAY-nyihn) was born Vladimir Ilich Ul-yanov (ewl-YAH-nof) in Simbirsk, a Russian town on the Volga River. He was the son of middle-class professionals who encouraged him in school. Lenin studied law in Kazan as a young man and became involved in a revolutionary student group in 1887. In that same year his elder brother Alexander was arrested for plotting against the czar and was executed.

Planning a Revolution

Lenin was a scholar, but his political gifts lay in organization and strategy. He learned these skills as a student in Kazan when he was arrested and exiled in 1887 for participating in student disorders. The czarist regime was repressive and even used secret police. Lenin found himself under constant surveillance. He completed his law degree in 1891, but he was also becoming a student of Marxism (theories of socialism based on the nineteenth-century writings of Karl Marx) and was active in the Russian Social Democratic Party. The years between 1893 and 1905 were ones of study, writing, activism, and frequent arrests and exile. In 1898 he married his lifelong partner Nadezhda Krupskaya, who joined him in exile to begin their life together.

During his many exiles, Lenin wrote about revolution, economics, and social democracy. In 1901 he began an extended period living abroad. This situation allowed him to meet other émigré revolutionaries and attend Russian Social Democratic Party conferences throughout Europe. The times in exile and as an émigré also helped Lenin develop an international reputation. He was a prolific writer and was well known among party activists in and outside Russia. Lenin began to

focus his energy on how to win a revolution. He learned to value secrecy, careful organization, and thoughtful leadership. Lenin began to see that Karl Marx's ideas could be applied to Russia only with modification, because Russia was an agricultural, even backward, country. Such conditions required a different kind of party organization. Communist survival and revolution could occur only if the leadership was a specially trained group of intellectuals who could guide Russia to the future.

Vladimir Ilich Lenin *(Library of Congress)*

The Bolsheviks

Before 1905 Lenin wrote on party tactics, including *What Is to Be Done?* (1902) and *One Step Forward, Two Steps Back* (1904). These pieces highlight his determination to create a party organized to succeed in Russian circumstances. In 1905 the Third Party Congress of the Russian Social Democrats was dominated by Lenin and a group who shared his beliefs. This group became known as the Bolsheviks. That same year there was a failed rebellion against the czar. This 1905 revolt signaled for Lenin the prelude to revolution. His writing took on a new cast, rallying his Bolshevik followers while viciously attacking his opponents, both within and outside the party.

Lenin developed a mode of behavior that was adopted by his followers. He argued that as long as Marx's writings were the ultimate guide, any means could be used to achieve the revolution. Lenin described the Bolshevik organizational principle as "democratic-centralism." In practice it meant that debate within the party should be vigorous, but once the party leaders make policy, all must

Soviet leader Vladimir Ilich Lenin in 1922 addressing a gathering in Petrograd. *(Library of Congress)*

The New Economic Policy

The Bolshevik seizure of power in 1917 was followed by three years of bitter civil war. Russian industry and agriculture were devastated. Several plans were tried unsuccessfully to stimulate the economy along communist lines. Since the beginning of the revolution, agricultural goods, especially grain, had been forcibly requisitioned from peasants. Most communists believed that farming and land should be run by the state as a collective enterprise.

The New Economic Policy (NEP) was announced by Vladimir Ilich Lenin and the young Soviet regime in 1921. The NEP was intended to raise grain and food production while alleviating peasant unrest in the countryside. The NEP allowed small-scale markets to open. Private agricultural enterprise emerged as an incentive to produce grain and support economic growth. The plan was flexible, and it worked. Within three years agriculture recovered and many peasants began to prosper. The method was antithetical to communist ideals, however. A new policy of collectivized agriculture began in 1928, despite the success of NEP.

be unified and never criticize the party. In planning the revolution this became a central tenet.

Lenin's theories often revised Marxism to suit the circumstances. Just before 1917, Lenin wrote *Imperialism, the Highest Stage of Capitalism* (1917). In this work he added a historical stage to Marxist theory: imperialism. According to Lenin, the powers of Europe were carving up the world in competition for empire. He argued that a Marxian revolution would therefore be delayed but would come after an imperialistic world war. Although many fellow Marxists disagreed with Lenin, he prepared his Bolsheviks for a seizure of power when the time was right. The Bolsheviks organized in the cities of Russia, recruited followers, and distributed propaganda. If an opportunity came, they would be ready.

Revolution

In March of 1917, a devastated Russia sued for peace with Germany to end its involvement in World War I. The czar had already been driven from power, and a provisional government was in place. Lenin secretly returned to Russia and began organizing the party. At midnight on November 6, the Bolsheviks, under Lenin's leadership, seized power at the Winter Palace in Petrograd. Now began the most difficult times of their struggle. Three years of civil war put the Bolsheviks to the ultimate test as Lenin promised the Russian people "peace, land, and bread." The party organization served him well, training Bolsheviks to be ruthless, disciplined, and unified. Lenin's regime successfully resisted internal opponents as well as armies sent by foreign powers. In the process, Lenin was wounded in an assassination attempt in 1918. He never fully recovered his health.

Lenin's Shadow

In the years after the civil war until Lenin's death in 1924, the Bolsheviks ruled with an eye to building socialism and making an economic recovery. They developed policies aimed at land redistribution, industrial growth, and greater equality and freedom. Lenin established an international communist movement, and his success inspired revolutions around the world. Unfortunately, Lenin did not live to see the early Bolshevik policies through, and many of his ideas for organizing a revolution were later used by Joseph Stalin to build a totalitarian state.

Lenin established communism as a distinct

Vladimir Lenin, leader and icon of the Bolsheviks, posing with a factory in the background to emphasize the importance of the workers in communist ideology. *(National Archives)*

The Bolshevik Revolution

The Bolshevik Revolution is the name given the successful communist revolution in Russia in 1917. Led by Vladimir Ilich Lenin, the Bolsheviks were a minority wing of the Russian Social Democratic Party. Ironically, the word Bolshevik means "majority" in Russian, but it referred to a single congress of the party in 1903 wherein Lenin and his followers laid down their plan for revolution.

The Bolsheviks believed in strict discipline, secrecy, and leadership by elite professional revolutionaries. They felt that this was the only way the czar could be overthrown in Russia. The idea was unacceptable to other Russian Social Democrats, but the plan proved successful. Using this type of organization, Lenin held his Bolsheviks together through the seizure of power and three years of civil war thereafter. The Bolshevik Revolution was the first communist revolution in history, and it began the split between socialism and communism as distinct ideas.

movement within socialism and created a new kind of revolutionary party that became the dominant communist model in the world. His stage of "imperialism" revised Marxism and became a justification for Third-World revolutionary movements. Lenin's idea of the seizure of power by an elite group of professional revolutionaries—rather than by the people at large—became the dominant model for socialist regimes. Although Lenin's ideas were reshaped under his successors, and his tactics were used for oppression and dictatorship, he left an indelible mark on Russian and world history.

Bibliography

Draper, Hal. *War and Revolution: Lenin and the Myth of Revolutionary Defeatism*. Atlantic Highlands, N.J.: Humanities Press, 1996.

Hill, Christopher. *Lenin and the Russian Revolution*. Harmondsworth, England: Penguin, 1971.

Nettl, J. P. *The Soviet Achievement*. New York: Harcourt, Brace & World, 1967.

Volkogonov, Dmitri Antonovich. *Lenin: A New Biography*. New York: Free Press, 1994.

Wilson, Edmund. *To the Finland Station*. New York: Doubleday, 1940.

Anthony R. Brunello

Jean-Marie Le Pen

Born: June 20, 1928; La Trinité-sur-Mer, France

French political figure, leader of National Front Party (1970's-1990's)

A former paratrooper who served in Algeria, Jean-Marie Le Pen (ZHO mah-REE leh PO) became one of the most controversial French politicians in the latter part of the twentieth century. From the beginning of his parliamentary career in 1956, he helped to redefine the Right in French politics. He brought to fruition a populist anti-immigrant emphasis that appealed to voters who resented residents who were not ethnically French. Le Pen's opponents accused him of pursuing divisive, if not neofascist, politics.

Opposition to de Gaulle

After graduating from law school, Le Pen was first elected to the French parliament in 1956 as a member of the Right. Among conservatives, he stood out for his vehement opposition to President Charles de Gaulle's Algerian program. Le Pen believed that de Gaulle's phased withdrawal from Algeria was a betrayal of France and the French citizens living in that North African nation. This stance earned him the support of many former colonialists who had returned from Alge-

Jean-Marie Le Pen (right) toasting his freedom in January, 1960; Le Pen had just been released after being jailed for suspicion of subverting the French government's efforts in Algeria. *(Library of Congress)*

916

ria after Algerian independence. By consistently taking an extreme right-wing position, particularly on matters concerning immigration and national defense, Le Pen distinguished himself from the more moderate conservative mainstream.

His racist rhetoric attracted many French voters who were most in competition with, or fearful of, the predominantly non-European immigrants who came to reside in the increasingly multicultural country. He argued that France was being overrun by foreigners—who, Le Pen argued, caused a disproportional amount of crime and unemployment and were leading to the decline of the nation's culture. By 1972, Jean-Marie Le Pen had become the undisputed leader of the far-right National Front. In addition to pushing for increased military spending, this party hammered away at the theme that the ex-

pulsion of immigrants would solve a whole range of problems ranging from crime to unemployment. By the late 1980's, Le Pen had led his party into the National Assembly, where it was

National Front president Jean-Marie Le Pen in 1997, in Strasbourg, France, for the tenth party congress. *(Reuters/Vincent Kessler/Archive Photos)*

The National Front

The far rightist National Front had become one of France's top four parties by 1996. Although party leader Jean-Marie Le Pen received only 15 percent of the vote in the 1995 presidential election, the National Front was able to influence the national agenda on topics such as racism, nationality, and immigration. Many critics argued that the party represents a threat to democracy and saw the National Front as belonging to the fascist tradition—a tradition that advocates strong central government, regimentation, and racial and national pride and that deemphasizes individual rights. This view was

exacerbated by the National Front's overtly racist programs, which declare that "immigration, unemployment, AIDS, and the decrease of the birthrate pose a real threat to the very survival of France." In early 1999, a splinter group of the National Front, the National Movement, was formed by former National Front deputy Bruno Megret and a number of other party bureaucrats. They proclaimed that Le Pen was no longer leading the party effectively. Many French political observers believed Megret to be even more right-wing than Le Pen.

Anti-National Front protesters marching in Strasbourg in 1997 in response to the party's congress being held there. *(Reuters/Jean-Christophe Kahn/Archive Photos)*

finally able to win seats under a revised system of proportional representation.

Although unsuccessful, Le Pen's presidential candidacies served as symbolic rallying points for the far Right in France. In 1988, for example, he received the votes of four million citizens in the first round of the presidential election. Moreover, beginning in 1984, Le Pen served as a member of the European Parliament. His success had peaked by the early 1990's when his movement stalled at being able to attract no more than 15 percent of the vote.

Increasing Difficulties

Le Pen encountered a series of difficulties as the twentieth century moved toward its end. In 1998, a French court stripped him of his political rights, banning him from running for office for two years, for physically attacking a female socialist candidate. This led Le Pen to announce that his wife would replace him as head of the National Front ticket at the next election. This announcement caused resentment among other party leaders. While still appealing the ban, he found his parliamentary immunity stripped by his fellow members of the European Parliament so that he could be tried for statements such as his remark that the murder of millions of European Jews by the Nazis was "only a minor detail of World War II."

Reaching the age of seventy in 1998, Le Pen faced internal opposition from those National Front members who sought increased legitimacy in the political arena. Many leaders privately complained that Le Pen's crude, blistering speeches only served to isolate the National Front from potential supporters. Regardless of the final conclusion of this power struggle, Jean-Marie Le Pen reshaped French politics.

Bibliography

Ardagh, John. *France in the 1980's.* New York: Penguin Books, 1983.

Marcus, Jonathan. *The National Front and French Politics: The Resistible Rise of Jean-Marie Le Pen.* New York: New York University Press, 1996.

Simmons, Harvey G. *The French National Front: The Extremist Challenge to Democracy.* Boulder, Colo.: Westview Press, 1996.

William A. Pelz

René Lévesque

Born: August 24, 1922; New Carlisle, Quebec, Canada
Died: November 1, 1987; Montreal, Canada

A founder and leader of Parti Québécois, premier of Quebec (1976-1985)

René Lévesque (reh-NAY leh-VEHK), a former premier of the province of Quebec, was born in Quebec in 1922. Lévesque chose journalism as his career. Fluent in both English and French, he demonstrated his unhappiness with the place of French Canadians in Canada by choosing to work for the United States as a reporter covering the events of World War II.

Cabinet Minister

After the conclusion of the war in 1945, Lévesque returned to his native Quebec and con-

René Lévesque *(Library of Congress)*

tinued to work as a journalist, this time on television, where he gained widespread exposure. This fame helped prepare his way for entering provincial politics in the early 1960's. The Quebec of that era was experiencing great change in what became known as the Quiet Revolution.

Elected in 1960, Premier Jean Lesage and his Liberal government brought in sweeping social and economic change. Lévesque played a role in this change when, as minister of natural resources, he introduced a bill to nationalize Hydro Quebec, the province's supplier of energy. This controversial measure brought the new cabinet minister national attention.

Despite the reforms, Lévesque remained unsatisfied. He wanted Quebec to have even greater control over its own affairs, but many in his party were opposed, as was the federal government. In 1967, Lévesque quit the Liberal Party and formed his own political organization dedicated to the creation of a sovereign (independent) Quebec. In 1968, it merged with several other smaller organizations to form the Parti Québécois. Lévesque was a natural choice for the new entity's leadership. At his core a democrat, Lévesque insisted that the only road to independence for Quebec would be through the ballot box.

In Power

After eight years of struggles, the Parti Québécois shocked Canada when it won the Quebec provincial election of 1976. The new government brought in numerous reforms in an effort to strengthen the French presence in Quebec. Most famous—considered notorious by many—was a language law entitled Bill 101. The bill restricted the English language in schools, the workplace, and public spaces; it sparked widespread protests in the English-speaking sections of the province. However, the real goal of the new government remained independence. In 1980, Premier Lévesque's government held a referendum asking the people of Quebec to provide it with a mandate to "negotiate" a form of "sovereignty association." Sixty percent of Quebec voters voted "no" on referendum day.

Final Years

Although the referendum was defeated, Lévesque and his party remained popular with the people of the province. He won another majority government in 1981. One more major battle, however, remained to be fought. The federal government, under Lévesque's rival, Pierre Elliott Trudeau, had long been attempting to revise Canada's constitution. Lévesque's government remained opposed. In 1982, the Trudeau government, with the assistance of the other Canadian provinces, circumvented Lévesque and his government and revised the constitution without their approval. Feeling personally betrayed, Lévesque began to experience the strain of his lengthy political career. His personal popularity decreased sharply along with the provincial economy in the early 1980's. Senior members of the party began to quit, unhappy with Lévesque's leadership and the fact that he had apparently given up on the idea of independence. Finally, Lévesque resigned as premier of Quebec in 1985, just before his party suffered a defeat in the provincial election.

Lévesque had little time to enjoy his private life. He died in 1987. His legacy, however, was a significant one. He had undeniably transformed the province of Quebec and, in many ways, the country as well. The place of Quebec and French Canadians in Canada could no longer be ignored.

Bibliography

Cook, Ramsay. *Canada, Québec, and the Uses of Nationalism*. Toronto: McClelland and Stewart, 1986.

Lévesque, René. *Memoirs*. Translated by Phillip Stratford. Toronto: McClelland and Stewart, 1986.

Linteau, Paul-André, René Durocher, Jean-Claude Robert, and François Ricard. *Quebec Since 1930*. Translated by Robert Chodos and Ellen Garmaise. Toronto: James Lorimer, 1991.

Steve Hewitt

Parti Québécois

Founded in 1968 by leading Quebec sovereignists, the Parti Québécois represented a merger of several small separatist parties, all of which sought independence for their province through democratic means. The most important individual in its creation was René Lévesque, a well-known Quebec journalist and politician who had quit the Liberal Party in 1967 to start his own party. Lévesque would serve as the party's leader for the next seventeen years. The Parti Québécois, although principally an independence party, also tended to be left-of-center politically, filling a void in Quebec politics. The party slowly gained political support after 1968; its popular vote increased in each election. The party's breakthrough occurred in 1976, when it won the Quebec provincial election. It held power until 1985. In 1980 it lost a referendum that was to have begun the move toward Quebec independence. It recaptured power in the 1990's and again lost a referendum—this time, however, by a closer margin.

Lin Biao

Born: December 5, 1907; Huanggong, Hubei, China
Died: September 12, 1971; near Öndörhaan, Mongolia

Chinese military leader and politician, vice chairman of Chinese Communist Party (1969-1971)

Lin Biao (LIHN BYOW), also written Lin Piao, was born the son of a factory owner in Hubei Province. He attended preparatory schools and the Whampoa Military Academy near Guangzhou. After graduating from Whampoa in 1925, he joined the army of the Kuomintang (KMT), or Nationalist Party, as a colonel and rose to the rank of major.

Military Career

After Kuomintang leader Chiang Kai-shek began to purge Communist elements in the army, Lin Biao joined the Communist Party. He helped to build the Communist "Red Army" in Jiangxi Province. As an aide to a general, Lin rose to the position of regional commander, gaining a reputation for enforcing discipline and for maintaining good relations with the local populations. By 1930, he was the commander of 100,000 troops in the Red Army First Group in the fight against Chiang Kai-shek's KMT. During 1934-1935, after the Red Army was almost completely encircled by KMT forces in Jiangxi, Lin helped to command the so-called Long March to Yan'an. When KMT and Communist forces joined to oppose the Japanese invasion in 1937, Lin Biao was wounded during the first joint Communist-KMT battle. After recovering from his wounds in Moscow, he served in a number of campaigns against the Japanese and worked to build military bases in Northern China. On October 1, 1949, Communist Party leader Mao Zedong announced the creation of the People's Republic of China (PRC), and Lin Biao was appointed the Commander of the Central China Military Region.

Becoming a Political Figure

As U.N. forces drove toward the Yalu River, Lin was selected to command a force of Chinese "volunteers" to oppose the American led U.N. force. After serving as vice premier, he became minister of defense and worked to remove Soviet influences after the split between China and the Soviet Union. By 1966, Lin Biao was one of China's most powerful political leaders. Mao Zedong, fearful of potential rivals and determined to sustain the communist revolution in China, chose Lin to serve as his protégé during the Great Proletarian Cultural Revolution. Along with Mao's wife,

Lin Biao *(Library of Congress)*

921

The Long March

The "Long March" of the Chinese Communist leadership during the period of 1934-1935 was a defining event in both the war against the Kuomintang (KMT), or Nationalists, and the emergence of Mao Zedong as the leader of the Chinese Communist Party. By 1934, Communist forces were concentrated in rural Jianxi Province in Southeast China after the establishment of the Chinese Soviet Republic in 1931. After moving from Shanghai, the Communist leadership was vulnerable to KMT forces, and by October the Communists were completely surrounded. Sensing weakness, Chiang Kai-shek's forces intensified attacks in an attempt to eliminate Communist opposition to the Nationalist government. Led by Mao, Communist troops broke out of the encirclement, and more than 150,000 Communists marched more than 6,000 miles (9,700 kilometers) and over eighteen mountain ranges in a running battle that concluded in the establishment of the Communist base at Yan'an in October of 1935.

Jiang Qing, Lin was one of the three main leaders of this political mass movement, which terrorized China for ten chaotic years.

In 1969, Lin was designated Mao's successor during the Ninth Party Congress. As the commander of the People's Liberation Army (PLA), Lin was given tremendous power in an attempt to reduce the social unrest unleashed during the Cultural Revolution. As the chaos subsided somewhat, Mao and his allies began to distance themselves from Lin. Lacking personal charisma and possessing peculiar personal habits related to his fear of illness, Lin was unprepared for his final battle. In 1971, Lin began to organize a coup code-named "Operation 571" that would assassinate Mao and propel Lin to the leadership of the Communist Party. The plan to bomb Mao's train was called off in early September. Fearful that the plot would be exposed, Lin Biao, his family, and a few advisers attempted to flee China in a daring flight to the Soviet Union. Lin Biao's plane crashed in Mongolia on September 12, 1971, killing all passengers. The cause of the crash remains a topic of controversy and is still being studied by historians.

Bibliography

Ming-le, Yao. *The Conspiracy and Death of Lin Biao*. New York: Alfred A. Knopf, 1983.

Salisbury, Harrison. *The Long March: The Untold Story*. New York: McGraw-Hill, 1985.

Lawrence Clark

Li Peng

Born: October, 1928; Chengdu, Sichuan Province, China

Premier of China (1988-1998)

The father of Li Peng (LEE PUHNG) was the famous Chinese communist martyr Li Shouxun, who was executed by Nationalist troops in 1930. As an orphan, Li became acquainted with Zhou Enlai, who later adopted him and became Li's political mentor. After World War II, Li was sent to Moscow for university training in electrical engineering. By the late 1950's, he was being groomed for leadership through positions in the electrical industry. Still protected as the adopted son of Zhou, Li survived the political and social chaos of the Cultural Revolution as an official in Beijing's electrical power administration.

Entering Political Life

In 1979, he was named the minister of electrical power, and by 1982 he was a member of the Communist Party's Central Committee. He was appointed to the State Education Committee in 1983, a position through which he earned a reputation for cautious conservatism. Described by some in the West as a "technocrat" with a political temperament similar to Soviet politicians of the time, Li's rapid rise to leadership and his extensive technical education suggested to some that a new style of Chinese leader might be emerging.

Li's Rise and Fall

Despite these predictions, the events of the late 1980's highlighted the party's adherence to the supremacy of the role of the party and its reluctance to enact political reforms. Li Peng continued to hold to the cautious conservatism that marked his rise through the Chinese Communist Party bureaucracy. Some in China and the West began to question whether Li's rise was attributable to his abilities or to his affiliation with Zhou and his *guanxi*, or connections within the party.

In 1987, conservative elements in the leadership backed him for the office of premier

Premier Li Peng at the opening session of China's 1993 National People's Congress. *(Reuters/Dennis Owen/Archive Photos)*

Li Peng officially ordering the blocking of one side of the Yangtze River at Sandouping in 1997. The river was being rerouted as part of the controversial Three Gorges Dam project. *(AP/Wide World Photos)*

(prime minister). Li became acting premier in 1987 and officially took office in 1988. In this position Li became a target for Chinese students, who began criticizing his failure to enact reforms in education. As he addressed delegates to the National People's Congress in 1988, students demonstrated outside the building during his speech. To student demonstrators tired of party corruption and the lack of free expression of grievances, Li personified everything that they considered wrong with the Chinese political system.

The 1989 Demonstrations

The reaction of Li Peng to the dramatic events of the spring of

The Socialist Market Economy

The endorsement of the so-called socialist market economy by China's National People's Congress in 1992 grew from the economic reforms of the late Deng Xiaoping. Deng was brought back to power in 1978 after being sent into political retirement during the Cultural Revolution. Faced with the potential collapse of China's economy, the Communist Party embraced Deng's "responsibility system." It involved beginning economic reforms that would end collectivized agriculture and introduce economic incentives for farmers.

Deng and his supporters argued that to modernize its economy China must embrace some free-market principles to reduce its reliance on costly and inefficient state-owned companies.

While more open markets did spur rapid economic growth in the 1980's and 1990's, the gradual shift to an emphasis on profits forced many state-owned companies to began to trim their workforces in order to compete. Although most Chinese people welcomed the rise in living standards that accompanied these reforms, the end of the promise of the "iron rice bowl"—lifetime employment— threatened social stability in China. No generally agreed-upon definition of "social market economy" exists, due in large part to the rapid embrace of economic liberalization in China. Perhaps the best definition was provided by Hong Ho, a Chinese government official: "It is a market economy that is subject to the regulation of a socialist country."

1989 marked the beginning of a decline in both Li's influence in the Chinese leadership and his popular image in China. Throughout the country, university students began marching to criticize government corruption, nepotism, and the lack of political reforms. Students eventually focused their protests on Beijing's Tiananmen Square in an attempt to gain attention during the visit of Soviet leader Mikhail Gorbachev.

By the end of April, the Chinese leadership felt threatened by the size of the demonstrations and the blunt criticism of party officials. During a televised meeting with student leaders, Li appeared angry and refused to accept student criticisms of party leadership. Li signed a declaration of martial law ordered by Deng Xiaoping on May 20, 1989, and by the beginning of June the party leadership had begun planning a forceful suppression of the demonstrations. Hundreds were killed (estimates of fatalities range widely) as troops in Beijing and other cities forcefully ended the student protests.

In the aftermath of the loss of life on June 4, Li Peng was closely linked with the forceful suppression of the demonstrators by Chinese army troops. By 1992, even members of the National People's Congress were expressing public displeasure with Li. They successfully adopted a resolution that forced Li to denounce hard-line political forces in the party. Li was branded the "butcher of Beijing" by Western critics of the student crackdown and was treated as a diplomatic pariah. In 1993, Li suffered a major heart attack, and many believed that he would retire

U.S. vice president Al Gore and Li Peng in Beijing in 1997, toasting the signing of a number of business agreements between China and American companies. *(Reuters/Paul Baker/Archive Photos)*

from the leadership. He returned to his post as premier, however, and served out his constitutional limit of two five-year terms. In 1998, when he was elected to the leadership of the National People's Congress, many observers were surprised at the two hundred members who openly voted in opposition to Li's candidacy.

Bibliography

Kristof, Nicholas, and Sheryl WuDunn. *China Wakes: The Struggle for the Soul of a Rising Power.* New York: Times Books, 1994.

Spence, Jonathan. *The Search for Modern China.* New York: W. W. Norton, 1990.

Lawrence Clark

Maksim Maksimovich Litvinov

Born: July 17, 1876; Białystok, Poland, Russian Empire
Died: December 31, 1951; Moscow, U.S.S.R.

Soviet diplomat, commissar for foreign affairs (1930-1939)

Maksim Maksimovich Litvinov (muhk-SYEEM muhk-SYEE-muh-vyihch lyiht-VYEE-nof) was active in the Communist Party and as a Soviet diplomat, holding the office of commissar for foreign affairs from 1930 to 1939. He was born into a Jewish family, and his original name was

Meier Moiseevich Wallach. Overall, he had a comfortable childhood as the son of the merchant and banker Moses Wallach and his wife, Anna. Litvinov served in the Russian army and then worked in a variety of clerical jobs, while active in party activities, until he became a member of

A crowd in Moscow celebrating the czar's declaration of liberty in November of 1905. Liberty under the czar was a false hope, however, and Litvinov soon began smuggling arms into the country. *(Library of Congress)*

the government. He married Ivy Low, a British citizen, and they had two daughters, Misha and Tanya.

Revolutionary and Party Activities

Litvinov's political views matured while he was a member of the Russian army. Soon after leaving the army, in 1898, he joined the Russian Social Democratic Labor Party (RSDLP) In 1901, while printing party leaflets, Litvinov was arrested and sentenced to two years in prison. He escaped, and in 1903, at the Second Congress of the RSDLP, he met Vladimir Ilich Lenin. From that time he was a strong supporter of Lenin and a faithful worker. For two years he smuggled party literature into Russia, and after revolutionary activities failed to change the government radically in 1905, he organized the smuggling of weapons. During this period, he began using the name Maxim Litvinov (in addition to several others) to escape arrest by Russian authorities. In 1908 he was expelled to Great Britain, where he lived until 1919. He was recognized by Lenin as a key interpreter of Bolshevik beliefs to Western Europe and as the party's representative to the International Socialist Bureau.

Governmental Positions

With the communist takeover of the Russian government, Litvinov was appointed ambassador to Great Britain, although he was never officially recognized by the British government. Ex-

Maksim Maksimovich Litvinov *(Library of Congress)*

Bolshevism in 1903

From July 30 to August 23, 1903, the Second Congress of the Russian Social Democratic Labor Party (RSDLP) was held in Brussels and London. Initially Vladimir Ilich Lenin and his supporters were in the minority. However, several groups became dissatisfied with the debates and left the meeting, allowing Lenin's faction to become the majority. Thus Lenin's supporters were able to elect the party officers and dictate much of the party's platform. This group was called the Bolsheviks (majority), and those who opposed them Mensheviks (minority). The Bolsheviks emerged from the Second Congress as a revolutionary Marxist group within the RSDLP. They were intent upon leading Russian workers to form a new socialist state rather than waiting for socialism to emerge democratically. All Bolsheviks were required to spend a substantial part of their time in party activities and to provide financial support. In 1917 this group officially became the Communist Party.

pelled from Britain in 1919, he began work within the Commissariat for Foreign Affairs. In 1922, Litvinov played a major role in negotiating the Treaty of Rapallo, which was the first formal recognition of the Soviet government by a major European power (Germany). From 1927 to 1930, he led the delegation that planned the League of Nations' World Disarmament Conference, a cause with which he became closely identified. As commissar for foreign affairs, he was the delegate to the Disarmament Conference in 1932. In 1934 he negotiated the normalization of relations between the United States and the Soviet Union.

During the mid-1930's Litvinov did not trust Nazi Germany and pressed hard for collective security treaties against the German government, even negotiating anti-German treaties with France and Czechoslovakia in 1935. Coming from a Jewish background and being identified as anti-German, Litvinov was dismissed as foreign commissar when Soviet leader Joseph Stalin decided to become more supportive of Germany and to sign the German-Soviet Treaty of Nonaggression. Litvinov remained an active member of the Communist Party until his membership was revoked in February, 1941: Stalin wanted to reassure the Germans of his commitment to the nonaggression treaty. In June, 1941, when Germany attacked the Soviet Union, Litvinov's party membership was restored, and he was appointed ambassador to the United States in November. He served in this capacity until August, 1943, when he returned to Moscow as deputy commissar for foreign affairs until his retirement in 1946.

Bibliography

Kennan, George F. *Russia and the West Under Lenin and Stalin*. Boston: Little, Brown, 1961.

Pope, Arthur Upham. *Maxim Litvinoff*. New York: L. B. Fischer, 1943.

Taubman, William. *Stalin's American Policy: From Entente to Detente to Cold War*. New York: W. W. Norton, 1982.

Ulam, Adam B. *Expansion and Coexistence: Soviet Foreign Policy 1917-1973*. New York: Praeger, 1974.

Donald A. Watt

Liu Shaoqi

Born: November 24, 1898; Ningxiang County, Hunan Province, China
Died: November 12, 1969; Kaifeng, Henan Province, China

Chinese political leader, chairman of People's Republic of China (1959-1967)

Principal organizer and ideologue of the Chinese Communist Party, Liu Shaoqi (LYEW SHOW-SHEE) was at one time the number-two leader of the People's Republic of China. Liu was born in Ningxiang County, Hunan Province. During his lifetime, Liu married five times and had nine children.

He joined the Chinese Communist Party (CCP) in 1921 while studying in the Soviet Union. Between 1921 and 1927, Liu worked as a labor union organizer and led a few major strikes in southern and central China. In 1932, he went to the communist Jiangxi Soviet Republic (in southern China) and became head of the national labor union. During the Long March in 1934-1935, when the Communists marched more than 6,000 miles (9,700 kilometers) from Jiangxi to Yan'an, Liu became an ally of Mao Zedong.

During World War II, Liu worked in northern China as a party organizer and an engineer of the anti-Japanese united front by working with forces that included local Chinese warlords. In

Soviet premier Leonid Brezhnev and Chinese chairman Liu Shaoqi, flanked by other officials, raise their arms at the Soviet-Chinese Friendship Meeting in Moscow in 1964. *(Library of Congress)*

1941, he helped rebuild the New Fourth Route Army, which had been decimated in a clash with the troops of the Nationalist government. In 1943, Liu returned to the Communist headquarters in Yan'an and became secretary-general of the Communist Party. In the same period, Liu proved himself a major ideologue through his works such as *How to Be a Good Communist* and *On Political Parties*. During the Chinese civil war, Liu headed the Working Central Committee of the CCP and was instrumental in the creation of such policies as the land law that contributed to the Communist victory in 1949.

People's Republic of China

After the founding of the People's Republic of China in 1949, Liu played a crucial role in such positions as vice chairman of the People's Political Consultative Conference, chairman of the Standing Committee of the People's Congress, member of the Politburo of the CCP, vice chairman of the CCP and, in 1959, chairman of the National Defense Commission and president of the People's Republic. From then on Liu was considered the heir apparent to Mao Zedong.

Between 1959 and 1962, Liu, with the assistance of Deng Xiaoping, led China to recovery after the traumatic industrialization of the late 1950's. Liu and Deng successfully pursued a policy of economic readjustment by deemphasizing heavy industry and increasing the production of consumer goods in the cities. They downgraded rural collectivism. At the same time, Liu worked tirelessly to promote Mao's position as an infallible sage.

Downfall in the Cultural Revolution

Liu's interest in the Soviet type of professionalism in economic affairs ran counter to Mao's revolutionary approach, which was based on mass mobilization. Liu therefore became

Young members of the Red Guards posing in army uniforms at Beijing's Tienanmen Square in 1966. *(Archive Photos)*

The Red Guards

The Red Guards were radical student organizations active from 1966 to 1969 during the Cultural Revolution. The Cultural Revolution was a large-scale campaign intended to eliminate misguided revisionists and "capitalist roaders" from the Communist Party. With their iconoclastic orientation, the Red Guards became the most powerful tool of Mao Zedong in his effort to debilitate his rivals in the party and the Chinese government—rivals such as Liu Shaoqi and Deng Xiaoping. The Red Guards were responsible for a wave of terror that led to the shutdown of schools nationwide and the persecution of millions of intellectuals in the name of the "continuous revolution."

By the end of 1968, the Red Guards had outlived their usefulness, as Mao had successfully removed his rivals from power. The students split and engaged in factional struggle that created anarchy. As they became an obstacle to the restoration of order, they were ordered by Mao to leave the cities for the countryside to receive so-called reeducation from farmers. The experiences of the Red Guards wrote the most dramatic chapters of the Cultural Revolution.

a principal target of the Cultural Revolution, which started in the summer of 1966. Without due process of law, he was found guilty of betraying the party and the Chinese people. At the Twelfth Plenum of the Eighth Congress of the CCP in October, 1967, he was not only expelled from the ruling party but also stripped of all positions in the government. For two years, he was subject to repeated harassment and humiliation by radical student organizations. Liu spent his last months in solitary confinement in Kaifeng, Henan Province, in central China, where he died of cancer in 1969. Liu was posthumously "rehabilitated" (that is, his reputation was restored) in February, 1980, at the Fifth Plenum of the CCP's Eleventh Congress. Liu's career and death epitomize the complex and tragic nature of the Chinese revolution.

Bibliography

Meisner, Maurice. *Mao's China: A History of the People's Republic of China*. New York: Free Press, 1977.

Spence, Jonathan D. *The Search for Modern China*. New York: W. W. Norton, 1990.

Peng Deng

David Lloyd George

Born: January 17, 1863; Manchester, England
Died: March 26, 1945; Ty Newydd, near Llanystumdwy, Caernarvonshire, Wales

Prime minister of Great Britain (1916-1922), champion of the underprivileged

David Lloyd George (DAY-vihd LOYD JOHRJ) was the son of William George, a schoolmaster whose early death left his widow and infant children dependent on her family. A brother, Richard Lloyd, a master shoemaker and Baptist lay preacher in a North Wales village, provided a home. "Uncle Lloyd" became surrogate father and mentor for David, whose youth was not quite as poor or rustic as he later claimed. He became a solicitor (lawyer) in 1884, and in 1888 married Margaret Owen, a farmer's daughter. This union produced four children and lasted until her death in 1941, despite Lloyd George's interest in other women, including his personal secretary (as of 1913), Frances Stevenson, whom he later married in 1943.

Political Rise

Lloyd George won election to Parliament in 1890 as a Liberal Party candidate for Caernarvon Boroughs. He advocated land reform and temperance, or abstention from drinking alcohol. He tried, with little success, to organize Welsh members into a nationalist bloc that he could lead. However, his opposition to the Boer War of 1900-1902 made him a national figure, supported by the pacifist wing of the Liberal Party. This situation helped him to a cabinet post in the Liberal government of Sir Henry Campbell-Bannerman in 1905. In 1908 Campbell-Bannerman's successor, H. H. Asquith, named Lloyd George chancellor of the Exchequer and thus responsible for the historic "Lloyd George budget" of 1909.

Lloyd George's speeches in Parliament were businesslike, but his public addresses, which were also covered by the press, were fiery, witty, and passionate in support of the budget and the Liberal program for workers. He attacked the House of Lords, the wealthy, and the privileged. As reports about his investments showed in 1913, Lloyd George was not personally committed to a life of poverty, but as a salesman urging benefits for the workers he was eloquence itself.

In 1911 Lloyd George became convinced that Germany was seeking war with France and that a German victory would endanger British pros-

David Lloyd George *(Library of Congress)*

perity and security. His July 21, 1911, "Mansion House speech" marked his new belligerency. Three years later, in the July, 1914, crisis preceding the outbreak of World War I, Lloyd George appeared to be undecided. However, when Germany invaded Belgium as he anticipated it would, he helped to create a cabinet majority for war with Germany.

World War I

As wartime chancellor of the Exchequer, Lloyd George moved swiftly to protect British finances from adverse speculation. He worked with bankers, business leaders, and Conservative Party politicians as partners in the war effort. In Asquith's coalition government of May, 1915, Lloyd George became minister of munitions, creating a new and effective department,

British prime minister David Lloyd George (far right), with French premier Georges Clemenceau (left) and Woodrow Wilson (center), leaving the Versailles palace afer signing the Treaty of Versailles. *(Archive Photos)*

The Budget of 1909

The Liberal budget for 1909 had to increase taxes in order to pay for the expanding costs of the Old Age Pension Act of 1908 as well as the new naval race with Germany. The bulk of the revenue increase came from an increase in income taxes, which was accepted by the House of Lords. However, the Lords broke precedent by vetoing the budget's new system of land valuation and taxes on mineral wealth or other "unearned increment." They also vetoed the luxury taxes covering motor cars, gasoline, cigars, distilled spirits, and other upper-class accessories. There was press speculation that the budget was

meant to tempt the predominantly Conservative House of Lords into trespassing onto the House of Commons' control of taxation, but not until this threat became real did Lloyd George deliver a speech attacking "the dukes." Part of the budget passed in 1909, but the budget and veto issues eventually led to two elections in 1910 and to the Parliament Act of 1911. Lloyd George's continuing attacks on wealthy landowners encouraged the workers' chant that "God gave the land to the people," while the landed aristocracy denounced Lloyd George as "the cad of the cabinet."

David Lloyd George speaking in 1929 at the launching of the Liberal Party's general election campaign of that year. By this time Lloyd George's influence had waned. *(Popperfoto/Archive Photos)*

Prime Minister

In effect, Law led the House of Commons, where Asquith maintained a "constructive opposition," while Lloyd George inspired the country and oversaw the war. In 1917 his support of France's calamitous Nivelle offensive and his reluctant agreement to the costly British Passchendale offensive showed his military limitations. However, by forcing the Admiralty to adopt a convoy system for ships, he helped overcome the acute submarine menace of that year. Also, his 1918 success in uniting British and American troops on the western front with French soldiers under the overall command of French Marshall Ferdinand Foch was an important contribution to Allied victory.

Postwar Career

In the election of December, 1918, the coalition Conservatives won a majority in Parliament, but they retained Lloyd George as prime minister. At the Paris Peace Conference of 1919, he was the chief proponent of moderate terms for defeated Germany.

From 1919 to 1922, Lloyd George faced a host of difficulties. At home, labor unrest, unemployment, and housing shortages posed acute problems. The partitioning of Ireland averted war, but Irish troubles lingered. Britain faced secessionist movements in India and Egypt, immigration controversy in Palestine, and indecisive conferences on war debts and German reparations. Lloyd George managed to survive this series of crises. However, when he backed Greece in a losing war with Turkey in 1922 (an event known

visiting factories to encourage production, and expanding the role of women in war production. With Field Marshall Herbert Horatio Kitchener's death at sea on June 5, 1916, Lloyd George was appointed head of the War Office. He found his ideas blocked by the leading generals. Frustrated by what he saw as indecisive cabinet leadership, Lloyd George in November, 1916, demanded a special war council under his own direction. Upon Asquith's refusal, Lloyd George resigned, thus bringing down Asquith's government. The Conservatives under Bonar Law declined to form a government, but they became the largest bloc supporting Lloyd George when he was appointed prime minister on December 6, 1916.

934

The National Insurance Act of 1911

This measure provided unemployment, sickness, and disability payments for workers. Unemployment benefits of seven shillings a week for fifteen weeks were made on an experimental basis for some two million workers, particularly in the building trades. Sickness benefits were ten shillings a week, and disability benefits five shillings a week for about fourteen million manual workers ages sixteen to seventy. Workers made weekly contributions—for sickness and disability insurance, contributions were four pence by the workers, three pence by the employer, and two pence by the government. David Lloyd George succeeded in outmaneuvering British Medical Association critics, but many workers objected to making compulsory contributions. When he argued to crowds that "nine pence for four pence is a very good bargain," the reply was likely to be "nine pence for no pence would be better." The 1911 act paved the way for the "dole" of the 1920's and later for the National Health Act of 1948.

as the Chanak crisis), the Conservatives withdrew from the coalition government. Lloyd George resigned on October 19, 1922.

Lloyd George spent a dozen years attempting a political comeback, but he had a shrinking number of followers. In the 1930's he produced extensive memoirs, masterfully written but not entirely accurate. His 1936 visit to, and brief enchantment with, Adolf Hitler showed faulty judgment. In 1940 he was forceful in urging Neville Chamberlain's replacement by Winston Churchill, but he refused office in the new coalition, which he viewed as ineffective. Shortly before his death in 1945, he was granted a peerage as First Earl Lloyd-George of Dwyfor and Viscount Gwynedd of Dwyfor. The Dwyfor, a small Welsh river, had been a favorite playground and fishing spot of Lloyd George during his boyhood.

Lloyd George twice became a legend in his own time. Before 1914, as "the people's champion," he made government benefit common workers. Thereafter, his leadership in the British war effort earned him renown as "the man who won the war." Despite these accomplishments, problems in the years following World War I ended public faith in the man known as the Welsh Wizard.

Bibliography
French, David. *The Strategy of the Lloyd George Coalition, 1916-1918.* Oxford, England: Clarendon Press, 1995.
Grigg, John. *The Young Lloyd George.* Berkeley: University of California Press, 1974.
_____. *Lloyd George, the People's Champion.* Berkeley: University of California Press, 1978.
_____. *Lloyd George from Peace to War.* Berkeley: University of California Press, 1985.
Owen, Frank. *Tempestuous Journey: Lloyd George, His Life and Times.* New York: McGraw-Hill, 1955.
Rowland, Peter. *David Lloyd George.* New York: Macmillan, 1976.

K. Fred Gillum

Henry Cabot Lodge

Born: May 12, 1850; Boston, Massachusetts
Died: November 9, 1924; Cambridge, Massachusetts

U.S. senator (1893-1924)

Henry Cabot Lodge (HEHN-ree KA-buht LAHJ) was the only son of a prosperous clipper-ship owner engaged in the China trade. His mother was the granddaughter of George Cabot, who had been a renowned Federalist senator. In 1871 Lodge graduated from Harvard College and married Anna Cabot Davis, his cousin and the daughter of a U.S. Navy admiral. Lodge graduated from Harvard Law School (1874) and passed the bar a year later. He was associate editor of the *North American Review* under Henry Adams, his

Henry Cabot Lodge *(Library of Congress)*

Harvard history professor. Lodge obtained a Ph.D. in political science (Harvard, 1876) and published the first of several historical and biographical books notable for vigor and clarity but reflecting an ultraconservative political philosophy. His most powerful friend was Theodore Roosevelt—younger, also scholarly, but more dashing. The two worked together to fashion Republican Party policies from the early 1880's.

Political Career

Lodge won election as a Republican to the Massachusetts House of Representatives (1879-1881), failed in a bid for Congress (1882), but continued to serve his party faithfully. He was elected in 1886 as representative from the Sixth District of Massachusetts and served as an eloquent, diligent leader until 1893. He supported African American suffrage through federal control of elections, as well as civil-service reform, against much southern opposition. He favored high tariffs to protect American laborers and industries. In 1893 he was elected senator from Massachusetts, retaining that powerful position for the rest of his life.

Lodge's remarkable career in national and international politics demonstrated an unwavering commitment to a strong federal government and to American expansion overseas. His most important domestic work included helping draft both the Sherman Antitrust Act (1890), outlawing any action in restraint of trade and rendering guilty anyone seeking to create a monopoly, and the Pure Food and Drug Act (1906), protecting the public against dangerous food, drugs, and medicines. His amendment to the Hepburn Act (1906), regulating interstate railroads, placed commercial oil pipes under Interstate Commerce Commission supervision. In international politics, Lodge favored a strong navy and opposed British attempts to define the British Guiana-Venezuela border (1895). He implemented efforts to annex the Hawaiian Islands (from 1893) and supported the Spanish-American War, the subsequent treaty (1898), and immediate annexation of the seized Philippine Islands. He also favored the Hay-Pauncefote Treaty (1901), which led to construction of the Panama Canal.

Lodge and World War I

Continuing to support American territorial and commercial expansionism, Lodge regarded Woodrow Wilson, the Democratic president elected in 1912, as timid and confused in a rancorous dispute with Mexico that year. He defined Wilson's neutral position when World War I erupted as insufficiently nationalistic and as condoning an unacceptable spread of German commerce and culture.

Lodge campaigned against Wilson's policies in 1916 and supported American interven-

tion in 1917. As chairman of the Senate Foreign Relations Committee, Lodge led two successful partisan fights. The first was against ratification of the Versailles Treaty (1918) as not harsh enough against a defeated Germany. The second was against the United States joining the League of

U.S. senator Henry Cabot Lodge was instrumental in passage of the landmark Pure Food and Drug Act in 1906. Here, three years later, federal marshals destroy worm-infested raisins seized from Washington, D.C., area bakeries. *(Library of Congress)*

The Pure Food and Drug Act

President Theodore Roosevelt assumed the leadership of reformers energized by "muckraking" journalists' exposés of corruption in politics, business, and finance. Henry Cabot Lodge orchestrated public indignation against the ineptitude of states and federal sluggishness, thereby helping to enact the Pure Food and Drug Act in 1906. This act prohibited the misbranding of food and drugs and outlawed the interstate transportation of such misrepresented items. Strengthened by modifications (1912, 1913, 1923) to cover cosmetics, obesity cures, mechanical curative devices, and new habit-forming drugs, this progressive law was perhaps Lodge's most important legacy to the American people.

The Panama Canal under construction in 1909. U.S. senator Henry Cabot Lodge was a strong proponent of the canal. *(Popperfoto/Archive Photos)*

Nations, which he reasoned would diminish American sovereignty. Lodge died in Cambridge, Massachusetts, following prostate surgery. Widowed since 1915, he was survived by a daughter, Constance, and a son, John Ellerton. His first son, George Cabot, the father of Senator Henry Cabot Lodge (1902-1985), predeceased him.

In the tradition of Daniel Webster and Charles Sumner, Lodge was a brilliant senator from Massachusetts—scholar, philosopher, and pragmatic politician willing to use less than scrupulous means to advance his jingoistic ends. Through it all, his sturdy patriotism was never subject to doubt.

Bibliography
Chalfant, Edward. *Better in Darkness: A Biography of Henry Adams, His Second Life 1862-1891.* Hamden, Conn.: Archon Books, 1994.

Garraty, John A. *Henry Cabot Lodge: A Biography.* New York: Alfred A. Knopf, 1953.

Hatch, Alden. *The Lodges of Massachusetts.* New York: Hawthorn Books, 1973.

Selections from the Correspondence of Theodore Roosevelt and Henry Cabot Lodge. 2 vols. New York: Scribners, 1925.

Young, James Harvey. *Pure Food: Securing the Pure Food and Drug Act.* Princeton, N.J.: Princeton University Press, 1989.

Robert L. Gale

Huey Long

Born: August 30, 1893; near Winnfield, Louisiana
Died: September 10, 1935; Baton Rouge, Louisiana

U.S. political leader and would-be economic reformer

Huey Pierce Long (HEW-ee PEERS LONG) was born in rural north-central Louisiana. He dropped out of high school and never attended college, but he enrolled under special arrangements allowing him to study for the bar exam at the law schools of the University of Oklahoma and Tulane University. He passed the exam in May, 1915. His real vocation, however, was politics. In 1918 he was elected to the Louisiana Railroad Commission (soon renamed the Public Service Commission). He was elected governor ten years later. He won a U.S. Senate seat in 1930 and was planning a campaign for the presidency when he was assassinated in 1935. He married Rose McConnell in 1913, and they had three children.

Career as Governor

Huey Long used the power of the governorship to improve society in Louisiana. His administration enhanced health care and education, provided assistance for the elderly, and built more roads and bridges than any previous administration. These programs became especially important after 1929 as the Great Depression destroyed many economic resources that Americans had enjoyed. According to his critics, Long also established a regime in Louisiana that destroyed democratic government. He persuaded the legislature to approve many questionable laws that allowed him to accomplish his purposes, and he transferred power from local governments to the governor's office.

Huey Long *(Archive Photos/APA)*

Long interfered with elections, dominated state court judges, demanded campaign contributions from state employees, and described himself as the new constitution of Louisiana—meaning that his wishes outranked the highest law of the state.

Conflict with President Roosevelt

When Huey Long assumed his seat in the U.S. Senate in 1932, the Great Depression had dramatically decreased living standards throughout the country. Long, because of his experience providing social improvement programs in Louisiana, wanted to use the power of the U.S. government to provide similar assistance on a national scale. He supported New York governor Franklin D. Roosevelt for the presidency in 1932 because he believed that Roosevelt would provide that assistance. He initially supported the president's reform programs, collectively called the New Deal, but soon concluded that its measures did

U.S. senator and Louisiana Democratic Party leader Huey Long in 1932 arguing for the seating of his group of delegates at the Democrats' national convention. *(AP/Wide World Photos)*

The "Share Our Wealth" Program

The Share Our Wealth movement was Huey Long's alternative program to President Franklin Roosevelt's New Deal. Long proposed the program to redistribute the nation's resources more equitably during the Great Depression of the 1930's. The plan included a proposal for the government to confiscate personal fortunes in excess of three million dollars. The money obtained would be used to provide every American family with $5,000 for shelter and transportation, to provide $30 monthly pensions to all persons over sixty-five years of age, to grant cash bonuses to World War I veterans, to guarantee a $2,500 annual income to workers, and to provide free college education to qualified students.

The idea attracted thousands of supporters nationwide. However, Long was assassinated before he had the chance to discover how much support the plan really had. Most economists who have studied the plan maintain that it was not economically viable—that confiscating all fortunes in excess of three million dollars simply would not have provided enough money to pay for the ambitious proposals.

not provide adequate relief. He therefore created an alternative social reform program, called Share Our Wealth, and became a vocal critic of the president. He eventually became disillusioned with both Democratic and Republican Party policies regarding the Depression. By 1935 he was preparing to establish a new political party and accept its presidential nomination. That effort ended when he was shot while in the Louisiana capitol building on September 8, 1935. He died two days later.

Huey Long's nationally broadcast radio speeches on social justice issues brought him thousands of letters of support. He became a symbol of hope for people whose finances had been destroyed by the Depression. His criticism, along with that of Francis Townsend and Charles Coughlin, helped to convince President Roosevelt to propose Social Security and higher tax rates on the wealthy. His legacy in Louisiana included concentration of power in a small political faction on a scale almost unparalleled in American history.

Bibliography

Dethloff, Henry C. "Huey P. Long." In *The Louisiana Governors*, edited by Joseph G. Dawson III. Baton Rouge: Louisiana State University Press, 1990.

Hair, William Ivy. *The Kingfish and His Realm: The Life and Times of Huey P. Long*. Baton Rouge: Louisiana State University Press, 1991.

Jeansonne, Glen. *Messiah of the Masses: Huey P. Long and the Great Depression*. New York: HarperCollins, 1993.

Williams, T. Harry. *Huey Long*. New York: Alfred A. Knopf, 1969.

Jerry Purvis Sanson

Erich Ludendorff

Born: April 9, 1865; Kruszewnia, near Posen, Prussia (now Poznań), Poland
Died: December 20, 1937; Munich, Germany

German military leader during World War I

Erich Friedrich Wilhelm Ludendorff's (EH-rihk FREED-rihk VIHL-hehlm LEW-dehn-dohrf) computerlike mind and compulsive work habits were among his talents that were polished at the prestigious Berlin War Academy. After attending the academy he was assigned to the German General Staff in 1904. There he worked with General Alfred von Schlieffen on a plan to handle a

Erich Ludendorff *(Library of Congress)*

two-front war. Promoted to lieutenant colonel in 1907, Ludendorff became even more involved with fine-tuning the famous Schlieffen Plan. However, he became increasingly worried about the manpower that would be needed to make the plan work. Politicking for personnel increases only succeeded in angering his superiors. Consequently, in January, 1913, Ludendorff was assigned the less esoteric duties of regimental infantry command.

World War I

At the outbreak of World War I in 1914, Ludendorff was appointed chief quartermaster of the Second Army, which headed to attack the heavily fortified Belgium city of Liège. Capturing Liège was a pivotal goal if the Schlieffen Plan was to succeed. Ludendorff was in charge of logistics, and he could not have imagined that the battle for Liège would make him a national hero. First Ludendorff's commander died and Ludendorff took over; then he managed to stumble across the perfect back-road route to the city. Finally, most of Liège's defenders evacuated the city to protect the more important fort network. By the end it seemed that the city had surrendered personally to him.

Meanwhile, in the east, two Russian armies were threatening to destroy the German Eighth Army. Germany's new hero was appointed chief of staff under General Paul von Hindenburg. They decimated Russian armies at Tannenberg in August, 1914, and at Masurian Lakes one month later. Ludendorff and Hindenburg were recognized as Germany's saviors. Ludendorff remained in the east until August, 1916, as the war turned into one of attrition. At this juncture Ludendorff and Hindenburg fought for having

Caporetto, 1917

Italy's entry into World War I against Germany in 1916 produced serious concern among Germany's war leaders. A particular worry was that the Austrian forces facing Italy were insufficient and poorly led. Erich Ludendorff's solution was to send seven well-equipped German divisions, incorporate Austrian forces into German forces, and take Italy out of the war with one stroke.

The blow was delivered on October 24, 1917, when, following intensive bombardment, combined Austrian and German forces attacked the Italians at Caporetto (then an Austrian town,

now Kobarid, Slovenia). Within twelve hours, one million Italian soldiers were in retreat and 350,000 had been taken prisoner. Forty thousand had been killed and another ninety thousand wounded. The retreat continued until November 12, when eleven Anglo-French divisions, withdrawn from the western front, reinforced the crippled Italian forces. Within weeks, Russia under Bolshevik leadership withdrew from the war. With these heartening developments, Ludendorff planned another massive strike—the spring, 1918, offensive—to drive England and France out of the war before full U.S. entry.

one command that could coordinate all war efforts. Germany soon entered a period of military control.

Total War

For Ludendorff, modern war was total war ending with total victory. On the home front, this meant control of national propaganda, economic production, and food allocations. Total warfare also included requisitioning labor forces to work in German factories. In foreign affairs it meant that occupied areas were to be fully exploited. Unrestricted submarine warfare would be used, and revolutionaries such as Vladimir Ilich Lenin could be unleashed to undermine Russia. Total victory meant striking decisive blows to smash enemy forces utterly. Such blows were delivered against Romania and Italy.

German general Erich Ludendorff (left) and other army officers attending the 1921 funeral of Bavaria's King Ludwig. *(Library of Congress)*

943

National Socialists (Nazis) attempted to seize power in Bavaria in an ill-conceived 1923 plan known as the beer-hall putsch. Erich Ludendorff was involved in the failed undertaking. *(Deutsche Presse Agentur/Archive Photos)*

Ludendorff also forced Bolshevik Russia to sign the Treaty of Brest-Litovsk, ceding to Germany one-third of Russia's most productive territory. In addition, Ludendorff helped found the Fatherland Party, which had equally comprehensive aims for the West.

Defeat

German war weariness and shortages stimulated Ludendorff's planning for an all-out offensive during the spring of 1918; the offensive was intended to end the war in a single blow. In spite of the offensive's initial success, an Allied counteroffensive doomed Ludendorff's plan. He resigned on October 26. Within two weeks the war was over, but Ludendorff had an excuse for the defeat: Germany had been "stabbed in the back" by politicians.

In postwar Germany Ludendorff was involved in the fiasco known as the Kapp putsch in 1920 and in Adolf Hitler's even more ludicrous Munich "beer-hall putsch" of 1923. Afterward, while Hitler sat in jail, Ludendorff was National Socialist Reichstag Deputy (1924-1928). He ran for president in 1925 but was defeated by Hindenburg. During the 1930's Ludendorff worked on his memoirs, published in 1933, and an exposition of his military doctrine, *Der Totale Krieg* (1935; *The Nation at War*, 1936). He put forth the ideas that war is natural to humankind and that modern war involves harnessing total national energy. Hitler read Ludendorff's books and attended his funeral.

Bibliography

Asprey, Robert B. *The German High Command at War: Hindenburg and Ludendorff Conduct World War I*. New York: Morrow, 1991.

Goodspeed, D. J. *Ludendorff: Genius of World War I*. Boston: Houghton Mifflin, 1966.

Parkinson, Robert. *Tormented Warrior: Ludendorff and the Supreme Command*. London: Hodder and Stoughton, 1978.

Irwin Halfond

Patrice Lumumba

Born: July 2, 1925; Onalua, Katako-Kombe Territory, Sankaru District, Kasai, Belgian Congo
Died: c. January 17, 1961; Katanga, Congo

First prime minister of independent Congo (1960)

Patrice Hémery Lumumba (pah TREES ay-meh-REE loo-MOOM-bah) belonged to the Batetela tribe of the Kasai region of the Belgian Congo. The Batetela suffered successive waves of invasions by Arab slave traders and colonizing Europeans. Born in an environment of uprootedness, Lumumba was a cultural orphan driven by a perpetual quest for identity. However, his Catholic upbringing made him favorably disposed to Christianity as well as to Western education. He belonged to the class of *évolués*—the partly westernized Congolese middle class—though he gradually grew to be an ardent nationalist.

Early Career

Growing up in Stanleyville (now Kisangani, Congo), a melting pot of different tribes and races, Lumumba recognized the need to transcend narrow ethnic and tribal loyalties. Additionally, his nationalism had been awakened as early as 1952-1953. After a brief stint as a postal clerk in Stanleyville in the early 1950's, and following a felony conviction, he relocated to Léopoldville (now Kinshasa, Congo) in 1957.

In 1958 the Belgian government announced a policy of decolonization, and on August 28 of that year French general Charles de Gaulle made an offer of complete independence to the French Congo at Brazzaville. These external events inspired political mobilization in the Belgian Congo, although none of the many political parties that mushroomed could boast of a national platform until the formation of the National Congolese Movement (the MNC) in 1958 under Lumumba's leadership. Lumumba attended the first All-African People's Conference in Accra, Ghana, in December of that year.

Though Lumumba was arrested in connection with a riot on January 4-6, 1959, he was released to participate in the Round Table Conference convened by the Belgian government in Brussels in January, 1960. The conference decided that June 30, 1960, would be the date for Congo independence. A constitution for the new independent state was promulgated in May. Joseph Kasavubu (who had formed an early Congolese independence association in 1950) became the president, and Lumumba the prime minister, of the independent Congo.

Patrice Lumumba *(Express Newspapers/Archive Photos)*

945

The Murder of Lumumba

Lumumba was ousted from government following the Katangan secession and the subsequent coup by the army chief of staff, Colonel Joseph Mobutu, on September 14, 1960. He then tried to join forces with Antoine Gizenga, head of the African Solidarity Party in Stanleyville. He was arrested by Mobutu's army, however, and imprisoned at Thysville. In January, 1961, he was flown to Katanga, escorted by soldiers from the Baluba tribe of the Kasai region. The Baluba had been persecuted, by Lumumba's order, a few months earlier. It is believed that Lumumba was beaten by his escorts during the flight and then murdered shortly after landing in Elizabethville on January 17, 1961.

Prime Minister of a Troubled Country

On July 5, 1960, six days after independence, the Congolese national army, the Force Publique, mutinied against their Belgian commander. On July 11, the Belgian navy bombarded the coastal city of Matadi, prompting further violence by the Congo's soldiers. On the same day, Moïse Tshombe, the governor of Katanga province, announced Katanga's secession from the Congo, apparently with the unofficial support of the province's Belgian residents as well as from the Belgian government.

Unable to cope with the situation, Kasavubu and Lumumba sought U.N. intervention. The United Nations sent troops to help expel the Belgians from Congo, but they refused to become involved in the Katangan secession issue. On August 8, the Congo suffered further disintegration when South Kasai announced its secession. With the help of the armies of several African states as well as help from the Soviet Union, Lumumba ended the secession of Kasai on August 26.

However, his government collapsed before he could mount an all-out assault on Katanga. Kasavubu, who had put up with his political rival Lumumba when the first national government was formed, dismissed the latter on September 5. Prime Minister Lumumba, in turn, issued a statement deposing the president. The United Nations decided to recognize the Kasavubu faction in October, but Lumumba fought on. In the ensuing power struggle, Lumumba was arrested in December, 1960, and transferred to Katanga, where he was assassinated, probably on January 17, 1961.

Bibliography

Kanza, Thomas. *Rise and Fall of Patrice Lumumba: Conflict in the Congo*. Boston: G. K. Hall, 1979.

Scott, Ian. *Tumbled House: Congo After Independence*. London: Oxford University Press, 1969.

Staff, Paul. *Patrice Lumumba*. Atlantic Heights, N.J.: Humanities Press, 1973.

Narasingha P. Sil

Albert Lutuli

Born: c. 1898; near Bulawayo, Rhodesia (now Zimbabwe)
Died: July 21, 1967; Stanger, South Africa

South African antiapartheid activist, winner of 1960 Nobel Peace Prize

Albert John Mvumbi Lutuli (AL-burt JON uhm-VUHM-bee luh-TEW-lee), also spelled Luthuli, was the son of a Congregationalist mission interpreter and the nephew of a Zulu chief. He attended mission schools for his elementary and secondary education, learned English, and became a teacher of Zulu literature and history. Seventeen years later, he was urged to accept a position as chief. He also began attending international religious conferences around the world. Lutuli studied Christianity and the use of nonviolence to combat oppression, and he served on various race-relations committees.

The African National Congress

In 1946 Lutuli joined the African National Congress (ANC) and quickly rose to prominence. When the ANC called on nonwhites in 1952 to violate unjust laws openly, Lutuli encouraged the Zulus to participate. Among such laws were those forbidding blacks to use public libraries, post offices, and railroad stations. These laws were part of South Africa's institutionalized system of racial oppression known as apartheid. The government ordered Lutuli to quit the ANC or resign as chief, but he refused, saying that a chief's first duty is not to the government but to his people. The government responded by taking away his chieftaincy and forbidding him to leave his home for one year. Tribal elders

Black South Africans burning their identity passes in protest in the 1950's. *(Archive Photos)*

947

The African National Congress (ANC)

In 1912, when the Union of South Africa was only two years old, a group of black Western-educated professionals formed the South African Natives National Congress to encourage the new white government to share benefits with nonwhites. Pixley Seeme, the organization's first leader, called for South Africans to share power equally, regardless of race, though he held little hope that this would occur. Later in the 1910's, the renamed African National Congress (ANC) staged unsuccessful nonviolent protests against the new pass laws. For three decades, while the white minority created ever more oppressive regulations to control the black majority, the ANC remained committed to nonviolence.

By the 1950's, most ANC leaders had been arrested or banned for their antigovernment stands, and a new, younger leadership formed alliances with communists and nonblacks. This contributed to the organization's formal banning by the government in 1960. Banning led the ANC to turn to sabotage and other violent acts, followed in turn by more repression and more anger among the repressed. With many leaders imprisoned or in exile, the ANC continued to lead the struggle against apartheid, with increasing international approval.

In 1990 Nelson Mandela, who had attained the role of legend in the ANC, was released from prison after twenty-seven years, and the ban against the ANC was lifted. Mandela ran for president on the ANC ticket in South Africa's first multiracial elections in 1994, and he won by a large margin. As a political party, the ANC played an important role in establishing a new multiracial government.

Albert Lutuli *(The Nobel Foundation)*

refused to name a successor as chief, and a month later Lutuli was elected president-general of the ANC.

Lutuli was banned (forbidden to speak to people in public) for two more years in 1954 and was arrested for treason in 1956. He continued to speak publicly against injustice, and he once publicly burned his identity pass, a document that all nonwhites were required to carry at all times. Large numbers of nonwhites, and later many whites, participated in his public meetings. In 1959 Lutuli was charged with promoting hostility between the races and banished to his village for five years. The ANC was formally outlawed.

The Nobel Peace Prize

While Lutuli was cutting sugar cane on his farm in 1960, he received word that he had been awarded that year's Nobel Peace Prize for his commitment to nonviolent struggle against injustice. He was allowed to leave his village long enough to accept the prize in Sweden, where he addressed an international audience on the evils of apartheid and the strength of nonviolent resistance. Returning to South Africa and the remainder of his banishment, he wrote an autobiography, *Let My People Go* (1962). That year, the government passed a law forbidding the media to print any quotations from Lutuli. During this period, the ANC entered a new era by turning to violence. In 1964 Lutuli was banished for another five years. He died in a train accident in 1967.

Nonviolent Resistance

For all his life, Lutuli remained committed to nonviolent resistance to injustice. His winning of the Nobel Peace Prize drew crucial international attention to oppression in South Africa, even as people of color within South Africa began to criticize Lutuli for being too passive. While he did not live to see the fruits of his struggle, Lutuli's contributions were invaluable in bringing about the peaceful end to apartheid in 1994.

Bibliography

Benson, Mary. *Chief Albert Lutuli of South Africa*. London: Oxford University Press, 1963.

Harcourt, Melville. *Portraits of Destiny*. New York: Sheed and Ward, 1966.

Luthuli, Albert John. *Let My People Go*. New York: McGraw-Hill, 1962.

Cynthia A. Bily

Douglas MacArthur

Born: January 26, 1880; Little Rock, Arkansas
Died: April 5, 1964; Washington, D.C.

U.S. military leader, commander of Pacific forces in World War II

Douglas MacArthur (DUHG-luhs ma-KAHR-thur) was one of the United States' greatest generals and war heroes. The son and grandson of generals, he spent his early years in southwestern Army forts. His mother was the daughter of a Virginia cotton merchant. Both parents had a strong influence in the development of MacArthur's lifelong character traits: a sense of personal responsibility, perseverance in reaching his goals, and belief in himself. He was a high achiever in military school in Texas and at the U.S. Military Academy at West Point. He graduated from West Point in 1903 with the highest scholastic record earned by any cadet in twenty-five years.

Early Military Career

MacArthur began his military service as a second lieutenant in the Army Corps of Engineers. In 1905 he was appointed aide-de-camp to his father, who at that time was on assignment in Japan to evaluate its war with Russia. The evaluation was extended to include Southeast Asia and India. MacArthur returned to Japan nine months later, where his cultural education was further enriched by firsthand experience and understanding of its citizens and the importance of their emperor.

MacArthur served with distinction in World War I. He was influential in forming and naming the famous Rainbow Division of the National Guard. Technically, MacArthur was the division commander's chief of staff, but that role did not keep him behind his desk. He was regularly at the front and in the trenches, directing, leading, and encouraging the troops. By the end of the war he had seven Silver Stars, two Purple Hearts, and several decorations from other countries.

Douglas MacArthur holding a press conference upon his arrival in Japan in August, 1945, at the end of World War II. *(National Archives)*

The Inchon Landing

At the outset of the Korean War, General Douglas MacArthur's U.N. forces were driven to a small perimeter at the extreme southern end of the Korean peninsula. Unable to break the resulting stalemate, MacArthur applied lessons learned during the island campaigns of the Pacific war with Japan. He conceived and executed a brilliant amphibious landing at the port of Inchon, 110 miles (177 kilometers) north of the existing U.N. position. The landing was designed to cut the Korean peninsula in half far north of the existing lines, thus trapping the North Korean army.

Because of numerous natural obstacles—including high tides, narrow approaches from the sea formed by a series of islands, and a dangerously rapid harbor current—Inchon was one of the last places the enemy would have expected MacArthur's forces to land. The key element was surprise. To help assure this, MacArthur's command staged an elaborate deception operation to make it appear that the landing would occur at Kansan, 105 miles (169 kilometers) south of Inchon. With a few minor exceptions, the plan worked. It resulted in the near-total destruction of the North Korean army and the liberation of South Korea.

The 1920's and 1930's

After the war, MacArthur was assigned to a job he did not want but did not refuse: superintendent of the military academy at West Point. With the job came confirmation of his temporary wartime promotion to brigadier general. At age thirty-nine, he was the youngest superintendent in the academy's history. He made many changes in its training system, curriculum, and rules, which he believed would better prepare the students for the changing military world awaiting them.

Following his work at West Point, MacArthur was posted to the Philippines. In 1930 President Herbert Hoover named him chief of staff, the youngest in the Army's history. MacArthur spent most of the next five years trying to get Congress to enlarge and strengthen the Army, but he had little success. The country was deep in economic depression, and there were many other priorities. When President Franklin D. Roosevelt replaced Hoover in 1933, MacArthur tried in vain to persuade him to increase military funding. Roosevelt was preoccupied with his "New Deal," his collection of domestic programs intended to help millions of Americans who had no money or jobs. MacArthur contributed greatly to this effort by putting into effect the Civilian Conservation Corps (CCC), which put unemployed young men to work in American forests.

When MacArthur's assignment as chief of staff ended, he accepted a job in the Philippines as military adviser to his old friend Manuel Quezon, who was expecting to be elected Philippine president. Quezon wanted MacArthur to help him plan military defenses for the Philippines that he believed would be needed when the islands became independent. On the boat to Manila, MacArthur met his future wife, Jean Faircloth. They married in April, 1937. Their son, Arthur, was born the following year.

World War II Service

On December 7, 1941, Japan bombed the United States' naval base at Pearl Harbor, Hawaii. The next day Roosevelt declared war on Japan and named MacArthur Allied commander of the Southwest Pacific. He fought first in the Philippines. He led a diverse force of Philippine and U.S. forces in a defense that delayed Japan's

Douglas MacArthur, as commander of the Allies, signing the agreement by which Japan formally surrendered at the end of World War II. *(National Archives)*

advance for three months, then escaped to Australia to direct that continent's defense. For the balance of the Pacific war, he led a brilliant campaign to expel the Japanese from all their island conquests, culminating in his return to the Philippines, as he had promised. In 1944 he was made a five-star general.

Early in August, 1945, the United States dropped two atomic bombs on Japan three days apart, ending the war. The Japanese officially surrendered to MacArthur on September 2, on the battleship Missouri in Tokyo Bay. Terms of the surrender provided for Allied occupation of Japan for five years. MacArthur directed the occupation. Using the knowledge of Japanese cul-

ture that he had gained years ago as his father's aide in Japan, he successfully blended Western ideals with Japanese culture to create a lasting democracy in Japan.

The Korean War

In 1950, when North Korean communist forces invaded South Korea, MacArthur became commander of the U.N. forces. They drove the North Koreans out of South Korea. MacArthur wanted to expand the war into North Korea, then China. The U.S. government refused to allow it. As a result of this and other disagreements, on April 11, 1951, President Harry S Truman relieved MacArthur of all commands. On returning to the

United States, MacArthur was met and cheered by thousands everywhere he went. He was the keynote speaker at the Republican National Convention in 1952.

Soldier-statesman Douglas MacArthur's most enduring legacy is modern Japan. The Japanese people were shattered and humiliated at the end of World War II in 1945. In five years he created a new Japan ready to take its place in the modern world as a successful, democratic state. His military campaigns in both the Pacific and Korean wars will be studied for years to come as examples of perfection in the military arts.

Bibliography

Blair, Clay, Jr. *MacArthur*. New York: Simon & Schuster, 1977.

James, D. Clayton. *The Years of MacArthur: Volume 2, 1941-1945*. Boston: Houghton Mifflin, 1975.

MacArthur, Douglas. *Reminiscences*. New York: McGraw-Hill, 1964.

Manchester, William. *American Caesar: Douglas MacArthur, 1880-1964*. Boston: Little, Brown, 1978.

Utz, Curtis A. *Assault from the Sea: The Amphibious Landing at Inchon*. Washington, D.C.: Naval Historical Center, Department of the Navy, 1994.

Ollie Shuman

Douglas MacArthur addressing a huge crowd at Chicago's Soldiers' Field in 1951, shortly after President Harry S Truman relieved him of his command of U.S. forces in Korea. *(National Archives)*

MacArthur in the Philippines

In 1937 Douglas MacArthur retired from the U.S. Army and was appointed field marshal by Philippine president Manuel Quezon. He was to organize the defense of the Philippine Islands, which were scheduled to become independent in 1946.

In July, 1941, MacArthur was recalled to active duty by the U.S. Army. When the Japanese attacked Pearl Harbor in December, 1941, MacArthur skillfully led his forces in a retreat to the Bataan Peninsula, which afforded a short line of defense. For four months they repelled a vastly superior Japanese force, seriously upsetting the enemy's timetable. At President Roosevelt's orders, in March, 1942, MacArthur, his wife, and son escaped to Australia in a dangerous journey by PT boat. Before his departure he promised President Quezon and the Philippine people that he would return. He kept his promise, triumphantly leading the U.S. Army back in 1944.

Ramsay MacDonald

Born: October 12, 1866; Lossiemouth, Morayshire, Scotland
Died: November 9, 1937; at sea, bound for South America

The first Labour Party prime minister of Great Britain (1924, 1929-1931)

James Ramsay MacDonald (JAYMZ RAM-zee mak-DO-nuhld), illegitimate son of Anne Ramsay and John MacDonald, studied at Drainie School and became a student teacher in Scotland in 1881. He left in 1885, at nineteen, for work in Bristol, England. There he first encountered socialist organizations. He returned to Scotland later that year. In 1886 he went to London, struggled for employment, became a clerk in a warehouse, and studied science so extensively that a collapse forced his return home. In 1888 he became secretary to Thomas Slough, parliamentary candidate for West Islington, and he held this post until 1891. He became active with the Fabian Socialists and the Social Democratic Federation.

In 1894 MacDonald joined the Independent Labour Party (ILP) and unsuccessfully ran for the Southampton seat in Parliament. In 1896 he met and married Margaret Ethel Gladstone, a social worker and the daughter of a prominent chemist. She brought her energy, sympathy for the socialist cause, and social gifts—as well as economic security—to the marriage. They traveled widely, to Europe, South Africa, India, Canada, New Zealand, the United States, and Australia. In 1900 MacDonald became secretary of the labour representation committee, an umbrella group of labour and socialist organizations that was to evolve into the Labour Party. He remained its secretary until 1912 and its treasurer from 1912 to 1924.

Parliament

Ramsay MacDonald entered Parliament in 1906 as a member from Leicester. The twenty-nine Labour Party members, with Keir Hardie as first chairman, were elected as the result of two developments in which MacDonald was a central participant. First, the Trades Union Congress (TUC) agreed to a levy on members to fund the party. Second, an informal deal was struck with the Liberals that allowed Labour to fight unopposed by Liberals in seats where they had the better opportunity of beating the Conservative Party candidates. This necessary partial alliance haunted MacDonald throughout his career, because it was seen by the far Left as compromising Labour. MacDonald's approach prevailed.

Ramsay MacDonald *(Library of Congress)*

However, MacDonald, who in 1911 became chairman of the Parliamentary Party, repeatedly refused a seat in Liberal cabinets and saw Labour as the eventual successor to liberalism. In 1911 MacDonald's wife died of blood poisoning, a blow that contributed to his growing sense of isolation.

World War I

MacDonald opposed the declaration of war that would bring England into World War I, but he undertook to support the war once it was declared in 1914. He resigned the party chairmanship in 1914 because he opposed the decision to support the government's demand for £100 million in war credits. His wartime position was consistently difficult, because he was portrayed as a pacifist and because his initial opposition to war was employed by German propagandists. He struggled to keep views of moderation toward the enemy in the foreground. However, his position was further damaged by his support of the Aleksandr Kerensky government in Russia—a provisional government that came to power upon the collapse of the czar's regime early in 1917—being misrepresented as support for the Bolsheviks.

The Run to Power

MacDonald lost his seat in 1918 but began to reinstate his national reputation by convincing both the ILP and the Labour Party to denounce communism officially in 1920. When the extremists seceded from these groups and attacked him, his national profile was greatly improved. He was returned to Parliament in 1921 and 1922, and in 1922 he was selected as leader of the official opposition. When the Conservative government lost a no-confidence motion on January 17, 1924, MacDonald was called to form the first Labour government. This minority government fell on October 8. From 1924 to his triumphant reemergence as prime minister in 1929, when Labour won 287 seats, MacDonald led the oppo-

Ramsay MacDonald tips his hat to a passerby in 1924, the year MacDonald formed Britain's first Labour government. *(Express Newspapers/Archive Photos)*

sition and helped create the party manifesto, *Labour and the Nation* (1928). Early in 1930 he oversaw the Naval Conference, which succeeded in setting ratios of naval armament for the major powers. Later in the year he oversaw the first Indian Round Table discussion. Then the Great Depression, which began in 1929 and was getting

British prime minister Ramsay MacDonald addresses the U.S. House of Representatives in 1929. *(Library of Congress)*

worse, caught up with him. When his cabinet could not decide on emergency measures to stave off a currency collapse, he tendered the resignation of his government to King George V.

National Government

MacDonald then accepted the king's wishes and became head of a national government on August 24, 1931. This role lost him the support of most of the Labour Party, and he and other Labour ministers in the cabinet were drummed out of the party. The national government collapsed on October 7. To his discomfort, MacDonald now found himself leading a Liberal-Conservative coalition against Labour to a resounding victory. His government undertook economic retrenchment, and MacDonald took the lead in foreign affairs at an international conference in 1932 and a disarmament conference in Geneva. He also oversaw a program of national rearmament that began in 1935 in response to Adolf Hitler's rise in Germany. On June 7, 1935, he resigned as

The Zinoviev Letter

Entering the October, 1924, election, Ramsay MacDonald's short-lived Labour government was being tested over its withdrawal of prosecution of a newspaper article inciting mutiny and over a proposed loan guarantee to Russia. Then the "Zinoviev letter" was revealed. Supposedly a message from the president of the Communist International (Comintern) in Moscow, it instructed the British Communist Party to prepare to take over British institutions. The letter was released by the British government, along with a diplomatic protest from the government at this interference in domestic affairs. However, because the newspapers got the letter for public release and because the government protest was dated long after the letter, it was seen as proof of Bolshevik sympathies in Labour ranks. Matters were further confused because MacDonald, doubting the letter's authenticity, had not initialed the draft protest for release and because he was caught away from London when the storm broke. This supposed "Red plot" played a major role in the subsequent Conservative victory. It is now known that the letter was created by White Russian émigrés and placed in Foreign Office hands with the help of the Conservative Party Central Committee and the intelligence services.

Britain's First Labour Government

Ramsay MacDonald formed Britain's first Labour government after the defeat of the Conservatives on January 7, 1924. It was a minority government that depended on Liberal Party support. He serve as prime minister and foreign secretary. In the latter post he distinguished himself by leading a successful negotiation to reduce Germany's war reparations to the Allies (owed after Germany's defeat in World War I). However, the issue of a loan to Russia in exchange for reparations for British property seized in the Russian Revolution of 1917 was deeply contentious. Then the government handling of the prosecution of a writer for the *Workers' Weekly*—who had written a letter apparently urging mutiny in the armed forces—brought about a motion of censure. The government fell on October 8, 1924. The Labour Party had proved that it could handle office, but its minority position had given it little leeway.

prime minister. He ran again and was defeated in November, 1935, but was returned in a by-election in January, 1936. He died late in 1937 of heart failure.

A Life

MacDonald was a lonely and sometimes bitter man, but his leadership of the Labour Party brought it into the government and placed it at the center of British political life. He never deserted the cause in his own eyes, but in heading the national government, he chose to act for the nation rather than the particular interests of his party.

Bibliography

Hamilton, Mary Agnes. *J. Ramsay MacDonald*. Freeport, N.Y.: Books for Libraries Press, 1971.

Marquand, David. *Ramsay MacDonald*. London: Cape, 1977.

Ward, Stephen R. *James Ramsay MacDonald: Low Born Among the High Brows*. New York: P. Lang, 1990.

Peter Brigg

Samora Moisès Machel

Born: September 29, 1933; Chilembene, Mozambique
Died: October 19, 1986; Mbuzini, near Komatipoort, Lebombo Mountains, South Africa

First president of independent Mozambique (1975-1986)

Samora Moisès Machel (sah-MAW-rah MOI-shays ma-SHEHL) was the son of peasants in the Limpopo Valley of southern Mozambique, and his family had a tradition of fighting the Portuguese colonizers. When Machel's brother died in a mining accident and the colonial government provided no compensation to his family, Machel's resentment increased. After attending a Catholic mission school for six years, Machel got a job and earned a nursing degree in night school. He moved to the capital, Maputo, and worked at a hospital. His unfair wages—much lower than those of his white coworkers—fueled his desire for revolution.

Joining the Liberation Struggle

In June, 1962, a group of Mozambican exiles in Tanzania, led by Eduardo Mondlane, formed the Front for the Liberation of Mozambique (FRELIMO). Machel had met Mondlane a year or two earlier and was impressed by his ideas. Soon after the formation of FRELIMO, Machel traveled to Tanzania and joined the fight. After training in Algeria, Machel commanded the first group of freedom fighters that crossed the border from Tanzania into Mozambique in September, 1964. He personally led the first assault on a Portuguese base.

During the next few years, Machel took on greater responsibilities for training troops in Tanzania. He became an important figure in the political wing of FRELIMO but continued to participate in military operations. Machel also began to spread Marxist notions, such as collective farming, among the peasants. In 1969, Mondlane was killed. Machel initially became one of three coleaders of FRELIMO, then in 1970 was elected president. Machel directed his followers through

four more years of war, but could not drive the Portuguese from the coastal region.

Victory and Independence

The turning point came in April, 1974, in Lisbon, when a group of military officers overthrew the Portuguese government. Portuguese representatives reached a settlement with Machel in September and agreed that Mozambique would become independent on June 25, 1975. At a celebration on that day in Maputo's stadium, Machel proclaimed independence. That night, FRELIMO's executive committee chose him to be the first president of independent Mozambique.

The end of the war against Portugal did not bring peace, however, as the fighting in neighboring Southern Rhodesia escalated in the late 1970's. Machel firmly supported Robert Mugabe's Zimbabwe African National Liberation

Samora Moisès Machel visiting a Mozambique village in 1974. *(Agence France Presse/Archive Photos)*

Army and allowed the organization to establish bases in Mozambique. As a result, the Southern Rhodesian security forces launched devastating strikes into Machel's nation. Zimbabwe's 1980 independence did not bring peace, either. South African security forces regularly raided Mozambique in the early 1980's in search of bases of its enemy the African National Congress. Furthermore, South Africa sponsored the operations of a group of rebels who sought to overthrow Machel.

The ongoing destruction, coupled with the legacy of poverty from the brutal Portuguese colonial regime, made Machel's goal of bringing justice to his people virtually impossible. Circumstances forced him to abandon some of his Marxist beliefs, and he sought aid from Great Britain and the United States. The Americans began to supply substantial assistance in 1983, and Machel even had a cordial meeting with Ronald Reagan in September, 1985. By then he had signed a treaty of nonaggression with South Africa, and progress toward real recovery in Mozambique seemed to be beginning. However, Machel's rule was cut short in October, 1986, when he died in a plane crash in South Africa. His second wife, Graca, and a son from his first marriage survived him. Samora Machel fought long and hard to bring justice to his land, and he can

Samora Moisès Machel (*Agence France Presse/Archive Photos*)

truly be considered the George Washington of Mozambique.

Bibliography

Christie, Iain. *Samora Machel: A Biography*. London: Zed Press, 1989.

Newitt, Malyn. *A History of Mozambique*. Bloomington: Indiana University Press, 1995.

Thompson, Carol. *Challenge to Imperialism*. Boulder, Colo.: Westview Press, 1985.

Andy DeRoche

The FRELIMO Freedom Fighters

On June 25, 1962, a group of Mozambican exiles in Tanzania formed the Front for the Liberation of Mozambique (FRELIMO) to fight the Portuguese colonial regime. The leader was Eduardo Mondlane, who labored to bring unity to the movement. In 1963 Samora Machel joined FRELIMO, and he led the first attack against a Portuguese base in Mozambique in 1964. During the next five years, the FRELIMO freedom fighters battled the Portuguese soldiers and instructed the peasants in Marxism. While they made progress, internal divisions racked the leadership, culminating in the assassination of Mondlane in 1969. Machel became the sole leader of FRELIMO in 1970 and expanded the military operations into much of rural Mozambique. The liberation army applied continual pressure on the Portuguese government, which was toppled in a coup in Lisbon in April, 1974. Mozambique officially gained independence in June, 1975: The FRELIMO freedom fighters had achieved their goal.

Harold Macmillan

Born: February 10, 1894; London, England
Died: December 29, 1986; Birch Grove, Sussex, England

Prime minister of Great Britain (1957-1963)

Maurice Harold Macmillan (MOH-rihs HEH-ruhld mak-MIH-luhn) was the son of Maurice Crawford Macmillan, a publisher, and Nellie Belles Macmillan, an American with musical and artistic interests. He was the third child and the third son; his brothers were eight and four years older than he. He was educated at Summerfields day school, Eton, and Balliol College, Oxford. Attaining the rank of captain during World War I, he received five wounds in combat, two of which resulted in some impairment for the rest of his

Harold Macmillan *(Library of Congress)*

life. He met Lady Dorothy Cavendish while each was residing temporarily in Canada, and they were married on April 21, 1920, at St. Margaret's Church, Westminster. Between 1921 and 1930, their son and three daughters were born.

Conservative Politician

Despite his having a perfectly good job as a publisher, Harold Macmillan decided to run for Parliament as a Tory (Conservative) in the general election of December, 1923. He came within seventy-three votes of winning the seat and was encouraged to run again in October, 1924. He was elected comfortably as part of a Conservative Party landslide and, at age thirty, his new life had begun.

Macmillan represented Stockton-on-Tees in the northeast, one of the most economically depressed areas of Britain. He soon became one of the more progressive Conservatives, coauthoring in 1927 *Industry and the State*, a manifesto of the progressive wing of the party. In 1929, following the worldwide financial crash, Macmillan was voted out of office. Also in that unhappy year, his wife began a long relationship with a dashing young man named Robert Boothby. Despite a collapse, which may have been a full-scale nervous breakdown, Macmillan was returned to Parliament in 1931, where he resumed his representation of Stockton until 1945.

Preoccupied with Britain's tremendously high unemployment rate, Macmillan began to express his ideas in tracts, pamphlets, and books. This writing culminated with *The Middle Way* (1938), in which he urged the adoption of a minimum wage and industrial reorganization with partial nationalization. The period 1931-1939 has been called Macmillan's wilderness years, for he was

The Profumo Affair

On March 21, 1963, rumors surfaced in the House of Commons regarding John Profumo, secretary of state for war in the Conservative government since 1960. Profumo's name was linked with that of Christine Keeler, identified as "a call girl." The next day, Profumo appeared in the Commons, with Prime Minister Harold Macmilllan at his side and admitted to a social acquaintance with Keeler. He denied any impropriety in their relationship. However, these rumors were followed by allegations that a Captain Ivanov, naval attaché at the Russian embassy and also a friend of Keeler, had asked her to obtain secret nuclear information from the secretary of state for war. By June 4, Profumo was forced to resign from the government. He denied any breach of security but admitted that his denial of a sexual relationship had been a lie. When the House of Commons reconvened June 17, Macmillan came under intense criticism. Though acquitted of any charges of dishonor, the prime minister's competence as a leader was questioned, even by members of his own party. Macmillan weathered this particular storm but survived as prime minister for only four months more.

too progressive to suit Conservative Party tastes and too conservative to suit the Labour Party. After Prime Minister Neville Chamberlain's Munich agreement with Adolf Hitler in September, 1938 (in which England acquiesced to Germany's demand to be ceded the Sudetenland), Macmillan was one of only thirty Conservatives who refused to support the pact in Parliament. He had served almost fifteen years in the House of Commons without holding a post in the government and seemed unlikely ever to do so.

Macmillan's Rise to Power

On September 3, 1939, Chamberlain announced that Britain was at war with Germany; World War II had begun. When Chamberlain's government fell on May 10, 1940, Winston Churchill became prime minister, and Churchill had a job—parliamentary secretary to the minister of supply—for Macmillan.

Macmillan later served as undersecretary at the colonial office, minister resident in French North Africa (where he met and worked with Dwight D. Eisenhower, Franklin D. Roosevelt, and Charles de Gaulle), U.K. high commissioner

British prime minister Harold Macmillan and U.S. president Dwight D. Eisenhower (left) giving an informal talk on television. (*Express Newspapers/D765/Archive Photos*)

to the advisory council for Italy, and later acting president of the Allied Council for Italy and secretary of state for air. In each succeeding post, he assumed greater responsibilities and grew personally closer to the prime minister.

War-weary Britain turned the Conservatives out of office in 1945, and Macmillan lost an election at Stockton for the third time in six campaigns (and lost his seat for a second time). However, within three weeks after the election, a "safe" seat at Bromley, a middle-class suburb of South London, came open because of the death of the incumbent. Macmillan won the seat comfortably and was back in Parliament, this time part of the opposition party. He soon established himself as one of the opposition's chief spokesmen on industrial and economic matters. In 1947 Macmillan and other leading Conservatives drew up an "Industrial Charter," generally accepting government control of the economy and some degree of nationalization of industry. Because of his wartime experience, he sometimes spoke on foreign policy as well. He pressed for a formal alliance with the Liberal Party, but it never came to pass.

The Conservatives regained power in October, 1951, with a scant majority of seventeen seats. With Churchill once again

Nikita S. Khrushchev with British prime minister Harold Macmillan (right) in 1960. *(Library of Congress)*

The Macmillan Publishing House

The Macmillans had been Scottish crofters (farmers) until Daniel Macmillan, grandfather of Harold, was, at age eleven, bound as an apprentice to a bookseller. The ambitious young man eventually moved to England, where he and his brother Alexander borrowed the money to set up a bookshop in Cambridge. Then, in 1843, the brothers established Macmillan and Co., publishers. The first book they published was *The Philosophy of Training*, by A. R. Craig, in 1847. It dealt with the "improvement of the wealthier classes" and established the high moral tone for which the firm would be known. Macmillan and Co. flourished and expanded into Canada and India as well as New York. In time, it attracted prominent authors, foremost among them Thomas Hardy. While other publishing houses incorporated or merged, Macmillan remained a decidedly family firm. Between the times of his service in World War I and the blossoming of his political career, Harold Macmillan worked as a junior partner in the family business.

prime minister, Macmillan was appointed housing minister, then minister of defense. Under Churchill's successor, Anthony Eden, Macmillan served as foreign secretary and chancellor of the Exchequer. Following the "Suez operation," a Middle East crisis in 1956 during which Britain and France failed spectacularly to assert themselves as powers in the region, Eden's premiership was in shambles. He resigned on January 9, 1957, citing illness.

The Premiership

At age sixty-two, Macmillan succeeded Eden as the result of his long service, wide experience, and brilliant achievement as minister of housing. His financial policy proved successful—the pound strengthened, and foreign trade dramatically improved. By April, 1959, the government was able to cut taxes substantially. In the general election of the following October, the Conservatives increased their majority. However, the economy turned down in October of 1960 and remained less than satisfactory for the balance of Macmillan's premiership.

The prime minister stood firmly behind President John F. Kennedy's policy during the Cuban Missile Crisis of 1962. He was also successful in negotiating the Nuclear Test Ban Treaty with the United States and the Soviet Union, signed July 25, 1963. On the other hand, he failed to usher Britain into the Common Market, a goal to which the Macmillan government had committed itself by 1961. The government suffered from sex-and-security scandals, and Conservative Party energy was obviously flagging after twelve years in power. On October 8, 1963, Macmillan was hospitalized for prostate surgery. Two days later, he notified the party conference at Blackpool that he was stepping down as prime minister.

Retirement and Writing

In the later years of his long life, Macmillan further exploited his natural bent for writing. He had always been inclined toward literature. He was a publisher and the son of a publisher. He had read Shakespeare's comedies and Samuel Richardson's *Pamela* while at the front during World War I. Throughout his political career, he had written pamphlets and books on policy matters. From 1966 to 1974, Macmillan produced six volumes of very readable memoirs, reflecting quite an engaging personality. He was made earl of Stockton in 1984.

Bibliography

Havighurst, Alfred F. *Twentieth-Century Britain.* 2d ed. New York: Harper & Row, 1966.

Horne, Alistair. *Harold Macmillan: Volume I, 1894-1956.* New York: Viking, 1989.

Macmillan, Harold. *Winds of Change 1914-1939.* New York: Harper & Row, 1966.

Patrick Adcock

Francisco Madero

Born: October 30, 1873; Parras, Coahuila, Mexico
Died: February 22, 1913; Mexico City, Mexico

Mexican revolutionary, president of Mexico (1911-1913)

Francisco Indalécio Madero (frahn-THEES-koh een-dah-LAY-thee-oh mah-THAY-roh) was the son of a wealthy landowner in the state of Coahuila in Northern Mexico. Madero attended business school in Paris and studied agriculture at the University of California at Berkeley. In 1893 Madero returned to Mexico to manage one of the family's properties at San Pedro de las Colonias. He exhibited great sympathy for the poor workers on the hacienda and frequently helped them. He and his wife, Sara Pérez, whom he married in January, 1903, gave money to support orphanages, hospitals, and schools in the area.

Opposition to Dictatorship

Madero first entered politics in 1904 when he ran for local office against the official candidate chosen by Mexico's long-time dictator, Porfirio Díaz. Madero lost the election but ran again in 1905 for state office, becoming one of the best-known opponents of the Díaz regime. In his 1908 book *The Presidential Succession of 1910*, Madero

Francisco Madero *(Library of Congress)*

warned Díaz that he needed to step aside to allow Mexicans to choose their own leader. In 1909 Madero founded the Antireelection Center in Mexico City. In 1910 Mexico held a presidential election, and Madero was nominated by the Antireelection Party as its presidential candidate. Madero held the hopes of all Mexicans that true reform would come peacefully through the ballot box. However, in June, 1910, Madero was arrested by the government and Díaz went on to claim reelection.

Madero Begins the Mexican Revolution

In October, 1910, Madero escaped and made his way to San Antonio, Texas, where he issued his *Plan de San Luis Potosí*, which called for the overthrow of the Díaz regime. Madero announced that the revolution would occur on November 20, 1910, and he attempted to cross into Mexico on that day. There was no uprising, so Madero fled to New Orleans, where he began to purchase weapons and coordinate his efforts with opponents of Díaz in Mexico.

In February, 1911, Madero and 130 men crossed the Rio Grande for an attack on Casas Grandes. The uprising had spread into several regions of Mexico by April, 1911, with Emiliano Zapata leading a movement in the southern state of Morelos. In May the revolutionaries attacked the city of Ciudad Juárez, across the Rio Grande from El Paso, Texas, and defeated Díaz's army.

Madero as President

The Treaty of Ciudad Juárez was signed on May 21, 1911, ending the insurrection. Díaz and his vice president resigned. Madero was elected president in November, 1911, and believed that he could make the changes outlined in his *Plan de*

Ciudad Juárez

Francisco I. Madero, who began the Mexican Revolution in November, 1910, triumphed in the battle of Ciudad Juárez in May, 1911. Revolutionary generals Pascual Orozco and Francisco (Pancho) Villa converged on Ciudad Juárez, an important city on the Rio Grande across from El Paso, Texas. The city was defended by General Juan Navarro. Madero had doubts about attacking the city for fear that inadvertent damage to El Paso might lead to U.S. intervention. In spite of Madero's misgivings, Orozco and Villa attacked the city. On May 10 the defenders, low on ammunition, surrendered. The victory was a dramatic event. Ciudad Juárez was a border town that gave Madero access to arms and support from the United States; moreover, it could serve as his provisional capital. Madero's success encouraged other attacks. Hermosillo, Durango, and other towns fell to the rebels and forced longtime dictator Porfirio Díaz to sign the Treaty of Ciudad Juárez, promising to step down before the end of the month. Madero's revolution had triumphed.

San Luis Potosí. He initiated a review of land reform but could not get it passed by the Díaz faction remaining in Congress. In the meantime, Zapata broke with Madero and began a rebellion against his government. Two conservative leaders rebelled as well: Bernardo Reyes and the former dictator's nephew, Félix Díaz. With so little support among the country's leaders, Madero's plans for reform languished.

Madero called on General Victoriano Huerta to defeat the conservative opposition. On February 19, 1913, however, Huerta secretly switched sides and arrested the president. Madero was taken from the National Palace, where he had been held prisoner, and murdered on February 22. The death of Madero marked the beginning of nearly a decade of violence as the Mexican Revolution continued.

Bibliography

Kendall, Jonathan. *La Capital: The Biography of Mexico City.* New York: Henry Holt, 1988.

Krauze, Enrique. *Mexico: Biography of Power, a History of Modern Mexico 1810-1996.* New York: HarperCollins, 1997.

Ross, Stanley R. *Francisco I. Madero, Apostle of Mexican Democracy.* New York: Columbia University Press, 1955.

James A. Baer

Street fighting in Ciudad Juárez in May, 1911. Revolutionary leader Francisco Madero was victorious in the battle of Ciudad Juárez, forcing dictatorial Mexican president Porfirio Díaz to sign a treaty on May 21 and agree to step down. *(Library of Congress)*

Ramón Magsaysay

Born: August 31, 1907; Iba, Philippines
Died: March 17, 1957; near Cebu, Philippines

President of the Philippines (1953-1957)

Ramón Magsaysay (rah-MOHN mag-SI-si) was born in the town of Iba, in Luzon, the northernmost of the main islands of the Philippines. He was the second of four children, and his father was a shopkeeper and landowner. Magsaysay worked his way through Rizal College, near Manila, and obtained a commercial degree in 1933. A relative helped him get a job as a mechanic with a bus company, and he rapidly rose to the position of general manager.

World War II

In 1941 war broke out between Japan and the United States. The Philippines was then an American commonwealth, a territory controlled by the United States. Japan invaded the Philippines in late 1941 and occupied the country in 1942. At the start of the war, Magsaysay, who was strongly pro-American, lent his company's vehicles to the American military and formed close ties with American officers. During the Japanese occupation, Magsaysay became leader of an anti-Japanese guerrilla force linked to the American army.

Magsaysay's war leadership led him to be appointed as military governor for his home province of Zambales after the war. When the Philippines became fully independent of the United States in 1946, the governorship of Zambales provided Magsaysay with a political base for running for office. He won election to the Philippine House of Representatives in 1946 and 1950.

Defense Secretary and President

During the late 1940's and early 1950's, the government of the Philippines came into conflict with communist-controlled guerrilla groups that had initially formed to fight the Japanese. In 1950

Ramón Magsaysay *(Library of Congress)*

President Elpidio Quirino appointed Magsaysay secretary of defense to solve the problem of the guerrillas, known as Huks.

Magsaysay recognized that the guerrillas were receiving support from the peasant population because the peasants had many legitimate grievances and because the peasants suffered abuses from a corrupt military. Relying heavily on advice and assistance from the American Central Intelligence Agency (CIA), Magsaysay undertook a campaign to win the support of the peasants and to demoralize and discourage the rebels. At the same time, he reformed the army, dismissed corrupt officers, and insisted that the military treat peasants with respect. By 1953 the Huks had largely disappeared as an effective force.

In 1953 Magsaysay was elected president of the Republic of the Philippines. Known to the Filipino public as "the guy," he was enormously popular, seen as a man of the common people. However, he was largely unsuccessful in his attempts to bring about meaningful reforms such as the redistribution of land, because he was opposed by powerful conservative interests. Before the end of his presidency, Magsaysay died when his airplane crashed while flying over the islands of the central Philippines.

Philippine president Ramón Magsaysay discusses security issues with Arthur W. Radford, chairman of the U.S. Joint Chiefs of Staff. *(Archive Photos)*

Historical Impact

Some Filipino nationalists have criticized Magsaysay for his close ties to the United States. His relations with the American Central Intelligence Agency, in particular, have led some to claim that he was an agent of American interests. He was also unable to overcome many of the problems of Filipino society, such as inequality of wealth and landownership. However, he did succeed in overcoming the Huk rebellion, lessening corruption in government and in the military, and in bolstering public confidence in the government of the Philippines.

Bibliography

Abueva, José Veloso. *Ramón Magsaysay: A Political Biography*. Manila, the Philippines: Solidaridad Press, 1971.

Karnow, Stanley. *In Our Image: America's Empire in the Philippines*. New York: Random House, 1989.

Kerkvliet, Ramon. *The Huk Rebellion: A Study of Peasant Revolt in the Philippines*. Berkeley: University of California Press, 1977.

Carl L. Bankston III

The Huk Rebellion

During World War II, some left-wing groups of peasants and workers in the Philippines formed a guerrilla organization known as the Hukbong ng Bayan Laban sa Hapon (People's Anti-Japanese Army), called the Hukbalahap or Huks. General Douglas MacArthur, commander of the U.S. armed forces in the Philippines after the war, saw these guerrillas as communists, and he ordered U.S. soldiers to disarm them. Many of the Huks hid or buried their weapons.

In 1946 Manuel Roxas was elected president of the newly independent Philippines. The Huks supported a rival of Roxas, Sergio Osmeña, because Roxas had cooperated with the Japanese during the war and because Osmeña supported new laws that favored poor tenant farmers. Following the election, the Huks, who favored redistribution of land and wealth, changed their organization's name to the Hukbong Mapagpalaya ng Bayan (People's Liberation Army) and began to wage guerrilla warfare against the government. Although the Huk rebellion ended by the early 1950's, scattered groups of Huks continued to operate through the 1960's.

Datuk Seri Mahathir bin Mohamad

Born: December 20, 1925; Alor Setar, Kedah, Malaya (now in Malaysia)

Prime minister of Malaysia (took office 1981)

Datuk Seri Mahathir bin Mohamad (dah-TOOK SEH-ree mah-hah-TEER bihn moo-HAH-muhd) was the first Malaysian prime minister to come from a nonroyal Malay family background. He successfully championed Malay causes in a country whose economy is dominated by its Chinese ethnic minority. Ascending to the position of prime minister in 1981, Mahathir served as prime minister longer than any of his three predecessors. Mahathir presided over the economic boom of the late 1980's and early 1990's. His response to dissidence and political opposition was often harsh, as it was during the economic recession of the late 1990's.

Early Life and Career

Mahathir was born into a family of modest means during the British colonial rule of Malaya. He attended Malay schools and the Sultan Abdul Hamid College in Alor Setar. He later studied medicine at the University of Malaya in Singapore, where he earned a medical degree in 1947. He served with the government medical service until 1957, the year of Malaysia's independence, when he entered private practice. His election to the national parliament in 1964 signaled the beginning of his active political career at the national level.

A young, brash, and outspoken member of the country's dominant political party, Mahathir incurred the party leadership's wrath by his criticism of its handling of the May, 1969, ethnic riots. After his expulsion from the party in 1970, he wrote his controversial book *The Malay Dilemma* (1970), which was a manifesto of Malay rights and privileges. Mahathir was restored to the United Malays National Organization (UMNO) in 1972 despite the sensation caused by the book. (The book was banned by the party because of

concern that it might provoke communal antagonism between the majority Malay people and the Chinese and Indian minorities.)

Rise to Prominence and Rule

Mahathir advanced rapidly in UMNO during the next ten years, holding positions in UMNO's Supreme Council and ministerial positions in trade and industry as well as education. He was named deputy prime minister in 1976, and when Tun Hussein Onn retired because of ill health, Mahathir became prime minister in 1981. Mahathir was viewed as a reformist with an uncon-

Datuk Seri Mahathir bin Mohamad *(Reuters/Archive Photos)*

968

The 1997 Currency Crisis

After a decade of spectacular economic growth, Malaysia experienced a major economic decline in 1997. During the period of growth, Malaysia, like other Asian countries, abandoned fixed exchange rates—in other words, it allowed its currency to change in value in relation to the global currency market. When Asian economies began to weaken in 1997, foreign companies converted portions of their holdings into stronger currencies. (They did this to hedge against possible declines in the values of Asian currencies.)

The currency conversions, combined with unscrupulous currency speculation, provoked a decline in the value of the ringgit, Malaysia's currency, and launched an economic crisis. Prime Minister Datuk Seri Mahathir bin Mohamad made bizarre claims of a foreign conspiracy to ruin Malaysia's economy. His statements raised international concern about the credibility of his leadership. However, his administration's imposition of stricter monetary policies helped to stabilize the situation during 1998.

ventionally brusque personality for a Malay leader. However, he managed to pursue pro-Malay policies that UMNO had already inaugurated in previous administrations without alienating the Chinese economic elite. He called upon Malaysians to reduce ties to Britain and Europe and to "look East" to Asia for examples of economic and political advancement.

In 1987, he cracked down on and detained political activists and opponents. With the economy growing dramatically for the next decade, however, most Malaysians were content to support his bids for reelection as prime minister. Still, an opposition Malay party was formed in 1988 by Tunku Razaleigh Hamzah, indicating that the Malay community was divided by both politics and personality.

The Economy Turns Sour

In 1995, Mahathir turned seventy and soon thereafter was elected to his fifth term as prime minister. However, in the late 1990's, Malaysia's economy turned sour, as did many Asian economies. The pressures on the Malaysian currency, the

Malaysian prime minister Datuk Seri Mahathir bin Mohamad in 1996, inspecting a model representing part of a unique multibillion-dollar building project. *(Reuters/Jimin Lai/Archive Photos)*

Datuk Seri Mahathir bin Mohamad in 1985 addressing the General Assembly of the Malay National Organization. *(Reuters/Goh Chai Hin/Archive Photos)*

ringgit, led to devaluation and to economic turmoil accentuated by political protests. The authoritarian streak in Mahathir's temperament resurfaced as he repressed opposition voices. After years of effective, if sometimes controversial, rule, Mahathir lashed out at foreign influences as the cause of his country's problems. He appealed to Malay nationalism and began tough economic policies designed to protect Malaysia from currency fluctuations; these approaches bolstered his popularity.

Bibliography

Gullick, John, and Bruce Gale. *Malaysia: Its Political and Economic Development*. Selangor, Malaysia: Pelanduk Publications, 1986.

Kahn, Joel, and Francis Loh Kok Wah, eds. *Fragmented Vision: Culture and Politics in Contemporary Malaysia*. Honolulu: University of Hawaii Press, 1992.

Mahathir bin Mohamad. *The Malay Dilemma*. Singapore: D. Moore for Asia Pacific Press, 1970.

Robert F. Gorman

John Major

Born: March 29, 1943; London, England

Prime minister of Great Britain (1990-1997)

John Roy Major (JON ROY MAY-jur), the prime minister of the United Kingdom between 1990 and 1997 and the nation's youngest leader in the twentieth century, had an inauspicious early life. Disciplinary problems led him to quit school at the age of sixteen. For the next few years he had a variety of occupations, even spending time un-

British prime minister John Major gives an impromptu speech in 1997. *(Express News/Archive Photos)*

employed collecting benefits from the state. Eventually he decided on banking as a career. He also married; he and his wife had two children.

Entry into Politics

In the 1960's John Major increasingly became interested in politics. His first taste of political life occurred when he was elected to a city council position. In 1974, as a member of the Conservative Party, he twice lost in attempts to be elected to the national parliament. He finally won a seat in 1979 and became a rookie member of Parliament in the Conservative wave that elected Margaret Thatcher as Britain's first female prime minister.

Advancing

Two years after Major's election, he took his first step up the political ladder when he was appointed as parliamentary secretary to a series of cabinet positions. Next came an appointment to a higher position, specifically as government whip. He served in this capacity from 1983 to 1985. The next move up was as a junior cabinet minister in an area involving social welfare policy. Finally, in 1987, just after the Conservatives won reelection in what would prove to be their last election with Thatcher as their leader, Major made it into the cabinet as chief secretary to the treasury.

Britain and the Persian Gulf War

On August 2, 1990, Iraq, led by Saddam Hussein, surprised the world by invading and annexing the tiny country of Kuwait. The immediate reaction of Western nations, led by U.S. president George Bush, was that the invasion would not be allowed to stand. Equally vocal in condemning Iraq's aggression and in demanding the freeing of Kuwait was the United Kingdom, under the leadership of Prime Minister Margaret Thatcher. Thatcher's words did much to convince Bush that he was following the right policy. She committed British resources, including ships, fighter aircraft, tanks, and seventy-five hundred military personnel to the coalition unit that was being formed. Thatcher, however, did not see the policy she had started through to its conclusion. In November of 1990, internal dissension forced her to resign the leadership of the Conservative Party. Her successor, John Major, would continue her fight. One of Major's first comments after becoming prime minister was to reiterate that there would be no change in Britain's Iraq policy. When hostilities began in January, 1991, Britain actively participated in the conflict. British pilots flew repeated sorties, and British ground forces were involved in the attack that was launched to expel Iraq. The popularity of Major and his government rose with the successful completion of the military campaign.

John Major *(Archive Photos/Popperfoto)*

Once in the cabinet, Major continued to advance, especially since he was looked upon favorably by Prime Minister Thatcher. In July, 1989, much to his surprise, Major was appointed to the important position of foreign secretary. He rose even higher just a few months later when he became the chancellor of the Exchequer, the equivalent of finance minister and the highest cabinet position behind that of prime minister. He spent his final twelve months as cabinet minister in this position. This period was marked by a concerted effort on the part of his ministry to deal with the problem of inflation.

Prime Minister

In November, 1990, after eleven years as prime minister and an even longer period in Parliament, Margaret Thatcher was forced out of office—not by the electorate, but by her own members of Parliament. A challenger had arisen to oppose Thatcher's continued leadership. A vote among her members of Parliament was required, with a majority voting in her favor. That majority was not enough, however, to prevent the necessity of a second ballot. John Major initially had been one of Thatcher's most vocal supporters. Even he hesitated, however, when he was asked to second her nomination for a second ballot. With growing signs that her support was waning, Thatcher elected to resign as Conservative leader; she then threw her support behind Major, who, as a compromise candidate, defeated two rivals on a second ballot to become leader of the Conservative Party and prime minister.

Thatcher's unexpected downfall was matched by Major's unexpected ascendancy. He quickly promised to maintain the United Kingdom's commitment to the international coalition that was being assembled to deal with Iraq's invasion of Kuwait. Two other contentious issues were his nation's place in a Europe that was increasingly moving toward integration and the continued problems with the place of Northern Ireland in the United Kingdom.

British prime minister John Major campaigning outside a mosque in East London in April, 1997, shortly before the general election. *(AP/Wide World Photos)*

The Major Era

Major's era was marked by successes and failures. An early success involved Britain's role in helping remove Iraq from Kuwait. In February, 1992, Major finally had to put his position to test in a general election. Polls indicated that he and

---

Great Britain and the Maastricht Treaty

Signed in 1992, the Maastricht Treaty set the conditions for those members of the European Community (the EC, which in 1993 became the European Union) who intended to replace their national currencies with a new multinational currency. The treaty's conditions revolved around issues of financial stability, including keeping inflation and government debt under control. The treaty proved controversial in many quarters. Opposition was especially strong in the United Kingdom. Historically aloof from the rest of Europe, many citizens of the United Kingdom saw themselves as distinct from the remainder of the continent. Opposition was primarily, but not exclusively, centered in the Conservative Party, which, under Prime Minister John Major, had signed the treaty in the first place. The "Euroskeptics," as opponents were nicknamed, remained a nuisance to Major throughout his term in office.

his party were heading to defeat despite conducting a spirited campaign. The polls proved wrong, however, as Major and the Conservatives won a majority government. Attempts at achieving peace in Northern Ireland gained some ground, including a cease-fire on the part of the Irish Republican Army (IRA). Eventually the progress ended, however, and the IRA started a new bombing campaign in 1996.

The other issue that continually troubled Major was the place of the United Kingdom in the European Union (the EU, known before 1993 as the European Community). Many members of the Conservative Party were opposed to further integration into the European system, especially the adoption of a universal European currency. In June, 1995, Major directly confronted these critics when he resigned and subsequently announced that he would be in the running for the party's leadership. Facing only one candidate, Major easily won the party leadership and emerged strengthened. The issue of Europe, like Northern Ireland, remained a problem for the Major government.

Political Defeat

After continual rumors of elections, and after waiting until almost the last possible moment, Major finally called a general election in early 1997. He had delayed elections in the hope that the Conservatives' low standings in the polls would turn around; that did not happen. Instead, his main opponent, Tony Blair, the leader of the Labour Party, enjoyed high public support and won a decisive victory over Major and the Conservatives. The latter quickly resigned as party leader and returned to private life.

Major's legacy as prime minister is an unspectacular one. In essence, he continued the policies of his predecessor. His government, despite its efforts, remained unsuccessful in handling British opposition to further integration into the European Union and the problem of Northern Ireland. The high point of Major's reign was his come-from-behind election victory in 1992, which demonstrated that he was not completely beholden to Margaret Thatcher.

Bibliography

Jenkin, John, ed. *John Major: Prime Minister*. London: Bloomsbury, 1990.

Reitan, E. A. *Tory Radicalism: Margaret Thatcher, John Major, and the Transformation of Modern Britain, 1979-1997*. Lanham, Md.: Rowman & Littlefield, 1997.

Thatcher, Margaret. *The Downing Street Years*. London: HarperCollins, 1993.

Watkins, Alan. *A Conservative Coup: The Fall of Margaret Thatcher*. London: Ducksworth, 1992.

Steve Hewitt

Makarios III

Born: August 13, 1913; Pano Panayia, Paphos, Cyprus
Died: August 3, 1977; Nicosia, Cyprus

First president of Republic of Cyprus (1959-1977)

Makarios III (mah-KAH-ree-os thuh THURD), originally named Mikhail Khristodolou Mouskos (mee-heh-EEL hree-sto-THEW-lew MEWS-kos), started life as the son of a shepherd on the island of Cyprus. He was ordained into the Orthodox Church of Cyprus in 1946 after an education at the University of Athens and the School of Theology of Boston University. In 1948, he became bishop of Kition (Larnaca). Two years later, on October 18, 1950, he was named Orthodox Eastern archbishop of Cyprus.

Struggle for *Énosis*

After World War II ended in 1945, Britain maintained an occupation force on Cyprus. During this time Makarios, as archbishop of Cyprus, took a leadership role in the island's struggle for *énosis* (union) with Greece. A precedent for this combined clerical/political role had been set during Turkey's earlier occupation of Cyprus, when the archbishop (the *ethnarch*) had politically regulated the Cypriot Greek Christian community.

Earlier, the Cyprus Convention of 1878 between Britain and Turkey had provided that Cyprus, an island located about 40 miles (64 kilometers) south of Turkey in the eastern Mediterranean Sea, would remain under Turkish sovereignty. However, it would be administered by the British government. Britain's purpose was to maintain a Mediterranean base against the threat of Russian invasion.

The situation changed during World War I (1914-1918). Britain and Turkey fought on opposing sides, and Britain annexed Cyprus, a strategic military location, as a Crown Colony in 1914. British occupation was initially welcomed by the island's Greeks, the ethnic majority, who are Orthodox Christians. They anticipated ultimately

the transfer of Cyprus to Greece. Cypriot Turks, the island's ethnic minority, are Sunni Muslims, and they remained adamantly opposed to the idea. Postwar Britain desired either to grant Cyprus independence or to grant the island British Commonwealth status. Turkey wanted to partition the island in an effort to protect the Turkish population. Civil unrest escalated, and ongoing annual petitions demanding unification with Greece were met by counterpetitions and demonstrations from the Turkish Cypriots.

Archbishop Makarios deemed it his religious and political duty to champion the hopes of the Greek Cypriots' dream of union with Greece. He met with Greek prime minister Alexandros Papagos in February, 1954. Continuing to declare "*énosis* and only *énosis*," he managed to achieve Greek support for the *énosis* movement. The Brit-

Makarios III *(Library of Congress)*

975

ish, however, met Makarios's position with hostility. They came to view him as a terrorist acting in conjunction with Greek army officer Colonel Georgios Grivas. Grivas was the Cypriot patriot head of the National Organization of Cypriot Struggle (EOKA), an underground nationalist movement of Greek Cypriots dedicated to the expulsion of the British from Cyprus and the union of the island nation with Greece. After attempts at peaceful negotiation failed, Makarios was arrested for treason in March, 1956, and exiled to the Seychelles. Terrorist activity escalated after his exile, in part as a result of the displacement of British soldiers during the Suez Crisis, a 1956 confrontation between Egypt on one side and England, France, and Israel on the other. Makarios was released from exile in March, 1957, and violence declined after his return to Cyprus that year.

Two years later, in February, 1959, Archbishop Makarios compromised, announcing his acceptance of an independent Cyprus rather than *énosis*. Thus, Cyprus gained independence, becoming the Republic of Cyprus in 1960. Makarios was named the first president (1959-1977) of an independent Cyprus; he had a Turkish vice president. Under the independence arrangement, Cyprus would not form a union with any other country, nor would it be subject to partition. Britain retained sovereignty over its two military bases there.

Continued Unrest

Things did not go smoothly for President Makarios, however, as Greeks and Turks continued to be divided over the question of union with Greece. Within three years, arrangements between the Greeks and Turks on the island had broken down. Public opinion in Greece and Turkey continued to be split in support of the two communities; the split resulted in protests that turned into riots. Turkey deported its Greek residents. U.N. intervention failed to solve the problem. In December, 1963, Greece and Turkey became actively involved in the ongoing conflict.

At this point, despite his earlier Greek leanings and involvement in the *énosis* movement, Makarios sought to unite the warring factions. He maintained a policy aimed at reducing conflict between the Greek Cypriot and Turkish Cypriot communities. Turkey resisted his attempts, however, as did leaders of the *énosis* movement, who now came to view him as a traitor. Makarios astonishingly survived four assassination at-

Cypriot Independence

In 1914, during World War I, Britain occupied the island of Cyprus and declared it a Crown Colony. British occupation was initially welcomed by the Cypriot Greeks, the island's Orthodox Christian ethnic majority, because they anticipated the transfer of Cyprus to Greece. The island's Turkish population, however, feared such an idea. Turkey wished to partition the island in an effort to protect its large Turkish Sunni Muslim ethnic minority. In February, 1959, Archbishop Makarios III announced that he would accept an independent Cyprus rather than continuing to insist on *énosis*, the unification of Greece and Cyprus. Official Cypriot independence came on August 16, 1960: Great Britain, Greece, and Turkey reached an agreement providing for a Greek president (Makarios III) and a Turkish vice president. Greek Cypriots would control 70 percent of the legislature's seats, with 30 percent for the Turks. Independence, however, was short-lived. Civil war erupted only two years later, and it resulted eventually in the partitioning of the island nation.

The Green Line

Civil war erupted between the Greek and Turkish communities on Cyprus only two years after the island nation achieved independence on August 16, 1960. At the time of independence, Great Britain, Greece, and Turkey had reached an agreement allowing for a Greek president and a Turkish vice president. A stalemate continued for more than ten years until July, 1974, when Turkish soldiers invaded Cyprus. The Cypriot government was overthrown, and the island was partitioned with what came to be known as the Green Line. It separated Cypriot Greeks in the south from the new Turkish Republic of Northern Cyprus in the north.

U.S. vice president Lyndon B. Johnson visits Archbishop Makarios III in Nicosia, Cyprus, in 1962. *(National Archives)*

tempts. In December, 1967, a Turkish Cypriot provisional government, responsible for Turkish minority affairs, was forced upon him.

Political and social strife and civil unrest continued to plague Cyprus, and negotiations between the groups remained stagnant. Nevertheless, Makarios continued in power, winning reelection in 1968 and again (in spite of minor bishops calling for his resignation) in 1973. In July, 1974, Greek Cypriots active in the *énosis* movement, under the leadership of mainland Greeks, attempted a coup. Makarios fled to Malta.

In response, Turkish forces landed in northern Cyprus. After a brief civil war, Cyprus was partitioned into two separate states—Cypriot Greeks in the south and the new Turkish Republic of Northern Cyprus in the north. The Turkish army occupied almost 40 percent of the land area of the island, despite the fact that the Turkish population numbered less than 20 percent. Greece responded with threats to invade and fight the Turkish forces, but the threats were not acted upon. Makarios III returned to Cyprus after the coup. The coup collapsed at the end of 1974, when Greece's ruling military junta fell, and Makarios resumed the presidency of Cyprus. He continued, unsuccessfully, his attempts to negotiate with Turkish representatives. Makarios was a charismatic Cypriot religious and political leader who attempted, despite several attempts on his life, to keep Cyprus independent and free from partition. He continued to argue against partition of the island until his death in 1977.

Bibliography

Meyers, Stanley. *Cyprus and Makarios*. London: Purnum, 1960.

_____. *Makarios: A Biography*. London: Macmillan, 1981.

Salem, Norma. *Cyprus: A Regional Conflict and Its Resolution*. New York: St. Martin's Press, 1992.

Vanezis, P. N. *Makarios: Pragmatism v. Idealism*. London: Abelard-Shuman, 1972.

M. Casey Diana

Malcolm X

Born: May 19, 1925; Omaha, Nebraska
Died: February 21, 1965; New York, New York

American black nationalist and Nation of Islam leader

Malcolm X (MAL-kuhm EHKS) was born Malcolm Little to Louise Little, a native of the West Indies, and Earl Little, a Baptist minister and organizer for Marcus Garvey's Universal Negro Improvement Association. One of Malcolm's formative memories was the violent death of his father at the hands of Ku Klux Klan members when Malcolm was six years old. This event was followed by the deprivations of the Depression and, some years later, the mental breakdown of his mother, after which Malcolm and his siblings became "court wards." A major turning point came when Malcolm was in the eighth grade: His older half-sister Ella invited him to live with her in Boston. Attracted to the city's bright lights, Malcolm was popular in area clubs and attracted to the "fast" life. He took a job as cook's helper on the Boston-New York City train. A second major turning point in his life came in 1946, when Malcolm was arrested and jailed for robbery. Prison ironically provided him with the time and inspiration to change his path in life radically.

Malcolm X *(Library of Congress)*

Religious Awakening

Prison changed the course of Malcolm's life. Some of his siblings had become members of the Nation of Islam, and they urged Malcolm to approach the religion with an open mind. Malcolm wrote a letter to Muslim leader Elijah Muhammad and read widely about world history, philosophy, and religion while still in prison. Paroled in 1952, Malcolm began his apprenticeship in the Nation of Islam in Detroit. Wallace D. Fard had originated the religion in that city in 1930. Working during the day as a furniture salesman, Malcolm became increasingly involved in the Black Muslim (Nation of Islam) movement. A watershed moment occurred when Malcolm first heard Elijah Muhammad speak in person.

Shortly after, he received his "X" (symbolizing the African name that had been stolen from American blacks brought to the United States as slaves). Malcolm suggested that the church mount an energetic campaign to attract young blacks to the Nation of Islam rather than waiting passively for converts to come to them. Almost single-handedly, Malcolm X galvanized and changed the significance of what had previously been a small subversive movement. In 1953 he became assistant minister at Detroit Temple Number One, and by 1954 Malcolm was minister of the important New York City temple. Malcolm's metamorphosis from street hustler to Muslim minister was

Malcolm X's image was adopted by many groups, as shown by this poster distributed by the Young Socialist Alliance, based in New York. *(Library of Congress)*

The Black Muslims

Wallace D. Fard laid the groundwork for the Nation of Islam, or the Black Muslims, in Detroit in 1930, when he began to preach a black separatist doctrine that combined religious elements and a philosophy of racial identity. Fard's message appealed to recent southern migrants to the north. Elijah Poole, a recent arrival from Georgia, took over leadership of the sect after Fard disappeared mysteriously in 1934. Poole became known as Elijah Muhammad and claimed it was his mission to lead American blacks from the bondage of whites and back to their "lost zion." Muhammad urged blacks to join forces based on their commonalities, and he enforced a work ethic requiring members to lead clean, abstemious lives. By 1952 the organization was under surveillance by the FBI. Nevertheless, a nationwide chain of stores (primarily dry cleaning plants, restaurants, and barber shops) and the Muslim newspaper *Muhammad Speaks* were parts of an economic empire that was worth about $70 million by the 1960's.

Malcolm X speaking at a Nation of Islam meeting. *(Archive Photos)*

complete, but other epiphanies remained.

Age of Martyrs

In January, 1958, Malcolm married Sister Betty X, a nursing student and instructor of women's hygiene in the Nation of Islam, as his career as a minister took off. The Civil Rights movement of the 1960's was partly responsible for Malcolm's rise to national prominence, as he often publicly took issue with the passive strategies of integrationists. Malcolm X's eloquence and confrontational stance made him a popular speaker; he spoke at many universities, especially enjoying the highly charged question-and-answer periods after his talks. A rift between Malcolm and the Muslim leadership developed over a charge of adul-

The Film *Malcolm X*

Before production began on the 1992 film *Malcolm X*, there were discussions and debates over how the film should treat its subject and who should be entrusted with the project. To a large extent these discussions mirrored racial conflict in the larger American society. African American film director Spike Lee, whose previous films had chronicled aspects of black life in the twentieth century, won control of the film from more mainstream nonblack directors. Lee's films were in the vanguard of black films seeking to turn the tide away from the images of blacks proliferated by 1970's "blaxploitation" films, which he charged continued stereotypical images that had

begun with the 1915 film *Birth of a Nation*. However, some within the black community protested that Lee was preoccupied with his own vision that depicted black men in ways that were also stereotypical. It did not help matters that Lee marketed T-shirts and caps emblazoned with an X in conjunction with the film. Almost three hours and thirty minutes long, the film presented both the facts and the myth of Malcolm X. Lee had absorbed the Malcolm X story during his childhood; he also drew upon Malcolm's 1964 autobiography, *Autobiography of Malcolm X*, which contains cowriter Alex Haley's own mythologizing touches.

tery against Elijah Muhammad. The rift was exacerbated by Malcolm's comment, when he was asked his thoughts on President John F. Kennedy's assassination, that "the chickens have come home to roost." Malcolm meant that the white hatred that had been allowed to run roughshod over blacks had finally killed a white leader, but the Nation of Islam officially "silenced" him for ninety days for that comment. During his suspension, Malcolm and his family vacationed with heavyweight champion Cassius Clay, who shortly afterward announced his conversion to Islam, his new name—Muhammad Ali—and his conscientious objector status regarding the Vietnam War.

The Black Muslim leadership was progressing with plans to oust Malcolm. Nevertheless, it was by now clear that he had gained the trust and support of the black masses. Malcolm therefore began to make plans to establish an organization geared toward the economic and political empowerment of blacks regardless of their religious affiliation. In 1964 Malcolm X made a pilgrimage to Mecca. The panorama of hundreds of thousands of faithful Muslims of all colors radically altered his spiritual perspective once again. He became El-Hajj Malik El-Shabazz and dedicated his life to achieving respect and equality for American blacks. He urged "sincere" whites to "convert" racist whites.

On February 13, 1965, Malcolm's house was firebombed, but he and his family escaped injury. Then on Sunday, February 21, 1965, as he opened his remarks on behalf his new Organization for Afro-American Unity at about 2:00 P.M. in Harlem's Audubon Ballroom, Malcolm X was assassinated while his children and his pregnant wife watched. Malcolm X was eulogized by leaders from all facets of black society, and the meaning of his life and death to the evolution of American religion and politics continues to be studied and analyzed.

Bibliography

Clarke, John Henrik, ed. *Malcolm X: The Man and His Times*. New York: Macmillan, 1969.

Clegg, Claude Andrew, III. *An Original Man: The Life and Times of Elijah Muhammad*. New York: St. Martin's Press, 1997.

DeCaro, Louis A., Jr. *On The Side of My People: A Religious Life of Malcolm X*. New York: New York University Press, 1996.

Gallen, David, ed. *Malcolm X: As They Knew Him*. New York: One World/Ballantine, 1992.

Malcolm X with Alex Haley. *The Autobiography of Malcolm X*. New York: Grove Press, 1964.

Dale Edwyna Smith

Georgi M. Malenkov

Born: January 8, 1902; Orenburg, Russia
Died: January 14, 1988; Moscow, U.S.S.R.

Soviet premier (1953-1955)

Georgi Maksimilianovich Malenkov (gyih-OHR-gyoo-ih mahk-see-meel-YAH-noh-vyihch mahl-yehn-KOF), a political leader in the former Soviet Union, was the son of lower-middle-class peasants. Still in school when the Bolshevik Revolution occurred in 1917, he joined the Red Army in 1919 to fight in the civil war (1918-1921) that erupted after the Bolsheviks' seizure of power in Russia. Admitted into the Communist Party in April, 1920, Malenkov served as a political commissar in the eastern and Turkestan districts.

Georgi M. Malenkov *(Archive Photos)*

In 1921 he resumed his education by enrolling in the Moscow Higher Technical College and was elected secretary of the Bolshevik students' organization. Graduating with an engineering degree in 1925, Malenkov was appointed then to an important political position under the Central Committee of the Communist Party. He came into direct association with the party's leader, Joseph Stalin, and became a member of Stalin's personal staff that year. By 1935 Malenkov was in charge of the Communist Party's personnel matters as director of the Organization Bureau.

Rise to Power

As a high-ranking specialist in party appointments and dismissals, Malenkov played a key role in the elimination of Stalin's opponents. In the purges of 1936-1938, Malenkov was involved in selecting communists for expulsion from the party. Large numbers of party officials—as well as their family members, friends, and acquaintances—were arrested or killed during this period.

When the Soviet Union entered World War II in 1941, Malenkov, now one of dictator Joseph Stalin's closest collaborators, was appointed to the State Committee on Defense, a group of five men that directed Soviet war efforts. He had been promoted to the inner circle of policy making. After the war, elevation to full membership in the Politburo (the leading policy-making body of the Communist Party) and deputy premier (deputy chairman of the government's Council of Ministers) were rewards for his loyalty to Stalin and his administrative abilities.

Stalin's Successor

At fifty-one years of age, Malenkov became head of the government as the premier and

Exile to Kazakhstan

Georgi Malenkov steadily lost influence over domestic and foreign affairs after February, 1955. Malenkov's opponents on the Presidium (formerly the Politburo) of the Communist Party were able to thwart his efforts to acquire more political power. Blaming Nikita Khrushchev for insufficient consumer goods, the Hungarian Revolution in 1956, and the too-rapid pace of uprooting Stalinist practices, Malenkov called for Khrushchev's resignation as head of the party on June 18, 1957. Initially, only three of the other ten full members of the Presidium opposed Malenkov's demand. However, Khrushchev refused to resign and called a meeting of the party's Central Committee to choose between him and the Malenkov-led group. Malenkov found himself isolated and in the minority during Central Committee deliberations. Malenkov was stripped of his high governmental and party offices in July, 1957. Subsequently he was exiled to Kazakhstan to manage a hydroelectric plant until he retired.

leader of the Communist Party of the Soviet Union as its senior secretary on March 6, 1953, one day after Stalin's death. He promised Russians peace and a happier life. However, Malenkov's power was not absolute, as Stalin's had been, and in the power struggle that followed his ascent to power, Malenkov's prestige and political authority gradually declined. On March 14, 1953, he was released from his post of party secretary in the name of collective leadership. An improvement in living standards, increases in investment in consumer goods, increased spending on housing and payments for agricultural products, along with a call for improved relations with the West were associated with Malenkov's administration.

Nikita Khrushchev, chief of the party's Secretariat since September, 1953, became Malenkov's chief rival. Khrushchev reasserted the priority of military armaments, heavy industry, agricultural production, and de-Stalinization in contrast to Malenkov's policies. Malenkov lost the power struggle and resigned as premier on February 8,

Soviet premier Georgi M. Malenkov (right) with other Soviet officials who fell from power. Vyacheslav Mikhailovich Molotov stands to his right. *(Archive Photos/Paris Match)*

1955. His position in the party decreased, until in July of 1957 he was sent to remote Kazakhstan to oversee a hydroelectric plant.

Malenkov's Contribution

Ambitious and endowed with administrative political skills, Georgi Malenkov represented a middle generation of reform-minded Soviet technocrats and intellectuals. He was instrumental in guiding Russia's industrial development and was directly implicated in the terror and hardships imposed on Soviet people during the Stalin regime. Yet Malenkov's emphasis on peaceful coexistence with Western nations, desire to increase the availability of consumer goods, and relaxation of Stalinism were strikingly similar to Russian reforms that finally occurred decades later.

Bibliography

Hough, Jerry F., and Merle Fainsod. *How the Soviet Union Is Governed*. Cambridge, Mass.: Harvard University Press, 1979.

Roeder, Philip G. *Red Sunset: The Failure of Soviet Politics*. Princeton, N.J.: Princeton University Press, 1993.

Schapiro, Leonard. *The Communist Party of the Soviet Union*. 2d ed. New York: Random House, 1971.

Steve Mazurana

Nelson Mandela

Born: July 18, 1918; Mveto, Umtata District, Transkei, South Africa

South African antiapartheid leader, winner of 1993 Nobel Peace Prize, president of South Africa (took office 1994.

Nelson Rolihlahla Mandela (NEHL-suhn ro-lih-LAH-lah mahn-DAY-lah), the son of a chief of South Africa's Xhosa-speaking Thembu tribe, received his early education in Methodist mission schools. He attended Fort Hare University College from 1938 until 1940. He was dismissed in that year for participating in a student boycott. Mandela then apprenticed in the office of a white law firm in Johannesburg and, by taking correspondence courses, qualified for the bachelor of arts degree from the University of South Africa in 1942. He enrolled at the University of Witwatersrand in 1943 and ultimately received a law degree from that institution. Shortly afterward, he opened Johannesburg's first law firm run by black Africans.

Early Political Involvement

Ever the foe of apartheid (South Africa's rigid system of segregation) and white minority rule in South Africa, Mandela, along with Oliver Tambo and Walter Sisulu, founded the Youth League of the African National Congress (ANC), a black political party in South Africa. He was elected ANC's general secretary in 1948 and its president in 1950. The ANC, representing South Africa's black majority, opposed the ruling National Party, which enforced apartheid and imposed upon blacks such oppressive requirements as internal passports. Blacks were required to live in separate communities, where services were inferior to those in white communities. Segregation was strenuously enforced.

Mandela attracted international attention in 1952 by spearheading the organization of the Defiance Campaign, which, committed to nonviolence, demanded equal rights for all South Africans. Thousands of blacks formally protested the minority control under which they were forced to live. Mandela, the movement's leading spokesperson, epitomized the ANC's threat to the racist regime that controlled South Africa.

The Suppression of Mandela

In late 1952, the ruling National Party prohibited Mandela from attending public gatherings, a ban that remained in effect for several years. In

Nelson Mandela *(Archive Photos/AMW Pressedienst)*

South African president Nelson Mandela signs South Africa's new constitution into law on December 10, 1996. *(Reuters/Adil Bradlow/Archive Photos)*

1953, Mandela was elected president of the Transvaal ANC, but shortly afterward he was forced by the National Party to resign from the organization. By late 1953, Mandela had been officially banned for two years from speaking at public gatherings, a ban that was later renewed for five years. Mandela and 155 other black leaders were accused of high treason and arrested in 1953. Nearly five years later, the defendants were acquitted of the charges against them. In 1956, Mandela met Nomzamo Winifred Madikizela, and they were married in 1958. Winnie Mandela became an anti-apartheid activist in her own right.

With the Sharpeville massacre in 1960, a year in which the National Party banned the ANC as well as the Pan-African Congress, Mandela and others formed a guerrilla branch of the ANC, the Umkonto we Sizwe (spear of the nation), which abandoned the ANC's earlier nonviolent posture. This or-

The 1994 Elections

In April, 1994, South Africa held its first truly democratic elections. Not surprisingly, the ANC won 64 percent of the seats in the newly formed National Assembly. Mandela was officially elected president by the National Assembly on May 9, 1994. He was inaugurated the following day. The first few years of Mandela's presidency were marked by an increase in trade and tourism. The relaxation of international economic sanctions against the nation led to a period of growth for South Africa as a whole. With the extension of equal rights to all minorities, the country emerged as a model to the rest of the world.

The Sharpeville Massacre

Under apartheid, South Africans of color were required to carry passes when they traveled within their own country. At its annual conference in December, 1959, the ANC urged its members to challenge this regulation and voted to institute a massive antipass demonstration to begin on March 31, 1960. The Pan-African Congress instituted its own antipass campaign at about the same time. Thousands of South Africans burned their passes in public. Many of them then traveled and presented themselves for arrest for traveling without passes.

On March 21, 1960, in Sharpeville, a small township about 35 miles (56 kilometers) south of Johannesburg, a group of several thousand unarmed and undocumented people of color surrounded the Sharpeville police station. The police force, numbering seventy-five, panicked at being so greatly outnumbered and fired into the crowd. By the time the shooting stopped, sixty-nine of the protesters had been killed by more than seven hundred rounds fired randomly by the police. Four hundred others were wounded. The following day, press stories and photographs of the massacre were front-page news around the world. International pressure against the National Party intensified substantially as a result of the massacre.

ganization committed various kinds of sabotage. The government issued warrants for Mandela's arrest, but it took the government a year to find him. In 1962, upon his return from travels throughout Africa and Britain championing his people's cause, Mandela was arrested and sentenced to five years in prison.

In 1963, Mandela and other members of Umkonto were convicted of attempting the violent overthrow of the government and received life sentences. Mandela was imprisoned until 1982 at the infamous Robben Island Prison, then was transferred first to Pollsmoor Prison and later to Victor Verster Prison. Strident international protests regarding his imprisonment and worldwide economic sanctions against South Africa eventually led to his being released without conditions on February 11, 1990. The following month, he was elected deputy president of the ANC, and the following year he was elected president at the ANC's national conference.

The Ascendancy of the ANC

With Mandela's release from prison, the National Party officially recognized the ANC.

Within a month of his release, Mandela toured Africa, Europe, and North America, where heads of state received him. Returning to South Africa, Mandela initiated talks with President F. W. de Klerk that led to the drafting of a new South African constitution. In December, 1991, Mandela and de Klerk convened a conference, at which people of color were represented proportionately, to consider drafting a new constitution. By February, 1993, Mandela had entered into an agreement with de Klerk in which the ANC and the National Party would, until May, 1999, share responsibility for forming a transitional government.

In July, 1993, Mandela and de Klerk toured the United States together, and the following September, Mandela addressed the U.N. General Assembly urging the withdrawal of economic sanctions against South Africa. Mandela and de Klerk shared the Nobel Peace Prize for 1993.

Central Contribution

Perhaps the best single adjective to describe Nelson Mandela is "tenacious." Through extremely difficult periods, always without regard

987

to his personal comfort and security, Mandela fought for the rights of his people. That his efforts succeeded is nothing short of amazing. Not only did Mandela gain control of his nation, but he also brought justice to a huge population suppressed since the arrival of white settlers in South Africa. Remarkably, he accomplished these ends with minimal bloodshed.

In 1998, Mandela celebrated his eightieth birthday among friends and family by marrying Graca Machel, widow of former Mozambique president Samora Machel. Mandela and his first wife, Winnie, had separated in 1992 and were divorced in 1996. Winnie Mandela had tirelessly promoted many of her husband's initiatives while he was in prison. However, she was arrested in 1988, and found guilty in 1991, of kidnapping and assault because of an incident involving her bodyguards. Her sentence was reduced to a fine, but the trial and conviction made her a very controversial figure.

Nelson and Winnie Mandela after Nelson's release from prison in 1990. *(AP/Wide World Photos)*

Bibliography

Mandela, Nelson. *Long Walk to Freedom: The Autobiography of Nelson Mandela*. Boston: Little, Brown, 1994.

_____. "Nelson Mandela: The Struggle Is My Life." In *African Philosophy: A Classical Approach*. Edited by Parker English and Kibujjo M. Kalumba. Upper Saddle River, N.J.: Prentice Hall, 1996.

Meer, Fatima. *Higher than Hope: The Authorized Biography of Nelson Mandela*. New York: Harper and Row, 1990.

Meredith, Martin. *Nelson Mandela: A Biography*. New York: St. Martin's Press, 1998.

R. Baird Shuman

Winnie Mandela

Born: September 26, 1934; Bizana, Transkei, South Africa

South African antiapartheid activist and political figure

Winnie Mandela (WIH-nee mahn-DAY-lah), born Nomzamo Winifred Madikizela (nom-ZAH-moh WIH-nih-frehd mah-dee-kee-ZEH-lah), grew up with seven brothers and sisters in a small South African village. Both her parents taught school. Winnie attended grammar school in Bizana and high school in Shawbury, then earned a diploma in social work in Johannesburg and a bachelor's degree in political science at the University of Witwatersrand. Her academic research and work as a medical social worker inspired her to join the fight against apartheid, her country's system of legal racism. Along with her husband, Nelson Mandela, she became a leader of that movement.

Antiapartheid Activism

While her academic work made Winnie aware of racial injustices, it was her experience as the first black medical social worker at Baragwanath Hospital in Soweto (a black residential township in South Africa) that showed her the actual impact of racism on most black South Africans. Infant mortality rates were extremely high, and those babies who survived often lived in poverty. Few opportunities existed for black young people to attend good schools, get good jobs, and pursue their dreams.

Apartheid, which had been officially adopted as government policy in 1948, when Winnie was an adolescent, was a strict system of racial segregation. It severely restricted black economic, social, and political rights. Winnie began protesting against those policies in the 1950's, becoming a member of the African National Congress (ANC) and other organizations dedicated to ending apartheid. She met Nelson Mandela through her ANC involvement, and they married in 1958. Four years later, Nelson Mandela was impris-

oned because of his anti-apartheid leadership. He remained in prison until 1990.

Winnie became an antiapartheid leader, too, but she affiliated with a radical wing of the ANC. As a result, she was arrested and imprisoned repeatedly. She was jailed for seventeen months in 1969-1970. From 1977 to 1985, she was forced to live in internal exile; she was sent to the remote village of Brandfort, where she was under constant surveillance and her activities were severely restricted. In spite of the government's

Winnie Mandela *(Archive Photos)*

989

efforts to suppress her, Mandela continued to resist its racist policies.

Primary among her concerns in Brandfort was the plight of black children, who suffered from poor nutrition, inadequate schools, and insufficient medical facilities. Working through the Women's League of the ANC, Mandela mobilized parents to work on self-help projects that would produce income while providing goods and services. One such project enabled women to sew school uniforms for children. Another involved organizing young people into groups to learn arts and crafts. Mandela's primary goal, however, was to end apartheid. She focused her energy on promoting resistance to those policies.

Mandela's reputation was tarnished in 1988-1989 by a violent incident involving the beating and kidnapping of four black youths. Mandela and her bodyguards were linked to the kidnapping, and one of the youths was killed by Mandela's chief bodyguard. In 1991 she was sentenced to prison for the kidnapping, but the sentence was later reduced to a fine.

In 1990, Nelson Mandela was released from prison as part of a negotiated end to apartheid. He was soon elected president of the new post-apartheid government. Winnie was elected to serve on the new parliament, and she continued her leadership role in the Women's League of the ANC. She also served as deputy minister of arts, culture, science, and tech-

Anti-apartheid activist Winnie Mandela in 1992, addressing strikers and demonstrators outside a hospital near Johannesburg. *(Reuters/Juda Ngwenya/Archive Photos)*

The Mandelas' Political Differences

Winnie and Nelson Mandela both wanted to end apartheid, but they had different ideas about how to combat it. Nelson believed that the best way to change the system was to work patiently to convince his opponents that it was in their own best interest to move toward racial integration. Winnie, however, supported those who were impatient with this gradual approach and who used confrontational, sometimes violent, methods of protest. Their fundamental disagreement represented the difference between moderation and a more radical approach to change. Sometimes significant political change only occurs when both methods are used, and it may be that it took both of the Mandelas' approaches to end apartheid.

nology until 1995, when Nelson Mandela expelled her from the cabinet. In 1996, her long, difficult marriage to Nelson ended in divorce.

Postapartheid Controversy

Following her divorce, Winnie began using her maiden name along with her married name, becoming known as Winnie Madikizela-Mandela. In 1998 Winnie was brought before the Truth and Reconciliation Commission, which was established to investigate human rights violations by both supporters and opponents of apartheid. Its goal was to grant amnesty to perpetrators who confessed their guilt and to award compensation to victims. Madikizela-Mandela was accused of perpetrating violence and intimidation through a group called the Mandela United Football Club during the final years of apartheid. She maintained that she was innocent of the charges.

Nelson and Winnie Mandela arriving at the Supreme Court in Johannesburg for the start of Winnie's 1991 kidnapping trial. *(Reuters/Juda Ngwenya/ Archive Photos)*

Bibliography

Gilbey. Emma. *The Lady: The Life and Times of Winnie Mandela*. London: Cape, 1993.

Harrison, Nancy. *Winnie Mandela*. New York: George Braziller, 1986.

Mandela, Winnie. *Part of My Soul Went with Him*. New York: W. W. Norton, 1984.

Vail, John J., and Arthur M. Schlesinger. *Nelson and Winnie Mandela*. New York: Chelsea House, 1989.

Susan MacFarland

Wilma P. Mankiller

Born: November 18, 1945; Tahlequah, Oklahoma

First woman principal chief of Cherokee Nation (1985-1995)

Wilma Pearl Mankiller (WIHL-mah PURL MAN-kih-lur), the daughter of a white mother and a full-blooded Cherokee father, was born into extreme rural poverty. At age twelve, Mankiller moved with her family to San Francisco, California. During the 1960's, Mankiller married and had two daughters. Increasingly frustrated with life as a housewife, she began taking college courses. The Native American occupation of Alcatraz Island, which lasted from 1969 to 1971, heightened Mankiller's interest in her heritage and marked a turning point in her life.

Native American Issues

Concerned with the problems that faced Native Americans, Mankiller became the director of the Native American Youth Center in East Oakland, California, and did volunteer work with the Pit River Tribe. After her marriage failed in 1974, she began visiting Oklahoma, and in 1977 she returned there to live. She worked as an economic stimulus coordinator (a low-level management position) for the Cherokee Nation until 1979, when her abilities as a grant writer led to a position as a program development specialist.

A nearly fatal automobile accident in late 1979 and the discovery in 1980 that she suffered from myasthenia gravis, a chronic neuromuscular disease, resulted in a spiritual awakening that strengthened her commitment to community involvement. In 1981 she established the Community Development Department of the Cherokee Nation. The Bell Community Project, a rehabilitation program that emphasized self-help, received national media attention and prompted Chief Ross Swimmer to ask Mankiller to run as his deputy chief in the 1983 tribal elections. Although some Cherokees opposed the notion of a woman holding high office, Swimmer and Mankiller won the election. Two years later Swimmer resigned, and in accordance with provisions in the Cherokee constitution, Man-

Wilma P. Mankiller *(AP/Wide World Photos)*

killer became principal chief of the Cherokee Nation, the first woman to hold such a position in any major American Indian tribe.

Chief Mankiller

As principal chief, Mankiller managed the operations of a tribe with more than 140,000 enrolled members. The Cherokees faced a host of problems, including inadequate health care and unemployment rates reaching 50 percent. Mankiller sought to foster an outlook of self-reliance among the Cherokees, encouraging them to take an active role in planning the tribe's future. She believed that traditional Cherokee values that placed importance on helping neighbors and respecting the land would aid her people in their struggle to improve their lives. Enjoying the challenges and opportunities which the office of principal chief offered, she sought election in her own right in 1987. Mankiller won a runoff election by a large margin. She regarded the vote as a mandate for her leadership that put to rest any doubts concerning the ability of a woman to lead a tribe.

Mankiller focused on economic development during her first full term as chief, founding the Cherokee Nation's Chamber of Commerce and using the methods of community development that she had practiced earlier in her career to

Wilma P. Mankiller between Angela Davis and Gloria Steinem in 1998. The three were featured speakers at a benefit for the Boston Women's Fund. *(AP/Wide World Photos)*

President Clinton and Tribal Leaders Meet in 1994

In the U.S. political system, Native American tribes have limited sovereignty, or powers, over their people and their lands. President Bill Clinton's April, 1994, meeting with tribal leaders reaffirmed the unique relationship between tribal governments and the federal government. Clinton pledged to fulfill the special obligations that the federal government has toward Native Americans. In addition, he signed two memoranda, one that instructed federal agencies to cooperate with tribal government in their use of eagle feathers in religious practices, and a second that required federal agencies to consult with tribes when making decisions concerning tribal resources. Clinton also promised to restore funding for the Indian Health Service. As the chief of one of the largest tribes in the country, Wilma Mankiller attended the meeting.

improve the economy in northeastern Oklahoma. However, she did not abandon her heritage, creating the Institute of Cherokee Literacy in order to promote the use of the Cherokee language. The Cherokees approved of her methods. In her 1991 reelection bid Mankiller won by a landslide, receiving nearly 83 percent of the vote. However, health problems forced her to forgo reelection for a third term in 1995. After leaving office, Mankiller accepted a fellowship at Dartmouth College. After a bout with cancer forced her to return to Oklahoma in 1996, Mankiller announced that she planned to volunteer at a women's shelter in Tahlequah. In 1998 President Bill Clinton awarded Mankiller the Presidential Medal of Freedom for her efforts on behalf of the Cherokees.

Wilma P. Mankiller, Cherokee principal chief, confers with Phillip Martin, chief of the Mississippi Band of Choctaw, at a 1989 U.S. Senate Indian Affairs Subcommittee meeting. *(AP/Wide World Photos)*

Bibliography

Mankiller, Wilma P., with Michael Wallis. *Mankiller: A Chief and Her People*. New York: St. Martin's Press, 1993.

Wallace, Michele. "Wilma Mankiller." *Ms.*, January, 1988, 68-69.

Thomas Clarkin

BIOGRAPHICAL ENCYCLOPEDIA OF
20th-Century
World Leaders

Index

In the following index, volume numbers and those page numbers referring to full articles appear in **bold face** type.

Abdulla, Farooq, **2:** 545
Abdul Rahman, **1: 1-3**
Abernathy, Ralph David, **1: 4-6**
Abuja, Nigeria, establishment as Nigerian capital, **1:** 8
Acheson, Dean, **1: 7-10**
Acquired immunodeficiency syndrome (AIDS), Zaire and, **4:** 1080; Zimbabwe and, **4:** 1106
Act of European Unity, **2:** 388
Adams, Gerry, **1: 11-13; 4:** 1314
Addams, Jane, **3:** 892
Adenauer, Konrad, **1: 14-17**
Affirmative action, **1:** 194
Afghanistan, Soviet invasion of, **1:** 198
Aflaq, Michel, **1:** 60
African Democratic Assembly, **3:** 724
African National Congress (ANC), **1:** 238; **3:** 948, 985, 989
African socialism, **3:** 830; **4:** 1159
Afrika Corps, **4:** 1315
Afro-Asian Bandung Conference, **5:** 1453
Agenda for Peace (Boutros-Ghali), **1:** 176
Agrava Commission, **4:** 1279
Aguinaldo, Emilio, **1: 18-20**
Airpower in the 1920's, **4:** 1073
Akihito, **1: 21-23; 3:** 694
Albright, Madeleine, **1: 24-26; 4:** 1137
Algeciras Conference, **1:** 226
Algerian coup of 1965, **1:** 171
Alianza Popular Revolucionaria Americana, **2:** 645
Allenby, Edmund Henry Hynman, **1: 27-29; 2:** 498
Allende, Salvador, **1: 30-33; 4:** 1236-1237
Alliance Party of Malaysia, **1:** 3
All-India Muslim League, **3:** 775
American Expeditionary Force (AEF), **4:** 1229
Americo-Liberians, **2:** 411
Amin, Idi, **1: 34-37; 4:** 1160, 1163
Anarchism, **5:** 1631, 1642
ANC. *See* African National Congress (ANC)
Andropov, Yuri, **2:** 574
Anglican Church, South Africa and, **5:** 1519
Anglo-French Entente, **1:** 98

Anglo-Iranian Oil Company (AIOC), **4:** 1094
Anglo-Iraqi Treaty, **2:** 500
Anglo-Japanese Alliance, **4:** 1056
Angolan Revolt, **5:** 1373
Annan, Kofi, **1: 38-40**
Anschluss, **4:** 1306
Antarctica, exploration of, **1:** 242
Anti-Ballistic Missile Treaty, **5:** 1417
Antitrust legislation, U.S., **3:** 814
ANZUS Pact, **4:** 1065
Apartheid, **1:** 237; **3:** 947, 985, 989; **5:** 1518, 1520; ending of, **2:** 385
Appeasement of Nazi Germany, **1:** 72, 93, 280; **2:** 464, 562
Aprista movement, **2:** 644-645
Aquino, Benigno, **1:** 41; **4:** 1030
Aquino, Corazon, **1: 41-43; 4:** 1031, 1279
Arab Federation, **3:** 745
Arab-Israeli wars. *See* Six-Day War; Yom Kippur War
Arab Revolt, **2:** 498; **3:** 904
Arab socialism, **4:** 1130
Arafat, Yasir, **1: 44-48; 4:** 1137
Arbitration, **3:** 886
Arias Sánchez, Oscar, **1: 49-51**
Aristide, Jean-Bertrand, **1: 52-54**
Arms Race, The (Noel-Baker), **4:** 1154
Arras, Battle of, **1:** 27
Arusha Declaration, **4:** 1159
Asquith, H. H., **1: 55-58; 3:** 901, 932
Assad, Hafez al-, **1: 59-62**
Asser, Tobias Michael Carel, **1: 63-64**
Astor, Nancy, **1: 65-67**
Astor, Waldorf, **1:** 65
Aswan High Dam, **4:** 1130
Atatürk, Kemal, **1: 68-71; 2:** 482; **3:** 755
Atlantic, Battle of the, **2:** 418
Atomic bomb. *See* Hiroshima and Nagasaki, bombing of
Atoms for Peace program, **2:** 475
Attlee, Clement, **1: 72-75**
Australian Commonwealth, establishment of, **1:** 103; **4:** 1294

Australian Council of Trade Unions (ACTU), **2:** 642
Australian Labor Party (ALP), **2:** 642; **3:** 810
Australian mining boom, **2:** 344
Australian navy, **2:** 505
Austria, German takeover of, **4:** 1306
Austro-Hungarian Empire, **2:** 514; ethnicity issues in, **2:** 512
Authenticité, **4:** 1078
Authoritarianism, **5:** 1630
Axworthy, Lloyd, **1: 76-78**
Aydeed, Muhammad Farah. *See* Aydid, Muhammad Farah
Aydid, Muhammad Farah, **1: 79-81**
Ayub Khan, Mohammad, **1:** 142
Azikiwe, Nnamdi, **1: 82-85**
Azócar, Patricio Aylwin, **4:** 1238

Babangida, Ibrahim, **1: 86-88**
Baby Doc. *See* Duvalier, Jean-Claude
Badoglio, Pietro, **2:** 380
Baghdad Pact, **4:** 1082
Baghdad Railway, **1:** 225
Bajer, Fredrik, **1: 89-90**
Bakr, Ahmed Hassan al-, **3:** 748
Baldwin, Stanley, **1: 91-94**
Balfour, Arthur, **1: 95-98,** 254
Balfour Declaration, **1:** 97, 124; **5:** 1561
Balkan Wars, **2:** 482; **3:** 755; **5:** 1534
Ballinger, Richard, **5:** 1465
Banerjea, Surendranath, **1: 99-101**
Bangladesh, establishment of, **1:** 143; **3:** 776
Bantu Education Act, **5:** 1518
Barak, Ehud, **4:** 1139, 1213
Barbot, Clement, **2:** 451
Barre. *See* Siad Barre, Muhammad
Barthou, Jean-Louis, **3:** 897
Barton, Edmund, **1: 102-104**
Ba'th Party, **1:** 60
Batista y Zaldívar, Fulgencio, **1: 105-108,** 268
Batlle Doctrine, **1:** 110
Batlle y Ordóñez, José, **1: 109-110**
Bay of Pigs invasion, **1:** 269; **3:** 821
Beer-hall putsch, **2:** 581; **3:** 695, 944
Beernaert, Auguste-Marie-François, **1: 111-113**
Begin, Menachem, **1: 114-117,** 262; **5:** 1365
Belfast peace negotiations of 1997, **1:** 12
Ben Bella, Ahmed, **1: 170-171**
Bendjedid, Chadli, **1:** 171

Benelux Charter, **5:** 1427
Benelux Economic Union, **5:** 1426
Beneš, Edvard, **1: 118-121; 4:** 1043
Bengalee, The, **1:** 100
Ben-Gurion, David, **1:** 115, **122-125; 3:** 680; **5:** 1570
Bennett, Richard Bedford, **1: 126-128**
Bennett, W. A. C., **1: 129-131**
Berber Dahir, **4:** 1107
Berlin, Battle of, **5:** 1624
Berlin Crisis, **3:** 820
Berlin Wall, **3:** 712, 820; **5:** 1525; fall of, **1:** 235; **2:** 577
Bernadotte, Folke, **1:** 228
Bernstein, Eduard, **5:** 1642
Besant, Annie, **5:** 1482
Betar, **1:** 115
Bethmann Hollweg, Theobald von, **1: 132-134**
Bhopal poison-gas disaster, **2:** 545
Bhumibol Adulyadej, **1: 135-137**
Bhutto, Benazir, **1: 138-141**
Bhutto, Murtaza, **1:** 140
Bhutto, Zulfikar Ali, **1:** 138, **142-145; 5:** 1626
Biafra secession from Nigeria, **1:** 85
Biko, Steve, **5:** 1519
Bill 101, **3:** 919
Bimini, Adam Clayton Powell and, **4:** 1258
Bismarck, Otto von, **1:** 224; **5:** 1577
Black, Hugo L., **1: 146-148**
Black and Tan War, **2:** 352, 394
Black and Tans, **2:** 341
Black Muslims, **3:** 979
Black Panther Party, **3:** 857
Black Star Line, **2:** 552
Black Thursday and Black Tuesday, **3:** 717
Blair, Tony, **1: 149-152**
Blamey, Thomas, **1:** 208
Blitz, the, **1:** 303, **2:** 563
Blitzkrieg, **2:** 582, 598; **3:** 835; **4:** 1232
Bloc Québécois, **1:** 166, 297
Bloody Sunday, **2:** 340, 648; **3:** 831; **4:** 1141; **5:** 1495
Bloomsbury Group, **3:** 837-838
Blum, Léon, **1: 153-156; 4:** 1075
Boer War, **1:** 163-164; **3:** 870; **5:** 1419; Canada and, **3:** 895
Bolshevik Revolution, **3:** 915. *See also* Russian Revolution
Bolsheviks, **1:** 220; **3:** 808, 831, 982; **5:** 1495
Bolshevism, **3:** 927
Borah, William E., **1: 157-159**

Borden, Robert Laird, **1: 160-162**
Bormann, Martin, **3:** 682
Boston police strike of 1919, **2:** 346
Botha, Louis, **1: 163-165**, **5:** 1420
Botha, P. W., **2:** 383, 385
Bouchard, Lucien, **1: 166-168**
Boumedienne, Houari, **1: 169-171**
Bourgeois, Léon, **1: 172-173**
Boutros-Ghali, Boutros, **1: 174-177**
Boxer Rebellion, **3:** 716, **5:** 1522, 1600
Bradley, Omar N., **1: 178-180**
Branch Davidians, FBI confrontation with, **4:** 1299
Brandeis, Louis D., **1: 181-183**
Brandt, Willy, **1: 184-187**
Branting, Karl Hjalmar, **1: 188-189**
Brasília, building of, **3:** 880
Braun, Wernher von, **1: 190-192**
Brazilian New State, **5:** 1530
Brazzaville Conference, **2:** 462
Brennan, William J., Jr., **1: 193-195**
Brest-Litovsk, Treaty of, **3:** 944
Bretton Woods Conference, **3:** 839
Brezhnev, Leonid Ilich, **1: 196-199**
Brezhnev Doctrine, **1:** 197
Briand, Aristide, **1: 200-203**; **2:** 652
Britain, Battle of, **2:** 563, 582
British Commonwealth, **2:** 479; **3:** 862
British East India Company, **4:** 1234
British Eighth Army, **4:** 1089
British Empire, Canada and, **4:** 1206
British Expeditionary Force, **1:** 205
British monarchy, **2:** 478
British navy, **2:** 559
Brooke, Alan Francis, **1: 204-206**
Brown, Elaine, **3:** 857
Brown, Willie, **3:** 764
Brown v. Board of Education, 1954, **4:** 1037; **5:** 1557
Bruce, Stanley, **1: 207-209**
Brundtland, Gro Harlem, **1: 210-212**
Brüning, Heinrich, **3:** 690
Bryan, William Jennings, **1: 213-216**
Brzezinski, Zbigniew, **1: 217-219**
Bugandan Rebellion, **4:** 1164
Bukharin, Nikolai Ivanovich, **1: 220-223**
Bulge, Battle of the, **4:** 1200, 1335
Bull Moose Party, **4:** 1326
Bülow, Bernhard von, **1: 224-226**; **2:** 485
Bunche, Ralph, **1: 227-229**

Burger, Warren E., **1: 230-232**; **4:** 1291
Burma, British colonialism and, **5:** 1472
Burma campaign, World War II, **1:** 35; **4:** 1098; **5:** 1403
Burnham, Forbes, **3:** 766
Bush, George, **1: 233-236**; **2:** 334, 415; **4:** 1156, 1226
Bustamante y Rivero, José Luis, **2:** 645
Buthelezi, Mangosuthu Gatsha, **1: 237-239**
Byng, Julian, **3:** 861; **4:** 1057; **5:** 1527
Byrd, Richard E., **1: 240-243**

Cairo Accord, **3:** 800
Callaghan, James, **1: 244-246**
Calles, Plutarco Elías, **1: 247-249**, 257; **4:** 1166; **5:** 1538
Cambodia, killing fields of, **4:** 1251
Campbell, Kim, **1: 250-252**, 260; **2:** 527; **4:** 1114
Campbell-Bannerman, Henry, **1:** 55, **253-255**
Camp David Accords, **1:** 116, 174, 262
Canada Council, **5:** 1440
Canadian Bill of Rights, **2:** 406
Canadian Medical Association (CMA), **2:** 528
Canadian New Deal, **1:** 127
Capital punishment, United States and, **1:** 231
Capitalism, **5:** 1638, 1641
Caporetto, **3:** 943
Cárdenas, Lázaro, **1: 256-258**
Carney, Pat, **1: 259-260**
Carranza, Venustiano, **1:** 247; **2:** 401; **4:** 1165, 1191; **5:** 1537, 1607
Cartel des Gauches, **3:** 676
Carter, Jimmy, **1:** 217, **261-264**; **3:** 864; **4:** 1104, 1196, 1287
Cassin, René, **1: 265-267**
Castillo, Ramón, **4:** 1223
Castro, Fidel, **1:** 106, **268-271**; **2:** 451, 601; **4:** 1177
Caudillismo, **5:** 1631
Ceausescu, Nicolae, **1: 272-275**
Central African Federation, **3:** 804
Central American Peace Accord, 1987, **1:** 50
Central Intelligence Agency (CIA), **1:** 32, 270; **3:** 821, 966; **4:** 1082, 1095
Central Treaty Organization, **4:** 1082
Chaco War, **5:** 1362, 1445
Chamber of Deputies, French, **3:** 676
Chamberlain, Austen, **1: 276-278**, 281
Chamberlain, Joseph, **1:** 281; **2:** 540
Chamberlain, Neville, **1:** 72, **279-282**; **2:** 464
Chamorro, Emiliano, **5:** 1422
Chamorro, Violeta, **4:** 1179

Chanak crisis, **3:** 935

Chao Tzu-yang. *See* Zhao Ziyang

Charles, Prince of Wales, **2:** 397

Charlottetown Agreement, **4:** 1112

Charter of Rights and Freedoms, **5:** 1502

Charter 77, **2:** 639

Chen Duxiu, **1: 283-285**

Cheney, Dick, **2:** 493

Ch'en Tu-hsiu. *See* Chen Duxiu

Chernenko, Konstantin, **2:** 575

Chernov, Victor, **3:** 833

Chiang Ch'ing. *See* Jiang Qing

Chiang Kai-shek, **1: 286-289**; **2:** 606; **3:** 921; **5:** 1458

Chiang Tse-min. *See* Jiang Zemin

Chifley, Joseph Benedict, **1: 290-292**

Chiluba, Frederick, **3:** 805

China, Republic of, establishment of, **1:** 289

China, U.S. opening of relations with, **4:** 1147

Chinese Communist Party (CCP), **1:** 284; **2:** 605; **3:** 770, 929; **4:** 1028, 1208; **5:** 1615

Chinese Red Army, **5:** 1616, 1619

Chirac, Jacques, **4:** 1076

Chisholm, Shirley, **1: 293-295**

Chou En-lai. *See* Zhou Enlai

Chrétien, Jean, **1:** 251, **296-299**; **2:** 527

Christian Democratic Party, Italian, **2:** 381

Christian Democratic Union (CDU), German, **1:** 15

Churchill, Winston, **1:** 72, **300-303**; **2:** 562

Chu Teh. *See* Zhu De

CIA. *See* Central Intelligence Agency (CIA)

Ciudad Juárez, Treaty of, **3:** 964

Civil Rights Act of 1964, **3:** 786, 825

Civil Rights movement, U.S., **1:** 4, **3:** 762, 856

Cixi. *See* Tz'u-hsi

Clark, Joe, **1: 304-306**; **5:** 1501

Clemenceau, Georges, **1: 307-310**

Cliche Commission, **4:** 1111

Clinton, Bill, **2: 333-336**, 337, 415; **4:** 1137, 1226

Clinton, Hillary Rodham, **2:** 333, **337-339**

Cliveden set, **1:** 67

Clodumar, Kinza, **2:** 429

Coalition for a Democratic Majority, **3:** 864

Coalition governments, **5:** 1643

Cold War, **2:** 595, 631; **3:** 820, 846; arms race and, **4:** 1123; containment policy and, **1:** 10; Haiti and, **2:** 451. *See also* Berlin Wall

Collins, Michael, **2: 340-342**, 352

Colorado Party, Paraguayan, **5:** 1446

Columbus, New Mexico, Pacho Villa's raid on, **5:** 1538

Common law, **3:** 707

Common Law, The (Holmes), **3:** 706

Common Market. *See* European Economic Community (EEC)

Communism, **5:** 1642

Communist International (Comintern), **1:** 222; **3:** 956

Communist Party, Chinese. *See* Chinese Communist Party (CCP)

Communist Party, French, **3:** 703; **4:** 1075

Conakat Party, Congolese, **5:** 1509

Confédération Générale du Travail (CGT), **1:** 308

Congo Crisis, **2:** 623

Congregation of the Missionaries of Charity, **5:** 1469

Congress of Racial Equality (CORE), **3:** 762, 857

Congress Party, Indian, **4:** 1133

Conservativism, **5:** 1638

Constantine, **5:** 1534

Constitution Act, Canadian, **1:** 296

Constitutional monarchism, **5:** 1632, 1637

Consumer Pricing Act, **3:** 789

Containment, **1:** 10; **3:** 787

Contra movement, **4:** 1178. *See also* Iran-Contra scandal

Cook, Joseph, **2: 343-344**

Coolidge, Calvin, **2: 345-348**; **5:** 1435

Co-operative Commonwealth Federation (CCF), **2:** 420

Copps, Sheila, **2: 349-351**

CORE. *See* Congress of Racial Equality (CORE)

Corporatism, **4:** 1120

Cosgrave, William T., **2: 352-354**

Coubertin, Pierre de, **2: 355-357**

Council of Economic Advisers (CEA), **2:** 592

Council of Europe, **5:** 1426

Cremer, William Randal, **2: 358-359**, 567

Cross of gold speech, Bryan's, **1:** 213

Cuban Constitutional Army, **1:** 107

Cuban Missile Crisis, **1:** 270; **2:** 548; **3:** 822, 847; **5:** 1434, 1472

Cuban Revolution, **1:** 107, 268; **2:** 602

Cultural Revolution, **2:** 392; **3:** 767, 931; **4:** 1027; **5:** 1617, 1621

Curtin, John, **2: 360-363**, 509

Curzon, George Nathaniel, **2: 364-366**

Cyprus, **3:** 975; **4:** 1188; independence of, **3:** 799, 976

Cyprus Crisis, **3:** 799, 976; **4:** 1188

Czechoslovakia, dissolution of, **2:** 641
Czechoslovakia, establishment of, **4:** 1042
Czechoslovakia, Soviet invasion of, **1:** 197

Dáil Éireann, **2:** 341, 352; **4:** 1173
Dalai Lama, The, **2: 367-370**
Daugherty, Harry M., **2:** 625
Dawes, Charles G., **2: 371-373**
Dawes Plan, **2:** 372, 651; **5:** 1443
Dawson, Anderson, **2:** 504
Dawson, Geoffrey, **1:** 67
Dayan, Moshe, **2: 374-377**
Deakin, Alfred, **2: 378-379**
December Revolution of 1905, Russian, **4:** 1141
Defferre, Gaston, **4:** 1076
Defferre Law, **4:** 1076
De Gasperi, Alcide, **2: 380-382**
de Gaulle, Charles. *See* Gaulle, Charles de
de Klerk, F. W., **2: 383-385; 3:** 987
Delors, Jacques, **2: 386-388**
Demirel, Suleyman, **4:** 1180-1181
Democracy, **5:** 1632
Democratic Unionist Party (DUP), Northern Irish,
    4: 1185
Deng Xiaoping, **2: 389-392; 3:** 925, 930; **5:** 1612
Department of Health, Education, and Welfare,
    2: 474
Depression. *See* Great Depression
Desai, Morarji, **2:** 539
Descamisados (shirtless ones), **4:** 1222
Desert Storm, **1:** 235; **2:** 493; **4:** 1261. *See also* Persian
    Gulf War
De-Stalinization, **3:** 846
Détente, **1:** 197; **2:** 535
de Valera, Eamon, **2:** 341, 352, **393-396**
Dewey, Thomas, **5:** 1508
Dia, Mamadou, **5:** 1391
Diana, Princess of Wales, **2: 397-399**
Díaz, Porfirio, **2: 400-403; 3:** 964; **5:** 1537, 1606
Diefenbaker, John G., **2: 404-407**
Dien Bien Phu, French defeat at, **5:** 1541
Diouf, Abdou, **5:** 1391
Djilas, Milovan, **2: 408-409**
Doe, Samuel K., **2: 410-413**
Dole, Robert, **2: 414-416**
Dole-Mondale vice-presidential debate, **2:** 415
Dollar diplomacy, **5:** 1437
Domino theory, **4:** 1252

Dönitz, Karl, **2: 417-419**
Douglas, Helen Gahagan, **4:** 1146
Douglas, Tommy, **2: 420-422**
Douglas, William O., **2: 423-424**
Douglas-Home, Alexander, **2: 425-427; 5:** 1583
Downer, Alexander, **2: 428-430**
Duarte, José Napoleon, **2: 431-433**
Du Bois, W. E. B., **2: 438-441; 4:** 1151
Dubček, Alexander, **2: 434-437**
Ducommun, Elie, **1:** 90
Due process of law, **3:** 707
Dulles, John Foster, **2: 442-445**
Dumbarton Oaks Conference, **2:** 594, 596
Duplessis, Maurice, **2: 446-448**
Duvalier, François, **2: 449-452**
Duvalier, Jean-Claude, **1:** 52; **2: 453-455**

Easter Rebellion, **2:** 341, 393
East Timor, Indonesian invasion of, **5:** 1450
Eban, Abba, **2: 456-459**
Éboué, Félix, **2: 460-462**
EC. *See* European Community (EC)
Ecumenism, **3:** 781
Eden, Anthony, **2: 463-466; 3:** 963
Edward VII, **2: 467-470**
Edward VIII, **1:** 94; **2: 471-472**, 561
Efendi, al-. *See* Karami, Rashid
Egyptian Expeditionary Force (EEF), **1:** 28
Eichmann, Adolf, trial of, **5:** 1575
Eisenhower, Dwight D., **2: 473-476; 5:** 1433
El Alamein, **4:** 1316
Elizabeth II, **2: 477-480**
El Salvador, civil war in, **2:** 432
El Salvador Peace Pact, **4:** 1216
Engels, Friedrich, **3:** 807; **5:** 1640
Enrile, Juan, **1:** 42
Entebbe airport hostage rescue, **3:** 679; **4:** 1212
Entente Cordiale, **2:** 469-470; **4:** 1235
Enver Pasha, **2: 481-483**
Equal Rights Amendment (ERA), **1:** 294
Erzberger, Matthias, **2: 484-486; 5:** 1442
Ethiopia, Italian invasion of, **2:** 616, 618
Ethiopian Revolution, **2:** 617
Ethnic cleansing, **4:** 1069
EU. *See* European Union (EU)
European Atomic Energy Community (Euratom),
    5: 1427
European Coal and Steel Community, **1:** 16; **2:** 382

European Commission, **2:** 386-387
European Community (EC), **2:** 386; Greece and, **4:** 1187; Turkey and, **4:** 1182
European Economic Community (EEC), **5:** 1427; Britain and, **1:** 246; **2:** 648
European Recovery Program (ERP), **4:** 1034
European Union (EU), **2:** 387; **3:** 876; Britain and, **1:** 151; Norway and, **1:** 211
Evangelium Vitae, **3:** 784
Evatt, Herbert Vere, **2: 487-488**
Evian, Agreement of, **1:** 169
Evita. *See* Perón, Eva
Evren, Kenan, **4:** 1180
Executive privilege, **1:** 231

Fadden, Arthur William, **2: 489-490**
Fahd, **2: 491-493**
Fahd Plan, **2:** 492
Fair Labor Standards Act, **1:** 146
Faisal (Saudi Arabia), **2: 494-497; 5:** 1592
Faisal I (Iraq), **2: 498-500**
Falangists, **2:** 519
Falkenhayn, Erich von, **4:** 1232
Falkland Islands, **4:** 1063
Falkland Islands War, **5:** 1475
Fall, Albert B., **2:** 627
Farabundo Martí Front for National Liberation (FMLN), **2:** 433; **4:** 1216
Fard, Wallace D., **3:** 979
Fascism, **4:** 1118, **5:** 1644
Fashoda Crisis, **1:** 96
FBI. *See* Federal Bureau of Investigation (FBI)
Fedayeen, **3:** 746
Federal Bureau of Investigation (FBI), **3:** 719; confrontation with Branch Davidians, **4:** 1300
Federal Parliamentary Labour Party, Australian, **5:** 1386
Federal Reserve Board, **2:** 591
Federal Reserve System, U.S., **2:** 593
Federation of Rhodesia and Nyasaland. *See* Central African Federation
Ferraro, Geraldine, **2: 501-503**
Fez Plan, **2:** 492
Fianna Fáil, **2:** 394; **4:** 1172
Field, Winston, **5:** 1412-1413
Fifth Amendment, **3:** 707
Fifth Republic, French, **2:** 556
Figueres, José, **1:** 49

Final Solution, **3:** 686, 899
Fine Gael, **2:** 353
Finnish civil war, **4:** 1020
Fisher, Andrew, **2: 504-505; 3:** 733
Foch, Ferdinand, **3:** 778
Ford, Gerald R., **2: 506-508**
Forde, Francis Michael, **2: 509-510**
Fortress Europe, **3:** 697
Four Modernizations, **2:** 390
Fourteen Points, Woodrow Wilson's, **2:** 516; **4:** 1133; **5:** 1587
Fourth Red Army, **5:** 1620
Fourth Republic, French, **2:** 555
France, Battle of, **1:** 204
Francis Ferdinand, **2: 511-513**
Francis Joseph I, **2: 514-517**
Franco, Francisco, **2: 518-521; 3:** 792
Frankfurter, Felix, **2: 522-523**
Franz Joseph I. *See* Francis Joseph I
Fraser, Malcolm, **2: 524-526**, 643
Free French movement, **2:** 460, 462, 554
Free German Youth (FDJ), **3:** 713
Free Officers' Organization, Egyptian, **5:** 1363
Free trade movement, Australian, **4:** 1295
FRELIMO. *See* Front for the Liberation of Mozambique (FRELIMO)
French Equatorial Africa, **2:** 461
Friendship, Treaty of, Soviet-Egyptian, **5:** 1365
Front for the Liberation of Mozambique (FRELIMO), **3:** 959
Fry, Hedy, **2: 527-528**
Fujimori, Alberto, **2: 529-532**
Fulbright, J. William, **2: 533-535**
Fulbright scholarships, **2:** 534
Fusion Party, Australian, **2:** 344

Gallipoli campaign, World War I, **1:** 68, 97, 301; **3:** 734
Galvao, Henrique, **5:** 1373
Gandhi, Indira, **2: 536-539**, 546
Gandhi, Mahatma, **2: 540-543; 4:** 1132-1133, 1197
Gandhi, Rajiv, **2:** 539, **544-546**
Gandhi, Sanjay, **2:** 539, 544
Gang of Four, **3:** 768; **5:** 1617
García Robles, Alfonso, **2: 547-549**
Garvey, Marcus, **2: 550-552**
Gaulle, Charles de, **2:** 460, **553-556; 3:** 916; **4:** 1074, 1253

Gaullism, **4:** 1255

General Agreement on Trade and Tariffs (GATT), **2:** 533

General strike of 1926, British, **1:** 92

General Theory of Employment, Interest, and Money, The (Keynes), **3:** 839

Geneva Conference (1954), **2:** 445; **3:** 705; **5:** 1540-1541, 1617

Geneva Convention, **1:** 112

Geneva Protocol, **4:** 1154

George V, **1:** 56; **2:** 557-560

George VI, **2:** 561-563

Germany, division into East and West, **5:** 1524

Germany, reunification of, **3:** 875, 877

Getty, Don, **3:** 873

Ghana, establishment of, **4:** 1150

Ghana, 1966 coup in, **4:** 1152

Gheorghiu-Dej, Gheorghe, **1:** 272

Giap, Vo Nguyen. *See* Vo Nguyen Giap

Glasnost, **2:** 575

Glenn, John H., Jr., **2:** 564-565

Gobat, Charles Albert, **2:** 566-567

Goddard, Robert H., **2:** 568-570

Goebbels, Joseph, **2:** 571-573

Golan Heights, **1:** 61

Goldman, Nahum, **5:** 1570

Good Neighbor Policy, **3:** 739

Goods and services tax (GST), Canadian, **2:** 351; **4:** 1113

Gorbachev, Mikhail, **2:** 574-577; **5:** 1392

Gore, Al, **2:** 578-580

Göring, Hermann, **2:** 581-583; **3:** 835

Gorton, John Grey, **2:** 584-585; **4:** 1054

Gothic Line, **3:** 836

Gouin, Paul, **2:** 447

Government of India Acts, **3:** 774; **4:** 1198

Gramsci, Antonio, **2:** 586-588

Grand Trunk Pacific, **3:** 896

Grau San Martín, Ramón, **1:** 105

Gray, Herbert, **2:** 589-590

Gray Report, **2:** 590

Great Depression, **3:** 717, 839; **4:** 1321; Canada and, **2:** 421; Germany and, **3:** 695; Hitler and, **3:** 690

Great Leap Forward, **2:** 392; **4:** 1027

Great Proletarian Cultural Revolution. *See* Cultural Revolution

Great Society, **3:** 786

Green Book, The (Qaddafi), **4:** 1268

Green Line, Cypriot, **3:** 977

Greenspan, Alan, **2:** 591-593

Grey, Edward, **1:** 55

Griffith, Arthur, **2:** 352

Gromyko, Andrei Andreyevich, **2:** 594-597

GST. *See* Goods and services tax (GST)

Guderian, Heinz, **2:** 598-600

Guevara, Che, **1:** 268; **2:** 601-604

Guillaume spy case, **1:** 186

Gulf of Tonkin Resolution, **2:** 535

Gulf War. *See* Persian Gulf War

Guo Moruo, **2:** 605-607

Gustav Line, **3:** 836

Guyana, independence of, **3:** 766

Habsburgs, **2:** 515

Habyarimana, Juvénal, **2:** 608-611

Haganah, **1:** 124; **2:** 374-375; **3:** 678

Hague Conference, 1899, **4:** 1297

Hague Conference, 1907, **1:** 64; **4:** 1297

Haig, Alexander M., **2:** 612-614

Haile Mengistu Mariam, **5:** 1398

Haile Selassie I, **2:** 615-618

Haiti, 1986 revolt in, **2:** 454

Halsey, William F., **2:** 619-620; **4:** 1145

Hammarskjöld, Dag, **2:** 621-624

Hanson, Pauline, **3:** 726, 811

Harding, Warren G., **2:** 625-628

Harriman, William Averell, **2:** 629-631

Hassan II, **2:** 632-634

Hassan, Mulay, **4:** 1108

Haughey, Charles James, **2:** 635-637

Havel, Václav, **2:** 638-641

Hawke, Robert, **2:** 524, 642-643; **3:** 810

Hay, John, **5:** 1436

Haya de la Torre, Víctor Raúl, **2:** 644-645

Health-care reform, U.S., **2:** 338

Heath, Edward, **2:** 646-649; **5:** 1583

Hebron Agreement, **4:** 1137

Helfferich, Karl, **2:** 485

Henderson, Arthur, **2:** 650-652

Herriot, Édouard, **3:** 675-677

Hertzog, James Barry Munnik, **5:** 1421

Herzl, Theodor, **5:** 1559

Herzog, Chaim, **3:** 678-681

Hess, Rudolf, **3:** 682-684

Hewson, John, **3:** 811

Hill, Anita, **5:** 1479

Index

Himmler, Heinrich, **3: 685-687**
Hindenburg, Paul von, **3: 688-691**, 695, 942; **4:** 1190
Hirohito, **1:** 21; **3: 692-694**
Hiroshima and Nagasaki, bombing of, **5:** 1437, 1506-1507
Hiss, Alger, **4:** 1051, 1146
Hitler, Adolf, **2:** 464, 571; **3: 695-698**; Sudetenland and, **1:** 120. *See also* Nazi Party; World War II, Germany and
Hoare, Samuel, **3:** 898
Hoare-Laval Agreement, **3:** 898
Hobby, Oveta Culp, **3: 699-701**
Ho Chi Minh, **3: 702-705**; **5:** 1617
Ho Chi Minh Trail, **5:** 1542
Hoffa, Jimmy, **3:** 824
Hohenzollern Dynasty, **5:** 1578
Holmes, Oliver Wendell, Jr., **3: 706-708**
Holocaust, **3:** 686, 698; **5:** 1571, 1575. *See also* Jews, Nazi genocide against
Holt, Harold, **3: 709-711**
Home, Lord. *See* Douglas-Home, Alexander
Honecker, Erich, **3: 712-714**
Hong Kong, return to China of, **3:** 771
Hoover, Herbert, **3: 715-718**; **5:** 1410
Hoover, J. Edgar, **3: 719-721**
Hoover Commission, **3:** 717
Houphouët-Boigny, Félix, **3: 722-724**
Hourani, Akram, **1:** 60
House Committee on Education and Labor, **4:** 1257
House Committee on Un-American Activities, **4:** 1052
House of Lords, British, **2:** 426
Howard, John, **2:** 428; **3: 725-727**
Hsuan-tung. *See* Pu-yi
Huerta, Adolfo de la, **4:** 1167
Huerta, Victoriano, **1:** 247; **3: 728-729**, 965; **4:** 1165, 1191; **5:** 1537, 1606
Hughes, Charles Evans, **3: 730-732**
Hughes, William Morris, **3: 733-736**
Huk Rebellion, **3:** 967
Hull, Cordell, **3: 737-740**
Hull House, **3:** 892
Humanae Vitae, **4:** 1203
Hume, John, **1:** 12
Humphrey, Hubert H., **3: 741-743**
Hungarian revolt, **4:** 1125, 1127

Hussein I, **3: 744-747**
Hussein, Saddam, **1:** 235; **3: 748-751**; **4:** 1261
Hutus, **2:** 611
Hutu-Tutsi conflict, **2:** 609

Ibn Saud, **2:** 494
Ideology, definition of, **5:** 1633
Ikeda, Hayato, **3: 752-754**; **5:** 1377
Il duce. *See* Mussolini, Benito
Immigration Restriction Act of 1901, Australian, **3:** 710
Imperial Conference of 1926, **3:** 862
Imperial War Cabinet, **1:** 161
Imperialism, **5:** 1638
Imperialism, the Highest Stage of Capitalism (Lenin), **3:** 914
Inchon landing, Korean War, **3:** 951
India, independence of, **2:** 563; **4:** 1097
India, state of emegency in, 1975-1977, **2:** 537
Indian Home Rule Leagues, **5:** 1482
Indian National Congress, **1:** 100; **4:** 1133, 1197
India-Pakistan War, **2:** 537
Indochina War, **3:** 704
Industrial Relations Act, British, **2:** 648
Inkatha Freedom Party, **1:** 238
İnönü, İsmet, **3: 755-757**
Institutional Revolutionary Party (PRI), Mexican, **5:** 1609
Intermediate Range Nuclear Forces Treaty, **4:** 1260
International Arbitration League, **2:** 359
International Atomic Energy Agency, **2:** 475
International Disarmament Conference, **2:** 652
International Olympic Committee, **2:** 356
International Peace Bureau, **1:** 90; **2:** 567
International Peace Conference, **1:** 112
Interparliamentary Union, **1:** 90; **2:** 359, 567; **3:** 890
Intifada, **1:** 48; **4:** 1274
Inukai, Tsuyoshi, **3:** 692
IRA. *See* Irish Republican Army (IRA)
Iran, Islamic revolution in, **3:** 842; **4:** 1275; OPEC and, **5:** 1594
Iran-Contra scandal, **1:** 234; **4:** 1289; **5:** 1424
Iranian hostage crisis, **1:** 263
Iran-Iraq War, **3:** 751, 843; **4:** 1276
Iraq, U.N. sanctions against, **1:** 39
Irgun Z'vai Leumi, **1:** 114
Irish arms-smuggling scandal of 1970, **2:** 635-636
Irish Free State, **2:** 342, 394

Irish Land Purchase Act of 1903, **1:** 96
Irish Republic, establishment of, **2:** 395
Irish Republican Army (IRA), **2:** 341, 352, 394. *See also* Sinn Féin
Irish Volunteers, **2:** 393; **4:** 1171
İsmet Pasha. *See* İnönü, İsmet
Isolationists, U.S., **1:** 159
Israel, establishment of, **1:** 124
Israeli independence, war of, **1:** 125
Israeli Intelligence Service, **3:** 680
Itaipú Dam, **5:** 1446
Italian Communist Party (PCI), **2:** 588
Italian Popular Party, **2:** 381
Italian Socialist Party (PSI), **2:** 586
Italian Somaliland, **5:** 1397
Itō Hirobumi, **3: 758-761**

Jabotinsky, Vladimir, **1:** 123
Jackson, Jesse, **3: 762-764**
Jagan, Cheddi, **3: 765-766**
Janata Front, **2:** 538
Jaruzelski, Wojech, **5:** 1548
Jaurès, Jean, **1:** 153
Jeanneney, Jules, **3:** 677
Jewish Documentation Center, **5:** 1573-1574
Jewish Legion, British, **1:** 123
Jews, Nazi genocide against, **3:** 686, 698, 899. *See also* Holocaust
Jiang Qing, **3: 767-769**
Jiang Zemin, **3: 770-773**
Jinnah, Mohammed Ali, **3: 774-776**; **4:** 1097
Joffre, Joseph-Jacques-Césaire, **3: 777-778**; **4:** 1232
John XXIII, **3: 779-781**
John Paul II, **3: 782-784**
Johnson, Lyndon B., **3:** 741, **785-788**
Jones, Paula, **2:** 336
Jordan, Barbara, **3: 789-791**
Juan Carlos I, **3: 792-794**
Juárez, Benito, **2:** 400
Judicial activism, **2:** 424
Judiciary Act of 1925, **5:** 1465
July Agreement of 1936, **4:** 1306
July 26 movement, **1:** 106-107
Jutland, Battle of, **2:** 562

Kabila, Laurent, **4:** 1080
Kádár János, **3: 795-797**
Kagera Basin Organization (KBO), **2:** 610

Kagera River Basin, **2:** 610
Kanakas, **1:** 103
Kapp, Friedrich, **5:** 1387
Kapp putsch, **3:** 944; **5:** 1387, 1442
Karamanlis, Constantine, **3: 798-799**; **4:** 1187
Karami, Rashid, **3: 800-802**
Karmal, Babrak, **5:** 1369
Kasavubu, Joseph, **2:** 623; **3:** 945; **5:** 1510
Kashmir, Pakistani invasion of, **1:** 143
Kashmir, unrest in, **2:** 545
Katanga, **2:** 624; secession of, **3:** 946; **5:** 1509
Katangan Republic, **5:** 1510
Katipunan, **1:** 18
Katzenbach, Nicholas, **5:** 1552
Kaunda, Kenneth, **3: 803-806**
Kautsky, Karl, **3: 807-809**
Keating, Paul, **3: 810-812**
Keeler, Christine, **3:** 961
Keiretsu, **3:** 753
Kellogg, Frank B., **1:** 202; **3: 813-815**
Kellogg-Briand Pact, **1:** 158, 202; **3:** 813; **5:** 1444
Kennan, George F., **3: 816-818**
Kennedy, John F., **3: 819-822**
Kennedy, Robert F., **3:** 720, **823-826**
Kenya, independence of, **3:** 828
Kenyatta, Jomo, **3: 827-830**; **4:** 1162
Keppler, Wilhelm, **4:** 1306
Kerensky, Aleksandr Fyodorovich, **3: 831-834**
Kerensky government, **3:** 955
Kerr, John, **5:** 1569
Kesselring, Albert, **3: 835-836**
Keynes, John Maynard, **3: 837-840**
Khan, Ishaq, **1:** 140
Khartoum, **3:** 870
Khmer Rouge, **2:** 508; **4:** 1250; **5:** 1401
Khomeini, Ayatollah. *See* Khomeini, Ruhollah
Khomeini, Ruhollah, **1:** 263; **3: 841-844**; **4:** 1084, 1275
Khrushchev, Nikita S., **1:** 196, 270; **3: 845-848**, 983, **4:** 1086; **5:** 1624
Kiesinger, Kurt, **1:** 185
Kikuyu, **3:** 827
Killing fields, Cambodian, **4:** 1251
Kim Il Sung, **3: 849-852**
Kim Jong-p'il, **4:** 1194
King, Charles, **5:** 1512
King, Ernest Joseph, **3: 853-855**
King, Martin Luther, Jr., **1:** 4; **3: 856-859**; J. Edgar Hoover and, **3:** 721

King, William Lyon Mackenzie, **1:** 126; **3: 860-862;**
    4: 1056; **5:** 1439
King-Byng affair, **3:** 861
Kinkaid, Thomas, **2:** 620
Kinneret Operation, **2:** 457
Kirkpatrick, Jeane, **3: 863-865**
Kirov, Sergei, **5:** 1431
Kissinger, Henry A., **3: 866-869,** 908; **4:** 1104
Kitchener, Horatio Herbert, **3: 870-872**
Klaus, Václav, **2:** 641
Klein, Ralph, **3: 873-874**
Kleindienst, Richard, **4:** 1291
Kohima, Battle of, **5:** 1403
Kohl, Helmut, **3: 875-878**
Konoye, Fumimaro, **5:** 1491
Korean Commission, **4:** 1302
Korean War, **1:** 9; **3:** 851, 951-952; **4:** 1303, 1310;
    China and, **4:** 1208; settlement of, **2:** 443
Koresh, David, **4:** 1299
Kosovo, **4:** 1068
Kreisky, Bruno, **5:** 1575
Kristallnacht, **2:** 572
Kruger, Paul, **1:** 164; **5:** 1419
Kubitschek, Juscelino, **3: 879-880**
Kuomintang (KMT), **1:** 286; **2:** 605; **3:** 921; **5:** 1458
Kuo Mo-jo. *See* Guo Moruo
Kuroki, Tamesada, **4:** 1230
Kuwait, invasion of, **1:** 235; **2:** 493; **3:** 749
Kwangtung Army, **3:** 850; **5:** 1492
Kwasniewski, Aleksander, **5:** 1550

Labor Party, Australian, **2:** 361
Labour Party, British, **2:** 651; first government of,
    3: 957
La Follette, Robert M., Jr., **3: 881-884**
La Fontaine, Henri-Marie, **3: 885-886**
La Guardia, Fiorello Henry, **3: 887-889**
Lancaster House Agreement, **4:** 1104
Land for peace agreements, **4:** 1137
Land mines, **1:** 77; **2:** 398
Lange, Christian Lous, **3: 890-891**
Lansdowne, Lord. *See* Petty-Fitzmaurice, Henry
Lansdowne letter, **4:** 1235
Lateran Treaty, **4:** 1119, 1241
Lathrop, Julia C., **3: 892-893**
Laurier, Wilfrid, **1:** 160; **3:** 860, **894-896**
Lausanne Conference of 1932, **2:** 652; **4:** 1193
Lausanne Peace Conference of 1923, **3:** 756

Laval, Pierre, **3:** 677, **897-900**
Law, Bonar, **1:** 91; **3: 901-902**
Lawrence, T. E., **1:** 28; **3: 903-905**
League of Nations, **1:** 173; **4:** 1153; **5:** 1587
Lebanese Civil War, **3:** 801
Lebensraum, **3:** 682
Le Duc Tho, **3:** 868, **906-908**
Lee Kuan Yew, **3: 909-911**
Leghari, Farooq, **1:** 140
Lend-Lease Act, **2:** 630
Lend-lease program, **1:** 8; **2:** 630
Lenin, Vladimir Ilich, **1:** 220; **3: 912-915; 5:** 1428,
    1495
Leopard Battalion, **2:** 455
Leopold II, **1:** 111
Le Pen, Jean-Marie, **3: 916-918**
Lerdo de Tejada, Sebastian, **2:** 400
Lévesque, René, **3: 919-920**
Lewinsky, Monica, **2:** 336
Leyte Gulf, Battle of, **2:** 620
Liberal Party, Australian, **2:** 525; **4:** 1066
Liberal Party, Canadian, **5:** 1500
Liberal socialism, **2:** 409
Liberalism, **5:** 1635
Liberia, U.S. aid to, **2:** 412
Likud, **1:** 116
Limann, Hilla, **4:** 1283
Lin Biao, **3: 921-922**
Lin Piao. *See* Lin Biao
Li Peng, **3: 923-925**
Little Entente, **1:** 119
Litvinov, Maksim Maksimovich, **3: 926-928;**
    4: 1086
Liu Shao-ch'i. *See* Liu Shaoqi
Liu Shaoqi, **3: 929-931**
Lloyd George, David, **1:** 55, 161; **2:** 366; **3:** 902,
    932-935
Locarno, Treaty of, **1:** 202, 277; **3:** 691; **5:** 1444
Lodge, Henry Cabot, **3: 936-938**
Löhr, Alexander, **5:** 1545
Long, Huey, **3: 939-941**
Long March, **3:** 922; **4:** 1025; **5:** 1615, 1619
L'Ordine Nuovo, **2:** 587
Lougheed, Peter, **3:** 874
Ludendorff, Erich, **3:** 688, **942-944**
Luftwaffe, **2:** 582
Lumumba, Patrice, **2:** 623; **3: 945-946; 5:** 1509
Lusitania, sinking of, **1:** 134

Luthuli, Albert. *See* Lutuli, Albert
Lutuli, Albert, **3: 947-949**
Lynching, **5:** 1564

Maastricht Treaty, **3:** 876, 973
MacArthur, Douglas, **3: 950-953**
MacDonald, Ramsay, **1:** 72; **2:** 650-651; **3: 954-957**
Machel, Samora Moisès, **3: 958-959**; **4:** 1104
Macmillan, Harold, **2:** 646; **3: 960-963**
Madero, Francisco, **2:** 401; **3:** 728, **964-965**; **5:** 1537, 1606
Madrid Peace Conference, **4:** 1138
Maginot Line, **4:** 1233
Magloire, Paul E., **2:** 449
Magsaysay, Ramón, **3: 966-967**
Mahathir bin Mohamad, Datuk Seri, **1:** 2; **3: 968-970**
Major, John, **3: 971-974**
Makarios III, **3:** 799, **975-977**
Malaysia, founding of, **3:** 910
Malaysian currency crisis of 1997, **3:** 969
Malcolm X, **3: 978-981**
Malenkov, Georgi M., **3: 982-984**
Manchukuo, **3:** 693; **4:** 1264
Manchuria, Japanese invasion of, **3:** 693; **5:** 1436
Mandela, Nelson, **1:** 238; **2:** 385; **3: 985-988**, 989; release from prison of, **2:** 385
Mandela, Winnie, **3:** 986, **989-991**
Manhattan Project, **4:** 1308
Mankiller, Wilma P., **3: 992-994**
Manley, Michael, **4: 1017-1019**
Mannerheim, Carl Gustaf, **4: 1020-1022**
Mannerheim Line, **4:** 1021
Manning, Preston, **1:** 306; **4: 1023-1024**
Mao Tse-tung. *See* Mao Zedong
Mao Zedong, **2:** 389; **3:** 767, 921; **4: 1025-1028**, 1208
March on Washington (1963), **3:** 858
Marcos, Ferdinand E., **1:** 41; **4: 1029-1031**, 1279
Marcos, Imelda, **4:** 1029
Marne, Battles of the, **3:** 778
Marshall, George C., **2:** 473; **4: 1032-1035**
Marshall, Thurgood, **4: 1036-1038**; **5:** 1478
Marshall Plan, **2:** 621, 629; **4:** 1034; **5:** 1507
Martin, Paul, **4: 1039-1040**
Marx, Karl, **3:** 807, 912; **5:** 1640
Marxism, **1:** 153; **2:** 587; **3:** 807, 912; **5:** 1640; Lenin and, **3:** 914
Marxism, revisionist, **5:** 1641
Marxist-Leninism, **5:** 1642

Masaryk, Tomáš, **1:** 118; **4: 1041-1043**
Massé, Marcel, **4: 1044-1045**
Massey, Vincent, **4: 1046-1047**
Massey, William Ferguson, **4: 1048-1049**
Massey Commission, **4:** 1047
Matignon Agreements, **1:** 155
Mau-Mau Uprising, **1:** 34; **3:** 827
Mauriac, François, **5:** 1571
Maximato, **1:** 248
Mayaguez incident, **2:** 508
May Fourth Movement, **1:** 283
Mayling Soong, **1:** 287
McCarthy, Eugene, **3:** 743, 788, 825; **4:** 1175
McCarthy, Joseph R., **4: 1050-1053**; **5:** 1417
McCarthyism, **4:** 1051
McFarlane, Robert, **4:** 1289
McGovern, George, **4:** 1149
McMahon, William, **2:** 524; **4: 1054-1055**
McVeigh, Timothy, **4:** 1299
Meech Lake Accord, **1:** 166, 306; **4:** 1112
Meighen, Arthur, **4: 1056-1057**
Meiji Constitution, **3:** 760
Meiji Restoration, **3:** 759
Mein Kampf (Hitler), **3:** 696; **4:** 1306
Meir, Golda, **4: 1058-1061**
Menem, Carlos Saúl, **4: 1062-1064**
Mengele, Josef, **5:** 1575
Mensheviks, **3:** 808, 831; **5:** 1495
Menzies, Robert Gordon, **2:** 489; **3:** 735; **4:** 1054, **1065-1067**
Mexican Civil War, **3:** 728
Mexican peso crash, 1995, **5:** 1610
Mexican Revolution, **1:** 247; **2:** 401-402; **3:** 965; **4:** 1165; **5:** 1537, 1606
Mexico, U.S. invasion of, **3:** 729
Mfecane, **1:** 238
Midway, Battle of, **4:** 1145
Militias, private, in U.S., **4:** 1299
Milner, Lord, **5:** 1604
Milošević, Slobodan, **4: 1068-1071**
Miners' strike of 1906, French, **1:** 308
Minto-Morley Reforms, **4:** 1198
Mitchell, William, **4: 1072-1073**
Mitterrand, François, **4: 1074-1076**
Mobutu Sese Seko, **4: 1077-1080**
Mohammad Reza Pahlavi, **1:** 263; **4: 1081-1084**, 1094, 1275
Molina, Arturo, **2:** 431

Molotov, Vyacheslav Mikhailovich, **4: 1085-1087**
Monarchical absolutism, **5:** 1635
Mondale, Walter F., **2:** 503; **4:** 1289
Mondlane, Eduardo, **3:** 959
Monnet, Jean, **5:** 1427
Montagu-Chelmsford Reforms, **4:** 1198
Montevideo Conference, **3:** 740
Montgomery, Bernard Law, **1:** 179; **4: 1088-1090**, 1201
Montgomery Bus Boycott, **1:** 4; **3:** 856
Morgenthau, Henry, Jr., **4: 1091-1092**
Morgenthau Plan, **4:** 1092
Moro Islamic Liberation Front, **4:** 1280
Moro National Liberation Front (MNLF), **4:** 1031
Mosaddeq, Mohammad. *See* Mossadegh, Mohammad
Moscow Conference of Foreign Ministers, **3:** 740
Mossadegh, Mohammad, **4:** 1081, **1093-1095**
Motherland Party, Turkish, **4:** 1181
Mother Teresa. *See* Teresa, Mother
Mountbatten, Louis, **2:** 563; **4: 1096-1098**
Mubarak, Hosni, **4: 1099-1102**
Mugabe, Robert, **4: 1103-1106**; **5:** 1413
Muhammad V, **4: 1107-1108**
Muhammad, Elijah, **3:** 978
Muldoon, Robert, **4: 1109-1110**
Mulroney, Brian, **1:** 166, 250, 259, 305; **4: 1111-1114**
Munich Agreement, **1:** 120, 282; **2:** 464
Museveni, Yoweri Kaguta, **4: 1115-1117**
Mussolini, Benito, **2:** 380; **3:** 898; **4: 1118-1121**, 1241
Mutesa II, **4:** 1164
Muzorewa, Abel, **4:** 1104; **5:** 1414
Myrdal, Alva, **4: 1122-1123**
Myrdal, Gunnar, **4:** 1122

NAACP. *See* National Association for the Advancement of Colored People (NAACP)
NAFTA. *See* North American Free Trade Agreement (NAFTA)
Naguib, Muhammed, **5:** 1364
Nagy, Imre, **4: 1124-1127**
Nalundasan, Julio, **4:** 1029
Nasser, Gamal Abdel, **1:** 45; **2:** 465; **4: 1128-1131**; **5:** 1363, 1365
Nation of Islam, **3:** 978-979
National Aeronautics and Space Administration (NASA), **1:** 190
National Association for the Advancement of Colored People (NAACP), **2:** 439; **4:** 1036-1037

National Democratic Party (NDP), Rhodesian, **4:** 1103
National Front, French, **3:** 917
National government, British, **1:** 93
National Guard, Nicaraguan, **5:** 1423
National Health Service, British, **1:** 74
National Insurance Act of 1911, British, **1:** 56; **3:** 935
National Insurance Bill, Israeli, **4:** 1060
National Liberation Front (FLN), Algerian, **1:** 169
National Liberation Front (NLF), Vietnamese, **3:** 705
National Party of Australia, **2:** 525
National Party of New Zealand, **4:** 1110
National Resistance Movement (NRM), Ugandan, **4:** 1116
National Security Council (NSC), **2:** 613; **3:** 869; **4:** 1289
National Socialist Party, German. *See* Nazi Party
National Socialists, German. *See* Nazi Party
National union government, French, **4:** 1247
Nationalism, **2:** 516; **5:** 1637
Nationalist Party, Australian, **3:** 735
Nationalist Party, Chinese. *See* Kuomintang (KMT)
NATO. *See* North Atlantic Treaty Organization (NATO)
Nautilus, USS, **4:** 1309
Nazi Party, **2:** 581; **3:** 685, 691, 695; propaganda of, **2:** 571. *See also* Hitler, Adolf
Nazi-Soviet Nonaggression Pact, **4:** 1086, 1306
Négritude, **5:** 1391
Negro World, **2:** 550
Neguib, Muhammad, **4:** 1128
Nehru, Jawaharlal, **4: 1132-1135**
Neoconservative movement, **3:** 863
Netanyahu, Benjamin, **4: 1136-1139**
Netanyahu, Jonathan, **4:** 1136, 1212
New Deal, **3:** 732, 951; **4:** 1091, 1322; **5:** 1460
New Democratic Party, Canadian, **2:** 421
New Economic Policy (NEP), Soviet, **1:** 221; **3:** 913
Newfoundland, **5:** 1407, 1440
New Guinea, **2:** 362; Australia and, **2:** 362
New State, Portuguese, **5:** 1372
Newton, Huey, **3:** 857
Niagara Movement, **2:** 439
Nicholas II, **3:** 831; **4: 1140-1143**
Nigerian Civil War, **1:** 84
Night (Wiesel), **5:** 1571
Nimitz, Chester W., **3:** 854; **4: 1144-1145**

Nixon, Richard M., **1:** 231; **2:** 612; **3:** 820, 867; **4: 1146-1149**, 1273; pardon of, **2:** 507. *See also* Watergate scandal
Nkomo, Joshua, **4:** 1103; **5:** 1413
Nkrumah, Kwame, **2:** 440; **4: 1150-1152**
Nkumbula, Harry, **3:** 803
Nobel Institute, **3:** 891
Nobel Peace Prize, **3:** 891
Noel-Baker, Philip John, **4: 1153-1154**
Nol, Lon, **5:** 1401-1402
Nonalignment, **4:** 1134
Noriega, Manuel, **4: 1155-1157**, 1260
Normandy invasion, **1:** 179; **2:** 474; **4:** 1089
Norris-La Guardia Act, **3:** 887
North, Oliver, **4:** 1289
North African Socialist Federation, **1:** 171
North American Free Trade Agreement (NAFTA), **1:** 297; **2:** 333; **4:** 1113; **5:** 1610
North Atlantic Treaty Organization (NATO), **1:** 9; Bosnia and, **4:** 1070; Canada and, **5:** 1441; establishment of, **4:** 1207
Northern Expedition, **2:** 606
Nuclear Arms Reduction Treaty (INF treaty), **4:** 1290
Nuclear Nonproliferation Act, **2:** 565
Nuclear Test Ban Treaty, **2:** 595, 630
Nuremberg Trials, **2:** 418, 582; **3:** 683; **4:** 1193, 1307
Nyerere, Julius, **4: 1158-1161**

Obote, Milton, **1:** 34; **4:** 1115, **1162-1164**
Obregón, Álvaro, **1:** 247; **4: 1165-1167**; **5:** 1537
O'Connor, Sandra Day, **4: 1168-1170**
Oder-Neisse line, **1:** 185
Official Languages Act, Canadian, **5:** 1517
Ogaden War, **5:** 1396
Oil embargo, 1973, **5:** 1592
O'Kelly, Seán T., **4: 1171-1173**
Oligarchy, **5:** 1630
Olympic Games, **2:** 356
Omdurman, Battle of, **3:** 871
O'Neill, Thomas P., Jr., **4: 1174-1176**
One Nation Party, Australian, **3:** 726, 811
One Nation policy, Australian, **3:** 811
OPEC. *See* Organization of Petroleum Exporting Countries (OPEC)
Operation Breadbasket, **3:** 762
Operation Overlord, **2:** 474
Opus Dei, **2:** 521

Orange Free State, **5:** 1420
Organization of African Unity (OAU), **4:** 1152
Organization of American States (OAS), **1:** 306
Organization of Petroleum Exporting Countries (OPEC), **2:** 496; **5:** 1592-1593
Orozco, Pascuál, **3:** 728; **4:** 1165; **5:** 1537
Ortega, Daniel, **4: 1177-1179**
Oslo Accords, **1:** 47; **4:** 1136-1137
Ostpolitik, **1:** 185
Otlet, Paul, **3:** 885
Ottawa Agreement, **1:** 93
Ottawa Treaty, **1:** 77
Ottoman Empire, **1:** 27, 68, 225; **3:** 755
Ouchy Convention, **5:** 1427
Özal, Turgut, **4: 1180-1183**

Pahlavi. *See* Mohammad Reza Pahlavi
Paisley, Ian, **4: 1184-1185**
Pakistan, establishment of, **3:** 776; **4:** 1097
Pakistan People's Party (PPP), **1:** 138-139
Palestine Liberation Organization (PLO), **1:** 45; **3:** 746; **4:** 1137
Palestinian National Congress, **1:** 46
Pan-African Congress, **3:** 828, 986; **4:** 1151
Pan-Africanism, **4:** 1151
Panama, U.S. invasion of, **4:** 1156
Panama Canal, **4:** 1327
Pan-American Conferences, **3:** 739
Panjat Sila (five principles), **5:** 1452
Papa Doc. *See* Duvalier, François
Papandreou, Andreas, **3:** 799; **4: 1186-1189**
Papandreou, George, **3:** 799
Papen, Franz von, **4: 1190-1193**
Papua, **2:** 362
Paris Peace Conference, **1:** 309; **3:** 934. *See also* Versailles, Treaty of
Paris Peace Talks (Vietnam War), **3:** 868, 907
Parizeau, Jacques, **1:** 167
Park Chung Hee, **4: 1194-1196**
Parks, Rosa, **1:** 4
Parliament Act of 1911, British, **1:** 56, 255; **3:** 901
Parliamentary system of government, **5:** 1633
Parti Québécois, **1:** 166; **2:** 447; **3:** 920
Pasha, Jemal, **2:** 498
Pasok party, Greek, **4:** 1187
Passy, Frédéric, **2:** 359, 567
Patel, Vallabhbhai Jhaverbhai, **4: 1197-1198**
Patton, George S., **4: 1199-1201**

Index

Paul VI, **4: 1202-1204**

Pearce Commission, **5:** 1414

Pearl Harbor, Japanese bombing of, **3:** 738; **4:** 1144; **5:** 1590

Pearson, Lester B., **4: 1205-1207**; **5:** 1499

Peng Dehuai, **4: 1208-1210**

P'eng Te-huai. *See* Peng Dehuai

People's Army of Vietnam (PAVN), **5:** 1540

People's Liberation Army (PLA), Chinese, **3:** 922; **4:** 1209; **5:** 1621

People's National Party (PNP) of Jamaica, **4:** 1018

People's Progressive Party (PPP), Guyanan, **3:** 766

People United to Save Humanity (PUSH), **3:** 762

Peres, Shimon, **4: 1211-1214**

Perestroika, **2:** 575; **5:** 1370

Pérez de Cuéllar, Javier, **2:** 531; **4: 1215-1217**

Permanent Court of International Justice, **3:** 886; **4:** 1330

Perón, Eva, **4: 1218-1220**, 1222

Perón, Juan, **4:** 1218, **1221-1224**

Peronism, **4:** 1222

Perot, H. Ross, **2:** 334; **4: 1225-1227**

Pershing, John J., **4: 1228-1230**; **5:** 1539

Persian Gulf War, **1:** 235; **2:** 493; **3:** 749, **4:** 1261; Britain and, **3:** 972; Morocco and, **2:** 634. *See also* Desert Storm

Pétain, Philippe, **3:** 676, 898; **4: 1231-1233**

Petrov affair, **4:** 1066

Petty-Fitzmaurice, Henry, **4: 1234-1235**

Philippine insurgent movements, **4:** 1031

Philippine Insurrection, **1:** 19; **4:** 1228

Philippines, martial law in, **4:** 1030

Ping-pong diplomacy, **3:** 867

Pinochet Ugarte, Augusto, **1:** 32; **4: 1236-1239**

Pius XI, **4: 1240-1242**

Pius XII, **4: 1243-1245**

PLA. *See* People's Liberation Army (PLA), Chinese

PLO. *See* Palestine Liberation Organization (PLO)

Pluralistic government, **5:** 1631

Podgorny, Nikolai, **5:** 1365

Poher, Alain, **4:** 1255

Poincaré, Raymond, **4: 1246-1249**

Poindexter, John, **4:** 1289

Point Four, Truman foreign-policy plank, **1:** 8

Pol Pot, **4: 1250-1252**

Pompidou, Georges, **4: 1253-1255**

Poole, Elijah, **3:** 979

Popular Front, French, **1:** 154

Popular Front for the Liberation of Palestine (PFLP), **3:** 746

Powell, Adam Clayton, Jr., **4: 1256-1258**

Powell, Colin, **4: 1259-1262**

Powers, Gary Francis, **3:** 847

Prague Spring, **2:** 435, 638

Prats, Carlos, **1:** 32

Pratt, Hodgson, **1:** 90

Pravda, **1:** 221; **4:** 1085

Presidential system of government, **5:** 1633

President's Summit for America's Future, **2:** 579

Princeton University, **5:** 1586

Profumo scandal, **3:** 961; **5:** 1583

Progressive Conservative Party, Canadian, in Alberta, **3:** 874

Progressive movement, **1:** 214; **3:** 883

Prohibition, **2:** 627; **5:** 1409-1411, 1587

Pure Food and Drug Act, **3:** 937

Pu-yi, **3:** 693; **4: 1263-1265**

Qaddafi, Muammar al-, **4: 1266-1268**

Quebec independence referendum of 1995, **1:** 167; 299

Quebec separatist movement, **1:** 166; **3:** 920; **5:** 1500. *See also* Bloc Québécois; Parti Québécois

Quezon, Manuel, **3:** 951; **4: 1269-1271**

Quiwonkpa, Thomas, **2:** 412

Quotations from Chairman Mao Zedong, **4:** 1026

Rabin, Yitzhak, **4:** 1213, **1272-1274**

Rabuka, Sitiveni, **2:** 429

Raeder, Erich, **2:** 417

Rafsanjani, Hashemi, **4: 1275-1278**

Railroad strike of 1910, French, **1:** 201

Rainbow Coalition, **3:** 763

Rakosi, Matyas, **4:** 1127

Ramos, Fidel, **1:** 43; **4: 1279-1280**

Rankin, Jeannette, **4: 1281-1282**

Rapallo, Treaty of, **3:** 928

Rathenau, Walther, **5:** 1442

Rawlings, Jerry John, **4: 1283-1286**

Reagan, Ronald, **1:** 234; **2:** 612; **4: 1287-1290**

Rebellion of 1914, South African, **1:** 164

Red Army, **5:** 1497

Red Guards, **3:** 767, 931

Red Record, A (Wells-Barnett), **5:** 1564

Re-establishment and Employment Act, **2:** 510

Reform Party, Canadian, **4:** 1023

Reform Party, U.S., **4:** 1226
Rehnquist, William H., **4: 1291-1293**
Reichswehr, **5:** 1387
Reid, Escott, **5:** 1441
Reid, George Houston, **4: 1294-1295**
Rejection Front, Algerian, **1:** 169
Religious Freedom Restoration Act, **4:** 1169
Renault, Louis, **4: 1296-1297**
Reno, Janet, **4: 1298-1300**
Reparations, German, for World War I, **2:** 371;
  4: 1193; **5:** 1443
Republic, **5:** 1632
Republic of Ireland Act, **2:** 395
Reynaud, Paul, **2:** 554
Rhee, Syngman, **3:** 851 **4:** 1194, **1301-1304**
Rhineland, **3:** 697
Rhodesian Front, **5:** 1413
Ribbentrop, Joachim von, **4:** 1086, **1305-1307**
Rickover, Hyman G., **4: 1308-1309**
Ridgway, Matthew B., **4: 1310-1312**
Roberts, F. S., **3:** 871
Robinson, Mary, **4: 1313-1314**
Rockefeller Foundation, **5:** 1360
Röhm, Ernst, **3:** 685
Röhm purge, **4:** 1191
Romanian constitution of 1965, **1:** 273
Romanian Winter Revolution, **1:** 274
Romanov Dynasty, **4:** 1142
Rommel, Erwin, **3:** 835; **4: 1315-1316**
Roosevelt, Eleanor, **3:** 721; **4: 1317-1320**
Roosevelt, Franklin D., **1:** 303; **3:** 951; **4:** 1091, 1317,
  1321-1324; **5:** 1437; Court-packing plan of, **3:** 731
Roosevelt, Theodore, **4: 1325-1328**; **5:** 1464
Root, Elihu, **4: 1329-1331**
Rope and Faggot: A Biography of Judge Lynch (White),
  5: 1566
Ross, Nellie Tayloe, **4: 1332-1333**
Rough Riders, **4:** 1327
Roxas, Manuel, **3:** 967
Royal absolutism, **5:** 1631
Ruhr region, French occupation of, **4:** 1193, 1249
Rundstedt, Gerd von, **4: 1334-1336**
Rusk, Dean, **5: 1359-1360**
Russia Leaves the War (Kennan), **3:** 817
Russian provisional government of 1917, **3:** 832
Russian Revolution, **1:** 220; **3:** 914; **5:** 1497. *See also*
  Bolshevik Revolution; Bolsheviks; December
  Revolution of 1905, Russian

Russo-Japanese War, **4:** 1141, 1230
Rwanda, genocide in, **2:** 611

SA. *See* Storm troopers (SA)
Saavedra Lamas, Carlos, **5: 1361-1362**
Sabry, Ali, **5:** 1365
Sacco and Vanzetti case, **2:** 523
Sadat, Anwar el-, **1:** 262; **5: 1363-1366**
Sahara, western, **2:** 633
Saint-Mihiel, **4:** 1035, 1072
Saipan, fall of, **5:** 1493
Sakharov, Andrei, **5: 1367-1370**
Salazar, António de Oliveira, **5: 1371-1374**
Salisbury, Lord, **1:** 95, 253; **2:** 364
SALT. *See* Strategic Arms Limitation Talks (SALT I);
  Strategic Arms Limitation Talks (SALT II)
Samouth, Tou, **4:** 1250
Sandinistas, **4:** 1177; **5:** 1375-1376, 1424
Sandino, Augusto César, **5: 1375-1376**, 1423
Sandline crisis, **2:** 429
Satō, Eisaku, **5: 1377-1379**
Satyagraha, **2:** 541-542
Saud, **2:** 494
Sauvé, Jeanne Mathilde, **5: 1380-1381**
Schacht, Hjalmar, **3:** 690
Schleicher, Kurt von, **4:** 1190
Schlieffen, Alfred von, **3:** 778
Schlieffen Plan, **3:** 942
Schmidt, Helmut, **1:** 186
Schröder, Gerhard, **5: 1382-1384**
Schuman, Robert, **1:** 16; **5:** 1426
Schuman Plan, **1:** 16
Schuschnigg Kurt von, **4:** 1306
Schwarzkopf, Norman, **4:** 1261
SCLC. *See* Southern Christian Leeadership
  Conference (SCLC)
Scopes "monkey" trial, **1:** 215
Scullin, James Henry, **5: 1385-1386**
Seale, Bobby, **3:** 857
SEATO. *See* Southeast Asia Treaty Organization
  (SEATO)
Second Turkish Army, **3:** 756
Second Vatican Council. *See* Vatican II
Seeckt, Hans von, **5: 1387-1388**
Seeme, Pixley, **3:** 948
Selassie. *See* Haile Selassie I
Senghor, Léopold, **5: 1389-1391**
Seven Pillars of Wisdom (Lawrence), **3:** 903

Shaba, **4:** 1080; **5:** 1510
Shah of Iran. *See* Mohammad Reza Pahlavi
Shamir, Yitzhak, **4:** 1213
Sharansky, Nathan, **4:** 1137
Share Our Wealth movement, **3:** 941
Sharpeville Massacre, **3:** 987
Sherif, Nawaz, **1:** 139
Sherman Anti-Trust Act, **3:** 814
Shevardnadze, Eduard, **5: 1392-1395**
Shining Path, **2:** 530
Shipley, Jenny, **4:** 1110
Shukairy, Ahmad al-, **1:** 45
Siad Barre, Muhammad, **1:** 79; **5: 1396-1399**
Sihanouk, Norodom, **5: 1400-1402**
Sikh Rebellion, **2:** 546
Silver Jubilee of George V, **2:** 560
Simpson, Wallis Warfield, **2:** 472, 561
Sin, Jaime, **1:** 42 **4:** 1031
Singh, V. P., **2:** 545
Singh, Zail, **2:** 545
Sinn Féin, **1:** 11, 151; **2:** 352, 394; **4:** 1171
Sino-Japanese War, **3:** 759; **5:** 1620
Sison, José Maria, **4:** 1031
Six-Day War, **2:** 377; **3:** 746; **4:** 1131, 1272
Sixteenth Amendment, **3:** 738
Sixth Plan, Georges Pompidou's, **4:** 1254
Six-year plan, Mexican, **1:** 257
Slim, William Joseph, **5: 1403-1405**
Smallwood, Joseph Roberts, **5: 1406-1407**, 1440
Smith, Alfred E., **5: 1408-1411**
Smith, Ian, **3:** 805; **4:** 1103; **5: 1412-1415**
Smith, John, **1:** 149
Smith, Margaret Chase, **5: 1416-1418**
Smuts, Jan Christian, **5: 1419-1421**
SNCC. *See* Student Nonviolent Coordinating
    Committee
Social Credit Party, Canadian, **1:** 131
Social Democratic Party (SDP), German, **1:** 184;
    3: 807
Social Democratic Party, Swedish, **1:** 189
Socialism, **5:** 1639; scientific, **5:** 1640; utopian,
    5: 1639
Socialist market economy, Chinese, **3:** 924
Socialist Party, French, **1:** 153; **4:** 1075
Socialist Unity Party (SED), East German, **3:** 712
Solidarity movement, **5:** 1547-1548
Solidarity Party, Polish, **3:** 783
Somalia, famine in, **1:** 81

Somme, Battle of the, **1:** 204
Somoza García, Anastasio, **4:** 1177; **5:** 1375, **1422-1425**
Song Jaioren, **5:** 1458
South Africa, formation of, **1:** 165
South African coalition government of 1933, **5:** 1420
South Africa's Truth and Reconciliation Commission
    (TRC), **1:** 239, **3:** 991, **5:** 1521
Southeast Asia Treaty Organization (SEATO), **2:** 444
Southern Christian Leadership Conference (SCLC),
    1: 4-5; **3:** 762, 856
South Korea, economic growth in, **4:** 1195
South Korea, 1961 coup in, **4:** 1194
South Pacific Summit of 1997, **2:** 429
Soweto Uprising, **2:** 384
Spaak, Paul-Henri, **5: 1426-1427**
Spain, democratic monarchy of, **3:** 793
Spanish-American War, **4:** 1228
Spanish Civil War, **2:** 518-519; Portugal and, **5:** 1372
Spencer, Diana. *See* Diana, Princess of Wales
Spirit of Independence, The (Rhee), **4:** 1303
Sri Lanka, Indian intervention in, **2:** 546
SS, **3:** 685
Stalin, Joseph, **1:** 221, 303; **3:** 982; **4:** 1085;
    5: 1428-1431; Tito and, **5:** 1489
Stalingrad, Battle of, **5:** 1624
Standard Oil, **3:** 814
Starr, Kenneth, **2:** 335
Stevenson, Adlai E., **5: 1432-1434**
Stimson, Henry L., **5: 1435-1438**
Stimson Doctrine, **5:** 1436
St. Laurent, Louis, **5: 1439-1441**
Stockholm Conference, **2:** 651
Storm troopers (SA), **2:** 581; **3:** 682, 685
Strategic Arms Limitation Talks (SALT I), **1:** 197;
    2: 597; **4:** 1148
Strategic Arms Limitation Talks (SALT II), **1:** 219, 263
Stresemann, Gustav, **1:** 202, 277; **5: 1442-1444**
Stroessner, Alfredo, **5: 1445-1447**
Student Nonviolent Coordinating Committee
    (SNCC), **3:** 856
Submarines, atomic, **4:** 1308
Submarine warfare, **1:** 133; **2:** 417; **3:** 688
Sudetenland, **1:** 120, 282; **4:** 1086
Suez Crisis, **2:** 445, 465, 476, 623; **4:** 1130
Suharto, **5: 1448-1451**, 1454
Sukarno, **5:** 1448, **1452-1455**
Sun Yat-sen, **1:** 286; **2:** 606; **5: 1456-1459**, 1601
Sun Yixian. *See* Sun Yat-sen

Suttner, Bertha von, **1:** 90
Sykes-Picot Agreement, **2:** 499
Syndicalism, **5:** 1631, 1643

Taba dispute, Israeli-Egyptian, **4:** 1100
Taft, Robert A., **5: 1460-1462**
Taft, William Howard, **1:** 181; **5: 1463-1466**
Taft-Hartley Labor Relations Act, **5:** 1461
Taiwan, Republic of China and, **1:** 288
Tammany Hall, **3:** 887
Tanganyikan African National Union (TANU),
    4: 1160
Tanks, developmnent of, **2:** 598-599
Tannenberg, Battle of, **3:** 688
Taschereau, Louis Alexandre, **2:** 446
Taylor, Charles, **2:** 413
Teapot Dome scandal, **2:** 346, 627
Tehran Association of Militant Clergy, **4:** 1277
Teng Hsiao-ping. *See* Deng Xiaoping
Tenth Indian Division, **5:** 1404
Teresa, Mother, **5: 1467-1470**
Tet Offensive, **3:** 788; **5:** 1541
Thailand, independence of, **1:** 136
Thant, U, **5: 1471-1473**
Thatcher, Margaret, **3:** 971; **5: 1474-1477**
Theocracy, **5:** 1631
Theodore, Edward Granville, **5:** 1386
Thieu, Nguyen Van, **3:** 908
Third Army, U.S., **4:** 1200
Third International, **1:** 222
Thomas, Clarence, **5: 1478-1480**
Tiananmen Square demonstrations and massacre,
    2: 391; **3:** 925
Tibet, communist Chinese invasion of, **2:** 367-368
Tilak, Bal Gangadhar, **5: 1481-1483**
Timoshenko, Semyon K., **5:** 1623
Tirpitz, Alfred von, **5: 1484-1486**
Tito, Josip Broz, **2:** 408; **5: 1487-1490**
Tlatelolco, Treaty of, **2:** 548
Togliatti, Palmiro, **2:** 588
Tojo, Hideki, **5: 1491-1494**
Tokes, Laszlo, **1:** 274
Tolbert, William, **2:** 411
Tongogara, Josiah, **4:** 1106
Tonton Macoutes, **2:** 450
Torrijos, Omar, **4:** 1155
Totalitarianism, **5:** 1630
Trade Disputes Act of 1906, British, **1:** 255

Trade Union Council, British, **1:** 92
Trades Union Congress (TUC), **1:** 245; **3:** 954
Trans-Canada Pipeline, **5:** 1440
Transvaal, **1:** 164; **5:** 1420
Travel rorts affair, Australian, **3:** 726
Trench warfare, **3:** 777
Trident Conference, **2:** 474
Trilateral Commission, **1:** 218
Tripartite Pact, **5:** 1492
Triple Alliance, **1:** 224; **2:** 469
Triple Entente, **1:** 224
Trotsky, Leon, **1:** 221, 284; **5: 1495-1498**
Trudeau, Margaret, **5:** 1499
Trudeau, Pierre Elliott, **1:** 304; **2:** 589; **3:** 920;
    5: 1499-1502, 1516
Trujillo, Rafael, **5: 1503-1504**
Truman, Harry S, **2:** 445; **3:** 952; **5: 1505-1508**
Truman Doctrine, **5:** 1507
Truth and Reconciliation Commission. *See* South
    Africa's Truth and Reconciliation Commission
    (TRC)
Tshombe, Moïse, **2:** 623; **3:** 946; **5: 1509-1511**
Tubman, William V. S., **5: 1512-1515**
Túpac Amaru Revolutionary Movement (MRTA),
    2: 531
Turkey, Greek invasion of, **5:** 1535
Turkish coup of 1960, **3:** 757
Turkish Revolution, **2:** 483
Turkish war of independence, **1:** 70
Turner, John Napier, **2:** 590; **5: 1516-1517**
Tutsis, **2:** 608
Tutu, Desmond, **5: 1518-1521**
Tweed, William Marcy, **4:** 1331
Twelfth Army Group, **1:** 179
Tydings-McDuffie Act, **4:** 1270
Tz'u-hsi, **5: 1522-1523**

U-boats, **2:** 417
Uganda People's Congress (UPC), **4:** 1163
Ulbricht, Walter, **3:** 712; **5: 1524-1526**
Umkonto we Sizwe, **3:** 986
U.N. General Assembly, **2:** 488
U.N. General Assembly Resolution 3379, **3:** 679
Uniform Crime Reports (UCR), **3:** 719
Union Minière du Haut-Katanga, **4:** 1079
Union Nationale Party, **2:** 447
Union Treaty, Soviet, **2:** 576
Unionist Party, British, **1:** 281

United Arab Republic (UAR), **3:** 745; **4:** 1130

United Federal Party, Southern Rhodesian, **5:** 1413

United Malay National Organization (UMNO), **1:** 1; **3:** 968

United Nations, **2:** 488; establishment of, **1:** 265; **2:** 596; Indonesian withdrawal from, **5:** 1454; management problems of, **1:** 176; Spain's entry into, **2:** 520

United Nations dues, United States and, **1:** 25, 40, 175

United Nations Educational, Scientific, and Cultural Organization (UNESCO), **1:** 266

United Nations Emergency Force (UNEF), **2:** 623

United Nations Palestinian Commission, **1:** 228

United Somali Congress (USC), **1:** 79

United States-Japan Security Treaty, **5:** 1378

Universal Declaration of Human Rights, **1:** 266; **4:** 1318

Universal Negro Improvement Association (UNIA), **2:** 551

U.N. Resolution 242, **2:** 458

U.N. Security Council, **2:** 488

U.S. Children's Bureau, **3:** 893

U.S. Department of Health, Education, and Welfare (HEW), **3:** 700

U.S. Joint Chiefs of Staff, **3:** 854; **4:** 1260

U.S. Mint, **4:** 1333

U-2 incident of 1960, **3:** 847

Vanier, Georges, **5: 1527-1528**

Vargas, Getúlio, **5: 1529-1531**

Vargas Llosa, Mario, **2:** 529

Vatican City, establishment of, **4:** 1120, 1241

Vatican neutrality in World War II, **4:** 1245

Vatican II, **3:** 780; **4:** 1202

Velasco Ibarra, José María, **5: 1532-1533**

Velvet revolution, **2:** 437, 639-640

Venizélos, Eleuthérios, **5: 1534-1536**

Verdun, Battle of, **4:** 1232

Versailles, Treaty of, **1:** 282, 309; **2:** 484; **4:** 1330; violation of, **2:** 463, 561; **3:** 697; war reparations and, **4:** 1193; Woodrow Wilson and, **5:** 1588. *See also* Paris Peace Conference

Vichy government, **3:** 677, 898; **4:** 1233; French colonies and, **2:** 460

Victor Emmanuel, **2:** 380

Victoria, **2:** 468

Vietminh, **3:** 703-704; **5:** 1540

Vietnam War, **2:** 535; **3:** 705, 788, 907; **4:** 1175; **5:** 1541; Australia and, **2:** 584; **3:** 709. *See also* Paris Peace Talks (Vietnam War)

Villa, Pancho, **4:** 1165; **5: 1537-1539**

VIP affair, **3:** 709

Vo Nguyen Giap, **3:** 704; **5: 1540-1543**

Voodoo, **2:** 450

Vorster, John, **4:** 1104; **5:** 1414, 1518

V-2 ballistic missile, **1:** 191

Vyshinsky, Andrei, **5:** 1429

Wafd Party, **5:** 1604

Waldheim, Kurt, **4:** 1216; **5: 1544-1546**, 1575

Wałęsa, Lech, **5: 1547-1550**

Walker, James J., **3:** 887

Wallace, George C., **5: 1551-1553**

Wang Ching-wei. *See* Wang Jingwei

Wang Jingwei, **5: 1554-1555**

War on Poverty, **3:** 786

Warren, Earl, **1:** 194; **4:** 1291; **5: 1556-1558**

Warsaw Pact, **4:** 1126

Washington Arms Limitation Conference, **3:** 732

Watergate scandal, **1:** 231; **2:** 507, 612; **3:** 789; **4:** 1148

Weimar Republic, **5:** 1443, 1485

Weizmann, Chaim, **5: 1559-1562**

Weizmann Institute of Science, **5:** 1561

Wells, Ida Bell. *See* Wells-Barnett, Ida B.

Wells-Barnett, Ida B., **5: 1563-1564**

West African Pilot, **1:** 83

White, Walter Francis, **5: 1565-1567**

White Australia policy, **3:** 733; **5:** 1568

White Guard, Finnish, **4:** 1022

White Revolution, Iranian, **4:** 1083

Whitlam, Gough, **2:** 524; **3:** 710; **4:** 1055; **5: 1568-1569**

Wiesel, Elie, **5: 1570-1572**

Wiesenthal, Simon, **5: 1573-1576**

Wilhelm II. *See* William II

William II, **1:** 224; **5: 1577-1580**

Wilson, Harold, **1:** 246; **5: 1581-1584**

Wilson, Woodrow, **1:** 182; **3:** 729, 937; **4:** 1330; **5: 1585-1588**

Wingate, Reginald, **5:** 1604

Women's Army Corps (WAC), **3:** 699

Women's Franchise Bill of 1918, **1:** 162

Worker priests, **4:** 1244

Workmen's Peace Association, **2:** 359

World Bank, **4:** 1045

World Court. *See* Permanent Court of International Justice

World War I, **1:** 27; assassination of Francis Ferdinand and, **1:** 133; **2:** 512; **5:** 1579; Australia and, **1:** 208; **3:** 733; Britain and, **1:** 56; **2:** 558; **3:** 871, 933; France and, **4:** 1231, 1247; Germany and, **1:** 133; **3:** 688, 942; Greece and, **5:** 1534; Italy and, **2:** 556; South Africa and, **5:** 1420; Turkey and, **2:** 481; United States and, **4:** 1229; **5:** 1587. *See also* Gallipoli campaign, World War I; Versailles, Treaty of

World War II, **2:** 473; **3:** 697; Australia and, **2:** 360; Britain and, **1:** 72, 204, 301; **2:** 562; **4:** 1088, 1097; Douglas MacArthur and, **3:** 951; French Equatorial Africa and, **2:** 462; Germany and, **2:** 417, 598; **3:** 835; **4:** 1315, 1335; Hungarian resistance during, **3:** 796; Ireland and, **2:** 395; Italy and, **2:** 380; **4:** 1120; Japan and, **3:** 693; **5:** 1493, 1589; Philippines and, **3:** 966; Portugal and, **5:** 1373; Soviet Union and, **5:** 1623; United States and, **1:** 178; **3:** 854; **4:** 1144, 1200. *See also* Burma campaign, World War II; Hitler, Adolf

World Zionist Organization, **5:** 1559

Wye River Agreement, **1:** 47; **4:** 1137

Xuantong. *See* Pu-yi

Yalta Conference, **2:** 596

Yamamoto, Isoroku, **5: 1589-1591**

Yamani, Ahmed Zaki, **5: 1592-1594**

Yeltsin, Boris, **2:** 576; **5: 1595-1598**

Yemeni Civil War, **2:** 496

Yilmaz, Mesut, **4:** 1181

Yom Kippur War, **2:** 376; **5:** 1364

Young Egypt Party, **5:** 1364

Young modernists, Egyptian, **5:** 1605

Young Plan, **5:** 1443

Young Turks movement, **1:** 68-69; **2:** 481; **3:** 755

Yüan Shih-kai. *See* Yuan Shikai

Yuan Shikai, **5:** 1458, 1554, **1599-1602**

Zaghlūl, Saʿd, **5: 1603-1605**

ZANU Liberation Army (ZANLA), **4:** 1106

Zapata, Emiliano, **3:** 728, 964; **4:** 1165; **5:** 1537, **1606-1608**

Zedillo, Ernesto, **5: 1609-1611**

Zhao Ziyang, **3:** 771; **5: 1612-1614**

Zhou Enlai, **2:** 445; **3:** 867, 923; **5: 1615-1618**

Zhu De, **4:** 1208; **5: 1619-1622**

Zhukov, Georgy Konstantinovich, **5: 1623-1625**

Zia-ul-Haq, Mohammad, **1:** 138, 144; **5: 1626-1628**

Zikist movement, **1:** 83

Zinoviev letter, **3:** 956

Zionist movement, **1:** 114, 122; **2:** 456; **4:** 1058; **5:** 1559-1560

Zulu Rebellion, **2:** 541

Zulus, **1:** 237